Table of Contents

PROLOGUE

PART 1   –   ENGLAND
PART 2   –   AUSTRALIA
PART 3   –   ENGLAND again
PART 4   –   CANADA

EPILOGUE

ISBN: 9781520258218

PROLOGUE

The Wheel turns full circle

It all began late in the 17th century with a group of German sword makers who, to escape religious persecution in Europe, settled beside the spring waters of the River Derwent in the village of Shotley Bridge, which was nestled in the Derwent valley in the northwest corner of County Durham, England. Legend has it that a Mr. Oley of this group entered a worldwide contest to find the best sword, and when he came before the judges not carrying anything he was asked, "Why have you entered this competition? Where is your sword?" In response, he very quietly removed his top hat and took out a curled sword that immediately uncurled into a straight blade. Everyone was amazed and astounded at the suppleness and strength of the steel that he won the competition outright, and for 150 years the quality of his steel was known throughout the world for its excellence.

It was only in 1839, after the ingredients to make iron, such as ironstone, ore, coal, bauxite and dolomite were discovered in the area that a small group of men, who'd heard the story of the special spring steel sword, decided to take advantage of the renowned local waters. They started a tin plate company in the village of Consett, high on the hill above Shotley Bridge, and they named it 'Consett Tin Plate Company.' At that time, Consett was still a farming village and it lay 900 feet above sea level, on the east bank of the beautiful River Derwent valley, in the northwest corner of County Durham in England, and was surrounded by farms and vast areas of untamed moors.

The Company grew and, after another couple of name changes, finally settled on the name 'Consett Iron Company' when they changed from making tin plate to making iron and steel. After a number of years of making iron and steel, local supplies of iron ore ran out and, because the investment in the steelworks was so great that they couldn't just close it down they had to find new supplies from other countries. Iron ore was bought from Sweden and as far away as the Americas, and it came by boat to Newcastle docks, about 14 miles away. It was unloaded into Company-owned railway cars, and traveled on North East railway lines, snaking their way through towns and villages to the steel works. Even though transporting iron ore across country to Consett made it a very inconvenient place to conduct business, the Company prospered, and its name became acclaimed throughout the world for manufacturing the best iron and steel in the world.

It was Consett specialized steel that built the very first English Polaris submarine, HMS Resolution. It was Consett steel that built the Canadian ship; The Empress of Canada, and Consett steel was used to build the Sydney Harbour Bridge in Australia. (When I was born in the early 1940's I would never in my wildest dreams have dreamt that I, born and raised in Consett, would live my life in all three of these countries.)

From 1840 to the middle of the 1900's, the Company owned nearly all the land and nearly all the property within a 12-mile radius of Consett. Whole families were imported from across the country and Ireland to become totally dependent for their livelihood and the 'tied' roof over their heads. It was very 'Dickensian' but this arrangement was advantageous to everybody. It meant that the Company could rely on a stable workforce and people could rely on 'cradle to grave' employment. Children were schooled for employment within the steel works or in one of the Company's thirty-seven coal mines which fed the steel works, and it was not unusual to find three generations or more all working for the Company at the same time. Long service awards of 65 years were not uncommon. Yes, that's correct, 65 years or more. Men were known to start work at the age of 12 and drop dead on the job in their early 80's.

As the company expanded, more and more houses and villages were built to accommodate the workers. All of them were encamped in a circle around the hill looking upward towards Consett who was in the topmost position.

Templetown was created to house workers at the Brick works. Delves Lane, Crook Hall and Villa Real were built to provide housing for pitmen for various coalmines. Berry Edge, Blackfyne and Blackhill were all steelworker villages. Moorside and The Grove were the last villages to be built to support the Company, this time by the local council. Castleside village lay beyond Moorside, but it was in existence long before the Company came along but, even so, lead hands, supervisors, and managers took it over and the area was known as 'a cut above' the rest.

There was never any doubt in anybody's mind as to who the boss was and who 'ruled the roost.' It was a Company town. Life was very harsh with most people working 10 hours a day, six days a week, but grateful to have a job and a roof over their heads. If you were unlucky enough to be fired from the Company, there was very little hope of alternative employment of any kind in the area. Their immense influence extended well beyond the iron & steel works and coal mining industry, so you might as well 'pick up sticks' and move to another part of the country. No improvement in housing, schooling, higher education, health care, and recreational facilities was conducted without Company approval and financing.

The Company, as well as Consett, grew and prospered. It was a typical working class town with more churches and public houses than food shops. There were so many pubs that road directions were given not by actual road or street name, but by the name of the pub, "go left at The Burton, pass The Freemason's Arms, and turn right at The Black Horse." Every Friday afternoon the men would be paid in cash and lots of wives, from young to old, would hang around the Company entrance gates in order to get the weekly housekeeping money as quickly as possible from their husbands. It was quite common to hear loud arguments between husband and wife as to the amount - with the men arguing that they wouldn't have enough left for the Friday night pub-crawl. One often heard the joke that Consett working man would get drunk on Friday night, beat the wife on Saturday, and pray for forgiveness in church on Sunday. Many a true word spoken in jest! You'd see the same women week after week trying to keep bruised faces hidden with headscarves as they shopped at the stalls in the market square on Saturday after they'd been roughed around by a drunken husband the previous night. Believe it or not, earlier in the century, the drunkenness was so bad that the Company refused to pay some men their wages on the grounds that, "they'll just drink them away" and were taken to court to be forced to pay them by law.

It was a dirty, mucky place when the furnaces were going full blast and the whole area was blanketed in red iron ore dust that could be seen from miles away. On washing days, women had to be very careful which way the wind was blowing when they put their clothes out on the lines to dry or they'd be covered in 'the red menace.' The majority of houses were built of beige sandstone and were not only ingrained with black soot from the coal fireplaces but had a daily topcoat of red dust, and when it rained, it rained red water. The local park was the only place in the world with red grass. It was known as Consett Park or Blackhill Park, depending upon where one lived, because it ran down the hill parallel to the road and joined the town of Consett to the town of Blackhill, east of Consett. Everyone within a seven-mile radius of Consett lived on the side of the hill and everywhere one walked, it was either uphill or downhill.

Many people had a house with a bit of a garden, but if you weren't that lucky, as a lot of people weren't, then the Company would rent families a small piece of land, called an allotment, so that people could grow their own food and augment their wages. The staple food of the day was meat, vegetables and potatoes, minus the meat in a few houses. Every kind of vegetable that would survive in the severe northern climate such as potatoes, turnips, cabbages, carrots, cauliflowers, peas, and beans were grown, and somewhere, hidden of out sight of his neighbor, somewhere in the bottom of the garden, was the obligatory bed of jealously guarded 'prize-winning' leeks. You'd never see flowers growing in an allotment, or backyard garden, because they'd take up too much valuable space, and if it couldn't be eaten, then it wouldn't be planted.

Wives expected their husbands to work hard in the garden. Even before the last frost disappeared you'd see rickety old windows made into 'cold frames' which magnified the sun's heat to germinate the seeds. Once the seedlings started to show some strength they would be carefully put out in the garden and would be measured for daily growth and it would not be unusual to pass by somebody's allotment thinking that the man of the house was beating the wife to death only to realize his tirade was against snails, caterpillars or earwigs munching on his lovingly tended plants. No part of the vegetable was wasted. Inedible parts such as the leaves of a cauliflower or the outer skin of a turnip were put to one side to feed somebody's pigs.

Life's priorities for the man were his work, the pub, the garden, racing pigeons, religion, and then the family. It was a man's world and women and children knew their place – right at the end of the line. Men never hesitated in stopping a woman on the street to give her a good telling off for not being in control of a misbehaving child, and in not teaching the child to mind his/her manners, and to be seen but not heard. Mind you, if the husband was told about it he'd go looking for the fellow and thump him black and blue, and let him know in no uncertain terms that he should mind his own business. Then, after he'd had a beer or two, he'd go home and thump the wife for putting him in a position where he had to thump another fellow.

The vast majority of people lived from hand to mouth or from payday to payday, and anything other than the basic necessities of life was considered to be a waste of money. The class system was rife and the pecking order very clear. Instead of a woman congratulating another woman on getting a new coat, the comment would more likely to be "Come into money have you?" or, "You're getting a bit above yerself aren't you!" Clothes were usually home-made and were shortened, lengthened, patched and passed from the eldest to the youngest and at the absolute end of their useful life were made into rugs for the floor. Nobody had much of anything and nothing was wasted.

If you didn't have a garden, which was definitely frowned and commented upon as being lazy, then you had to rely on the shops in Front Street or Middle Street. There were no refrigerators so meat and fish had to be bought as you needed them - pork came from Yagers, beef came from Askew's, and fish came from Maggie Lister's the wet fishmonger; and – God forbid - if you had to buy bread then it came from Hanson's bakery. For general provisions, you went to the small grocery store, put the order in, and waited for the clerk to fill it. If you couldn't get what you wanted in either Front Street or Middle Street, then you had to make the 14-mile bus trip by the 'high road' along the top of the hills to Durham City or by the 'low road' through the valleys to Newcastle upon Tyne.

It was the woman's job to make a luxurious meal out of nothing, such as scrag-end of mutton, and have it hot and ready for her man coming home from the pub, whenever he showed up. Most women had to fight for housekeeping and rent money, and it wasn't unusual for Sunday church clothes to be at the Pawnshop from Monday until Friday when the husband got paid and they could be redeemed. If life was hard for men, it was twice as hard for woman. Not only did she have to make ends meet with very little money, but also housework was physically very hard.

Clothes were washed in the poss-tub, and were bashed up and down with a long broom handle with a round block of wood attached to the bottom of it. Monday's were wash days, and heaven help the woman who didn't do her wash on that day as she was branded by other women as being 'bone-idle lazy.' Irrespective of the weather, the wash had to be done and hung out on the line, or draped over a 'clothes horses' in front of the coal fire to dry, and a flat iron heated in the fire to iron the clothes. She cooked the meals over the coal fire and maybe, if she was very lucky, she had an oven attached to the side of the fireplace. If she didn't have water piped into the house, then water had to be brought from the communal tap in the village and it had to be boiled before use. Brooms were used to keep the floors clean and whatever small amount of furniture she had was polished until you could see your face in it. Women had a very rough life and it didn't ease up much until the 1950's.

The police themselves were judge, jury and executioner. Rather than haul a miscreant into court for a minor offence, and have all the paperwork to do, they would take them round the back of the nearest shed and beat the living daylights out of them, and warn them what would happen if they did it again.

Times were especially tough during the World War of 1939 to 1945 because most meat, wheat, sugar and fruit were imported from other countries and the ships were constantly attacked and blown up. Even though money was available because the men who were making armaments in the steel works were exempt from joining up as soldiers, food was rationed to each person. Those people savvy enough to stockpile non-perishables, and there were quite a few of them, survived the war and rationing without a great deal of hardship. For instance, if you were friendly with a local farmer then meat could be bought, at a price, but under veiled threat if you were foolish enough to broadcast the fact that you'd gotten something you shouldn't.

The Company was an important target for the Germans as they were producing steel for armaments, but no matter how hard they tried to bomb the steelworks, they always missed. Even though the town of Consett was located on the top of the hill, the steel works were nestled into the side of the hill and, with a total blackout in effect, the planes couldn't see the steel works until they'd flown passed them. It also didn't help them that there was a squadron of British fighter planes based about 10 miles further up the Derwent valley whom not only protected the steel works, but also the shipbuilding docks at Newcastle. The area didn't get off scot-free though. The Germans, flying in grid patterns over Consett, dropped several bombs on Blackhill cemetery and many a coffin was blown out of the ground and, on the other side of Consett, many a cow was blasted to smithereens in the fields behind Delves Lane.

It was just after the war that the Company's stranglehold on the area began to loosen. Lots of young men and women who had chosen to join the war effort experienced a different way of life outside of Consett and found it very hard to settle down again within the confines of steel making or coal mining. Transportation had improved enormously with regular bus services to the cities of Newcastle and Durham so people could travel further afield to work, and the Company, even though locally they were still in charge, found themselves in the position of trying to get the horse back into the barn after it had bolted. The 'Dickensian' era had finally come to an end; however, the Company, and Consett, were prospering so people were being paid more of what they were worth and life in general eased up, with not too many people leaving the Company's security blanket of 'cradle to grave' employer.

It was in the late 1940's that the villages' horticultural shows became popular, and each one was timed to take place just before the Company-sponsored 'Consett & District Horticultural Show.' The local shows, which were only held on a Friday and Saturday, were great social events and almost everybody in the village entered something to be judged. Whether it was vegetables, pies, pastries, jams, jellies, hand-made rugs, hand-stitched embroidery, roses, flowers, homemade wine – the categories and entries were endless. Anything and everything was entered in order to vie for a prize. It wasn't just the monetary award attached to winning; it was also the status. The 'one-upmanship' on your neighbor. It was terribly snobbish, but having a husband or wife who consistently won prizes was a huge status symbol within the community.

Consett & District Horticultural Show was something else. It was a week-long event that nobody, absolutely nobody, missed. It was the social event of the year! People traveled great distances to attend. Consett soccer pitch was commandeered to use as the Fairground and, with great anticipation, young and old people stood and watched the Ferris wheels, Dodgem cars, and shuggy boats being assembled. Sideshows magically appeared decked out with expensive-looking cheap toys to win. A marquee was erected to hold all the men's garden produce and the women's contributions ready for judging. Fencing was erected to accommodate all the finest cows, bulls, horses, goats, sheep, rabbits, hens, and pigs that had been brought in from near and far and spruced up for the Judges. In the North East of England, this was the Show of Shows. Bar none!

Leeks had a show all to themselves, and the vast majority of households grew leeks in one place or another in the hopes of winning. The prize money was quite substantial, much more than that awarded at local village shows, and it came with a lot of publicity and distinction for the person who won so it's easy to see how men guarded the size of their leeks from everybody else. But you needed to grow a leek in the range of 5 to 6 lbs. before you stood a chance at the prize. One year, the weather was so bad that gardeners everywhere were having a tough time growing anything and one highly optimistic man (my future uncle-in-law) showed up with his offering for the 'big show.' All the officials took one look and burst out laughing -- his leeks were so small that he was able to carry both of them in his top jacket pocket -- and when one official finally found his voice he said, "Eeh lad! You should enter them as Spring Onions!"

Life was good, the skies were clear, God was in his Heaven, and all was right with the world, and there was a continuum to life in Consett that everybody thought would go on forever. But, in 1970, after more than 140 years in existence, the Labour Party government irrevocably nationalized Consett Iron Company and it became just a division of the British Steel Corporation.

Everybody at the time thought that it was a good thing; that job security and wages would meet higher standards; that life in general would be on par with the rest of the country. How little everyone knew at the time. Although it was always referred to as The Company by the locals, slowly and surely the Company lost its individual identity and, through time, became just another cog in the great British wheel of steel making.

It is hard to believe, but a scant 10 years later, in 1980, the unimaginable happened. Newspapers reported that the Company was to close down. By now the Conservative Party was in power and they decided to make each of its divisions, all over the country, into specialized manufacturing plants. 'They' decided that Consett was to become a Billet-making plant only, which meant nearly 5,000 people, out of the 7,500 people who worked at the Company, would be out of work within a short period of time. Once the news leaked out, The Amalgamated Steelworkers Union dug their heels in and fought the Conservative Party, and refused to have anything to do with any plant closure or loss of jobs of any kind, which ultimately led to the government decision to close everything down. No manufacturing of any kind! Nothing! 150 years of manufacturing history wiped out by the stroke of a pen. What a mind-numbing resolution. Unfortunately, no amount of talking would undo the decision. It was all over bar the shouting, and shout they did. Hundreds of desperate men and women walked the length of England from Consett to London to protest the closure but the government wouldn't listen.

In September 1980, life, as everybody in Consett and district knew it, came to an end. After 150 years in the iron & steel making business, making spring steel that nobody else in the world could match, the British government closed the Company down and threw 7,500 people out of work.

Everyone felt, and rightly so, that if the government hadn't nationalized the Company it would have remained a thriving entity. It had gotten along very nicely for 140 years without any government involvement, why hadn't they just left it alone? Men of all ages would spend the next few years looking for non-existent work. People would commit suicide. Young people would leave school and hang around the government owned Job Centre hoping for an apprenticeship of any kind, in any place. Families would pack up and move away. Consett would become a hotbed of previously unheard of crime with young people taking their frustrations out on the old, and for quite a long-time life languished in Consett.

Over the next few years, Consett Council systemically demolished all evidence of the steel works from the blast furnaces, steel mills, billet mills, railway lines, power plants, to the Hownsgill Plate Mill. The mill, which was only 20 years old at the time, was the first revolutionary four-high roller mill in the world and it was so huge that it could have stored the Queen Mary and the Queen Elizabeth ships, minus their stacks, side by side.

The black soot of the coal chimneys and the 'red menace' has gone and most of the houses have been sandblasted back to their original warm colour of sandstone beige. After 150 years of industry, there are meadows of fresh green grass in this part of the Derwent Valley where the world famous and once proud 700-acre steel works stood.

The wheel turned full circle.

Arial view of where the 700 acre Consett Iron Company/division of British Steel site was.

PART 1 - ENGLAND

Templetown

It was into this Company town and social environment that I literally arrived on Thursday, March 4, 1943 and nobody had a hint of what was to come. I was born in a bedroom in my Grandads' house at 2 Engine Shed Houses, in the village of Templetown, in the town of Consett, in the County of Durham, England, and was the second female born out of wedlock to his daughter, Beatrice Mary Buckett. My older sister, Nora, was born two years earlier, and when I was two years old, our mother, who was ready to give birth to a third child, a boy, married his father, Bill Dodds, and went to live in her mother-in-law's house, and Nora and I were left behind with our grandparents.

The grandparents had each been married before and between them had seven children, all of whom were adults and married with their own homes by the time I was born, and when the grandparents got together they had four more children: Marjorie (married but visited daily), Jimmy, Billy and Lorna and they still lived at home, and my sister and I were raised to believe the grandparents were our Mam and Dad, and our aunts and uncles were our sisters and brothers, and this is my life story, as I remember it, and for simplicity's sake I give my grandparents their proper title.

You couldn't really call Templetown a village, because that implies amenities such as butchers and baker's shops, and there weren't any. Other than one enterprising person who adapted their living room into a small convenience store for essentials such as candles and potatoes, all 200 villagers trailed up the hill into Consett for supplies.

Templetown was also home to the Company's power plant. It stood guard at the top of the hill, keeping vigil over the four or five supervisor's houses that faced the road in order to watch the workers coming or going to work. Below these houses were five or six streets of workmen's houses all running parallel to each other, and behind them were acres of land on which cattle and sheep grazed. Running past the power plant were railway lines that traversed the steel bridge spanning the road into Templetown, carrying iron ore wagons into the steel works. At the end of the stone wall and attached to pylons was a 6-foot high barbed wire security fence that ran the length of the village and enclosed all the Company's property. Once the fence reached our house, which was about a quarter of a mile past all the other houses in the village, two 6-foot wide gates replaced it, and the right-hand side gate was fastened to our backyard wall. These gates were never closed which was just as well because we had to go through them and round by the backyard to enter the house by the kitchen.

My home

Facing up the road towards the village of Templetown, and like an eagle with its wings outstretched waiting to pounce on unsuspecting workers, my home stood just inside the Company's security gates, guarding the entrance to the Brick works, Tar works, and the Engine Sheds. We lived in the right wing, with the beak being the dividing stone wall in the backyard between our house and Mr. Garoodes house in the left wing, parallel to the road. It was built as two separate, but joined at the hip, Manager or Gaffer's houses, and I lived in our half for the first sixteen years of my life.

When I was very little opening the gate, and walking down the backyard to enter the house by the kitchen door was not as simple as it sounds. It was a mental and physical obstacle course. The heavy wooden gate was as tall as the six-foot high stone walls surrounding it, and it was hung on very secure hinges so that once the latch was lifted it swung with ease but it took some effort to open. I would always push so hard that it would bang against the washhouse wall and bounce back with such force that it would either knock me over, or clasp me tight between it and the concrete step leading up to the outside toilet. Once the challenge of actually opening the gate without doing myself any physical damage was accomplished, I was ready for the next part. The backyard, with its high stone walls, was always in deep dark shadow, and to a small child with a vivid imagination scary monsters were everywhere. To get to the sanctity of the kitchen I had to race past the dirt encrusted eyes of the washhouse, ignore the black cavernous coal house dungeon; and fly like the wind down the concrete backyard away from the eerily silent open mouth of the air-raid shelter. Finally, with arms outstretched before me I'd fling open the kitchen door and shout, "Gran! Gran! I'm home! I'm home!" like some expeditionary leader back from darkest Africa. Her reply was always the same, "You're gonna take that door off its hinges someday hinny!"

The house, which was built of stone instead of the normal brick, was built in the late 1800's for 'upper-crust' people who worked for the Company and it had distinct living areas for both Master and servant. The kitchen, complete with a walk-in pantry, was the servant's domain, and it was located at the back of the house (backing onto the road) with its own private set of stairs leading to a double bedroom above. The rest of the house was the Master's. His very large living room was at the front of the house overlooking the garden, and his dining room was behind the servant's kitchen; both rooms being at opposite ends of a long hallway. Leading upstairs from the front entrance door was the Master's set of stairs that led to two double bedrooms and a bathroom that contained a bath, a sink, and a huge wardrobe. The toilet was outside by the back gate. (When I lived there an extra door had been put into the bathroom wall on the kitchen side so it became possible to do a complete circuit of the house without going outside.)

The kitchen was the only room that was heated, and had a permanent light fixture. Heat came from the coal fire, and light came from a flickering gas mantle -- and when the very fragile mantle burned out Grandad used to light the Tilly oil lamp or, if there was no oil left, candles. It was a large room, and it did double duty as a living room. On the kitchen side, there was an 8-seater wooden table and a very large sideboard that held all the dishes, a black-leaded fireplace with an oven to one side, a one-ring gas burner, and a kitchen sink which stood on top of a cupboard which held the pans. All the cooking and baking was done on the fire and in the oven so most of the heat went into making food. On the living room side, there was a three-seater horsehair sofa, an upholstered rocking chair, a long padded wooden bench, and a car battery-operated wireless. Linoleum covered the original flagstone floor, while 'clippie rugs' made from old worn out clothes and empty hessian flour bags gave the illusion of some warmth. We sat as close to the fire as we could, and while the front part of the body roasted quite nicely, the back part froze.

The dining room with its window looking into the backyard was never used for its intended purpose because it was never furnished and to my recall, it was mostly used as a starter home for young married relatives. The living room, also in name only, was a very pleasant sunny room at the front of the house underneath the front bedroom and was used for Grandad's aviary of Budgerigars and Canaries. The 'servants' bedroom window looked into the backyard, and was equipped with two double beds complete with extra old squeaky springs, a wardrobe, a chest of drawers and bare wooden floor. This room belonged to our Lorna, Nora and myself. The first of the 'Masters' bedrooms also looked into the backyard and had the obligatory old squeaky double bed, a chest of drawers, a wardrobe and another bare wooden floor, and belonged to Jimmy and Billy. The remaining bedroom, the actual Master's bedroom overlooked the front garden. It had a lovely double bed with a 'Down' mattress and comforter, a lovely old wardrobe and a chest of drawers but this room had linoleum on the floor, and obviously, this room belonged to Grandad and Gran.

I remember our house being so cold that even in the thin English summertime Lorna would wrap an oven shelf in a towel to heat the bed before Nora and I got into it, and put our overcoats on top of the blankets in the winter. I used to look forward to Sunday mornings because I'd run along the hallway, right through the middle of the bathroom, and jump into the grandparent's bed and snuggle down between them and the down mattress and covers, warming my cold feet on them. For years, I believed Gran when she said I had ice in my veins because I was always so cold. She had a lovely sense of humour, and after we'd all get up, she would shake the mattress and covers high into the air to fluff them. Then I'd jump into the bed between the mattress and the covers and she'd poke me and say, "Well, I didn't shake those covers very well, there's still a big lump in there, and I'd better get a big stick and flatten it!" I would shriek with delight, "No, No Gran, it's only me!" And we'd both chuckle at our huge joke and play it again the next Sunday.

Downstairs, behind the kitchen, was a small walk-in pantry and an access door to the bottom hallway and hanging on the wall at the far end of the hallway near the front door, was a set of buffalo horns. Now, if I was frightened running the outside obstacle course to get into the house, nothing was as bad as having to traverse this bottom hallway when the wind was blowing – which it always was. It was the scariest place on earth. The wind used to moan its way through the creaks and crevices of the front door, turn right at the bottom of the front stairs, and make the most eerie howling heart-stopping sounds through those Buffalo horns that you could ever imagine. I used to be petrified of having to go along that bottom hallway for most of my young years because one never knew when a wailing Banshee was going to jump out and grab you. Unfortunately, I had to go halfway along this hallway in order to go out of the side door into a small garden in order to feed the young chickens which were housed in a dinky little shed and, boy, I was quick on my feet. Also on this side of the house on some Company land, Grandad had built a large barn and that is where he raised rabbits, both for the pot and for competition. Every inch of the garden at the front of the house was planted with vegetables and row upon row of potatoes, and the only way our garden differed from anyone else's was the fact that we had room for a rock garden. I guess all those rocks were once removed from the vegetable side, and to make them attractive they were planted with small alpine flowers.

As my address suggests, the Engine Sheds were close by and railway lines ran along the bottom of the garden. Day and night, coal-fired engines would shunt into the Engine Sheds where the engine drivers would then physically turn the engine around on a huge turntable to face back the way he'd come. Then he'd pick up a number of full coal wagons that were waiting patiently on the sidelines, from various pits in the area, and bring them back along the bottom of garden and into the steel works a couple of miles away. Many a time I've heard the secret whistle and had to duck to avoid being hit by a 'roundie' of coal thrown into our garden, courtesy of one of our engine driver relatives.

My Immediate Family background

My Grandad was Herbert William (Billy) Buckett, and he was born in 1883 in the university town of Oxford in the south of England. His occupation for most of his life was professional

Cricket Player, and Grounds man, and he played 'County' cricket for the Headingly/Leeds Cricket Club for a lot of years. Now that doesn't seem much of an occupation when you really think about it, but at that time County Cricket was a gentlemen's sport and you had to be independently wealthy to afford the time to play; and even though Grandad came from a very well to do family, he himself was not terribly wealthy so the cricket club employed him as grounds man to supplement his income. This also sounds a bit mundane until someone tells you that this job was reserved for the very best players to ensure they stayed with the club, and Grandad was well known throughout England as being one of the best fast bowlers of his time. Towards the end of his professional career he was approached by the Company, who offered to create a job for him in order to entice him north because they wanted him to play cricket in the state-of-the-art Cricket Club they had just built in Consett. They hoped that by having a professional cricket player settle in Consett, other professional players would come and their club would gain recognition as a County Cricket Club, and it did.

In 1909 he married Laura Martha Hilsden, also from the south, but it was only after they moved north that their three children, Gladys, Beatrice and Mabel were born. They had a fourth child, Elsie, but she died in infancy and tragically, Grandad's wife died in 1924 at the very young age of 37. As well as playing cricket, the Company created the job of 'Gaffer' for him at the Brick works and Tar works and after his wife died, he found himself with a seven, five, and three-year-old on his hands and couldn't cope. This is where the only mother I have ever known enters the picture.

Elizabeth Mary Barron, or Lizzie as she was known, was born in 1888 in the farming community of Allendale and moved to Consett when she married Miles Barron and they had three children, Bill, Bob and Betty. I don't know what occupation Miles Barron held, but I know that Lizzie was employed as Seamstress to my Grandad's family for a number of years before his wife died. I'm not sure whether Miles had died at this point, but Lizzie moved into Grandad's house and took on the responsibilities of housekeeping and raising his three children while her three children, who were much older, were raised by her father, Granda Robson, until they were adults.

Billy and Lizzie, my grandparents, were together for 44 years, and had four children: Marjorie, Jimmy, Billy and Lorna. In most household's, they have 2 parents; I had 6-1/2 as I am including the motherly protection of my sister, Nora. It wasn't easy being the butt of most of the adults' tempers, but I mostly learned to live with it, or learned to ignore it. In writing my story, I choose to ignore the really bad bits in the spirit of "if I don't remember it, then it didn't happen." But let me tell you that being chastised by an articulate Oxford educated Grandad was much more devastating than being physically hit by one of the others; and I must have been a real dim-wit when I was little not to realize that the lovely gray-haired old people were actually my grandparents, but I didn't. There was nothing to suggest that these people were other than what they seemed to be, my Mam and Dad, and brothers and sisters. It wasn't until I reached the ripe old age of nine that the carefully woven fabric of my familial relationships would be torn apart at the seams.

I really only first remember Grandad after he retired. He was a very tall proud man, with thin graying hair, and not much spare flesh on him. He always very well dressed in the best quality clothes and had a cultured soft spoken south of England voice, totally opposite to the loud colloquial 'Geordie or Pitmatic' voices spoken in the North. Grandad was highly intelligent and when he spoke, everybody listened. His word was the law, and nobody dared argue with him as he had a very vicious bad temper, 'The Buckett Temper,' and even though he was retired his needs were still seen to before everybody else. We had to stand back from the table until Grandad was seated and then he would give permission for us to sit because nobody was allowed to sit down before him, even the grown-ups. The food on the table was passed to him first so that he could take his pick and only when his plate was sufficient were the rest of us allowed to partake. Nobody was allowed to talk during the meal, and more than once I remember getting his cane wrapped across my knuckles for either talking out loud, or eating with my mouth open. I was told that Grandad had been a real tyrant with his much older children but that he'd mellowed by the time I was born, so even though I experienced his bad temper now and again, my mind would block the nasty times for the most part. The only real autocratic thing that I can remember about him is that Nora and I had tin plates to eat off, and if we scraped them during eating we would have our meal taken away. He was gruff, stern and a strict disciplinarian and insisted on getting his own way, but I loved him. I loved him even more when I learned as a grown-up that he insisted upon my sister and I being raised by him and Gran and of not being put into an orphanage as was the custom for any unwanted children.

Gran was totally opposite to Grandad and was the peacemaker of the family, and whereas Grandad wouldn't back down to anybody, Gran gave in to everybody. She was only about 5' tall when I first remember her, and she had a cuddly round figure and was the personification of love and kindness. Her long white waist-length hair was tied up in a bun at the back of her neck, and she always wore a wrap-around apron to protect her black dress. She had lots of patience and was very easygoing, and nothing seemed to ruffle her feathers and there were always one or more children hanging onto her skirts so that it seemed she couldn't move for children. Gran was a great cook, and everybody who came to our home was invited to eat with us if they happened to come at mealtimes, which some people seemed to do most casually. The food was plain and simple such as sheep's head broth, suet dumplings, steak and kidney pies, rabbit pies, bacon and egg pies, and yeasty stotters (bread that hasn't been allowed to rise) just to name a few, but whatever Gran cooked was absolutely delicious and nobody could ever match her culinary skills either then or now. Gran acted as a buffer between Grandad and the grown-up children and how she stood it at times I don't know because all them inherited the 'Buckett Temper.' As they grew older and took over running the household, outbursts became more and more frequent until it was like living beside Mount Vesuvius.

Sometimes, after being punished for something and not allowed any supper, Gran would quietly sneak up the stairs with a piece of bread and dripping hidden in her apron, and shout to whomever was listening downstairs that she was just going to check that the bedroom candle had been put out. Then she'd say, "Nan, hurry up and eat that hinny before anyone catches you, or there'll be trouble!" She was my earth angel, and I loved her with all my heart and never could I have wished for a better person to raise me. The grandparents never turned anyone away who needed help and whatever they had, they shared, and their home was open to anybody and everybody all their lives. They didn't have much in the way of worldly goods or possessions, but all their children were raised to be honest and decent people and I'd like to think they raised me the same way. It's strange now that I think about it, but I had no trouble in addressing their older children from both sides as Aunt or Uncle but for some reason the third set of their children were my brothers or sisters. Life can be so confusing at times.

Marjorie was the eldest of this relationship, of slim build and around 5'3" in height, she was quite attractive, always well dressed and, without a doubt, in her generation, she was the nemesis of the Buckett family. There always has to be one member of the family willing to stir things up, just to let the rest of us know we're alive I think, and she was certainly the one. She had inherited the 'Buckett Temper,' in spades, and was argumentative and stubborn all her life and was always falling out with somebody, mainly Grandad when he was alive. I don't think she had an easy time growing up with him because given her combustible nature, and his controlling attitude to life, they constantly butted heads. Even after she married Ken Lowther and left home, she used to visit nearly every day, and invariably those visits ended up with Marjorie and Grandad arguing, and of him telling her to go home, and not come back. She would deliberately get him all riled up, slam the kitchen door, and storm off, and the rest of us would have to listen to Gran trying to calm Grandad down because what he would have loved to do to Marjorie left nothing to the imagination. Honest, there were times that Nora and I wished she'd go home and stay home and let the rest of us live in peace.

Jimmy came next. He was around 6' tall, slim just like Grandad, and soft spoken. He took after Gran in temperament because he never got angry except for the time when Nora took a hacksaw to the crossbar of his cherished possession, his bike, to make it into a girl's bike. The 'Buckett temper' was very much in evidence that day. Apart from that one time, he was always cheerful and kind and he loved life and lived his short life to the fullest. He used to remind me of John Wayne, the movie star, the way he talked with a slow kind of drawl, and walked with the same kind of lazy stroll. He joined the navy for his National Service after World War II to "see the world" and spent his tour of duty as a trained Cook on a ship stationed in the Mull of Galloway up in Scotland. He was not impressed, but Gran was grateful.

Then came Billy, nearly as tall as Jimmy but with a little bit more flesh on him and he was also a happy person. He had a beautiful singing voice something similar to the famous crooner, Bing Crosby, and was always singing the latest song. He tells the story of having left school at 14 to work on Herdmans Farm below Templetown. His job was to harness the horses, cut and stack hay, and to help out quite often at Herdmans other farm that was about 20 miles away. After catching a bus for the first 15 miles of the journey, if the postman wasn't going that way to offer him a lift, then he had to walk the rest. Billy served his National Service time in the Durham Light Infantry and he really fancied staying on home ground but, as life can be ornery, he ended up in Malaya and Burma. The Durham Light Infantry were world famous for extremely fast marching at 120 steps per minute, and wherever Billy went, it was always in a hurry. I remember when he was courting his wife, June Hodson, and hadn't time to properly brush his shoes but was wiping them on the back of his trouser legs, and when I asked him why he was doing that, he replied, "Nan, I'm in a blooming big hurry and besides, a good soldier never looks behind."

In no time at all the boys got married, and it was left to Lorna, the youngest, about 5'4 tall, slim built and very attractive, to finish raising both Nora and I. Lorna was a teenager of 14 when I was born and was already working for a living. All the money she had to keep us was the grandparents' small pensions and what she made as a conductress with the Venture Bus Company, and the irregular money that my biological father was forced to pay by the courts. Not very much to keep five of us when there's rent to pay, groceries, clothes and school dinners to buy. Money was always tight, more so now that the lads had gotten married so didn't make any contribution to the household. But, Lorna managed somehow – how, I'll never know. She has been the family organizer all of her life and everything she has done, absolutely everything, has been with other people's interests at heart. There's nobody quite like Lorna, she's a unique person, and I love her dearly and as Gran was getting older, Lorna became mother to my sister Nora and I, in every way other than biological.

Nora, about 6 yrs old

My sister Nora was a stocky child; not fat, just well built. I mean you couldn't eat all that rib-sticking food without some of it being left behind on the body. She had bright ginger hair and was a very stubborn, demanding, creative and questioning child. Her nickname was either 'Ginger' because of the colour of her hair, or 'Tuppence' because when she was born, it was said she was so small that she could fit into a pint-pot. Grandad used to say that she would try the patience of a Saint and, as long as I can remember, Nora never got along with Grandad and would be defiant towards him at every opportunity as she'd also inherited the infamous temper. She just had a stubborn streak that wouldn't go away. He would ask her to do something and she would just stand there and totally ignore him until he was driven crazy by her insubordination. Then he would grab hold of her long plaits and bang her up against the nearest piece of furniture or wall until she cried, and did as she was told.

It was no wonder that she grew up being defiant, and as I learned how to be intimidated at a very early age, I was definitely the quiet obedient one. She was my sister, and I loved her, and I remember a time when it looked as though I was going to get a good hiding from Grandad when she put me behind her back and defied him to touch me, and he took his temper out on her. You can't go far wrong in life with a sister like that!

I was also a well-built child, not fat, just plenty of meat on the bones, and remember being told that I always looked like "a sack of taties, tied in the middle with a bit of string." I was a very quiet child, who saw life through rose coloured glasses and was something of a daydreamer. My nickname by the family was 'Mousy' because my long-plaited hair was mousy brown, and I was always curled up in a corner somewhere, with my head in a book, and would never make a sound. I could block out the background noise very effectively, and the grown-ups always had to shout to break my concentration. Very early in my life, Marjorie's husband, Ken, gave me the nickname of Dilly Dream. It was a comic book character who lived in a world all her own and this nickname was probably very apt as I sort of lived within myself. I could not have argued with anybody to save my life and I always did as I was told; and what small confidence I did have deserted me once I knew the truth of my birth. I was a very sensitive child who loved everybody and wanted them all to get along. But when the grown-ups argued, it would upset me so much that it would make me cry. I learned to cry quietly in my corner so as not to draw attention to myself because, if they noticed, it would give them a reason to say, "stop that crying, or I'll give you something to cry about!" There were lots of times that I got a smack across the head or had my knees nipped for no reason, and after asking, "What was that for?" being told, "That's in case you do something!"

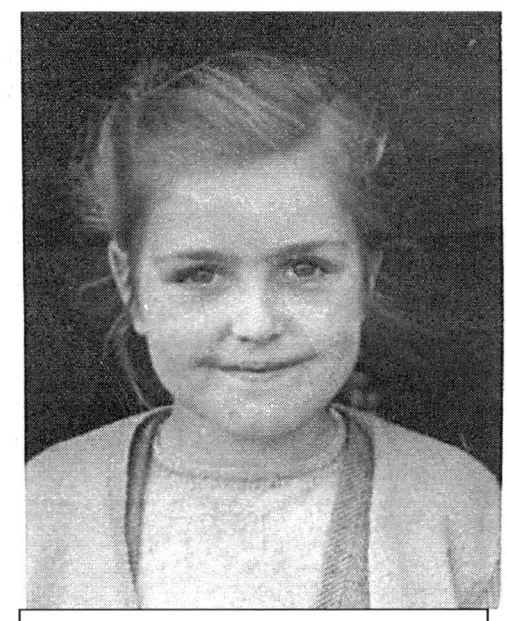

Nancy, me, about 4 yrs old

A Glorious Childhood

To the left of our house we had Company-owned manufacturing buildings, but to the right of us, and for miles down the road, we had countryside. With my back to the industry, I enjoyed the truly magnificent landscape of rolling hills and valleys, farms, fields, meadows, sheep, trees and green grass. There were fields to play in, trees to climb, small rivers and brooks to wade through, country walks, fresh air and sunshine. To be born in this part of the country was fantastic because there is no other area in the world that can outshine the World Heritage Site of the River Derwent Valley.

Life was pretty self-sufficient because Grandad cultivated every piece of land he could get his hands on. Apart from the hens, chickens and rabbits, he also raised pigs in a barn in the field across the road from us, and before he retired he also had a couple of cows and horses. Most of his retirement time was spent collecting waste scraps of food from houses in the village to feed the pigs. Each day he, or Gran, would light the fire under the copper boiler in the washhouse and boil all the waste scraps together, and then it would be mixed with mash and ladled into buckets. I remember the smell of the pig's food being so mouth-watering delicious that I wondered why Gran couldn't make some for us to eat. One time when Grandad was ill with Bronchitis it was left to me to feed the pigs because everybody else was at work, and it had been raining very hard for a few days so the field was very muddy. Gran said I should put a pair of rubber boots on and when I reminded her that I didn't have any, she said to borrow Jimmy's big man-sized rubber boots. Now my feet were very small because I think I was only about 7 years old at the time, and Jimmy's boots came all the way up to my backside. What a hoot! I can't for the life of me think how I managed to walk the ½ mile down a wet bank in huge rubber boots, carrying a pail of sloppy pig food in each hand without coming a cropper, but I must have managed somehow because I can remember the little piglets climbing over each other to get to the trough.

It wasn't long after this when Grandad had a young pig killed and I saw it hanging on a hook on the back of the washhouse door being 'cured.' Curiosity made me go and find Grandad to ask him if it was one of the pigs I had recently fed because I was feeling very sad about it, and I think that was the only time in my life that I remember him being deliberately horrible towards me. He very nearly leaped out of his chair as he grabbed me by the arm and swung me round to face him, then he told me in no uncertain terms what he'd do to me if I opened my mouth and told anybody about a dead pig hanging in our washhouse, and I have never been so frightened of him in all my young life. While still holding me tight by the arm, he raged on and on about how the police would come and take him away, and every ounce of blood must have drained from my body because I thought I was going to pass out from fear. I didn't know that war rationing was still in effect, and that it was illegal to kill any animals for your own personal use, and that the pig should have been handed over to the local government. If I was shy and quiet before, you'd have thought I'd turned invisible after that outburst and it took me the longest time to forgive him.

Another of Grandad's interests was in raising and judging pedigree rabbits such as Chinchillas and Angoras and he was very well known at shows all over the North and even as far away as the Midlands. All the rabbits were extremely well cared for and fed only the freshest Dandelion leaves, and their fur was brushed daily. They had new straw every day, and the floors were kept clean and the walls were made as draft-proof as possible. My cousin, Johnny Barron, came over from Delves Lane, the next village to ours, two or three times a week to catch the mice with his bare hands as you couldn't put mousetraps in with long-haired rabbits. I especially loved the Angora rabbits with their beautifully long silky hair and was in my element if Grandad would let me brush them. It was easy to become attached to these lovely tranquil creatures, and heart-breaking, when I was much older, to realize that one of my favorites, now too old to compete in shows, was the rabbit pie we were having for supper. However, being ever practical, one of us was going to get a pair of new winter gloves made by Aunt Mabel after the rabbit skins had cured.

Every so often, Grandad would let the hens sit on their eggs so that we would get new chickens. Once they'd sat on them for a while he'd quietly remove the live eggs and replace them with pot eggs so that the hen would still think she was brooding, then he would put the live eggs into an incubator which stood at the far end of the bottom hall, and once they were about to hatch, and providing we were extra quiet, Nora and I were allowed to watch the fluffy yellow chickens emerge from their shells.

During the summertime, I always seemed to be in the company of Grandad when I was little, and one of the things we got pleasure out of was visiting Stockdale's farm which lay about two miles past our house, further on down the hill. Just behind the farm, through a couple of fields and over by a bank of trees ran a small babbling brook called the Beck and it was great for splashing around in or for catching baby fish called tiddlers. While Grandad talked with the farmer or helped him groom the big Shire horses, I would tumble around in the hay barn and just generally make a quiet nuisance of myself until Grandad called for me to come. One time I remember being finally tall enough to look into the bullpen and of being mesmerized by the bull's enormous size when he spotted me and started snorting and pawing the ground. He was getting really angry but before I could move my feet Grandad yanked me away and shut the top half of the stall door to calm the animal down again. Boy, did I get my backside spanked for that.

After visiting the farm, we would climb through the fence and walk over the fields to inspect the Beck, or we would check the bushes around there to see if any berries had ripened enough to pick. If it was an especially lazy day, we may just continue walking around the bottom of hill and back up the other side into Delves Lane, then come back to Templetown via the black path – sort of like walking a triangle with the top cut off. The black path so named because of the cinders that were scattered on it from the Coke Works. I couldn't go home without taking some flowers for Gran so Grandad would keep an eye open for primroses and buttercups or, if he was getting desperate, dandelions, because I would only pick 'gold' flowers for the longest time, the others weren't good enough.

Every school morning Grandad would get up well before us and have the coal fire blazing and the oatmeal bubbling away in the pot because Nora and I were never allowed to leave the house without something in our stomachs. He used to check our heavy brogue shoes to make sure there were no holes in the soles and, if there were, he used to cut up pieces of cardboard to put inside them until he could fix them properly with a 'slap on' rubber sole. I used to hate those heavy serviceable brogue shoes because I would kick the insides of my ankles when I walked, and my ankles would be sore, bloodied, and very painful in no time. Grandad used to say that I should stop walking like a Red Indian who placed one foot directly in front of the other and try walking like Farmer Plod and sway from side to side. I did try, honest I did, but walking that way made me look as though I'd messed my panties and Nora would walk away from me so as not to be associated with me.

One of my most cherished memories was the day I had the grandparents all to myself and we were sitting around the fire singing old-time songs while the dinner was cooking. I can still feel the warmth of Gran as I cuddled into her on the horsehair sofa. I can still hear the poker rattling in the grate as Grandad encouraged the old ashes to drop through to keep them from dampening down the fire. I can still smell the delicious aroma of the sheep's head broth simmering away in the big cauldron sitting on the ruby red coals, and a momentary twinge of sadness as the kitchen door swung open to burst that little bubble of tranquility, but then a surge of happiness at seeing Jimmy, with his gun broken over his arm, swinging a brace of rabbits in the other, and of Gran, now giving full attention to the wild rabbits and saying to Jimmy, "Well done lad!"

Everybody had the same need to bring home whatever food they could find, and we were no exception. We had certain areas where we'd pick blackberries, bilberries, elderberries, rosehips and mushrooms, and anything and everything that was edible or good for the pot was gathered enthusiastically. Billy was great at finding mushrooms and he would often trail Nora and me with him to help carry them. Those were great days, we'd tramp up and down the hill and over the fields, and when we'd find a stash of them you'd think we'd found white gold. Boy, field mushrooms were good, and it never bothered me at the time that the best ones were found in a platter of cow dung, but it was a good thing I never learned till later in life that the little white wriggly things were actually maggots.

Friday was baking day and Gran and Lorna used to bake everything you could think of from bread, to pies, to sweet pastries. Cakes were not unheard of, but when it came to filling the stomach, good old pastry did the trick. We might not have been rich, but we were never ever hungry. Lorna used to shop for staples such as flour and yeast on a Friday but didn't buy much because we used to have everything we needed from Grandad's small holding. Bless her heart, it didn't matter how little money she had, Lorna always brought Nora and I a bag of Smith's crisps with the salt wrapped separately in a blue paper package, and some comic books which everyone read, even Billy and Jimmy. There wasn't much money for luxuries such as sweets, so we loved to get a stick of young Rhubarb out of the garden and dip it into some sugar to make it extra sweet; or cocoa powder and sugar mixed together that we'd dip our fingers in and suck. Sometimes, just sometimes, we'd get a 'store bought' treat of Licorice Root, something like a small branch broken off a bush, and when we sucked like mad on the yellow woody substance, it really did taste like licorice. Other times we would pinch the sweet new peas out of the peapods growing in the garden with one of us acting as 'look-out' in case any grown-ups caught us.

Saturday morning Gran always took the bus to the big city of Newcastle to the Quayside to buy bags of fresh fish, lobster, crab, periwinkles, and mussels for Saturday evening tea, and after she'd been away for a couple of hours, I'd be sent out to watch for her coming home again. Darky, our big huge, really huge, black Labrador dog, and I used to sit on the roadside watching and waiting for any sign of Gran walking down the road, and as soon as she was in sight, I'd give a hoop and a holler and the two of us would sprint up to meet her. He always used to beat me to her, but as I got faster and he got older I beat him more than once.

Darky was my constant companion. He was the most kindhearted animal you could ever wish to meet and was my pal from when I was born until he died peacefully at the very old age of 17 when I was a teenager. I've never met another animal with such a gentle and loving nature as his and I think it's maybe because a beautiful spirit like him only comes along once in a lifetime. One time, as he watched over me when I fell asleep outside, and contrary to his nature, he showed his teeth and really growled at a villager whom he'd known all his life, for wanting to take me home. The villager was reported as saying, "There's no way I was going to touch her to wake her up, because he'd have gone for my throat!" Darky knew everybody in the village, and everybody knew him, but he was especially known for swiping pans from backyards. Lots of women had spoiled him by saving the old bones for him after they had been boiled for soups or stews, but if they weren't careful he'd bring the pan as well as the bones home. People used to say we trained him to deliberately take the cauldron as well as the bones - they were wrong, but they always knew where to come to get their pans back.

It was great being able to help Gran carry the bags home. She always looked exhausted with the weight of them and relieved to see us, even though by that time she was probably only 100 feet from the back door. She'd give Darky the heaviest basket, and I'd take one or two of the lighter string bags, and between the three of us we'd casually stroll the remainder of the way home with the catch of the day. Me pounding Gran with umpteen questions as to what she'd bought, and her answering, "Nan, let me catch my breath hinny and let me put my feet up." Once we'd gotten into the kitchen and dropped the bags onto the kitchen table, with a sigh of relief, she would drop onto the couch and lift her feet up so that I might take off her black laced shoes and rub some feeling back into her sore feet. Nora and I used to think we must be really poor because we had to eat all that fish on a Saturday – how ignorant can you be as a youngster? We ate like Kings and didn't know it!

We didn't have a rich household by any means but what we had we shared, and most of the time you had to 'make do and mend' and to have something 'shop bought' was very unusual. Neither Nora nor I were used to having bought things, so when Billy came home from his two-year National Service with gifts for us from Malaya, we were thrilled to bits. I remember sitting there when Billy gave me my gift and of having to be prompted by him to open it, "Go on Nan, it's for you, really, you can open it, it's okay." It was a lovely little monkey on a ladder that climbed up and down when it was moved from side to side, and Nora's gift was a small beautifully engraved leather wallet and they were our most treasured possessions for years.

We had great fun with the lads, they were as generous as they were loving, and if they had anything in their pockets such as a sweet or a couple of pennies they would share it with Nora and me. We worshipped both of them and were only too pleased to be included in anything they were doing, even though they were much older than we were. I remember one-day Jimmy bet Billy that he could run faster than him and before we knew it, Nora was on Jimmy's shoulders and I was on Billy's. Both of them took off like madmen over the field where our pigsty was and, as the ground was very uneven, I had to hang on for dear life. I was bent nearly double with my hands around Billy's neck because he was bouncing me around all over the place and all the while shouting, "Nan, you're bloody choking me, get yer hands off me neck – get hold of me hair!" I was far too frightened to let go and Jimmy won the race and it took Billy ages to get his breath back because I really had nearly choked him!

Nora and I would explore the countryside and have adventures most every day and it didn't matter if the weather was fine or raining we were nearly always outdoors. One of our more favorite things to do was to have a picnic and we would set off down the hill with our bread and jam lunch in a brown bag. If we walked long enough, we would reach Stockdale's farm and go through the fields to the Beck. After we'd had a plodge or two, or fished for tiddlers, we'd have our lunch then stop and pick primroses, buttercups and violets on the way home for Gran and Lorna. We'd be away from home for hours, but we were always home in time for tea.

My sister was also blessed with a vivid imagination and I remember once playing pirates in the huge barn in the far corner of the field across the road from us. About eight of us were there, and Nora, being the boss pirate, and wanting to show off to the others, had climbed up into the rafters, lost her footing, and fell into what was just a smattering of hay. I thought she was dead and I started to weep because I didn't know how I was going to tell them at home what had happened. She lay there for the longest time without moving and, while I was now in the act of becoming hysterical, she came round and told me to shut up I was scaring the piglets in the shed attached to the barn. I nervously said, "What piglets?" She answered, "The ones that Grandad said we were not go near because any noise would put them off their food and Mr. Holmes, his best friend, would be furious!" Nora certainly liked to live on the edge!

There were also a couple of cows residing in the same field as our pigsty and Mr. Holmes' barn, and the older kids used to pretend that they were bulls, and one of the 'gang' initiation rites was to see how close you could get to them. I was pretty feint-hearted as a youngster and I was just pretending to be brave, because I wasn't really a brave person when I accepted the challenge. But, after being prodded and goaded by them, I cautiously ventured into the field a short way, when the faintest sound of a 'moo' from one of the 'bulls' sent me flying back. I struggled to get in between the barbed wires of the fence and, while doing so, ripped my brand new homemade dress from hem to waist. When I very tearfully showed Gran what I'd done, no amount of sobbing that, "They made me do it!" had any effect and I got a well-deserved punishment. "If they put their heads in an oven, would you Nan? Think before you do daft things!" she said in an annoyed voice. This was about the only time I ever heard her raise her voice to me.

I often played on my own because Nora would quietly slip away to go and play with her best friend, Anne Clarke. Now there aren't many games you can play by yourself, but juggling balls was one that I never tired of. I would be quite absorbed in bouncing three balls up against the coal house door, to the beat of rhythmic drumming, and chant to myself, "Ickle Bockle, Black Bottle, fishes in the sea. If you want a pretty maid, please choose me!" Before long the kitchen door would open and in a very loud voice, Grandad, or one of the lads, would shout, "Quit that bloody racket before you get your head in your hands with your brains to play with!" Then I'd creep quietly outside the back gate and commence my game again, but this time on the back wall where there was no echo, and with one eye watching out for the Company trucks coming in and out of the big gates.

If money was available, then Saturday mornings were a real treat for Nora and I with a trip to the Rex Cinema at the top of the market square in Consett, to see all the children's serials such as Roy Rogers, Superman, or The Perils of Pauline. Week by week all the children would line up with great excitement just to see what happened to their favorite character, and last week's show would be discussed and acted out in great detail before entering the movie house. I used to get so engrossed in the movie that I just couldn't stand the suspense of what ill was going to befall the character that I used to irritate Nora no end by asking her to tell me, through covered eyes, "What's happening?" I know I drove her crazy and she would threaten not to take me anymore, but she did.

Religious education was mandatory in our house, and Grandad insisted that Nora and I attend Sunday school every Sunday. Consett must have been a very religious town because there were seven places of worship: Catholic, Protestant, Chapel, Gospel Hall, Methodist, Baptist, and Presbyterian. The only one we were not allowed to attend was the Catholic Church because we were raised as Protestants and as the town was split into two camps you were either a 'Proddy Dog' or a 'Catty Cat' and you didn't mix with each other if you could help it. As Nora was older (she would probably be about 5 years old and me 3 years old when it was decided she was old enough to go to church on her own with me in tow), she decided that we should attend all the Churches to make our own minds up about religion. I just tagged along behind. We started with the church of our birth, the Church of England, and every few weeks we would change and, through the process of elimination, our preference became The Gospel Hall. This choice might have had something to do with the fact that if you attended six times in a row, you received a bar of toffee!

Easter was very special as Lorna and Gran would take us to the big city of Newcastle, the capital of Geordie Land, to get new clothes for Easter Sunday. Now in those days our clothes were made for practicality and long life, and Lorna used to make most of our clothes but bless her, she wasn't very good when she first started, so Nora and I would baulk at anything homemade. But Easter! Boy, we looked forward to Easter. Easter Sunday was always very special and God knows how Lorna managed it, but she made sure we were outfitted like little princesses for the Easter Sunday Service, at whatever Church we were attending at the time. There was always great anticipation in the air before Easter, and lots of preparation. It wasn't enough that we had new clothes, we were allowed to boil eggs and get up to our eyeballs painting and staining them, then there was the surprise of whether we'd get a chocolate Easter egg, or a sugar mouse, or a sugar pig. It was a great time, Easter!

We had a lot of cheap day trips away from home in the summer usually on a Sunday because kids traveled free on the 'Sunday Seaside Special' train. Lorna would get Nora and me ready and tell us not to move from where she'd put us, and then once she'd gotten herself ready we would make the two-and a half hour train trip from Consett train station to the beach at Whitley Bay. What an adventure! What resilience Lorna had! She'd spend the previous day making up sandwiches and cakes and pack them into empty biscuit tins to take with us because we couldn't afford to buy food when we were there. Then, like a female sergeant major, she would get Gran and Nora and I, and all of our bags to the seaside via bus and train – not an easy task, and she certainly earned those stripes! Mind you, eating sandwiches on the beach was not my idea of fun because no matter how hard they tried to prevent it, either Nora or I would kick sand up where the food was and you'd end up with more sand than sandwich. If I didn't know that it was the Earl of Sandwich who invented the sandwich, I would swear 'sandwich' was named after a beach somewhere.

One of the most memorable experiences of my young life took place in the long tall grass in the field opposite our house, and it happened on the most perfect summer's day that I have ever experienced. The sun was shining and the air was radiantly warm, the sky was the most beautiful azure blue, and little white cotton wool clouds drifted aimlessly overhead. I had no housework to do, it was all done. My time was my own and I had the day to myself. I had brought a book to read but my mind kept straying towards the different shapes that the clouds were making, first a face, then an animal, next a car. It was abstract art at its most magnificent. Peace, quiet and pure contentment crept over me as I enjoyed a little piece of heaven.

For two weeks, every October, when the schools were closed down for harvest time Nora and I would go potato 'tatie' picking at Stockdale's farm. We'd make about three pence a day plus a bucket of potatoes in payment, but what started out as a full bucket was mostly empty by the time I trailed the three miles back up the hill to home. Nora would turn around periodically and say, "Where's your taties? You'll get a clip round the lug (ear) if you've got none left by the time we get home!" I would then have to scamper back to where I'd thrown them in the grass and retrieve them, but the bucket used to get so heavy that I don't think I ever brought a full bucket home. We would sit and rest near a field of turnips, which just happened to be halfway home, and the thought of eating juicy tender young flesh was so great that Nora and I would 'snag' a turnip. It took some smashing against the rock to break it open, in order to get to the juicy fleshy part, but desperate times called for desperate measures, and we lulled our guilty consciences by saying, "Ah, the farmer won't miss just one!" I don't ever really remember enjoying tatie picking but as Nora wanted someone to go with her, I always got suckered into going with the promise of a ride out to the potato field on the farmer's tractor and trailer.

Christmas and New Year were glorious events in our house. We counted the days until a week before Christmas when Nora and I, and any other children we could get to accompany us, would go around as many houses as we could to sing Christmas carols. It didn't matter if you had a voice like a frog, so long as the numbers were there, and people appreciated the effort of you standing there in the freezing cold, singing your heart out. One person, usually Nora, would collect all the money and it would be shared out at the end of the evening. She was tough, and if you didn't sing you didn't get a share, but you were okay if you hummed loud if you didn't know the words.

Lorna used to make up our Christmas stocking that was either one of Billy or Jimmy's knee socks, and put it on the bottom of the bed ready for when we awoke on Christmas morning. With this being just after the war, goods were still rationed in England so there wasn't a lot to be had, but Nora and I whooped and hollered over our oranges, apples, nuts, and chocolate bars stuffed into the sock. "Look what I've got!" "Yes, but look what I've got!" You could have heard us for miles. Our presents were pretty much the same each year - some sort of reading material, even if it were only comic books that everybody used to read; a new set of underwear; and a new set of doll's clothes made by Lorna for our one and only doll. We figured we were pretty lucky and that Christmas was a fantastic time. The chicken, or piece of pork, would be cooking in the oven, the plum duff would be steaming away on the fire, and the pantry would be overflowing with goodies that Gran and Lorna had stood for days and baked, and all the relatives would be present. Who could ask for anything more?

New Year was extra special. There were two old, falling to pieces, leather armchairs set either side of the drain in the backyard, and you could bet your bottom dollar that by the time Billy and Jimmy, and brother-in-law Ken came home from the pub, one of them would have to throw up some of the beer just consumed. We'd hear the gate crash against the washhouse wall, and they would come stumbling, laughing and giggling all the way down the back yard and settle in an armchair. The one who was least drunk would be admonishing the other two, saying, "Eeh, can you not hold it man, that's a lot of good money yer getting rid of!" Or, "You'll be sorry in the morning that you spent so much money whetting your whistle only to hoy it all doon the drain!"

One year they were so plastered that a full bottle of Whisky fell onto the floor in the kitchen and broke, and before anyone could stop them, the dog and all three of them were down on their hands and knees trying to lick the booze up before it 'evaporated,' totally oblivious to broken shards of glass. Or the New Year that Ken was so happily drunk that it took both Billy and Jimmy to get him up the stairs and into bed. But as soon as they put him in one side he got out the other, and everyone was called upstairs to see his antics. Ken, with a silly grin plastered on his face, was thoroughly enjoying himself doing somewhat of a Charlie Chaplain routine and he had everyone in stitches. It was the only night of the year that they were allowed to get rip roaring drunk because Grandad would not have tolerated it at any other time of the year.

Nora and I would be tucked away on the bench by the fireplace, trying to keep out of sight so that the grown-ups would let us stay up to watch and listen. Oh, those were the days. Everyone would sing his or her heart out. Jimmy would be the first to start singing, then Billy. It never failed, ever, but that we'd all end up in tears when Billy started to sing *MOTHER*. *M is for the million smiles you gave me. O is that you're growing very old. T is for the tears you shed to save me. H is for a heart as good as gold. E is for the eyes that shine so brightly. R is right, and right you'll always be. Put them all together and they spell Mother, and she's the only one for me.* I'll probably always be able to hear him sing that and see the love in his face while he sang this to Gran. Then everybody would start to get a little bit daft and do his or her 'party piece.'

Billy was famous for his interpretation of the Hunchback of Notre Dame and he would drop his left shoulder, start dragging his left leg, screw up his face and then go lolloping around the kitchen slurring his words and have his left arm swinging from side to side. He really did look the part of the hunchback and he used to frighten the life out of me, as well as the adults, because he was so good. Even though I knew it was him, I'd scream with fright when he came across the kitchen and I'd try to bury my head into Nora's back and I wasn't happy again until that piece of play acting was over.

His next party piece was a one-act play – it was always the same but it wasn't New Year if Billy didn't do it. He'd get a woman's hat and a pair of knitting needles and sit on a seat pretending to be an old woman doing her knitting. He'd wait for a few seconds then put those tools down, and then put on a man's hat and pretend to be the son. Then the play would begin. In between pretending to be the man or the woman he'd have to dress the part, and it would start with the son coming home and asking where the father was. *"He's in the barn!"* the mother would reply. *"What's he doing in the barn?"* asked the son. *"Hanging!"* said the mother. *"Have you cut him down!"* demanded the son. *"Nope!"* replied the mother. *"Why not?"* shouted the son. *"He ain't dead yet!"* replied the mother. Oh, the guffaws and hysterics that used to cause. We all knew it off by heart but it was hilarious to see it acted out.

Our Bramble Bush Family

We had such a mixed-up family, it was hard to figure out who was related to who, and Nora and I had more pseudo 'aunts' 'uncles' and 'cousins' than you could shake a stick at. Gran had family living all around us, and it was a sure bet that our New Year's Eve celebrations wouldn't end until the majority of them had visited and had a 'wee drink' to bring in the New Year. We were never short of relatives and both us of considered Gran's family to be our family. I wasn't to know any different for quite a few years. Gran had three sisters, 'Aunt Louise' married Jim Maguire and had children Lully, Raymond, Tommy, Jimmy and Sheila and they lived near us in Templetown. Her sister 'Aunt Laura' married George Winter and had Moira, Philip, Billy and Mabel and they lived at the Grove. Her other sister 'Aunt Mabel' married Ralph Maguire and had Brian and Eileen and they lived in Winlaton near Newcastle, and to differentiate her from Grandad's daughter Mabel, she was always referred to as 'Aunt Mabel from Winlaton.'

Gran's children, 'Uncle Bob Barron married Aunt Margy' and had Peggy, Esther, Robin, Johnny and Leslie and they lived in Delves Lane; 'Uncle Bill Barron married Aunt Anne' and had Sydney and Johnny and they lived in Moorside; and, 'Aunt Betty Barron married Uncle Frank Ronson' and had Jill, Jennifer and Billy. While Frank was in the Armed Forces, Betty and family roomed with Uncle Bob and Aunt Margy.

Other relatives of Grans were old 'Aunt Jemima' who lived at the top of Templetown opposite the Gospel Hall, and Nora and I visited every Sunday after Sunday school, and old 'Aunt Aggie' who lived in Knitsley hamlet about a mile and a half down the hill from us toward the farm and was always good for a refreshing drink on the way home from an adventure.

The only bona fide relatives that I ever knew from my Grandad's side were Aunt Gladys who married Uncle Wilf Ingram and they had Laura, Wilfred and Janet and lived in Castleside; Aunt Mabel married Uncle Joe Clark and they had Heather and Lesley and lived in Blackhill; and Aunt Beattie who married Uncle Bill Dodds, and they had Brian and Dorothy and lived in Ebchester, southeast of Consett on the road to Newcastle.

Of the four children the grandparents had together: Marjorie would marry Ken Lowther and have David, Kenneth, Ian, Lindsay and Nancy; Jimmy would marry Ruby and have Fiona; Billy would marry June and have Billy, Keith and Susan; and Lorna would have Ted.

The last child

Edward (Ted) 18 months old

The grandparents raised fourteen children altogether but I have only accounted for thirteen so far: Gladys, Mabel, Beattie and Elsie; Bill, Bob and Betty; Marjorie, Jimmy, Billy and Lorna; and Nora and myself, Nancy. The fourteenth child was Edward, or Ted as he is known, and he was born to Lorna when I was eleven. He just turned up one day and instantly became the apple of Gran's eye. Whether it was because she knew that he would be the very last child to be raised in our household, or what, but she absolutely adored him. I didn't see much of him for the first few years of his life because I was either going to school or babysitting for Marjorie; but he has played a big part in my life since we became adults. In a way, he had the easiest time of any of us growing up in this household. Maybe it was because Grandad and his temper weren't around for much of Ted's childhood; or maybe it was because Nora and I were getting older and not demanding so much of Gran's time that it let her give attention to only one child for a change. Whatever the reason, Ted was a fairly placid, easygoing child and we all loved him very much. He has grown up to be a handsome man, with a great sense of pride in his family, and a lovely generosity of spirit. By that I mean there is nothing he wouldn't do for his family – much like myself, and maybe that's why he and I get on so well. I loved him then, and I love him now.

So, there you have it. More relatives than most people I know, and certainly more than Nora and I were entitled to, but we loved every one of them.

School Days

I started school at the age of 4½ at Consett Council Infants School where I wasn't the brightest kid in the class but I do remember winning a big story book my first year. It was so big that I swapped Marjorie McDonald for her much smaller one because I had a two mile walk home from school and my book would have been too heavy. The only other thing I can really remember about the Infants School was that I was in the school 'band' and played the Triangle, and that our headmistresses' name was Miss Bloomfield, which she lived up to because she was a big woman. By the time I was seven I was very skinny, extremely agile, and bursting with energy. To everyone's surprise, even my own, I enjoyed sports and earned a Defensive spot on the Netball Team, and played all through my junior and senior years for the school. I captained my team more than once so I must have been good at it, and we traveled everywhere in the district playing against other school teams, often winning the yearly school tournaments.

At first, I didn't mind school because there were always lots of books to read, but I was not a brilliant scholar. My best subjects were English, Music, sports, and Geography, and that should tell you where my interests lay. My quixotic Dilly Dream character meant I could read a book; hum the latest record by the famous singer, Dean Martin, and mentally run with abandonment on a white sandy beach in Jamaica – all at the same time. I wasn't a dummy; it wasn't allowed as the teachers constantly meted out corporal discipline if the work wasn't done to their satisfaction. I had one male teacher who used an old narrow chair leg that he called 'Horace' to deliver instant punishment, and when he smacked it against the back of the leg, it jolly well hurt and left black and blue bruises! Another male teacher had a very thin branch from a willow tree. He would march up and down the aisles swishing his rapier in the air and, like a swordsman of old, would assault the knuckles of any child who dared to look up from their paperwork. They taught by fear! They were gods in their own time, and heaven help the child who complained about being punished at school, because after being cross-examined as to why the wrath of the teachers had been incurred, you stood a great chance of getting another good hiding for shaming the family!

I'm afraid that apart from my love of Netball (basketball), English, Music, and Geography, my school years were a daily endurance and fortitude test. No matter how much I pretended that my stomach hurt, or that I was dying from dengue fever complete with contrived cough, Gran used to frighten me into going to school because she said the Schoolboard Inspector would take her to jail if I didn't attend. My attitude towards school must have had something to do with the way I was taught - with fear instead of encouragement, because I've had a passion for learning ever since I left those particular nightmare days of my youth behind.

A Dose of Reality

Given my 'Dilly Dream' nature of living in a world of my own making, up until the age of nine I thought I'd had a great childhood, in stark contrast to my sister Nora's memories; however, in my innocence I didn't know that it was all about to change, that my rose coloured glasses would fail me when slapped across the face with sharp reality. What I didn't know, and never could have imagined was that my safe and secure little world was marching steadily toward destruction!

For reasons I didn't understand at the time, Nora and I had to make regular visits to Aunt Beattie and Uncle Bill, and cousins Brian and Dorothy, a long way away in Ebchester. It used to take at least an hour to get there because from Templetown we had to catch the bus to Consett, then wait for another bus to Medomsley which dropped us about two miles away from their house. After a long downhill walk, and just as the road dropped steeply away into the valley, we branched off to the right and walked about ½ mile along a treed laneway to where the relatives lived in 'Wyncliffe House.'

It was a very large stone-built house standing right on the top of the hill, overlooking part of the Derwent valley. Nora was 7 when she was allowed to take me on my own, I was 5, Brian was 3 and Dorothy was 2 years old. We visited them every couple of weeks throughout the summers and even stayed for a week or so which was great fun, until I was nine years old. I didn't know why we had to visit 'Aunt' Beattie and Uncle Bill so much, I just thought they liked us.

The kids sort of teamed up into pairs. Brian and I would always be together, as would Dorothy and Nora. Even though I was a very shy child, Brian and I used to get up to all sorts of mischief because I'd go along with anything; not because I was brave, just the opposite in fact, I was too scared to say no.

Entertainment was provided by our own imaginations. I remember one time walking back to the main road and further down the hill a bit because there was a big house with a garden full of crab apple trees, and Brian got it into his head that he would climb the 6-foot-high wall surrounding the property and 'snag' some apples. He put the fear of death in me when he shinnied up the wall and wanted me to do the same but I couldn't get a grip and had to wait patiently until he came back. He seemed to take forever, and I can remember being very anxious because there were dogs on the property, when his face suddenly appeared at the top of the wall and I shrieked with fright, because I thought it was the owner of the house. "Brian, Brian, come on, come on down. I'm scared! I'm never ever going to pinch anything ever again. If you want to pinch things, you'll have to do it on your own!" He replied, "You're no fun, no fun at all, they're not going to eat them, they're just crab apples, no good for anything but pinching!" Just as he spoke, the lady owner came out of the house and shouted something that neither of us had time to hear because we took off like the wind. She knew who we were because we were the only kids in the area and for the rest of the afternoon we sort of skulked around the house waiting for her to show up, but she never did. Apart from the couple of times that Nora and I 'snagged' a turnip from the farmer's field, that was the last time I ever tried to pinch anything. In fact, it was about that time that I realized that I didn't need anything so bad that I'd steal for it – words I've lived my life by.

On the hillside below Wyncliffe House were lots of hazelnut trees, and one of my greatest pleasures was to go hunting for them, and if Dorothy and Nora weren't interested, then Brian and I would go on our own and could spend all day just rummaging around the area. The two of us would spend hours just searching for ripe nuts and would have most of them eaten before we got home, and it was the same story if we went blackberry picking. Most mornings Aunt Beattie would give us a two-pint tin mug and Brian and I would get up very early, probably around 6:30 am, and scour the hill looking for mushrooms. We usually found the best mushrooms in the field behind the house, the same field that the local farmer's cows had pastured in, but when you're young that doesn't matter. It gave them a great flavour!

Brian was great at creating a fantasy game out of nothing and just below the hazelnut trees was a Nunnery, and Brian and I would pretend we were foreign spies. We would secretly watch the nuns going about their daily chores and make reports in our little notebooks, such as "Black Nun #1 came and got some cabbages to make poison to kill the villagers." Or, "Black Nun #2 is secretly pinching tomatoes off the vine to sell to the local grocery store in order to buy ice cream!" Or, we'd pretend we were explorers and climb over the stones and through the nooks and crannies of the old stone quarry that was opposite their lane where it split off from the main road. Mind you, we had to be careful not to be spotted because Uncle Bill's sister, Eleanor, lived opposite the quarry. She lived in a farmhouse just bordering the lane that led to Wyncliffe House and we'd be in for a good telling off if she saw us, because there was an old coal shaft under the quarry somewhere and it could have fallen in at any time. Most of the time she was great fun to visit, and she always asked if we were hungry, which we always were, so she'd make us a sandwich to 'keep us going until tea' as she said. She kept a couple of milking cows and made her own butter and I remember the first time I tasted hers because she mixed the creamy pale butter with too much carrot juice and it was the only time I've ever eaten 'orange' butter.

If we were all bored and could find nothing to do, which was most unusual, then Aunt Beattie used to give us sixpence and suggest we make an excursion to the actual village of Ebchester to buy either an iced lollipop or an ice cream at the Village Store. The village lay at the bottom of Ebchester Hill which was well known for its share of fatal tragedies over the years, as cars with dicey brakes often ended up in the River Derwent which ran parallel to the 'low road' to Newcastle at the bottom. After being admonished a number of times for running and not being able to stop ourselves, and ending up crashing into the gorse bushes on the side of the hill, we knew to take it easy and walk slowly. With that knowledge, Aunt Beattie knew that the walk down the hill and back again would take us at least 1½ hours, so she would get some guaranteed peace for a while.

Nora and Dorothy were of like mind. They both loved crafts, and whereas Brian and I didn't have the patience, both Nora and Dorothy would sit for hours making things. Their favorite things to make were Snow-White and the Seven Dwarfs ornaments. Aunt Beattie had gotten the rubber molds and some Plaster of Paris stuff, and the two of them would churn out mold after mold and sit for ages painting them and getting them just right. Their other favorite ornaments were three ducks, each one smaller than the one before, and I'm pretty sure they could have stocked a shop with them because they made so many. Or the two of them would dress up in old Victorian hats and pretend they were having a tea party in the shed half way down the garden, which had a couple of seats and a small table and an old gramophone that only played '78s. I can't remember the title, but I do remember some of the words of one particular record because it was Dorothy's favorite, *"You were meant for me. I was meant for you. Nature fashioned you and when she was done, you were all the sweet things rolled into one. You're like an aching melody, that never sets me free; but I'm content the Angels must have sent you and they meant you just for me."* They would exuberantly wind the gramophone up but if you didn't watch over it, it would soon lose speed and the voice would go from a high-pitched Tenor to a barely understandable Bass. Then we'd all make a mad dash to wind the thing up again but invariably in our hurry we'd over-wind it and for a while the singer would sound like a chipmunk.

t was towards the end of a perfect Sunday dinner of Jersey potatoes straight from the garden, roast beef and Yorkshire pudding, and Aunt Beattie's special mint and green onion sauce that my 'Dilly Dream' world shattered. Our 'cousin', Peggy Barron, had already told Nora that she was Beattie's daughter but hadn't said anything to me because I was so young so I was totally unprepared for what came next. One minute we were all enjoying the beautiful spring day, the glorious smell of daffodils and crocus in their pots on the window ledge, and thoroughly enjoying a lovely meal when, in a moment of silence, Uncle Bill said, *"Your Mam is not your Mam you know – she is!"* Nobody moved or breathed. It was as though somebody stopped the hands of time and everything was happening in slow motion. I remember my head turning gradually toward him because even though I hadn't been looking at him, I knew he was talking to me. I just knew it! Somewhere in the recesses of my mind all the nasty little incidents in my past were coming together and the whole assembly of thoughts were pushing themselves to the surface. Nora sat next to me with a look of total horror on her face as Uncle Bill repeated yet again, *"That's your mother sitting at the end of the table! Beattie is your mother!"*

My mother Beattie and her husband, Bill Dodds

Somehow my body rose and pushed itself away from the table, crashing the chair and stumbling on its feet like some small infant not sure of its first steps. My fantasy family world exploded into a million pieces. I felt as though somebody was pulling my stomach out through my throat, and I managed to stumble into the garden before I threw up. I thought I was never going to stop. I could hear Beattie shouting at Bill in the background and by now Nora had her arms around me telling me everything was going to be okay, but that I had to find out sometime. I can still see Brian and Dorothy, my new brother and sister, sitting at the table open-mouthed and dumbfounded. I couldn't believe it; yet, at the same time things were starting to make sense. The girls in school used to ask how come I had a very old mother when she had to come to school for Parent/Teacher days. I had just never thought about it.

What an awful way to find out about my true parentage. To be so young and have the security of my Mam and Dad ripped away without warning. I was more than heart broken. I was desolate and inconsolable! What was I to do? Where was I to go? Where did I belong? It wasn't as though he was giving me anything in their place. He didn't go on to suggest that I come and live with them, no; he just exploded my world and mentally left me with no home and no parents! I was totally embarrassed because I didn't know what to say or how to act with this new knowledge. Until that moment in time I was happiest when I had my head in a book, exploring with Nora, picking wildflowers for Gran and Lorna, going for long walks with Grandad, or helping him tend the animals. What a horrible way to find out that I'd been living a huge lie.

Automatically Nora put my hat and coat on, and we left to walk up the hill to catch the bus home. I had a thousand questions I wanted to ask her, but couldn't find the words through my tears. I had started weeping after I'd thrown up, and just couldn't stop. I was still desolate as Nora told Gran what had happened because we were home a couple of days earlier than we should have been. I remember hiding behind her just in case Gran said, "Well, you'd better take her back to her mother now that she knows!" but she didn't. She put her warm and loving arms around me and cuddled me for ages, with me still half sobbing. I was so worried that I didn't have a Mam any more that I asked her if I had to call her Gran now but she said, "No hinny, I've been your Mam all your life, and I always will be!"

The world had suddenly become a very frightening place and life didn't stop because I was now lost in a sea of people that I was somehow cast adrift from. I still wasn't old enough to understand the relationships between all the people in my life, how they all melded together, so I clung to Nora. She was the only person that I knew without a doubt belonged to me. 'Aunt' Beattie came within the next few days to see Gran and tried to explain that Uncle Bill had blurted it out before she even knew he was about to say anything, and that she was sorry it had to come out like that, but it was time I knew. I don't suppose she gave a second thought as to how I felt about the relationship change because she ignored me all the while she talked to Gran. So, after all the fuss and weeping was over, nothing changed. I still lived in the same house, and I still considered her to be my Aunt Beattie, and even though they were now officially my grandparents, Gran was still Mam and Grandad was still Dad. Marjorie, Billy, Jimmy and Lorna were still my brothers and sisters, and remained so all my life.

However, some things did change and I became more mentally aware, and a lot of things that had happened in the past started to take on new meanings, such as other people's attitudes toward me and my sister, for one thing. One child born illegitimate could be reasoned with, but a second child, born to a different father. Never mind other people wanting to know how it happened. It would take a lifetime to explain my existence to my satisfaction! Up until now I'd never understood the threat from the grown-ups that I'd be sent back to Beattie, or be put in the Cottage Homes (our local orphanage), if I misbehaved because I couldn't think why they would say such things. But, after learning the truth about my birth, those threats definitely took on a new significance, and for the next while I certainly lived up to the old saying of, "Children should be seen and not heard!"

As I said, Templetown was a small village. It didn't matter how much protection both Nora and I received from the family, in the early 1940's, being illegitimate was something to be discussed and dissected by all and sundry. We lived in 'holier than thou' times, and the pure spitefulness of some women in the village had to be experienced to be believed. When I was out and about with Grandad people would be very respectful and polite, but it was totally different when I was on my own. Often there would be a small group of maybe two or three women standing chatting near the small 'living room' shop in the village, and having to pass them to get into the shop was horrendous at times. I'd hear the 'stage whisper' comment of, "There goes one of Beattie's bastards" and hadn't a clue what they were talking about because at that time, I didn't know I was illegitimate or in their eyes, a bastard. But once I knew the devastating truth, their remarks hit like lightning bolts. I was an undesirable. The lowest of the low! Definitely an unwanted second pregnancy! Upon realizing this, I started to grow the most awful inferiority complex.

Nora and I would talk about our birth's all the time, either away from the house, or under the bedcovers at night, but never in front of the others. She told me that she'd heard her father was a soldier but that he'd been killed in the war, and both of us reasoned that if he'd come back he would have married our mother and at least Nora would have had parents, and they would have been such a happy family.

In the late 1930's our mother was a housemaid in a hotel in Blackpool, a much-celebrated seaside town in Lancashire on England's northwest coast, when she fell pregnant in 1940 and Nora was born in May 1941, and to give you an idea of just how deeply Nora was hurt by the fact that she was illegitimate she wrote a poem:

It's the war boys, it's the war.
Johnny, are you keeping score?
Cross that one off my list
She's been sent home, she's been dismissed.
That seed I planted that September day
Will bring forth fruit early in May.
It's the war boys, it's the war

Johnny, are you keeping score?
No, I will not marry the mother
I am engaged to another.
No, I won't give the baby my name
Let it live a life of shame!

It's the war boys, it's the war
Johnny, what was the score?
We were young and full of pride
Oh, the things we had to hide!
Was it a girl, or was it a boy?
How it would have brought me joy.
It's the war boys, it's the war!

It was easy to believe that Nora's father had been a soldier and that he'd been killed in the war, seeing has how she was born in the middle of World War II, but what had she heard about my father? I was born toward the end of the War so in my mind he was a soldier too. But was he? Where was he now? Where did he come from? If he was still alive, why hadn't he married our mother? There was nobody we could have asked who would have answered those questions, so it settled in my mind that there would never be an explanation for my existence. I really was a mistake! A 'nobody' to be palmed off onto anybody who would have me. Totally unwanted, and totally unloved by the woman who had carried me for nine months and given birth to me.

The biggest change that came over me was that a lot of things that I had been grateful for in the past now made me feel rotten. Aunt Mabel used to buy beautiful clothes for cousins Heather and Lesley, and would send for me to come and see if I could fit into any of them after they'd been outgrown, and until now I had been very happy to receive them. I used to prance around in front of Heather, Lesley and Nora in the hand-me-down clothes, pleased as punch to have something 'new' to wear. But now that I knew where I stood in the world, having to hold my hand out for other peoples used clothing was nauseating. The last time I ever went to Aunt Mabel's to pick up a 'new' hat and coat that had belonged to Heather, I was so physically ill that I vomited right down the front of it before I got to the bus stop to go home and I don't remember ever wearing it again. I swore to myself that when I grew up I would never again take 'hand-outs' from anybody. I would buy my own things, and they would be new things, not somebody else's cast-off clothing! It was very hard being just nine years old and realizing that everything I wore was thanks to somebody's generosity, either from immediate relatives, or friends of relatives, and sometimes from 'superior' people from the village, but never from the people who should have been providing for me, parents.

Responsibility came early

I always loved children and babies and, because I had such a quiet and soothing nature, they seemed to gravitate towards me, as opposed to Nora who was more aggressive. Somewhere round this age my name changed from Nancy to Nanny, and because Gran used to tell everyone that I was, "Nanny by name and Nanny by nature," I became the official child minder of the Buckett family. Up until now I had only looked after the children who had come to our house, but by the time I was ten years old, I was considered grown up enough to become resident babysitter for Marjorie and Ken's two-year-old son David, at their house. I wasn't asked if I'd like to give up my weekends and summer holidays to babysit - I was just told that I was going to do it - so for the next five years, until I was fifteen years old, every weekend I made the five-mile bus trip from Templetown to Blackhill via Consett, and then back again on Sunday evening to get ready for school the next day.

Marjorie & Ken's house in Chapel Street was located halfway down, and behind, the main street, Derwent Street, in Blackhill and their front door opened into the back lane that ran behind the stores. There were only two houses left as all the others had been demolished, and they lived in the first one. It was an old decrepit house with no front garden and only a small concrete backyard that accommodated a fly-ridden midden (outhouse) that was shared with the people next door. Ken tried to keep the odors down by covering the effluent with ashes from the fire but it wasn't very effective and, when he was a young man, it was my Uncle Joe's job to empty the middens with a shovel and a horse and cart and put the effluent on farmer's fields as fertilizer.

The house had no saving graces as it was in the last stages of decay, and it was an awful ugly place to try and raise children, but they were only living there temporarily so as to be first in line for a new Council-built house once this one was demolished. It was known as a one up, one down house - one-bedroom upstairs, and one living room downstairs with no permanent light fixture. The kitchen was nothing more than half a shed leaning tiredly up against the outside house wall. It had one tap for cold water, a sink with a bucket underneath to catch the waste, and a one-ring gas burner, so most of the cooking was done on the fire or in the oven attached to the fire. They didn't have much furniture, only a very highly carved sideboard for dishes and matching table and chairs, and two very old horsehair brown leather armchairs, one at either side of the fireplace, which they'd push together to make a bed for me each night. The house was so old and damp that I swear the old timbers had rheumatism. In 'bed' at night, small fingers of light from the damped down fire would make flickering shadows on the deteriorating plaster ceiling and with my imagination, it was very hard to get to sleep.

Marjory wasn't an easy person to get along with. It wasn't that she was unlikable; she just had a demanding and critical nature which, combined with the Buckett temper, didn't make for a harmonious environment at times. One minute she would be happy and laughing, and the next she would be giving me a tongue-lashing for no good reason, and it wasn't until I was much older that I realized that I had served the last of my childhood years as an indentured servant in her home. I didn't like her very much when I was a child and did my best to stay out of her way as much as possible.

Back row: Marjorie, Ken, Ian,
In front of them: Kenneth & David
Front row: Ted and Gran Buckett.

Ken, on the other hand, was the most cheerful happy person you could ever wish to meet and I always thought his personality was completely opposite to Marjorie because, where she could be difficult and complex, he was always down-to-earth and lovely to be around. He was tall and handsome, and had wavy brown hair that he combed constantly to try and keep it in check, but it still bounced all over the place. He was joyful, easy-going, and generous, and I have never heard him say a bad word about anybody. His nickname should have been 'Curious George' because Ken was absolutely curious about everything and his pockets were always full of stuff that 'might come in handy.' All his life he had to know how things worked and would take things to pieces before putting them back together again, usually with great improvement. He started his working life in the Blacksmith's shop for the Company and could create anything, even without the aid of architectural drawings. He was a terrific cook and when he came home each night, he would start making the supper, and I never heard him complain about having to do so. His imagination knew no bounds and you never knew what he would make, such as mushrooms and onions in gravy over mashed potato, and it was just too bad if you didn't like onions, because he put masses of them into everything. I think I was only about 4 years old when I told him that I was going to marry him when I grew up.

I used to love to go with Ken and the children to visit his mother, Nanna Lowther, or Florence Robson Lowther as she was correctly known. Nanna was a lovely woman who had a very hard life when she was younger. Ken was only one-year-old when his father died of a heart attack at the age of 43, and Nanna was left with her children Robson 12, Freddy 11, Harry 9, Jean 6, Lesley 3, and Ken 1, to raise on her own. Frederick, his father, worked as a Mining Engineer for one of the Company-owned pits, 'The Victory Pit' in Crookhall. After he died, Nanna was told to vacate the Company's cottage because if you didn't have anyone in your immediate family working for either the Company or in one of their coal pits, then you weren't entitled to a house from them. It's hard to believe that our local employer could be so ruthless as to throw a family out on the street after suffering the devastating loss of their father and wage earner, but they did, and Ken's mother, sister and brothers endured this fate. After splitting up all the children between her relatives for a couple of years, Nanna Lowther rented a pub and managed to get them all back under one roof. Now whether it was because of the trauma in her life or whether it was because it was so near to hand, but Nanna drank a bottle of Guinness every day of her life and remained in excellent health well into her 90's.

Marjorie & Ken's firstborn, David, was the most beautiful baby I've ever seen. He was the epitome of a perfect boy child with his blond naturally curly hair and brilliant blue eyes, and everyone loved him. He was always giggling and laughing, and he warmed my heart like the rays of the sun. I loved him like a mother bear loves its cub. He had a thirst for learning that was beyond his years, and the two of us would settle into one of the big armchairs by the side of the coal fire and read storybooks for hours. I was in seventh heaven. This is what I was born to do! We spent most days on our own because Marjorie used to leave quite early for her daily visit to Gran, and on the days she was at home, usually rainy days, I would automatically get David dressed for the outdoors. He and I would either spend a few hours playing in the children's playground in the park or, if I didn't feel like getting dirty from the red dust off the Company's blast furnaces which was everywhere, we would saunter up and down Derwent Street, window shopping, dodging in and out of the shop doorways to avoid getting wet. In between minding David, I would have to help with the housework and couldn't leave for home on a Sunday night until I'd polished every nook and cranny in the highly-carved sideboard.

Kenneth was born when David was about three, and he had light brown fairly straight hair and green eyes. There was nobody happier than David when he came along. He absolutely idolized his young baby brother and would do anything for him and when they were older, maybe about 6 and 3, Kenneth actually took the lead and he would instigate the mischief making. Ian was born a couple of years after Kenneth and he was not as boisterous as the other two; he was a much gentler child and more sensitive, thank goodness. He took after David in looks though, being a bonny child, and although his hair was also blonde it was fairly straight. Ian was a bit intimidated by the rambunctious goings on of his older brothers and he was happiest when he was either reading or painting when he was a bit older, and while the other two were tossing each other like wrestlers in the ring, he and I would quietly enjoy non-violent games. If David and Kenneth were running around Blackhill Park like wild animals, I would push Ian on the swings and we'd both pretend we didn't know such unruly children until it was time to go home. There was no activity that could wear David and Kenneth out, they would be on the go from sun up to sun down and just being around them was enough to exhaust anyone. Ian and I would sit on a park bench and read stories while the other two would be digging their way to China and getting up to their eyeballs in dirt. Then I'd take them home and Marjorie would say, "which pit have you two been digging coal from today? Get the tin bath out Nan; they need to soak that muck off them!"

The two elder boys were perhaps the most imaginative children I have ever come across. They could make a game of Cowboys and Indians last all morning with the table being the Coach, and the sideboard being the Saloon. They would come out from behind of the Saloon and pretend to be drunken outlaws, staggering around the room before falling down in a theatrical pose. I would have to sit 'in' the Coach and with my 'Sharpshooter' (my finger) pick them off one by one and they would dodge the 'bullets' and laugh, "you missed me, you missed me!" After doing this about a dozen times they'd get bored and pretend to be hit so that they could yell their heads off while 'dying' most dramatically. Life was never dull around those two. David I could reason with sometimes, but Kenneth had a stubborn streak and he would dig his heels in if he didn't want to do something, and if his mind was set, you couldn't change it for love or money. He was a typical boy, doing typical boy things. Before I could wash his clothes, I'd have to turn his pant pockets out because I'd find dead worms, birds eggs, nails, candies, bits of stick, and anything you can think of stuffed into them. He took after his father, and his nickname was Dennis the Menace because he too liked to take things to pieces, only he couldn't put them back together again.

Kenneth had a passion for Heinz Tomato Soup; it had to be Heinz, and nothing but Heinz, that's all he would eat for lunch, and we had Heinz Tomato Soup and bread for lunch – day in, and day out, week in, and week out. It seems strange now that I think about it, but I wasn't allowed to use the gas ring in the kitchen, but could keep the coal fire burning and that's how I heated the soup, in a pan over an open fire. The other children would like a change, even if it was only a jam or banana sandwich but not Kenneth, all he would eat was Heinz Tomato Soup. To this day, I never see Heinz tomato soup without thinking of Kenneth, and even though this beautiful child returned to heaven at the young age of nine, I bet he's still having Heinz Tomato Soup for lunch.

It's hard to believe that any parent would do so now, but whenever Marjorie and Ken had a party, they'd bring the two older boys downstairs, let them have a small drink of beer, and encourage them to do their 'party piece.' On the promise of getting a sixpence, both boys would sing songs from the radio and everybody would go wild.

I remember taking them both to the Barber's for the first time and Kenneth, who didn't want his hair cut, made such a fuss that the Barber conned him into sweeping David's hair up off the floor, to keep him quiet. Every time we went to the Barber's after that Kenneth would just go and get the broom and start sweeping the hair up without being asked. We were all laying bets that he'd end up being a Barber himself because he took so much pride in getting every last hair off the floor, much to the amusement of the other patrons as he'd tell them to lift their feet so that he could sweep underneath them.

If the two of them didn't want to go outdoors for the day, they became the most darned awkward kids ever. Each of them would wiggle and squirm and it was like trying to harness an unbroken pony and, as soon as I got one dressed, the other would be in a state of undress. That is unless they wanted to go outdoors, then they would stand as still and as quiet as two statues until we were all dressed –at these times I used to tell them they were my two little angels – with black wings! Ian was still a baby at this time, and with him in the big Silver Cross pram and David and Kenneth holding onto each side, I would take them to the children's playground so that they could burn off some energy, then we'd maybe have a bread and jam picnic. I used to make a game of everything, even the pram – it was our chariot and both children had to help me push the King on his outings to see his subjects. It must have seemed strange to see a huge pram coming toward you because I was hidden behind it, and it must have looked as though two small children and a pair of legs were propelling it on their own.

Sometimes Marjorie would tell me to get the three children ready and meet her in Templetown at Gran's house. Between David and Kenneth, who weren't really much help, and myself, we struggled to push that big old pram up the hill into Consett. I always had to stop about halfway up because not only was the pram very heavy, it was a steep hill. Thank heavens it was a downward run into Templetown. After her visit, Marjorie would bring the children home on the bus and I would have to push the empty pram all the way back to Blackhill to be ready for the next time. Five miles was an awful long way to push a pram even without two little ones hanging onto the handle and it wasn't a trip that I enjoyed.

Marjorie wanted David to have some sort of education before he had to go to school, and she was so convinced that the earlier her boys started learning the better off they would be. So, most days I had a curriculum of sorts set up, such as an hour's reading or writing, then half an hour doing sums, and maybe an hour playing with crayons, although the only paper available for use was the inside of cereal boxes or newspapers and while it was very serious teaching David the basics, the other two boys played around. All the boys loved their 'pretend school' during rainy weather, but it was a tussle getting them to do their work on sunny days.

Back LtoR: Ian, Kenneth, David Lowther and cousin Ted Buckett

My life revolved around the three Lowther boys and every waking moment was taken up with seeing to their needs. I had no life of my own, nor did I expect one. I didn't grumble, I just did as I was told. Now and again I'd be given an afternoon off and, with a sixpence from Ken, I'd either go to the local movie house for a Saturday afternoon matinee, or I'd spend the lot on sweets for the children, and we'd have a picnic on a blanket in the backyard. I was too young to see it as work; to me it was a labour of love which was just as well because I never ever received any babysitting money from Marjorie. I think that my inferior complex was so great it never crossed my mind that I deserved to be paid; in fact, I considered myself to be extremely fortunate if she gave me bus money to get home on a Sunday night because most times I had to make the long walk home, in the dark wintery nights, all on my own with my vivid imagination of spooks and ghosts popping out everywhere.

There were some bright spots and I did get to enjoy three holidays in a row with the family in the seaside town of Silloth which nestled on the shores of the Solway Firth, backed by the Lake District Fells, and that was a real treat because not everybody could afford to go away on holiday. It never dawned on me that they still needed a resident babysitter; all I knew was that we were all going on holiday to the seaside. The first year they rented a cottage outside of town and, as there wasn't a bus service, we walked three miles there and back to get supplies and halfway home had to carry the children as well as the groceries. The next year they booked a cottage that was totally overrun by earwigs: they were in the bed, under the pillows, in the sugar bowl, in the toilets – everywhere! And the last year, the rental cottage turned out to be someone's converted garage. Even though this sounds awful, it was opposite the beach, and the owner had a small convenience shop in her living room so even though the living quarters were cramped at least we didn't have to carry groceries very far. These three experiences were enough to put me off ever going back to Silloth even though it is a beautiful place to visit. My last memory of Silloth is of Ken when he took the children and me fishing. He was great at catching plaice or small cod, and after he'd cleaned them we'd have fresh fish for supper. One day the boys and I were digging in the sand for bait worms, or lug worms as they were known, and Ken was clowning around pretending to bite the end of a worm when he accidentally did. Yuck!

My life altering moment

The family gave me the nickname of 'Mousy' as an infant; Ken changed it to 'Dilly Dream' as a young child, and Gran miraculously changed it to 'Smiler' just before I left school at the age of 15. I was having a 'feel sorry for myself day' and was silently watching the flames licking against each other in the fire, when Gran, in her sweet soft voice said, "Nan, you've got a face like a wet weekend, have you lost a pound and found a penny? What's the matter?" I gave an involuntary sigh and replied, "I was just wondering why I was put on this earth Gran!"

What happened next totally changed the way I looked at myself. This normally gentle-hearted lady rounded on me with such a start at my musing and cried out, **"*You're as good as everybody Nan, no better, but as good as everybody else on this earth and don't you ever forget it!*"** Wow! It took a second or two to register that Gran, of all people, had verbally hit me over the head with a hammer, but once I got over the shock of being pounced on, I thought about what she had said. Gran was right! Damn it, I was as good as everybody else. I hadn't asked to be born. I had no choice in it. What made it so right for others to be born, but not me? I thought about all those people who had passed rotten remarks about me within earshot, and thought who were they to sit in judgment on whether or not I should have had the right to be born! Nobody is any better than the next! We all breathe the same air! It wasn't as though some upper-class echelon was saying, "Hey, leave that pocket of air alone, it's mine!" No, everybody on this planet was the same as everybody else; everybody required the same basic necessities of life - to breathe air – God's lowest denominator. Gran was definitely right. I *was* as good as everybody else on this earth – no better – but as good as! And if ever there was a moment in time that that changed my perception of myself, then that was it!

I will never forget Gran's words of wisdom as long as I live; they are burned forever in my brain. To hear those words pounding over and over was the most mentally stimulating and liberating moment of my life! From that moment on I gave myself permission to stop being ashamed and embarrassed about being illegitimate, and the inferiority complex that I had been carrying around since I was nine years old started to crack and shift a little from my shoulders, and you know what? For the first time since I learned of my true parentage, I found I didn't care anymore, that it really didn't matter, that other people's opinions really didn't matter! It was only my opinion that counted! And it wasn't my fault! What a relief to be able to shout that out loud! It wasn't my fault! I had nothing to be ashamed of! I hadn't made the mistake, my mother had!

What a life-altering day that turned out to be. I jumped up off the sofa and hugged Gran until she begged me to stop, and I had a smile on my face as wide as the Grand Canyon that stayed put for the next few years. That was the day Gran gave me the nickname of 'Smiler' because she said I had a grin on my face like a Cheshire Cat. I vowed I'd never be ashamed of my birth again. I would look people in the eye and say, "No, I didn't have a mother or a father, I had grandparents who loved me!" I straightened up and walked tall. I looked everybody in the eye, and if they didn't like me for who I was, or had a problem with the stigma of illegitimacy, then they weren't invited into my life! I treated everybody as I expected to be treated -- with respect, kindness, and consideration. I promised myself that I would be the very best person I could be and hoped that when it was my turn to stand in front of God he'd say, "Well, I certainly tested you, but you did okay, Kiddo!"

Finally, all grown up

I had been quietly drowning in a sea of self-pity when Gran threw me that lifeline. She will never know what a tremendous impact those words had on me and would continue to have for the rest of my life. Since I heard those blessed words, "You're as good as…." I had undergone something of a personality change regarding the acceptance of my birth, and I now walked towards the rest of my life with a smile on my face. Finally, at the age of 15 I could leave school, find work, pay my own way, and be responsible for myself. It was my time now, my time to show the world what I was made of. I was a slim young girl with an 'hourglass' figure and my waist-length thick brown plaits had been cut into a shoulder-length pageboy style. Very grown up and mature! I was still painfully naïve and shy with outsiders, and cursed to blush like crazy at the comments some of the unknown workmen coming in through our gate used throw over their shoulders, "My, she's a bonny lass?" or, "Jane Russell's got nothing on her!" or, "What a bobby dazzler!" but I'd be greeted with a big grin and "Hello Smiler" from workmen who knew me and my family.

In 1958, when I was just about to leave school, Grandad who had worked a great deal of his life for the Company told me to go to the Personnel Office and sign on for a job then wait to see if I received a call for an interview. I received a summons in the mail and at the appointed time, I met the Personnel Officer and the only thing he asked was, "Are you related to Billy Buckett?" And when I replied yes, he was my grandfather, he said, "You start here on the Monday after you leave school!" I walked on air all the way home and thought what a great way to get a job, no interview, no testing, no nothing - apart from having grandfather as my grandfather. Brilliant! When I got home and gave them the news that I'd been hired, Grandad burst my bubble a little bit when he said sharply, "I'm only going to tell you this once: *Never get fired, and never be ashamed to hold your hand out for a pay cheque!*" I didn't really understand the second part of his dictum at that particular time, but I must have learned because I have always given good measure for money, and those words from Grandad would also stay with me forever.

Down a long and drawn out road, the 'General Offices' building was built of solid stone in 1885, in a blunt tipped triangle shape, at the apex of the steel works. It stood with imperial majesty in its robe of dirt and grime, and in its crown, was a huge clock tower that could be seen from half a mile away. It outgrew itself, and even though there was an ugly huge red brick extension built onto the right-hand side, housing the telephone exchange, sales department, and the Doctor's office, some departments had to be moved into buildings dotted throughout the works. To the right, in a separate building, was the Planning department. To the left, the drafting, engineering, and printing buildings squatted in between the new Power Station and three Blast Furnaces, and to their immediate left lay the sinter plant and the original plate mill now being used as a steel storage area. Running around the entire works and encircling all the offices, was a multitude of shunt trains in perpetual motion on Company-owned railway lines. These trains fed the Blast Furnaces as well as the new steel making plant located behind the general office, consisting of an Open-Hearth Plant, state-of-the-art Electric furnaces, and Slab and Billet Mills.

The Managing Director's office was on the second floor with the window facing the main road, and as he had a bird's eye view of every activity taking place within his realm there wasn't much he missed. In his eyes, being late for work was absolutely unacceptable. If his chauffeur-driven Bentley was parked at the front door, nine times out of ten he would be standing at the top of the stairs making note of who was late, and if he caught you more than once, you'd be out of a job.

The Reception area was at the tip of the blunt triangle on the ground floor. Four massive revolving glass and brass doors opened into an enormous room giving the impression of entering a Cathedral as the floor was covered with oak parquetry, and the walls and ceiling were made of carved panels of solid oak. There was a floor to ceiling window, only missing the stained glass to complete the church-like setting, and there was a solid oak Scarlett O'Hara staircase, with highly polished brass treads and handrail that glistened like gold in the sunlight. This regal staircase led to the Managing Director's office, before branching out at both sides to the minion's offices. The reception area was a declaration in affluence, and everyone who passed through spoke in reverent whispers not only because of its intimidating nature, but also because the slightest sound echoed around its corridors.

As requested, on the Monday after I left school I walked into this overwhelming room and reported for work. I felt like a million dollars because Lorna had bought me a new faun, pale blue and delicate pink plaid coat with a belt that fastened around my waist, a blue woolen straight skirt with a pleat in the back, and a beautiful pale blue woolen twin set. To complete the picture, I wore a pair of light gray shoes with a small heel, and carried a matching handbag and gloves. I could have met the Queen! I had no idea where, or for whom, I was going to work, only that I had to report to the Receptionist at least 10 minutes before the hour of 8:00 am. I remember being told to sit and wait for my new boss to come and get me, and I sat cautiously on the edge of an overstuffed brown leather chair, just in case I fell in and couldn't get out. Before long a very thin decrepit old man with an ill-fitting and slightly stained suit shuffled over to greet me. He said his name was Mr. Jack Latham, and he was head of the mail room, and that is where I would begin my working life. In the mail room, the same place as every other person just leaving school and destined to work in the Company's offices had started. Right at the bottom!

Mr. Latham would have been tall if he hadn't been so seriously round-shouldered, and he was an ill-tempered character with poor health. He used to sit on a big stool at the mail sorting counter and throw out orders to anyone within earshot. There was no politeness in him. He just shouted,

"You! Go here, go there, do this, do that!" and he was such an unpleasant man that it was hard to find any sympathy for him when he'd have to cough up phlegm and spit it into a glass jar beside him. It was worse still if you happened to be standing next to him, waiting for his order, because it was absolutely repulsive. To hear him struggle to clear his lungs was bad enough, but to see the spittle sliding down the rim of the glass jar was enough to make the most disciplined stomach heave and he tested the mental and physical strength of quite a few people in his time.

To be the new kid on the block meant fun and games for the rest of the young people in the mail room, and there were certain initiation rites that had to be carried out, with the blessing of the boss, of course. The first rite of passage was to be sent to see the boss of the payroll department and to ask him for a Long Weight. I thought it was something to do with the Envelope Plate Stamping machine that sat in the corner but it wasn't until the boss of the payroll said, "Okay, Nancy, you've had a long wait you can go back to the mail room now, that the penny dropped. Duh! I was a quick learner, but I must admit to feeling a little bit unsure of myself when I refused to get some White Ink and an Indian Vanishing Rubber from the supplies department for Mr. Latham. Fool me once, shame on you! Fool me twice, shame on me!

Obviously, working as a mail room clerk didn't pay very well, only 8 shillings for a 50-hour week, but armed with the knowledge that everybody who worked in the offices had started in the same way, made it normal. I worked there for two weeks before I received one week's wages, because they always held one week back and you'd only receive it if you left the Company which was practically unheard of. I danced with joy when I handed over my hard-earned money to Gran and received a shilling in return. A whole shilling! I'd never had so much money in all my life! And what a marvelous feeling that I had monetarily contributed to the household.

I was informed by Mr. Latham that everybody who was employed by the Company was required to further their education until the age of 21 and that I'd better read the booklets he had given me as to what courses to choose. Since I was now no different to anybody else, for the next five years I studied Shorthand, Typing and English on Monday, Wednesday and Friday evening classes at Consett Technical College. Enrollment was not cheap, and it was always a near impossibility to save the 18 shillings or so needed to pay for books and tutoring out of my one-shilling weekly pocket money and I always ended up begging for help from Gran or Lorna. It was the one time of year that it was almost always impossible to convince them that paying for Company-dictated education was a prerequisite of my employment. The questioning didn't stop with Gran or Lorna as to why I had to attend evening classes; I was grilled and questioned by Mr. Latham as to what courses I was taking and what my progress was. Attendance at night school was mandatory and strictly monitored by the Company. They were informed on a weekly basis as to whom had missed a class or whom was not doing well with their studies, and I well remember a couple of young girls being shown the exit door because they'd lost interest in their education. It was a lesson learned early in my employment and well-remembered whenever I felt like skipping a class to go to the movies.

Mr. Latham was a hard taskmaster, but for those eager to learn he had a modicum of patience. His motto was, "Listen, and do things right the first time I tell you!" If you didn't listen, you didn't last long in his department and could find yourself shipped out into a dirty works office some place, never to be seen again. There were 7,500 people constantly working for the

Company in one area or another and the split was 2,500 management and office staff, 2,500 maintenance and support workers, and 2,500 production workers. In effect, 2,500 production workers keeping the other 5,000 of us gainfully employed. The girls in the mail room only delivered mail within the main office, but the boys had to go out into the works to deliver mail to the outlying offices.

I was a serious worker having been taught by Grandad that when you were at work, you worked for the money they paid you, and you played around in your own time after work, and I got on as well as anybody could with Mr. Latham. In fact, he thought I was a pretty decent typist and gave me most of the typing to do, which I thought was great. One of the girls didn't like the fact that I was being singled out to do most of his work and, in a very belittling tone of voice, told me I was in danger of becoming a 'Teacher's pet' and that Mr. Latham was 'learning' me to her disadvantage. I quietly laughed and told her that Mr. Latham couldn't 'learn' me anything. He could 'teach' me but it was up to me to 'learn' and if she wasn't happy about it, then she should voice her criticism to Mr. Latham, because nobody was going to stop me from doing what was asked of me.

It never ceases to amaze me, but it doesn't matter where you go in life, or whom you work for, there is always, positively always, one person in close working proximity who continuously whines and moans about his/her lot in life and is never happy.

I'd been employed in the mail room for about six weeks before Mr. Latham considered me knowledgeable enough to sort the mail by person, and office. Then, trusting me not to get lost in the maze of corridors and offices, he sent me out to complete the exercise by delivering the stuff. I'd been concentrating on completing my duties, when a handsome young man came out from one of the offices and turned towards me. I stood entranced. Coming toward me was an Adonis, somebody out of the pages of a romance novel. He was tall and slim, dressed in gray knife-creased trousers, wearing a brilliant white shirt and maroon tie, underneath a navy-blue blazer. His blonde hair bounced around, and his sapphire blue eyes caught the light and twinkled. He stopped and introduced himself, "Hello there, I haven't seen you around before, my name is Brian Shaw, what's yours?" Hesitantly, and trying to find some moisture for my suddenly dry lips, I shyly replied, "Nancy Buckett."

Brian Shaw, 23 yrs old on our wedding day in 1963.

He walked along the corridor with me to the elevator and pressed the button for me to go to the ground floor. I managed to side-swipe the wall before getting the cart into the elevator and that might have had something to do with the fact that I was still blushing when I got back to the mail room. A couple of the girls looked up as I rushed in to put the cart in its place, and ran out again to go to the Ladies bathroom. I was still standing by the sink with my hands over my eyes, my heart was racing, my face was scorching, and I felt very foolish and very young, when the door opened and the two girls came in to see if I was okay. I said everything was all right, and there was nothing to worry about, but they wanted to know what had happened to embarrass me so. I was feeling pretty upset with myself for blushing so hard, and I really didn't want to admit to them that I was so naïve that all it took to make me blush was a young man stopping to speak to me, but they wouldn't leave me alone. "Well, then" I said. "A really handsome young man stopped me in the corridor outside the Cost Office and started talking to me, asking me things, and I got really embarrassed because I couldn't get my thoughts together to answer him. He must think I'm an ignoramus." In a chorus, they said, "Oh! You've met Brian Shaw!" I didn't know it at the time, but I'd just met my future husband!

Everything changes!

I came home to Templetown from work one day to find Grandad closeted in his bedroom refusing to come out because he'd had a difference of opinion with Lorna. It was one of those stupid silly arguments over who should clean up and it got blown out of all proportion and the next thing we knew Aunt Mabel came and took Grandad to live with her at Castleside. After three months of living there, he moved to Consett and lived with Billy and his wife, June, for another three months. What a muddle! After forty-four years of life together, Grandad was now estranged from Gran and his health problems of a bad heart and pleurisy had really deteriorated. He was in a really bad state and during a visit from Lorna he asked if he could come home again, and he did. Only our 'home' was no longer in Templetown. I'd been working for the Company for a year when they asked us to move out of the house I was born in and move into a house in one of six parallel rows of houses they owned at the bottom of Blackhill bank. This politely veiled request was still in the days of, "You'll do as you're told, and you'll like it!" so we had no choice but to move to Cort Street and this is where Grandad came back to us.

The streets were built on the lower side of Blackhill bank and our house was the tenth house down from the top in a street of twenty houses. The even numbers were on the right side and the odd numbers, where Marjorie and family now lived at the bottom of Cort Street were on the left. Surprisingly, they were fairly large houses, maybe about 20 feet long from the front to the back door. It had a garden of about 16 feet square at the back, an outside toilet and a coal shed at the bottom of the garden, plus a gate leading into the back lane. You walked in the front door, along a very dark hallway, past the living room and just before the bottom of the stairs turned right into the kitchen. As usual, this was the main living area of the house and again, it was the only room that was heated. Compared to my first home this was definitely modern. It had electricity in all the rooms and even though we still did most of our cooking on the fire, we now had an electric stove in the lean-to kitchen attached to the house. The front living room window looked into the street, as did the main bedroom above it, but the kitchen and the other two bedrooms looked into the garden -- not much of an improvement but it beat the streetscape.

We'd only been settled in the new house for a few weeks and Grandad had only been back home for four days when he died. Even though I knew he would never get better, I hadn't really thought about him dying and I was devastated. He'd been far too ill to manage the stairs so Lorna had put a bed in the living room, tucked up against the wall to give him some security, and

I had gone in to see if he needed anything before going to work that morning. I knocked gently on the door and went in quietly so as not to disturb him if he was still sleeping. Usually he was awake, and he'd ask me to empty his urine bottle from the night before and to refill his water bottle, but this time he didn't. I stood there looking at him, wondering whether to touch him to see if he'd wake up, and then it occurred to me that there was a funny smell in the room. It smelled a bit like rotten eggs and then it hit me what had happened. Grandad was dead! He was never going to ask me for anything ever again. I remember running back upstairs to tell Gran and Lorna that there was something wrong with Grandad and blurted out that I thought he was dead. What terrible news to give to somebody still slumbering in sleep, but Lorna hastily scrambled out of bed and threw herself down the stairs to see if there was anything she could do, but it was too late, he'd left us, he was gone. If any of us had known he was so near to death we'd have sat with him, but sadly he died in his sleep, all on his own. Aunt Mabel and Aunt Gladys came to the house to 'lay' Grandad out by washing him all over and dressing him for his coffin, then he lay in an open casket in the living room, for the three days before his funeral.

All my life I had been Grandad's constant companion and even when he lived away from home I visited him, and I know he loved me and I was shattered by his death. I spent the next couple of days in silent anguish; not feeling like anybody understood why I was so upset. After all, as they frustratingly said, "Didn't you know he was dying?" "No, I didn't!" was my heart broken response. When the day of his funeral came, Aunt Gladys was in the house and she sharply told me to hurry up and finish dressing but I couldn't find a hat to wear. Nora had found one, and I wanted it. I thought that as I had loved Grandad more than she had, then I should get the hat. Figure that one out! Maybe it was because my love for Grandad was not taken seriously by the others, or what, but I threw the first tantrum I'd ever thrown. I remember stamping my feet and screaming at Nora, "I'm not going to see Grandad off without a hat! Give me that hat! Give it to me or I'll knock you into next week!" And with arms flaying in the air, I went to grab the hat off Nora's head and the next thing I knew Aunt Gladys came over and hit me hard across the face and told me to stop it, Nora was wearing the hat. What a shock to the system that was. I always sensed Aunt Gladys really didn't like me very much, and when she swiped me across the head, I felt the weight of 16 years' worth of anger behind it. However, it had the desired effect. I did stop the tantrum and found a scarf to cover my head for Grandad's funeral. In later years, I was told she never forgave her sister for having me, so I was right in believing she didn't like me.

It seems strange now, but on looking back, I don't think I saw much of my mother, Beattie, from the day I found out she was my mother until years later at Grandad's funeral. I don't think it was deliberate on my part not to have anything to do with her, I think it was just the circumstances of babysitting for Marjorie and Ken until I left school, then going to work, and then of courting Brian. The only momentous thing to report was that just days after Grandad died, Gran was really upset about something when I came in from work, and when I asked her what the matter was, she said, "Beattie and Bill have just left. They want you to go and live with them now." They had made the same request of Nora when she was 16 so it was hardly unexpected, but it was still a bit unbelievable! I repeated to Gran exactly the same words that Nora had said two years previous, "They have done nothing to help raise me for 16 years and now that I'm working and contributing to the household, they want me! No chance!" Years and years later, Bill Dodds said that he had wanted to bring both Nora and I with Beattie when he married her but Grandad wouldn't let him. On the other hand, Marjorie said Bill Dodds would only marry my mother, who she was pregnant with his child, on the condition she left both Nora and I with our Grandad! Who knows anymore?

Life goes on, and my stint in the mail room ended soon after Grandad's death, and I was told to report to Mr. Harold Rutter, the boss of the Invoice Department, on the second floor. There were about 28 people all working in this department, and in my section of the large open room, there were four rows of metal desks, with four desks in each row, for a total of 16 typists. I was given a desk in the row farthest from the window and an old Underwood manual typewriter, but sitting next to me was Barbara Lough who had worked with me previously in the mail room. This was great because Barbara and I had become firm friends, and I felt very comfortable working beside her. I also got a salary increase from 8 shillings to 12 shillings, which meant my pocket money increased to 2 shillings a week.

Mr. Rutter was a gentleman and, away from work, he was a lay preacher in the Presbyterian Church. Not only was he extremely soft spoken, but he also walked softly which could be a bit unnerving because he'd suddenly show up out of nowhere. I'd just about jump out of my skin to find him standing behind me and speaking so quietly I'd have trouble hearing him. He was a lovely man but after working for him for a few months, he upset me a few times by volunteering my services to whatever department needed help. I used to think it was because I was the newest of his employees so therefore my skills were expendable in his eyes, but after a while I gathered up some courage and said, "Mr. Rutter, Sir, is it possible for you to send somebody else this time?" And when he answered, "Sorry, no. You're the only one I can trust to do a good job!" I became the 'floating secretary' for the Company for the eight years I worked there. When I got used to the idea of 'temping' for the other offices it wasn't too bad and I began to enjoy the variety and the experience, and it certainly helped me to become more proficient and confident in my abilities, and having my skills recommended by a lay preacher was quite a boost to my self-worth.

On the other hand, Mr. Jimmy Oliver, who was my immediate supervisor, was a tarter, a real horror of a man to work for. He was as round as he was tall, and he was a chain-smoker who never removed a cigarette from his mouth. He could talk and drink tea with a lit cigarette hanging onto one side of his lip, and just as he was finishing one, he'd light the new one from the old one. He had it down to a fine art and it was something to see the finesse in his timing, because he never had to stub the old cigarette out, it burned out on its own, standing upright on his desk. I never saw him shake the ash off a cigarette either, he'd just stand over a wooden wastebasket and give a small puff out of the side of his mouth and the ash would fall directly into the basket. How nothing caught fire is beyond me. Even though I was always wary of him and his big booming voice, it was just after I reached the age of 17 that he promoted me to Shipping Invoice Clerk. Now this may not sound like much of a promotion, but believe me it was huge! The previous girl, who was 24 years old, had to voluntarily leave because her pregnancy was becoming obvious and she was at the point of embarrassing the male colleagues. It was a sign of the times that the moment a woman showed her pregnancy she was expected to give up her job because it was not socially acceptable for an obviously pregnant woman to work. So, this position became open and the fact that Mr. Oliver recommended me for the job was unexpected and a little bit embarrassing. After all, there was the promotional pecking order to consider. There were at least 15 girls who held seniority over me who should have been considered before me but, as Mr. Oliver was the ruling overlord, he insisted in giving me the job, and a salary increase to 20 shillings a week, of which I received three shillings' pocket money.

It was an enormously responsible job and, in the beginning, I doubted my abilities to do it and it took a while to become comfortable with the immense paperwork attached to it. Every piece of paper regarding shipping every piece of iron or steel came across my desk. I had to produce Proforma's which was a pre-shipment document showing the minutest details of the steel, Customs documentation, shipping invoices, Bills of Lading, and then final Invoices for all the steel being shipped throughout Europe and around the world, and I had to copy type in the language of the country it was being shipped to and it had to be letter perfect. I was given the very first IBM electric typewriter to be bought by the Company, and as photocopiers hadn't yet been invented, nor had fax's, everything had to be perfectly typed on a stencil and run through a very smelly machine to get enough copies. In slow periods, I was still volunteered to help in other departments, so I was constantly juggling work but what a marvelous experience in responsibility for a young person. Without question, the challenge of this job set me up for life because I never again doubted my abilities where there was a keyboard involved.

My cousin, Lesley Clark, worked with me in this department for about four years, and she was a bit rebellious, not daringly open, just quietly behind Mr. Oliver's back. She would go down to the Ladies Room and stay for ages, until Mr. Oliver would notice she was missing, and then he'd shout right across the office, "Hey, you over there! Go and get your Lesley's hat and coat and take them down to her and tell her not to come back here, but to go home!" Everybody would stop working to listen to him, and not being in a position to argue, I'd go to the coat rack, remove Lesley's things and start walking toward the door. Then, without fail, he'd further shout, "Put the bloody things back, but go and get your Lesley and tell her if she's not back in five minutes, not to come back!" Eeh, honest! That man used to drive me crazy. I used to plead with Lesley not to spend more time than was necessary in the Ladies, but she just used to laugh because it became a battle of wits between the two of them, with me caught in the middle. She must have had enough hassle from Mr. Oliver during the time she worked at the Company to last her a lifetime, but she was never as intimidated by him as much as I was.

I made good friends with some young people in this department, Margaret Harrison, Barbara Lough, even my cousin Lesley Clark, Joyce Kendall, Josh, I can't remember his last name, and Gerald McNally and we decided to form an alliance to help raise money for B.E.L.R.A. This stood for British Empire Leprosy Relief Association. Gerald was the leader, and a very good one at that. Every Saturday after work, and whatever the weather, we would stand outside various pubs begging for money for B.E.L.R.A. We became so good at it that a famous English film star, Miss Anna Neagle, who was playing at the Newcastle Royal Theatre, heard about our success and decided to visit us in Consett. When word got out about the impending meeting you can just imagine the excitement that caused and thousands of people turned up to line the streets, and Tyne Tees Television came with their cameras. The noise was absolutely deafening as her limousine drew up to the front door of the Freemason's Arms Hotel and she stood for a while waving to the people before following us inside to the Ballroom. It was a bit surreal actually. Seven young teenagers from Consett got to meet the famous Miss Anna Neagle, and the television cameras recorded the event for the evening news. Unfortunately, the crew lost the tape and it was never shown on the television that evening, nor any other evening, which was a big disappointment because we wanted the publicity for our cause, B.E.L.R.A. I think it was Andy Warhol who said that everybody would have 15 minutes of fame in life – well that was mine and it got lost!

My life had been one series of orders after another since the age of 10 and when I was nearly 18 years old I began to feel as though my life was one grind after another. Go to work, go to night school, come home, clean, iron, wash dishes, baby-sit for Marjorie at the drop of a hat, go to bed, go to work, ad infinitum. At that time, I had an enormous jump in salary to thirty shillings a week and was receiving five shillings' pocket money, out of which I was buying my own clothes, and I felt that I should not have to hand every penny over to Gran and Lorna. Nora, at the age of 20, paid a set amount for room and board and was allowed to keep the rest and I wanted the same privilege. I'd put to the back of my mind all that had been done for me since my birth. I'd conveniently forgotten that Lorna had to go to work at the age of 14 to help support Nora and I. That it was Lorna who had really raised us, who had put her own life on hold for us, and that now I was able to help make her life financially easier I didn't want to hand over my whole pay. Talk about biting the hand that fed you. I felt like a rotten ungrateful teenager! But it didn't help the rebelliousness go away, it just got worse.

Leaving home, the first time

One Saturday afternoon, after work, when I was 18, Marjorie came in. She still lived at the bottom of our street and she was in a bit of a mood and passed some disparaging remark about dishes still being in the sink. For the first time in my life I retaliated, "You're always here, why don't you wash them!" Nevertheless, I went into the lean-to kitchen where the sink was and started to wash them when one slipped against another and made a noise. She came running in shouting something about not taking it out on the dishes and hit me squarely across the face, swiping my glasses onto the stone floor where they broke in two. "My new glasses!" I cried. "I don't care if they are new, you'll not talk to me like that!" she said. I'd had to save for months to get those fashionable glasses to replace the ugly 'porthole' ones the National Health Service handed out, and I was absolutely distraught! For one thing, I couldn't believe she'd hit me and for another, I couldn't see without glasses and I had to fumble around on the cold floor trying to find both pieces. Then I thought about it. How dare she hit me! I wasn't a kid anymore! I was a grown-up! But not in her eyes obviously. With that slap across the face she affirmed, at least in her eyes, that I was still a nobody. Well that was the last straw! She would not get the chance to make me feel inferior ever again. I was leaving! I'd had enough of feeling like a skivvy. Nora didn't like housework or babysitting and I'd always had to do her share, but not anymore. I was leaving home! Yes, finally, I was angry enough to leave home.

After I shouted my announcement Gran broke into tears and asked me not to go, but I said I had to, I was not going to be a doormat for Marjorie any more. Meanwhile, she was standing with her back to the fire shouting, "Let her go Mam! Who cares! Let her find out that it's not so easy out in the big world, she'll be back! You'll see!" Hell would have frozen over before I would have given in and stayed so that she could gloat over me. Then Gran asked me where I was going to go but I hadn't a clue. Since the first time I saw him in the corridor when I was delivering mail, Brian Shaw has been the mainstay of my life. It took him a while to persuade me to go out with him, but I've been by his side ever since. I had been going with Brian for about 3 years at this time and I knew he was playing in a tennis tournament in Blackhill Park so I walked out of the house and up to where he was playing and told him I'd left home. He was surprised to say the least, but promised to help me find somewhere to live. Well, my best friend, Anne Gowland had just moved into an apartment with her friend June Cleghorn, so after Brian drove me back home to pick up my clothes he dropped me at Anne's place. I told Nora where I was staying but asked her not to say anything; I lumped them all together in my anger, and if they didn't want me, I didn't want them! Funnily enough, the apartment was in a house at the bottom of the street where Billy lived and he never knew it. Anyway, I lived with Anne and June for about 3 months, and then found lodgings with a spinster, Miss Elsie Price, in Shotley Bridge where steel was first invented by the German sword makers. Elsie was in her early 60's, very set in her ways, but a lovely person and I think she adopted me the way she fussed over me. Her father had died about a year prior to me moving there and I was given his room, but she put the fear of death in me when she said, "Don't worry if you hear footsteps on the stairs, it's only Father!"

It was a small but nicely proportioned house, with a kitchen, living room and two bedrooms, but no bathroom of any shape or size, and the toilet was outside in the backyard. I'd never given it much thought as to how I would bathe myself but between us we worked it out that Monday, Wednesday, Friday and Sunday were my nights to get a full wash down in the kitchen sink and the other nights were hers. By agreement, either Elsie or I would make ourselves scarce by going into the cold living room and waiting while the other one got washed. Primitive, but it worked. She was retired when I lived with her, but had been a professional seamstress and wasn't happy until she had taken my measurements and made me some beautiful stylish clothes. It was quite a tussle with her not to make them too form fitting as was the style then, and she continuously complained that it was a shame to be hiding my beautiful figure but I wasn't comfortable showing myself off. During the summer when I had no evening classes, she would put a fire on in the living room and she and I would sit in front of the black and white television and thoroughly enjoy watching the Ballroom dancing competitions. Because she was a dressmaker, she often said she would love to see the ballroom dresses in colour but didn't think that anybody would ever invent a colour television.

I'd been living with Elsie for about 3 months when Nora asked me to come home and visit Gran, and as I hadn't had any contact with any other family member for months, I was ecstatic that Gran wanted to see me! I had felt terrible about leaving home the way I did, but I was so mad at Marjorie that I could have spit blood or done murder at the time. Still, I wasn't sure how the rest of them, including Marjorie, would welcome me back into the family fold but everything went well, and nothing of our quarrel was mentioned which was usual when anybody had a fight. So, for the next 6 months I visited my Gran and Lorna once a week but continued living with Elsie and was back to babysitting Marjorie & Ken's children again – just as though nothing had happened.

It was while I was living with Elsie that Brian and I got engaged. He had given me a choice; he would pay for driving lessons or an engagement ring. Which was it to be? I chose the driving lessons. We were verbally engaged so there was no hurry for a ring. Choosing the driving lessons backfired on me because Brian had forgotten his annual car insurance bill was due for payment on the same day that the lessons had to be paid for in full, and he suddenly couldn't afford it, so I ended up paying for them myself. But, to make it up to me, he stopped smoking for six weeks in order to raise the money for a ring, which I took this time.

I'd only lived with Elsie for about nine months, when Jimmy's wife, Ruby, had a baby girl called Fiona. Ruby's health wasn't very good after the birth, so Jimmy asked me if I would move into their house to help take care of them and it would be most helpful if I still paid board money. Ruby came from a well-to-do family in Scotland and had been widowed at a young age. She had been used to a better standard of living than we were, and I think she looked down her nose at us and silently wished we weren't Jimmy's family. At that time, it was very prophetic because when Jimmy died of cancer in his early 40's she refused to let Nora or I know that he'd died because she didn't want us to attend his funeral as she said, "They are not his real sisters!" But that was all in the future.

They lived in a previous Doctor's house in an 'upper-crust' area in Blackhill and it was very elegant. The upstairs bathroom, complete with inside toilet, echoed with its floor to ceiling green marble tiles, and the bath and wash basin had hot and cold running water. All of the bedrooms were carpeted, as were the stairs, and the whole house felt more like a hotel than a home. The kitchen was so big that it held a full-sized billiard table complete with a wooden cover so that it could be used as a kitchen table, and the house had every modern household appliance of the day. I don't think I was much help with the baby as I was working full time and going to night school, but I did fetch and carry for nearly a year, when Ruby told me she could cope on her own, and I should find other lodgings. Having to find somewhere else to live caused me some anxiety because I couldn't go back to live with Elsie because she had died of a heart attack a few weeks earlier, but when Gran heard about it, she suggested I move back home, and I did.

Connecting with my mother

I think I was 19 years old at the time, and hadn't had much contact with Beattie since that disastrous day when I learned the unmitigated truth of my birth, but all that was about to change. Brian now had a car and we thrilled in the freedom of the roads. We went wherever our fancy took us, and that often meant driving the scenic route along the low road to the bigger shops in Newcastle. The road passed through the village of Ebchester and we got into the habit of stopping to visit Beattie and Bill. They always made us feel very welcome and, over time, when I really got to know my mother I decided that she was basically a very good person, and I liked her.

My mother was only about 5'3 in height, and depending upon whether she was dieting or not, she was stocky at times, but definitely not fat. She had a real flair for style, and would never consider herself properly dressed for the outdoors without her large brimmed hats. Beattie was a fairly attractive woman; she had a lovely smile, and though she was friendly with her neighbors she showed them a quiet and reserved nature. Most unusual when you consider her past, or maybe because of her past. Who knows? Indoors, she ruled. She had the typical northerner's sharp tongue and blunt speech and was not afraid to speak up for herself within her four walls, and it was rare to find her sitting relaxing. She was the proverbial whirlwind and if there was something to be cleaned, dusted, cooked or washed, she wasn't happy until it was done, and only then would she sit in an overstuffed chair by the fireplace and pick up a book to read. I was told by Gran that my mother would never be dead whilst I was alive and couldn't understand why she'd say that. I was nothing like my mother! And I never would be! I knew the old saying of, "What is bred in the bone would come out in the flesh!" and I had no intention of ever taking after my mother in any way, shape or form, and when I cried, "Never in this lifetime Gran!" she went on to say that I had the same "whirlwind cleaning nature just like my mother." Whew! Thank heavens for that. I wasn't being criticized. I was being praised!

Bill Dodds with a Roman pot found in the Roman Remains bath house on the property.

Bill Dodds, as well as being a Shunt Driver for the Company, was a perpetual handyman who had justifiably earned a reputation for not being very reliable. This is not to suggest that he was lazy, no, in fact, quite the opposite. He was very handy and didn't like to refuse anyone's request for help, so he'd start various projects all at the same time, and had to be constantly pushed into finishing them. However, he never needed prompting to 'set' his garden. He loved being outdoors and he'd be found either in the large garden or in the greenhouse. During the growing season, produce such as excess tomatoes, cabbages and cauliflowers would be sent across the road to Ebchester Post Office and to the Co-operative Store to be sold and he made extra money from his hobby. Bill had originated from Northumberland where the farmers had rich guttural, semi-Scottish accents, and because he hadn't many teeth left in his bottom jaw, it made his speech hard to understand. That was embarrassing to me at times because I'd not know whether he was asking me a question or telling me something and I'd have to ask him to repeat himself. He was a nice man with a ready laugh, and his very round belly used to shake in his dark blue overalls. The only time he'd ever be seen in a suit was either at the Bingo Hall in Consett on a Thursday night, or at a wedding or a funeral.

It's strange to meet up with people again that you've only known as a child, because the childhood memories are often wrong. I remembered them as being very dictatorial as a child, and they were nothing like that as an adult, and I found that my old 'set in concrete' beliefs about them started to crack a bit around the edges. They were a lovely couple and if it hadn't been for the constant interference of her sisters, Mabel or Gladys, who were always fighting with each other, I think life would have been very harmonious for them. From what I've learned I think Beattie had more heartache to contend with than will ever be really known, especially by my generation. Seemingly, she was easily persuaded as a young girl, and once she fell pregnant with her first child, her sisters made her life a living hell. Aunt Mabel and Aunt Gladys were terribly embarrassed about Beattie's first pregnancy, and absolutely mortified about the second one, and they ostracized her for months. My dear, kind, and loving Aunt Mabel, then went on to say it was a huge relief when Beattie finally married Bill Dodds and moved away, but that she'd had to live with the embarrassment of her sister being pregnant twice without the benefit of clergy, all her life. She ought to have walked in my shoes!

Beattie and Bill had moved from Wyncliffe House at the top of the hill where I knew them as a child, to a big stone farmhouse called 'Mains Farm' in the valley below, in the village of Ebchester. Now this house is worth mentioning because to have something like this happen was quite amazing. Bill was going to replace an old milking shed with a new greenhouse, when what he thought was just a lump of unmovable stone turned out to be the top of a thick stone wall. He went across the road to Ebchester Churchyard where he knew the man who looked after the graveyard was an amateur archeologist, and asked him to come and have a look and he confirmed that this was part of a part of a Roman fort building. Professional archeologists came and started excavating, and they realized they were in the area of the Commandant's House and the building was in fact a bathhouse. Bill let them excavate inside the milk shed and when they took up the cement floor, the complete bathhouse was brought to light. The stone piers of the bathhouse were still complete and, in some places, the original mortar floor could still be seen. Among the stone pillars were Roman footprints in cement, beautiful coloured glass, Roman coins, and a large amount of 4th century Roman pottery. There were so many artifacts retrieved from the site that the Company built a museum for them at the back of the house, and people such Spike Milligan, the famous English comedian 'Goon Show' member, was a frequent visitor. Bill and my brother Brian finished remodeling the farmhouse but the Roman Bathhouse had to remain as it was because the government designated it as an Ancient Monument. Fourteen years later this estate would shatter the illusions of any sibling acceptance that would take twenty years to heal… but more about that later.

Life with Brian

From the age of 15 when I was delivering mail, Brian became my friend first and over a period of five years, my boyfriend, my fiancé, and my husband, and our lives were inexorably linked together for fifty-three years. I was a dreadfully shy girl when I first met him and over the years he encouraged me to believe in myself, and supported me when I didn't, and he protected me physically and verbally from anything or anybody who would do me harm. He was the only person on God's earth who knew absolutely everything there was to know about me, and he will always be my best friend.

We had been going out together for about a year before I saw his mother, Ella Shaw, for the first time. She was tall, maybe 5'8", and fairly heavily built, with salt and pepper tightly permed hair, and she had on her face a pair of large red-rimmed glasses which came to flyaway points at the top. She was very well dressed in a navy Macintosh with a red headscarf over her head, and she wore matching navy shoes and handbag and somehow, I was a bit surprised to see her shopping at the stalls on Consett market.

Brian pointed her out to me but made no effort to introduce us so I was startled to see her standing at the exit of the Company's security gates in Blackhill a few weeks later. I was in a hurry because I'd to get home, grab something to eat, and get back to work, and intended walking past her because I didn't know why she should be standing there when she stopped me and said, "You're Brian's girlfriend aren't you!" "Yes," I replied. She hesitated a moment before saying, "Have you anything decent to wear to meet Miss Neagle?" "Pardon?" I answered. "I said, have you anything decent to wear when you meet Miss Neagle, because I have a twin set you can borrow," she replied. What on earth made this woman, who was a virtual stranger to me, think she could stop me in the street and demand to know what I was going to wear to meet England's famous film star? "Thank you for the offer, but I have a new twin set and skirt that I'm going to wear," I replied. "What colour is it?" she asked. "The twin set is pink and the skirt is brown," I answered. "Well that should be fine then," she said. I never gave her a chance to say anything more because we'd been walking along the road as we talked and I had to split off from her to turn down the street to my house. I left her standing at the bus stop to catch the bus back to Consett, then she'd have to catch another bus to get to her home to Delves Lane, and that's all the real contact I had with her for another year and a half. What a cheek!

Brian and I had been going together for over three years and had gotten engaged when he told me that he'd been requested to bring me to their home for formal introduction to his parents, and it was with a feeling of dread that I went. On future visits, we entered through the back door, but on my very first visit Brian was told to bring me in through the front door and we walked along the hallway into the living room. From the first minute I met Tommy, I loved him. He was sitting on a stool in front of the fire because he said he wasn't allowed to sit on the chair in case he creased the chair-back cover before I came, and I laughed. He was most irreverent toward Ella. He absolutely didn't give a damn if he upset her, and I thought he was so down to earth and natural that he was great. I was still very shy when meeting new people, but he jumped off the stool, grabbed me by the arm, and danced me round the room. He'd done that deliberately because he knew it would upset Ella's social protocol, and it wasn't long before he whispered in my ear that his nickname for her was, 'Cold Fish.' And after the carry-on in the kitchen I believed him.

Ella and Tommy Shaw, my in-laws

Ella held back, as only Ella could, then asked me to follow her into the kitchen. "Hold out your hands?" she asked. Puzzled, I did as she requested. "Oh good! Clean nails! I always judge a person by the cleanliness of their nails," she said. "Now take your engagement ring off and give it to me!" she demanded. I complied, and couldn't believe my eyes when she took a jewelers' eyepiece out of her apron pocket and proceeded to examine the diamond. "Not bad!" she pronounced, as she gave it back to me, and we both went back into the living room. Eeh lad! What a performance! As if I hadn't had enough of feeling inferior in my life she was determined to never let me forget that I still was.

They lived in a two-bedroom 'Pit' bungalow at the bottom of Delves Lane, just before the houses gave way to countryside. It was a nicely laid out house, with a central hall dividing the two front bedrooms, then a living room on the left at the back, a bathroom complete with toilet at the bottom of the hall, and a kitchen on the right. Out the back was a huge garden planted with vegetables, as usual. To say Ella was house proud is the understatement of the century; she was up at six every morning and the whole house had to be cleaned by eight and it didn't matter whether Tommy had just come in off nightshift or not, she never relinquished her routine. Then she'd spend the best part of the day doing the rounds of coffee and gossip in other people's houses. I never felt comfortable in her house because it was too manicured. Every time you got up off the settee to go to the bathroom or kitchen she would straighten the seat covers, and even though Tommy would tell her to leave them alone, she never listened.

Ella always thought of herself as middle class instead of working class like the rest of us because Tommy was a Deputy Manager in the pits and was next in line for a Pit Manager's job. It was his responsibility to work out the size of the charge that was going to shatter the coal face, and to clear the men out the area before it went off, and because he had men's lives in his hands, he was very well respected, and as most of the women Ella associated with had husbands who worked for Tommy, Ella considered herself to be better than them, and let them know it. She had a mean and vindictive nature and a malicious tongue that she was not afraid to use. Nobody was safe from her nasty remarks, and she was well known throughout all of Delves Lane as being a 'know-it-all' because there wasn't much she or her nosy neighbors missed.

Unknown to me at the time, Tommy and Ella had started their married life living in a house in Templetown and knew all about my family. She knew absolutely everything there was to know about me, and that was why she didn't exactly welcome me with open arms. She knew my mother, and that I was the second illegitimate child born to her and in her way of thinking, I was the Devil incarnate. Ella tolerated me at the best of times, and that's the most charitable thing I can say about her. She was somewhat successful in hiding her feelings towards me in front of Brian or his Dad, but never hesitated in showing her true colours towards me when I was on my own. She very rarely acknowledged my presence and if she had to talk to me, she struggled to be polite, and couldn't quite melt the ice in her voice, and her disapproval became permanent when she told me quite clearly and succinctly that Brian had gone against her wishes of not marrying Elaine Gray, an unofficial cousin to him, and a girl that Ella had had her eye on for years as a possible partner for him.

Tommy was small and slim for a man, only about 5'4", but he was a salt of the earth working man who'd worked hard all his life in one pit or another. He was so different in nature to Ella that everybody wondered what on earth he had seen in her to make him want to marry her. It wasn't as though she was even nice to him. She took every opportunity to berate his faults in front of anyone who stood still long enough to listen, and it could have been very embarrassing if he didn't stick up for himself. He would listen for a moment or two before sharply saying, "Get away with you, woman! Nobody is interested in what you have to say! Get about your business!" Then realizing she was showing herself up, she would fling herself off to the kitchen and slam a few pans around. Visitors didn't stay very long when Ella was at home.

Brian's dad was a studious man, well read, softly spoken, and he could hold an intelligent conversation on any topic. He was also a die-hard union man and the only time his voice was really raised was when he was arguing the merits of the Union, and when you heard of his early working life it was easy to understand why he felt so strongly about it. Tommy had started work in the coal mines around the age of 12, when the mines were still privately owned and the owners were greedy, and men had to work extremely long hours for very little pay. It was backbreaking dangerous work, with no regard to personal safety, and it was only when men fought to 'Unionize' that working conditions improved for the ordinary worker. He lived and breathed Union, and the only time he'd really get upset is when anyone dared to suggest that all Union's had outlived their usefulness.

It was a tradition for most pit men to stop in at the local pub, 'The Pitman's Arms' at the top of Delves Lane, for a beer after leaving work. This was probably to try and wash the coal dust from their throats, and Tommy was no different. He'd have a couple of beers, to the point of being fortified we used to think, before heading home for a bath and a clean set of clothes. Ella would watch for him coming down the hill then head back indoors to start filling the bath. Then she'd make him get out of his pit clothes by the back door so as not to bring any dirt into the house, and before he had eaten, he had to bathe. If the poor soul happened to bring a couple of bottles of beer home with him she thought it was absolutely wicked and wouldn't shut up about having the Devil's Brew in her house, until he'd drunk them. This fighting went on for years and years until he finally gave in and stopped drinking, or bringing beer home with him. Brian, who didn't drink himself, didn't agree with her stance, and saw nothing wrong in stopping at the Off-License Shop to bring his Dad an occasional beer. If Ella started to make a comment Brian would just say, "He's earned the right to have a drink whenever he wants it!" and she'd stand there with her lips pursed because she would never directly argue with him. He was her reason to live.

The only thing I didn't like about Tommy was that he wanted Brian to follow him down the pit and was very upset when Brian chose to work in an office environment. It stuck in his throat that his son was going into management because, in his eyes, management were on one side of the fence, and unions were on the other, and never the twain should meet, and so he refused to have anything to do with Brian's further education. It took Brian five years of part-time study at Newcastle University to complete his training as a Company Secretary (not the same as an ordinary secretary) and Tommy never acknowledged it when Brian passed his final exams, or ever paid for any of the costs involved. As he put it, "If you want something different to what I can offer you, then get it yourself!" Unwittingly, Brian's University degree built a psychological barrier between the two of them.

Not all of Brian's accomplishments were put down to his own personal ambitions. No. Some of them were attributed to his real father, Lewis Shaw. Brian was actually born to Tommy's younger brother, Lewis, who lived in the south of England, and during the war years, when the bombs were falling like raindrops on the south, Lewis had brought Brian, and his sister, Doreen, up to the north to be taken care of by their grandparents, who lived in a house at the top of Delves Lane. Seemingly, the two babies, 18-month-old Doreen, and three-month-old Brian, were too much for the grandparents, and Tommy and Ella took them to their house. Ella tells the tale of not liking girls, so she sent the girl back to her father, but kept the boy, Brian. Now the story gets weird, because Ella continues to say that Lewis never came back for Brian so they adopted him. Years later, Lewis told the tale of being hoodwinked by Tommy and Ella who lied about him being killed in the war and adopted Brian behind his back. Who knows anymore?

Anyway, Lewis had made a success of himself – in an office – whereas all the other brothers, Tommy, Jack and Mark had contented themselves by working in the coal mines. Hence, Tommy thought that Brian had more of his real father, Lewis, in him than he had of his adopted father, Tommy, and it rankled.

But with his blessing on our engagement, if not Ella's, we continued to go out together. We didn't have much money to spend on formal entertainment as we were both busy saving cash for our education, and his was much more expensive than mine, and on the only night we could get together, he'd walk the five miles from his house to my house in order to save the bus fare towards a car which would make getting around and amusing ourselves much easier. But before he got his own vehicle, there weren't many places we could afford to go, so it was either a walk in the park if the weather was good, or we'd sit and talk in Gran's unheated living room if it was raining. All the while watching the clock because Brian had to leave to get home in time for his 11 pm curfew. Years later Tommy told us he used to get quite anxious for Brian to come home, and he'd wait by the gate until he could hear Brian's steady footsteps coming down the hill, then quietly make his way back inside to sit ever so casually when Brian entered. Even in those days' parents kept a watchful eye on the children, it didn't matter how old you were.

My life was extremely busy in the winter as I had evening classes to attend on Monday, Wednesday and Friday evenings, which only left Tuesday, Thursday and Saturday free for romance and Brian wasn't available on Sunday's because he sang in the church choir, and really, Tuesday nights were out because I had to do housework and ironing, so that only left Thursday evening and Saturday for us to get together, and even Saturday evenings caused a problem in the beginning because I had to babysit for Marjorie. I was too young, in her eyes, to have a steady boyfriend, so he was not allowed to babysit with me, and he had to go home when it was time for them to go out. It was a case of, "everything in our favour was against us." Apart from the odd sixpence I got from Ken when I was much younger, I had never once been given any monies, or anything else for that matter, from Marjorie for all the years of babysitting, and after a few weeks I found the courage to tell her that after all these years I wasn't going to be available anymore, so she reluctantly relented and let Brian sit with me – which was worth more than mere money.

Thursday was really our only night out together, and we'd arrange to meet at the Co-op Dance Hall in Consett. Brian, and five of his best friends, would all stand outside waiting for me to arrive, and like the Queen of Sheba I was escorted into the dance hall with six young men, to the envy of quite a few young ladies. Not bad for a very shy young lass eh? Apart from Brian, all the other lads would surreptitiously glance around the room and talking behind their hands would quietly comment on the available 'talent.' "Cor, she looks great; I think I'll ask her for a dance!" "No way man! She's out of your class, she'll never dance with you, you gormless idiot!" "Why not man? I can dance as good as any of yer." "I'll bet you five shillings that you'll not get her to dance with the likes of you!" "Yer on!" Next thing I'd be pulled out onto the dance floor for an 'exhibition' dance in front of the desired female and would be swung around and around until the band of five musicians stopped playing. Once the ice was broken with the ladies Brian's friends used to vanish, but not before I was danced off my feet.

It was a different story altogether in the summer as there were no evening classes to attend, which meant that I was free most of the week. I still did my share of the housework and ironing on a Tuesday evening, and the compulsory babysitting on a Saturday night, but the rest of the week was my own, nevertheless our time together remained very simple because we were always cash-poor. Brian's university education cost a lot of money and it was very hard for him to save while courting me. However, he managed to save up an extra 20 pounds to buy what I thought was a 'clapped out' car from a man down the street from him. It was an old Standard, Flying 9, a pre-war car, the kind of car with running boards on the bottom of the doors that you see in the old movies and I instantly nicknamed it, "Rolls Canardly." Meaning it would roll downhill okay, but could hardly get up the other side and it stopped every time I got into it. We would confidently head out into the countryside and always, absolutely always, that blasted car would stop halfway up the hill and there was no choice, I'd have to get out to lighten the load so that it could make it to the top. Time after time he'd be assured by the previous owner, who'd be constantly fixing things, that it was 'now' in great running order, but it never ever got me to the top of a hill once. I always had to get out and walk up myself. He only had it a few months but that was enough time to get used to the freedom of the roads and he did, as everybody in that day and age did, he traded it in and made monthly payments on a second-hand forest green Austin A40 van. He had extra seats put in the back and for the next four years that little van took us all over England.

Once Brian had reliable wheels it simplified our lives a lot. We still didn't have much money between us, and after pooling what we had to fill the gas tank, we'd take his university books and head for the moors. Brian was granted 'day release' from the Company to attend University, and because he had to work as well as study for his degree, his workload was enormous. With a full-time degree pushed into two working days each week meant that he had to study both summer and winter if he hoped to accomplish anything. This would have made courting very difficult if he had not bought the van but, as he did, it meant we could go someplace quiet so that he could study, and I contented myself sitting beside him reading my books. When he thought he'd read enough, he'd give me his books so that I could bombard him with questions so that he'd get the answers right for his exams. I think I could have earned a Degree in Commerce from the University of Newcastle with all the knowledge I gained.

I think I was nearly 17 before Brian finally convinced me to take up Badminton, a sport that he loved and had managed to find time to continue playing during courting me. It was a winter sport and it fit in well with my evening classes, being held every other night, so I joined the club and learned to play on Tuesday and Thursday nights and Saturday afternoons. Even though we agreed on most things, Brian and I couldn't agree as partners, and I was teamed with Stan Thomas, while Brian used to partner other women. We became such good players that we were always on the tournament team. Three couples made up the tournament team: Stan and I were always the first couple, Brian and his partner the second couple; and the third couple used to change all the time. For the seven years I played with Stan we used to win most of our matches. I loved the sport. I never thought about beating the other couple, I just loved to play and would even cheer if the other side made a good shot. One of the highlights of playing badminton with Stan was the time we won the North of England 'Under 23-year-old' mixed doubles championship the only time we entered. Quite exciting!

My best friend was Anne Gowland, the girl who gave me shelter when I left home, and she and I would enjoy a friendship that would last all of our lives, even unto this day. Anne was courting Alan Rowland at the time and as he happened to be Brian's best friend since the age of 5, the four of us became inseparable and even though we were all destined to live in other countries, we stayed good friends. In our salad days, nobody had a clue that Alan would die an untimely death of a heart attack at the age of 37, and Anne would marry Jimmy Campbell ten years later, but in our early days we lived, loved and laughed our way through life. Our favorite haunt was the Lake District and on an occasional Sunday the four of us would drive the hour and a half up country to either Lake Ullswater or Lake Windermere where we would hire a rowing boat and go out on the water for a couple of hours. Even though everywhere we wanted to go was quite a drive to get there, we had a ball. I remember the time we all went to St. James' in Newcastle to watch an All-In Wrestling match. I really wasn't very keen on going, even after Brian explained that it was all showmanship, it was just that wrestling didn't appeal to me. However, after hiding behind my hands for a couple of bouts I got into the action and this very shy and quiet person surprised everyone by continuously shouting, "Pull his arm out and hit him with the soggy end!"

Anne Gowland, Rowland, Campbell

Anne and Alan married two years before us, and they bought a small house in the village of Stanhope, about 15 miles away, over the moors. It was a lovely little cottage, just one-bedroom upstairs and a living room, small dinky kitchen, and a bathroom downstairs. It was straight out of an Emily Bronte novel. It had flagstones throughout the downstairs and a cold water tap in the kitchen and Alan asked Brian to help him remove the flagstones and replace them with a concrete floor. Goodness knows how many eons they had been down there because those stones refused to budge very easily and there was more cussing and swearing went on during the couple of week-ends that it took to clear the place than I've ever heard in my life. I wasn't much use to either Alan or Anne and it was only if a flagstone broke that I'd be able to lift it into the wheelbarrow and as Anne was the ultimate organizer, she'd have lunch or dinner prepared before I even thought about it. Still, some nights, late in the evening, I was able to walk beside the van, shining a torch on the shoulder of the road, as the fog rolled in and over the moors like a thick pea soup, and Brian couldn't see to drive, so I did have my uses.

Maybe it was because Alan was like a brother to Brian, and Anne was like a sister to me, but we had some of the best times of our lives with them. We'd do the daftest things when I think about it. Like 'going out' for a fish and chip supper. Neither of the lads liked going to the local fish and chip shop. No, we had to drive 15 miles across the moors, all the way to the country village of Hexham to get the chips, and after they'd been consumed, drive all the way back, plus a further 15 miles in the other direction to the country town of Barnard Castle to get the fish. Crazy, but lots of fun. We'd sing our heads off all the way there and back, and the evening was not complete without Alan treating us to 'Old Man River.' What a voice he had. He was a slim man, and not very tall, but to hear him singing this song rivaled Paul Robeson, the famous deep baritone who originally recorded it.

Our other best friends were Paul and Allison Richardson. Paul had also grown up with Brian from a young age, and the three of them, Brian, Alan and Paul were friends for years, even after they were all grown and married. Paul was one of those people who constantly tried to get rid of his 'Geordie' accent and he really did sound as though he had plums in his mouth. He was constantly ribbed about it, but he didn't care. If we weren't out with Anne and Alan, then we were with Allison and Paul. One time Paul and Allison, and Brian and I went to the Town Moor in Newcastle. This had grown to be the biggest agricultural show in the north of England, as well as the northeast's biggest fair with loads of sideshows and rides, overtaking Consett Show by a mile. Allison was a lovely girl, very prim and proper girl, well spoken, and raised within a very strict Chapel family, but very friendly and easy to get along with. We were all just walking around watching people have fun when the two lads took off at a run to get tickets for one of the side shows. When they came back and showed us the tickets we were flabbergasted. They had bought admission tickets for a strip show! Neither of us could quite believe that our well-behaved, well brought up boyfriends, could have possibly expected us to go with them to 'see' this show. But they egged us on to be good sports and so we went in. The 'strippers' stood frozen and the stage revolved, and while only the upper part of their bodies were exposed Allison and I were mortified and tried to leave but the place had filled up behind us with other people. So, both of us hid behind Paul and Brian's backs, blushing like crazy and really embarrassed. I have never felt so uncomfortable in my life. Needless-to-say, both men loved it.

Now that Brian and I were engaged and, with his Mother and Father acting as chaperones, we traveled all over England and Scotland in 'our' van. The British Isles isn't all that big, so we'd leave after work on Friday and visit lots of places before returning home on Sunday, and we all got to see much more of the country than any of us would have thought possible just a short two years previous. I now had my driver's license so could take turns in driving and I remember being so nervous the first time I drove his parents, that I forgot to take the hand brake off and drove all the way home from a seaside resort with the brake on. No wonder the car didn't feel too swift on the hills.

Family has been important to me all my life, and I thought that now Brian and I were engaged I would be treated as one of the family by Ella. Not so, and I found that out the hard way. One of our more memorable weekend trips, this time with his Mother and his Aunt Olive in tow, took us to the seaside resort of Blackpool. Honest, the things I had to put up with were nobody's business. There was a bus trip going from Delves Lane to Blackpool, but Ella didn't want to travel by 'lowly' bus any more, she wanted to be chauffeur-driven by Brian now that he had a car. The intention was to drive the four of us to Blackpool but to stay in the same hotel as her friends and neighbors so that she could meet up with them, and that's what we did.

It was a nice hotel with a large fashionable foyer and a reception desk to the left, and stairs leading up to the bedrooms on the right. It must have been a big hotel, because as well as continuing down a long hallway on the second floor, the stairs initially branched off to some rooms at the side and front. I wasn't too pleased to find out that I had to share a bedroom with both Ella and Aunt Olive but Brian asked me not to cause a fuss because there was probably a 'shake-me-down' mattress on the floor, and besides which, it was only for two nights. We

collected our overnight bags and stepped up the stairs, turned right at the top, and walked along the open landing with its wrought iron banister rail to the bedroom overlooking the road, and I was totally aghast when we opened the door. Horror of horrors! There was only one supposedly double bed squashed up against the wall, and absolutely no room at all for another mattress, and it was obvious that the three of us were going to have to snuggle up real close because there wasn't much room. I was not a happy camper! Brian was only slightly better off than we were; he had to sleep in a double bed with a stranger! His bedroom was along the same landing as ours, but set back into an alcove, next to the general bathroom, and his roommate happened to be the driver of the bus that had brought the people from Delves Lane.

Because it was a long drive, it was fairly late when we got there and every other room in the hotel was taken so there was no choice but to share the bed with Ella and Olive. It was the most uncomfortable and embarrassing situation that I'd ever been in and I don't suppose it was much better for either of them. Here I was, squashed into a bed with a future Aunt-in-law and a future mother-in-law who made no pretence of liking me; who tried constantly to maintain an air of superiority over me; who, at the best of times, suffered my presence; who -- now had to remove her false teeth to soak them in a glass of water on the table beside me -- What! The irony and humour of the situation hit me like a ton of bricks. At first it wasn't very pleasant to see or hear Ella without her teeth in, because her face seemed to collapse into itself and her words became unintelligible.

No comedy writer could have written a better bedroom farce. Here I was, 18 years old, sharing a double bed with two middle-aged women, both of whom had no teeth in but persisted in carrying on a conversation with each other that sounded as though they were speaking to each other through an asbestos wall. "Sot su say Llla?" asked Aunt Olive, "I say, se so shop smorra?" Ella replied.

Oh, it was purgatory trying to decipher the words and the more they tried to speak the more I tried not to laugh to the point that my chest muscles hurt. You know when you're trying to suppress laughter and it just sort of sits there in your mid rift bubbling away until you're frightened to open your mouth in case it just comes blurting out? Well I was actually perspiring from trying to keep the laughter in. Seeing and hearing this very opinionated, straight-laced, highly judgmental, cold-hearted woman trying to make herself understood after she'd took her teeth out was absolutely hysterical and I'll never forget it. However, after an exhausting night, we managed some sleep and after breakfast the next morning the four of us split up with Ella and Aunt Olive going to the shops and Brian and I going for a very bracing walk along the seafront.

I know I'm being sarcastic here, but you haven't lived until you've done the annual pilgrimage of visiting Blackpool Illuminations in the middle of winter. Blackpool, the northerner's seaside dream vacation, consists mainly of side-shows and Disney-like lights all along the seafront which are illuminated each night, hence the term 'Blackpool Illuminations.' When I think about it now, somebody from that area had to have the greatest marketing talent ever known, because only a genius could promote an English seaside town as a holiday destination in the dead of winter. (As an addendum to this my sister, Nora, was unintentionally born in the ballroom of Blackpool Tower in 1941, in the middle of WW2.)

So anyway, here we were, Brian and I, freezing our butts off trying to keep warm by walking briskly along the seashore and back, and we were nearly back to our hotel when I became desperate for the bathroom. With Brian close at my heels, I ran up the stairs and into the bathroom trying to hurry because Brian needed to go also. As I came out I was re-fastening my coat as I walked so as not to hold Brian up, when a blood curdling, ear splitting, banshee-type wail erupted from the bottom of the stairs below me, "You Slut! You dirty rotten Slut! You're just like your Mother! I knew you were as common as muck from the first time I saw you. You dirty rotten Slut! You're nothing but a Prostitute!"

I turned to see who was the recipient of this cacophony of evil, and was absolutely horror-struck to learn that it was me, and that those appalling words were being thrown at me by Ella. Her face was contorted like some sort of a demonic gargoyle and from her expression she couldn't wait to get her hands on me. I was frozen to the banister rail, and struck absolutely dumb by her vehement attack. It was as though I was in the abstract, faintly listening to the ravings of a lunatic in the distance, along with an audience of people I vaguely knew. There were quite a few people from Delves Lane either coming up or going down the stairs, and everybody stopped to listen to her. We were all like transparent ghostly figures watching the last vestiges of self-delusional upper crust veneer fall away from Ella Shaw. She was like an enraged pit bull with a voice!

She had no sooner reached the top of the stairs when Brian came out of the bathroom and it mobilized her into more vitriolic speech. Not looking at him, but directly at me with her chest heaving, face distorted and finger wagging violently in my face she said in a highly derisive tone,

"You've been in the bedroom with Brian, haven't you! Don't lie to me! You've been in the bedroom with Brian! I might have known it; you couldn't wait until you got him on his own!" Brian walked toward me with a totally perplexed look on his face. He hadn't heard anything that had been said prior to him coming out of the bathroom. "What are you talking about Mother?" he asked. "You've been together in your bedroom haven't you? You've been having sex!" she said contemptuously. "What! Don't be stupid! No, we haven't been in the bedroom, and we haven't been having sex! We've been for a long walk along the seafront and had to run back to use the bathroom!" he said angrily. "Well I can see *you've* just come out of the bathroom, but *she* hasn't! *She* was fastening her coat up and has just come out of your bedroom!" she snarled.

I remember feeling very faint and just wanted to sit down somewhere. Ella was still foaming at the mouth, and his very subdued Aunt Olive stood to one side looking at me as though I was something the cat had dragged in. Brian took me by the arm and started to lead me to his bedroom that was nearer than mine but I tried to pull away from him, I didn't want to go into his room, especially not after the scene that had just taken place. Very gently he said, "Hang on a minute Nan, everything will be okay, you'll see, just wait until I get this door open." He put his key in the lock and turned it, but nothing happened; it wouldn't open. I was as puzzled as the others, but Brian turned to his mother and said, "It won't open because it's locked on the inside!" Ella with steam still coming out of her ears said scornfully, "Well, no wonder you can't get in she must have locked it on the inside when she came out!" Brian was starting to get really angry now, "Neither of us have been in this bedroom this morning Mother, stop it, you don't know what you are talking about!" He again turned to the bedroom door and this time knocked very loudly. Ella, still with a defensive tone to her voice said, "I don't know why you are doing that, there's nobody in there, you're both out here!" Ella had forgotten that Brian was sharing his bedroom with the bus driver from Delves Lane.

Brian remembered that the bus driver said he was going back to bed after breakfast for another few hours' sleep and when he unlocked the bedroom door from his side you could have driven his bus through Ella's open mouth. She recovered quickly and demanded, "How long have you been in there?" He rubbed his eyes and looked at all the people gathered around before answering, "I came back to bed after breakfast at 8:00 am. What's the matter? What's the problem?" Ignoring his response completely, and brandishing her finger at me, she said, "Are you sure that *they* haven't been in there?" In an instant the bus driver picked up on what was going on, and with an icy tone to his voice replied, "Perfectly sure Madam! Now if you and everybody else are quite satisfied, I'm going back to bed!" And with that, he slammed the door in her face.

There we all were our party of four and nearly a busload of people standing on the landing, on the stairs and in the reception area, listening to this woman verbally hack me to pieces for about 10 minutes. She never said a word in response to the bus driver's involuntary alibi. She just stood there looking at me as though I'd just slithered out from under a rock, totally vexed. No apology. Nothing. Nobody moved for a few seconds and I think they were all waiting to see if I was going to lift my fist and punch Ella, but I was still a very demoralizingly shy person and incapable of retaliating at that age. What should I do now then? Now that it's been proven beyond the shadow of a doubt that Brian and I were not having sex in his bedroom? I couldn't stay here. I had to go home. I lifted my head towards Brian and quietly said, "I'd like to go home. I don't mind catching a bus if you'll take me to the bus station." "Let's just get out of here for now," he replied. The shock of what had happened began registering itself and I started to quietly cry but I was not ashamed of my tears. I held my head high and with tears streaming down my cheeks, I looked every person in the eye as I pushed slowly through the middle of them, down the stairs, and out of the hotel.

For over two years Ella Shaw had thoroughly disliked me, had made no apologies for her feelings toward me and even though I had done my best to prove to her that I wasn't what she thought, it was to no avail. She had a base opinion of me that was never going to change – ever! It had been building up in her for over two years and the scenario in the hotel had been the catalyst for eruption, but how to react to her unfounded allegations caused me a huge problem. After we'd left the hotel Brian found a small café and ordered a cup of tea. If I'd been a drinker and old enough, I'd have ordered something much stronger like a brandy to calm my shattered nerves. However, a cup of tea is the Englishman's way of curing anything that ails you and he was hoping that it would settle me down in order to discuss what had happened. My only interest was in getting away from his Mother as soon as possible, and I insisted he take me to the bus station so that I might find my own way home. I didn't even want to go back to the hotel to collect my clothes. I just wanted to get away from Blackpool and from the close proximity of his Mother.

Brian, with his analytical brain and cool logic, said that this was a make or break time in my relationship with his folks, and that if I didn't find it in my heart to forgive his Mother, then he didn't know what was going to happen. He had no idea how he could explain to his Dad that I never wanted to see his Mother ever again. It was screaming in my head that I would never forgive her, that hell would freeze over before I'd ever want to see or talk to her again. My brain was getting more and more scrambled, the more I thought about it. We left the café and walked along the seafront, me in automation putting one foot in front of the other. Brian talking quietly about the ramifications of a split between his folks and me. He asked me to look at the bigger picture, our life together. I wasn't marrying his Mother, I was marrying him, and he didn't want to have to fight with his folks beforehand, "Couldn't you just pretend it never happened? That is was all a bad dream?" he asked. To make him happy I let myself be persuaded to stay until the next morning when we were all due to return home. If I'd had a whisper of a backbone I'd have crawled home on my hands and knees rather than face Ella Shaw again after those horrible accusations, but at that age I was still very pliable and open to Brian's desperate persuasion.

That night, getting ready for bed, Aunt Olive, who was a quiet and reserved woman, gave me a hug in front of Ella and told me it was all right, it was all over, and she bolstered my courage with her sympathy. Ella ignored me as though nothing had happened, and I thought to myself that even though Brian did his best to convince me it was a bad dream, I couldn't wait to get home. The next day, after an enormously strained and silent three-hour drive, Tommy smiled at us when we entered his house and said, "Well, you look as if you've had a good time." Nobody corrected him. I've had to swallow some pretty awful accusations from Ella Shaw throughout my life, just to keep the peace, but the visit to Blackpool stands out as one of the worst. The only positive side to all of this was that my innocence was quickly proven, and in what should have been a very humiliating way to her.

After Brian drove me home, I hurried along the hall into the kitchen to tell Gran what had happened, and after she listened to the whole story, she said, "Well Nan, that's the kind of woman she is, so forewarned is forearmed, and least said, soonest mended. Give her no more thought Nan, she's a nasty woman. Always has been, always will be!" These revealing words came out of the mouth of my gentle Gran who never said an unkind word about anyone. Then I thought about it. Of course, Gran knew Ella from when she lived in Templetown – everyone knew Ella Shaw! It took a few weeks of persuasion by Brian to visit his folks again, and by this time he had run out of excuses to his Dad. His Mother wasn't bothered, but it upset Tommy that I kept turning down his invitation to Sunday tea. Of course, he was still in the dark and had no idea of what had transpired in Blackpool and, as nobody had told him the truth, he thought I was refusing to go because I didn't like him. Consequently, I was put in a position where I had to put up with her, so as not to upset him. It was going to be left to me to try and mend the huge gaping chasm between Ella and me. So, after trying to visualize the bigger picture as Brian had suggested, I made the conscious decision to close that chapter in my life and start a new one. It was the only time in my life that I had no choice but to invite somebody into my life who hated me.

It was with great trepidation that I slowly entered their home the next Sunday to find his Mother busily putting food on the kitchen table, and when she saw who it was, she turned towards me and with a hesitant smile said, "Well hello there. How are you? We've missed you. Have you been busy?" You could have knocked me over with a feather and I said nothing for a moment or two, wondering how to respond. I had been arming myself to do battle, but she handed me an olive branch instead, and as I listened to Gran's advice going over and over in my head of, "Least said, soonest mended" I held out my hand and shook hers. All might be forgiven, but I would never forget it. However, over the next few months, we managed to redeem something of our 'arm's length' relationship and my regular Sunday visits became much more harmonious. Once she accepted the fact that I was going to be a fixture in her life, she became more friendly and courteous toward me, and that was an enormous relief. I, in turn, endeavored to help her when she needed a much younger pair of hands around the house, and got into the habit of helping her deep clean her home twice a year. This meant physically grappling and maneuvering wardrobes, dressers and beds out into the hallway so that she could change the carpets around, and before putting them back, help her put fresh wallpaper on the walls.

Being accepted into her home meant that Brian and I visited more often, especially during the summer months, and to Tommy's delight we'd help him in the garden. It was a huge garden and with Parkinson's disease starting to rear its ugly head, Tommy found it hard to get the entire garden weeded and that's where 'our expertise' came in. He'd sit on a stool directing our attention to this, that or the other weed and with his good nature, he'd laugh at our inane attempts to recognize them first. He said it was as good as a Pantomime watching the two of us decide what was a weed, and what wasn't, and he nearly fell off his stool laughing when Brian said, "Its simple Dad. If it comes back, it's a weed!"

Marjorie, Ken and children emigrate to Canada

Except for the three months when I wasn't speaking to her after I left home, Brian and I babysat Marjorie and Ken's children most Saturday nights. There was never much conversation between us as it seemed they were ready to leave the moment we got there, and Brian had to leave the moment they got back, so it ca me as a big shock to learn they had been planning on emigrating to Canada for some time. They had met all requirements for immigration and everything was in motion to move to where Ken's brother, Harry, lived in Toronto, but they had a problem with selling the house. They had bought the house at #35 Cort Street when the Company offered some for sale, but it was on condition that they kept the house for five years before selling it to anyone else. This was a problem because the house was 'tied' for another couple of years and because they didn't want to leave it standing empty, it was arranged that, after they left for Canada, Gran, Lorna and her young son Ted, and Nora would move into it and keep up the mortgage payments. I was still living in Shotley Bridge with Elsie.

I remember going to see the three boys, David, Kenneth and Ian, on their last night in England and of emotionally telling them that if they didn't like it in Canada then I would come and rescue them. "If you don't like it there just let me know and I'll come and get you!" I cried, as if traveling between England and Canada was a normal everyday thing. The next morning came all too soon, and after all the hugs and kisses, and with tears of sadness in everyone's eyes, they were waived off to begin a new life away from the dirt and grime, and rain-soaked skies, and nobody, absolutely nobody other than God, could have possibly known that it would be the last time any of us still in England would ever see nine-year old Kenneth alive again.

They had only been in Toronto for a few weeks when they moved into a house near to Lake Ontario and from what we learned in later years, Kenneth went to play with a new friend from one street over and they ended up at the lake. David was sent to "keep an eye" on his brother but he never tracked him down, and although he witnessed the commotion at the lake, he never quite connected it to Kenneth and was shushed away by the police. At the time of Kenneth's death nobody wanted to talk about what happened, or how it happened, or why it happened - everyone was in total shock. The only thing Marjorie ever said was that there were three policemen on the shoreline who refused to go into the Lake to rescue Kenneth because of the very deep holes in the lake, and that Kenneth had only gone down one time – drowning immediately. I remember a 'grown-up' David telling me that in his gut he just knew something was very wrong but was kept from looking for Kenneth by the police and that the guilt of not finding him and thereby 'saving' him haunted him for years, and it was left to the family doctor who told Marjory and Ken what had happened to Kenneth.

Our poor Marjorie, Ken, David and Ian. What on earth must they be going through? What a horrendous thing to happen just when they were looking for a better life! Nobody could do anything to ease their pain, we were on one side of the Atlantic and they were on the other. Nobody had a home phone installed, it just wasn't affordable, so the only correspondence between them and us was either by telegram or letter, and waiting to hear how they were all coping was dreadful. This all happened early in 1963, and the world wasn't yet small and air travel was not common, at least not for us. We'd have to travel to Canada the same way they did, by sea, and that was at least seven days on the ocean and not an easy thing to arrange, even if we could find the money for the passage. Everybody felt totally inadequate and absolutely bereft.

It was some weeks later that Gran showed me a letter she'd just received from Canada. Marjorie and Ken were doing their best to cope because they had to. Simple as that - they had to. They had two other young boys who needed them and no amount of begging or pleading with the Lord would bring Kenneth back, he was gone from their lives, if not their memories. Marjorie was in her early forties when she wrote that letter and, after the news of the day, written at the bottom of the page giving the impression of an afterthought, she surprised us all when she said she'd just found out that she was pregnant. She wrote of a hesitant joyfulness because there was an awful complication. Not only did her age play a role in complicating things but, as her pregnancy was unknown to the Doctors at the time of Kenneth's death, they had been prescribing Thalidomide in order to help her cope. She had been taking this terrible drug for weeks before the newspapers reported that it caused extremely debilitating deformities in children, and everyone had months of anxiety as we all worried about Marjorie, not only because of Kenneth, but also on behalf of the new baby. We lived on the edge of sanity until we heard by telegram that she had finally given birth to a normal healthy baby girl.

Ken with his 2nd family 'made in Canada': Lindsay and Nancy Lowther.

Lindsay, a beautiful bouncing healthy baby girl was a miracle baby, not only to be born when she was, less than a year after Kenneth's death, but also because she was born without effects of the Thalidomide drug. Three years later, in another surprise pregnancy, Marjorie gave birth to a second beautiful daughter, Nancy, my namesake, and between the two of them, gave Marjorie and Ken more reasons to live.

Marriage Ultimatum

I was now living back home in what was Marjorie's old house, and Kenneth's death and the subsequent birth of Lindsay forced the issue of marriage with Brian. I couldn't get it out of my head that I could have done something to prevent the tragedy and felt like Marjorie needed my help with the new baby. Nora and I were sleeping in the same bedroom that her boys had slept in, and I could still see the excitement of going to Canada in their eyes every time I set foot in that room. I could still hear myself say, "I'll come and get you!" and it preyed on my mind. I had looked after all of Marjorie's children starting with David, and wished desperately to help with Lindsay. It also preyed on my mind that Lorna said she was also thinking of going to live in Canada, and of taking Gran and Ted with her. As a result, it was with real emotion that I told Brian that, as there was no date set for our marriage, I was going to apply for immigration to Canada, to be with the family and I was deadly serious.

Brian thought about what I had said for a moment then replied, "Well I'd like to go to Canada also but I need to finish my education first." That seemed reasonable to me, and after agreeing to wait with him, I calmed myself down. After a few moments, he left to go to the bathroom I thought and when he came back, he shifted my focus altogether when he said, "Nan, do you want to get married first? All of our friends are married and settled. Let's get married so that we can go to Canada as a married couple." We had been going together for five years and every time the subject of setting a date to get married was mentioned, he'd always tell me why the timing was so bad. He had his degree to finish. We didn't have enough money. We had no house, no furniture, no nothing. But that was Brian. Once he made his mind up to do something, he was unstoppable.

"Guess what?" he said, when he came to see me three days later. "I've no idea," I replied. "We're getting married in three weeks' time, on the 21st December in my church in Consett. I've put the Bann's up and rented an apartment, so now we need to find some furniture to put in it," he replied. I could hardly believe my ears and asked him to repeat himself and instead of being thrilled at the news, the first words that came out of my mouth were, "Oh my God! Everyone will think I'm pregnant and have to get married." He looked at me as though I had finally driven him crazy before saying, "Nan, I don't care what other people think, and you shouldn't care what other people think either. They can just mind their own damn business. We've been together for five years and we want to get married, the arrangements have been made and we're getting married, and that's the only thing that matters," he responded. Trust him to get to the meat of the matter. Trust him to tell me what was important, and what was not. Trust him to tell me in covert words not to worry about what his mother thought. We were both old enough to know what we were doing, so together we broke the news to both sides about the wedding. Apart from Ella and some of my work colleagues quietly asking me if I was pregnant because the wedding was in such a rush, everyone else was happy for me. Except for my mother that is, and when Beattie heard that the first of the three Banns had been read, all hell broke loose.

Coming in from work, once again, I found Gran in tears. She told me that Beattie and Bill had just left and they were going to stop my wedding. Why was it that I was never at home when they called! "Why do they want to stop me from marrying Brian? Don't they like him? What reasons did they give Gran?" I asked. "No real reason that I could figure out Nan," she said. "Can they do that Gran; can they stop me from getting married?" I asked. "Well she's still your mother Nan, and you're not 21 yet, and you didn't ask her permission," she replied. "Brian asked for your permission," I said, remembering the night I thought Brian had just gone to use the bathroom, but had gone into the kitchen and asked Gran for her permission to marry me which I thought was a real gentlemanly thing to do. "Nan, she's still your legal guardian until you're 21 and Brian should have asked her instead of me," she replied sadly. I started to feel very upset. I was upset because Gran was upset, and she was upset because two people who'd had very little input into my life now wanted to step in and push her aside. Maybe there was a legal side to all of this, but morally – they had no right whatsoever to upset Gran. No right at all!

By the time Brian came later that evening I had worked myself up into a right state. My words were pounding over and over in my head like a wind smashed ocean against rocks. Who did my mother think she was! What right did she have to tell me she was going to stop my marriage! How dare she think she could dictate to me! And the more I thought about the situation, the angrier I got. She had done nothing to help raise me, absolutely nothing, and by the time I'd gotten washed and changed, ready to go out, I was ready to explode at the unjustness of it all. I had nothing to thank my mother for anything she'd done in the past, and here she was preparing to scuttle my future. Tears came and words tumbled out in distress as I told Brian what had happened, and we immediately left to drive to Mains Farm with him prepared to do battle with Beattie and Bill. He said he would sort it all out, that some mistake had been made and not to worry, he'd fix things. Thank heaven. I just couldn't handle confrontation. I hated fighting of any kind because I hated loud angry voices. If someone chose to pick a fight with me, I'd be the one to back off and apologize, and I'd never deliberately hurt anyone's feelings because I could never get passed my upbringing of, "if you can't find anything good to say, say nothing." So, when Brian said to calm down, he would fix things, I settled down a bit. However, I'd had a good two hours to get myself all churned up before he came to my house, and I didn't realize that my wrath hadn't gone away. It was still simmering close to the surface and, for the second time in my life, when my back was against the wall, I retaliated.

Both Beattie and Bill looked as though they expected us, and from the look on my face they must have sensed there was trouble ahead because the atmosphere quickened. I couldn't wait for Brian to ask for an explanation, but burst into the middle of the kitchen and fired the first shot, "What right do you have to interfere in my life?" "The right of a mother until you're 21!" she replied sharply. The battle lines were drawn. Up from the chair comes Bill, trying to be a peacemaker. "Now, now," he said. "Be polite. Be polite!" I was incensed. Be polite! I could have throttled the both of them. Where were they when I needed to be clothed and fed? Where were they when I needed to find money for my education? Where were they when I needed anything, period? I had never ever asked them for anything, and now they felt they had the right to tell me what I was, and wasn't going to do. I don't think so! It had been hard enough getting Brian to the altar without any interference from them or anybody else. We were paying our own way. We didn't ask for help from anybody. We were on our own, and we certainly didn't expect financial help from either of them. But neither did we ever expect any interference from them – especially not from a mother who had never been my mother!

Once the first round of initial anger dissipated Bill asked me to be quiet so as to give him a chance to explain. He said he'd been told that Brian and I intended to buy Marjorie and Ken's old house once Lorna, Gran and Ted had gone to Canada and he wanted to stop us. He thought it was a crappy house that would take forever to fix up and make nice, and he didn't want to see us start married life by taking on such an onerous task. It was a good job I liked Bill and listened to him but in the back of my mind I think my mother just wanted an excuse to flex her muscles over me, the only time she could. We didn't buy that house, not for their reasons, but because there were too many memories of Marjorie's children in it. Nevertheless, we went to see Mr. Armstrong, the Vicar, and told him everything, as we weren't entirely convinced Beattie and Bill agreed with us getting married. He managed to put our minds at ease somewhat when he said that as I was nearly 21, by the time it went to court I would be 21, and if they did stand up in church to object, he would ignore them. So, as my wedding day drew nearer and nearer, instead of being thrilled and excited by it all, I just wanted to get it over with.

Wedding Bells - and a Honeymoon?

I didn't expect to have a big wedding because of two reasons; first there was no time to arrange one; and second, we didn't have the money. There was no way Gran or Lorna could be expected to fork out for a big wedding so invitations went out to Aunts and Uncles only. Brian's mother wasn't too pleased that her only child was having such a 'hole in the corner' wedding, but it was all we could afford. I bought a navy blue and white suit to be married in and that was just fine with me but not so with Lorna. Her friend Beryl had gotten married not long before and told Lorna I could borrow her wedding dress, so Lorna whisked me off to Beryl's house without telling me why. Now, given my aversion to not wanting other people's clothes, I really didn't want to borrow Beryl's wedding dress. I was quite happy to get married in a suit, so long as it was in church, but Lorna would not be dissuaded, and to make both her and Gran happy I agreed to wear Beryl's dress and veil; so, with borrowed wedding dress and veil, new shoes, and best friend Anne in a lovely dress that she already owned, and best friend Alan by his side, Brian and I were married in Consett Parish Church of England on December 21, 1963.

LtoR: Ella Shaw, Jimmy Buckett, Brian Shaw, Nancy Buckett Shaw, Tommy Shaw, Gran Buckett, Alan Rowland, Anne Rowland, December 21, 1963.

It was a lovely old church, built in 1866, and the altar is actually built on top of a shaft in the #4 pit, but as no coal was ever mined there, we hope it will stand forever. All my apprehension left me as I walked through the church door. I was in the sanctity of God's house, and I realized in looking around, that it was all a bluff, my mother wasn't going to stand up and object, not in front of the rest of the family, so for the first time I looked forward to getting married.

For two youngsters getting married in such a hurry, we didn't do too badly. With our wedding taking place just before Christmas, the church was completely decorated in flowers for the upcoming services. Brian was still a member of the church choir and, to our complete surprise, the rest of them turned out to sing for us. I couldn't believe my eyes when I walked in the front door of the church and saw all the other choirboys and men, dressed in lily white smocks, waiting to lead me down the aisle and for a moment I thought I was at the wrong wedding.

Our photographer was a friend of my future brother-in-law Brian Stephenson, and 'Stivvie' as his nickname was, drove me to the church in his brand-new Hillman California car. Aunt Mabel created my beautiful wedding bouquet and buttonhole flowers for the family, and my brother Jimmy walked me down the aisle. When we came out of the church we had a surprise guard of honour made with badminton rackets held over our heads by our friends from our Badminton Club.

Even though it was a bit of a squeeze getting about 24 Aunts and Uncles in, our wedding reception was held in Gran's house. Lorna and Gran had baked for days, and Lorna had made and iced our wedding cake, and they had pulled out all the stops to give me a wedding feast beyond compare. It was so perfect that no paid caterer could have done better. We couldn't afford to go away for a honeymoon, so Anne and Alan, who had married two years before us, insisted we stay with them in their house near Stanhope moors. They gave up their bed for us while they slept downstairs on the bed chesterfield in the living room, and it was a good job that we were all the very best of friends because for three days we had a communal honeymoon. No sooner had Brian left home to get married than Ella moved Tommy out of her bedroom into Brian's bedroom, thereby reducing the risk of future physical contact. Years and years later she actually told me that she'd only ever had sex with Tommy once, and wouldn't never allow him to touch her again because she'd hated it, and that in all the years they were married she never allowed him to see her without clothes on. Tommy was right; she was a 'cold fish.'

When we returned from our three-day honeymoon, and even though our apartment was just along the road from them, they invited us to stay over at their home on Christmas Eve. It was probably because it would have been the first time in 24 years that Brian wouldn't be at home for Christmas morning, but I had to sleep with Ella, and Brian had to sleep with Tommy. We were married, but couldn't sleep together in the parent's house. My guess was that she was still letting me know that she didn't approve of us being together, ever.

On the Move

Christmas night came and we went to our new home and after putting the rest of the wedding gifts and Christmas presents away, Brian started to put his coat on. "Where are you going at this time of night, Brian?" I asked. "Well, it's nearly 10:30 pm and I have to get home before 11 pm," he replied. I burst out laughing, "You are home – this is your home now!" It took a few seconds for the statement to register, then he fell onto the sofa laughing and never since then has he had the urge to put his coat on at 10:30 pm to "go home."

We settled into our new apartment of one bedroom, living room, kitchen, and bathroom and we loved it. The only fly in the ointment, if you could call it that, was that his mother would visit at the most inopportune times. She made her displeasure of our marriage known to us very early, with the wedding gift of her old 20-year old horsehair chesterfield suite, after she had bought herself a new one. I swear she could see the dust before it settled on our furniture because she would cast her critical eye over everything and every time she came she would volunteer to come and clean for us while we worked, which I never accepted. I was raised to be clean and tidy and as a young housewife I wanted to look after my own home. Brian said not to worry if she didn't like how clean we kept our home, he'd been raised in a museum and if his mother didn't like the relaxed atmosphere of our house, then she didn't need to visit. I thought she was going to have apoplexy when he told her that, but it didn't stop her coming.

We'd only been living there for about three weeks when the young man who lived in the next apartment to us came hammering on our door and when Brian opened the door to him, he was covered from head to toe in blood! His wife had left him and he decided to commit suicide but after bleeding all over the place for ten minutes he changed his mind, and came looking for help. So, Brian grabbed the towels out of our bathroom and proceeded to put tourniquets on the young man's arms while I ran to the phone box to phone for an ambulance. They came within minutes, along with the Police because it was illegal to harm yourself, and bundled him off to hospital. Brian brought my brand new blue towels back and started to wash them in the bathroom basin and I told him to throw them out because I'd never be able to look at them again without remembering what that young man had tried to do to himself. After his family came and cleaned the apartment they took all the furniture away and we never saw any of them again.

Apart from that nasty incident, we had some great times living there and when Anne and Alan used to stay overnight, we'd strip our bed, put the mattress on the living room floor for them to sleep on, and then make the base into our bed. We traveled everywhere with our best friends and I remember one time we'd decided to try camping down the south of England. We'd been traveling a long time before pulling off onto the side of a country road to make ourselves something to eat, and while the camping stove heated up Anne sat down on a hillock. She'd only been sitting there for a few moments when suddenly she jumped up and started smacking herself all over her backside, waving her arms around crazily in the air, and shouting, "Help me! Help me!" The poor lass had mistakenly sat on a Red Ant hill. They were mean and horrible little creatures, and really bit when they were angry and quite a number of them had crawled up her trouser legs. No wonder she was jumping around. She couldn't get out of her clothes fast enough and as Alan was trying to help her, cars started slowing down to see what was going on. They must have wondered if the new sexual revolution was happening before their eyes because Anne finally stood on the side of the road in nothing but her underwear. All but Anne could see the funny side of it, and it took a while for her normally good humour to return. However, none of us was keen on sleeping outdoors after that and our 'camping' trip lasted only the first night as we decided none of us was cut out for camping, so we found Bed and Breakfast homes to stay in.

We also saw a lot more of my sister, Nora, and her boyfriend, Brian Stephenson, after we got married. It wasn't that we weren't close beforehand, it was just that she was busy courting and so was I so we never saw each other very much, except in the bedroom at night. Lorna had gotten rid of the old squeaky double bed when I moved back home, and we each had our own brand new twin bed complete with new dressing table and wardrobe, and as I was usually in bed and asleep before Nora came home, we were like ships that passed in the night, until I got married, that is. The four of us got into the weekly Tuesday night routine of playing cards in our apartment and we loved it. Every Tuesday night that God sent you'd find the four of us playing Bridge, snacking on cheese and crackers, or having a late-night supper of fish and chips from the local 'Chippie.' I was in seventh heaven and loved being married.

Nora Buckett Stephenson

Brian Stephenson (Stivvie)

I was still working for the Company, and once a week after work, I would visit Gran in Blackhill, and when Brian was finished for the day he'd come and pick me up. It was fantastic having the use of a car; it made life so much easier for all of us, including Gran and Lorna, but particularly Lorna. There was nothing I wouldn't do for either of them. If she needed to go somewhere, and it made it easier traveling by car, then all she had to do was mention it, and both Brian and I would be there, waiting to play 'Chauffeur.' We would take Gran, Lorna and Ted to places that had been just names on a map until now and explored with them, and it was especially nice to take Gran because she'd lived in villages all her life and hadn't traveled very much. Nora and Brian helped also. They did a good share of driving now that Stivvie looked like he was going to become a fixture in the family and one time they took Gran, Lorna and Ted, and Billy's youngest boy, 'Young Billy' up to a cottage in Silloth for a week's holidays, and as they had driven them up there, it was arranged that Brian and I would go and get them, and on the way back we all burst out laughing as 'Young Billy' startled us all by saying, "Look everyone, those two cows are playing Leapfrog!"

Gran was in her early 70's when she said she'd like to visit Marjorie and Ken in Canada and for someone who hadn't traveled very much, this was a pretty outstanding request to make. For the rest of us it meant a seven-hour car ride to Prestwick airport and back. But, no mind, if Gran wanted to visit Marjorie, then visit she would and with a full car of Brian and I, and Gran, Lorna, Ted and their dog, Kim, we set off for the airport which was in Scotland. There were no highways and lots of congested traffic, and we figured that by the time it took us the seven hours to drive home, Gran would be arriving in Toronto airport.

While Gran was away visiting Marjorie, Lorna asked us if we'd like to join her and her young 10-year-old son Ted for a caravan holiday in Wales. Ted was a lovely little boy who actually showed up out of nowhere when I was 11 years old but as all my spare time was spent in babysitting Marjorie's children, or working 6 days a week, I didn't see much of him while he was growing up. Anyway, although nervous about driving so far away from home than we had dared to travel before in our A40 van, we quickly found out that whether it was the highlands of Scotland or the mountains and valleys of Wales, the van, stacked to the roof with people, suitcases, and the dog, triumphed. We had a marvelous time even though the weather was not very good, and we must have climbed and picnicked on every mountain. We even walked across the swing bridge to the Isle of Anglesey, and I only mention it because Ted was frightened because it was swaying in the breeze, and Brian had to use all his powers of persuasion to conquer Ted's fear which he did, and we were proud of him. Even though Brian was not used to children, he liked being around Ted, and loved to fiddle around making toys for him such as rolling stock for his train set or model airplanes and ships.

Both Brian and I still worked at the Company, and had been living in our apartment for about a year when we got a huge surprise. Answering a knock on our door, we found Beattie and Bill standing outside. "We've just come to see how you're doing," my mother said. Unbelievable. To "just come …" meant catching a bus from Ebchester to Consett, then another bus to Delves Lane, then walking about ½ mile along the road to our home. "Well you'd better come in and see then," I replied. I was raised to respect others, and my manners were polished, "Would you like a cup of tea?" I asked. "Yes please," my mother replied as she sat down on our very ugly brown leather settee. "Did you buy this?" she asked. "No, Brian's mother gave it to us for a wedding present. It was her old one and she bought herself a new one," I answered. "Humph!" she said, and I could read her thoughts and could agree with her, what a rotten wedding present to give anybody.

Bill had been wandering around all the time we were speaking, and as there wasn't much to see, he turned to Brian and said, "When are you planning on moving?" That caught both of us by surprise and I jerked my head to look at Brian. "Not for a long time," he answered. Then Bill said, "I've got my eye on a bungalow for sale, part-way up Ebchester bank, are you interested?" Of course we were interested, but we couldn't afford to buy a house just then. Although my formal education was considered to be over as I was now over 21 years old, we were still paying University fees for Brian, so we had to tell him no, we just weren't in a position to buy it. I felt really bad that they had trailed all the way from Ebchester to Delves Lane just to tell us that they had spotted a good house for sale, but there wasn't much we could do about it. There was silence for a moment. "Could you manage the mortgage payments if I lend you the deposit," Bill asked.

There are some people in this life who just take the wind out of your sails, and Bill was one of them. He saw more than he ever let on, and did more for other people than anybody ever knew. He offered us more than the hand of friendship; he offered to set us on the right road for life. I thought we'd burnt any bridges between us the previous year, and here they were in our little apartment, offering to lend us some money to buy a house. How unbelievable is that? Very cautiously Brian asked what the catch was. "No catch, just offering to help you get on your feet because you're better off buying a house than renting one. You can either pay me back bit by bit, or when you sell the house and move up to something better," he said. Here was another one of those crossroads that we would encounter throughout life. Brian looked at me, and not even asking for my opinion, thanked them both most sincerely, as he accepted their offer. After they'd gone I told him he should have consulted with me first, but he said, "Look, we can't change what's happened in the past, but we can change our future, and its time you and your mother put the past behind you and moved on!" So, optimistically, the four of us went to see the house they'd mentioned, and it was true, it was a lovely little place and we liked it. Brian had been to see our Bank Manager in the interim and had been pre-approved for a certain amount of mortgage money, and we were all disappointed when the house auctioned off for more. Bill said never mind, there'd be other houses coming onto the market, so have patience, and he was right. With their help and blessings, we bought our first home in the little village of East Law, about two miles from their house.

East Law was about ten miles away from Consett, built on the side of a hill in the heart of farming country, a zillion miles away from industry. The 'low road' to Newcastle ran along the bottom of the community, with a road branching off up the hill to our house and it was so steep that for every six feet traveled it climbed one foot vertically. It felt as though I had to climb Mount Everest, especially when carrying grocery bags. It was a bedroom community with no shops or stores, but you could buy bread, vegetables, meat and fish from various motorized vans that came on Tuesday's and Thursday's.

It was a small upscale community of maybe 50 or so detached and semi-detached houses, and a few bungalows, and one set of four terraced houses at the very top of the hill, and we lived in the second terraced house. Bill, and my brother Brian, came and made some improvements for us. They replaced a couple of missing slates from the roof, and bricked up the doorway to the kitchen that was in the middle of the living room wall. Then he made a new doorway into the kitchen beneath the stairs, removed the living room door, and replaced both with sliding doors and cleverly hid them both behind a false wall. It was brilliant, and with both doors on the same wall, and not jutting out into the room, it made our living room much more spacious. It was our first taste of renovation. Nothing else needed to be done. It was a lovely well cared for home with a big bay window in the living room, and even though it only had a small kitchen, bathroom, bedroom, and a 'box' or half bedroom, it was ours – or it would be in 25 years!

The front garden wasn't very large, only 20 rose bushes planted in between paths made of broken concrete flagstones laid in a crazy paving pattern, but for non-gardeners like us it was perfect. We had a coal fireplace, with a very posh surround of porcelain tiles, hand painted with wildflowers. The kitchen, complete with electric stove, a free-standing food pantry, and a small two-seater kitchen table and chairs was small, but big enough for two of us. But, to one side of the kitchen was a door leading to a bathroom with hot and cold running water, and an inside toilet – pure luxury on cold winter nights! We traded in the old brown leather suite and bought a beautiful brand new three-piece suite whose arms were covered in charcoal gray material while the back and loose seats were covered in red fur. We had a wall-to-wall Axminster pure wool carpet installed that matched the furniture exactly, being charcoal gray with a splash of red in the shape of a feather. I made floor length curtains and cushions from heavy gold brocade and once it was all put together, it was stunning. We made the quantum leap from the dull and boring 1940's to the colourful psychedelic world of the 1960's in just one afternoon. The small backyard had a three-foot high wall of stone around it, and I could look out of the kitchen window over the rolling hills and dales. It was a well laid out house, small but not too small, and the air was so clean after Consett it was exhilarating. To complete our happy family, Lorna gave us a puppy from her dog Kim, whom we named Chick.

We held a New Year's Eve party the first year we were in this house and invited everybody we knew, including Brian's folks which made a lot of people nervous. Celebrating New Year's Eve was a big thing in our neck of the woods. I mean, everybody expected to get a bit sloshed at some point during the night, but those people who knew Ella, and of her often-voiced opinion against the Devil's Brew, were a bit cautious about coming. As it turned out they had no need to worry because thanks to a highly inebriated and jubilant Ella, we all had a terrific New Year's Eve. I had made a fruit cocktail punch in a huge bowl, and even though I tried to tell Ella that there was liquor in it, she insisted she didn't want the liquid, only the fruit at the bottom. Well, you can guess the rest. The fruit had been soaking in rum for a few hours and as she ate most of it and unused to liquor, she was intoxicated really quick. In no time at all she was singing her head off the same as the rest of us while, to Tommy's absolute amazement, topping up his beer glass. Quite astonishing. Everybody agreed that she should continue to live life in a drunken state because she was a much nicer person, and over the next few years' Tommy never let her live it down. Just the mention of that particular party used to drive her crazy and Tommy loved it. If she was getting a bit out of hand he'd mockingly say, "Away with you, you drunken woman. If I'd known you were a secret drinker I'd never have married you!" and all of us who knew about the party used to laugh, but at the same time thought it was poetic justice after her nagging him to death about an odd glass of beer.

We'd lived in that house for nearly a year when Brian said I didn't need to work anymore if I didn't want to, and after being employed by the Company for eight years, mostly in the Invoice Department, I resigned. I'd felt awful about working after I got married because there were so many school leavers looking for work that it started to prick my conscience and, besides that, I had a husband making very good money. I'd get Brian off to work, let the dog out the back to do his business and go back to bed for an hour. Then I'd make a leisurely breakfast, stoke the fire and put my head in a book until it was time to make supper. My days were my own! I had nobody shouting at me to break my concentration; nobody dictating my workload; nobody telling me what to do! I was in heaven!

For the three years we lived in East Law I got to know my mother, Beattie, very well. Now that I wasn't working any more, one or twice a week I would take Brian to work so that I could have the car, and Beattie and I went wherever the wheels took us. We wandered around the north east of England and sometimes even further. In fact, one day I had to call Brian to let him know I would be late picking him up as we were three hours away in Annan, in Scotland; he laughed and said he'd have to get an itinerary from us in the future.

Beattie and Bill only lived a couple of miles along the road from us and as it was such a beautiful scenic walk, I would take our dog, Chick, and visit them quite often. There was never any pressure from Beattie to recognize her as my mother; no, we'd just become good friends, and enjoyed each other's company. We'd arrange to catch the same bus, me at my stop and Beattie at her stop, and travel to Newcastle together and spend the day shopping, or just browsing around. After I persuaded her to let me cut her waist-length hair and perm it, I got the job of doing her sister-in-law Ellen Oats and daughter, Anne's hair on a regular basis so we became a traveling hair salon for a couple of years. By now, my brother Brian was married to a sweetheart of a girl called Rose who was only about 19 at the time, and both Beattie and I loved to visit her, and new baby Gary. She was a lovely gentle girl, but would get behind on her housework at times with having a new baby, so Beattie and I would help her by spring-cleaning. Poor Rose must have felt overwhelmed when she opened the door to us, because it was a case of, "you look after the baby, Rose, and we'll do the cleaning!" and, as I took after my mother in this respect, we were known as the 'Whirling Dervishes' of house cleaning.

My sister Nora and Brian Stephenson on their wedding day.

Brian and I had been married for two years when my sister Nora married Brian Stephenson, and to distinguish between the three Brian's in my life, my husband was called 'Shawsie', Brian Stephenson was called 'Stivvie', and my brother Brian Dodds was called 'Doddsie' so at least everybody knew to whom you were referring.

Nora did us all proud when she married and had a posh catered wedding. Every relative, blood or not, was invited, and it was beautiful. Her dress was made of very expensive white Italian silk, and I was Maid of Honour with Marjorie's 2½-year old daughter, Lindsay, as the bridesmaid. Our dresses were floor length turquoise Italian silk, and I had an arrangement of silk flowers in my hair that wouldn't stay put and constantly fell forward into my eyes; luckily, Marjorie had a small hat made of silk flowers for Lindsay and it stayed on, just. Lindsay was the most adorable little girl that you ever saw. She was her brother, Kenneth, reborn and we all swore that any mischief she could get into, she did. Lorna and I had gone to Newcastle airport to collect Marjorie and Lindsay in our brand-new Hillman Minx car, and she was such a mischief that every time I stopped at a traffic light, she would grab the keys and switch the car engine off. After doing that a couple of times I learned to keep my hand over the keys while driving so that she couldn't get to them, and what Marjorie must have gone through during a 7½ hour airplane trip with 'Miss Mischief' was anybody's guess.

Lindsay 2-1/2 yrs old, Nancy 22 yrs old.

Nora changed her religion from Protestant to Catholic to marry Stivvie, and as neither Jimmy nor I knew anything about a Catholic wedding service we were not sure when to sit or stand up. So, when Nora and Stivvie vanished behind the altar into a side room, both Jimmy and I, who had tight hold of Lindsay to stop her tap dancing on the flagstone floor, sat down in one of the pews, and Stivvie had to come running back to get us to go with them to sign the register. She got pregnant on her honeymoon and their first child Anthony was born nine and a half months later after a troublesome pregnancy. However, she was torn between being overjoyed at Anthony's birth and worrying whether other people thought she'd gotten pregnant before she was married, and it bothered her for years. She was always concerned about what other people thought and even though being born illegitimate was not our fault, she felt the social stigma much more than I did. All through her life she would try and hide her background and would never answer questions about her father. She wouldn't take out life insurance because she wouldn't fill the form in because she never wanted anyone to know she had no father, and whereas I now had the attitude to state bluntly who and what I was, and if you didn't like it, then the devil take you, Nora never found that same confidence.

But now that she was married, and had a home of her own in Belmont, Durham, Beattie and I would often drive over to visit with her, and new baby Anthony, and we three became firm friends. In getting to know Beattie as adults, both Nora and I used to wonder how on earth she'd gotten herself into trouble as much. I mean she just didn't look or sound the type to be used. By now she was brusque and had a fairly tough outer skin, and if she thought she was right, then she would have the last word; and she was certainly not a pushover by any means. But we were never able to ask our mother about the circumstances of our birth, because we both felt that if we insisted on having answers, it could possibly spoil our current friendship. So, unless Beattie herself volunteered the information, there was no way we could find out if the rumours we'd heard were true. We couldn't even ask other relatives because supposedly nobody else knew.

Anne and Alan had started the process of moving to South Africa with his company, Whimpey, around this time, so they faded out of our lives for a while and, as we saw less of them, we saw more of Nora and Stivvie. We'd either go to their house for a meal and play to cards on a Tuesday night, or they would come to us at East Law. If we wanted to go out to eat, we would go to the Chinese restaurant in Consett where Stivvie introduced me to his favorite white wine,

Asti Spumanti. I remember the first time I ever tasted it because I knocked the wine glass over and spilled it over the tablecloth. If we went to their house on a Saturday we were always, without exception, treated to Fish and Chips from their favorite shop called Stanton's, located in Milburn Gate in Durham City. If we went on Sunday it was always a Sunday dinner of roast beef and Yorkshire puddings, with mushy peas, and why I mention it is because Nora would plunk the entire items one on top of the other, so that it looked like a pyramid - cooking was not her idea of fun!

Other times we would meet up with them at Stivvie's family's pub in the mining village of Cornsay Colliery and were welcomed by his dad, Matt, his mother Ivy and his younger brother Frank who were very down to earth people. Frank worked in the pits while Stivvie worked in a bank and they were as opposite as you could get; Stivvie spoke very good English while Frank spoke pitmatic, and you had to listen very carefully when he talked. It was lovely visiting them and even though neither Brian nor I were pub drinkers we thoroughly enjoyed going there. We played dominoes, cards, or darts and, just before leaving, Ivy would let us raid the pub garden for anything in season. Stivvie's mother was a most gentle, kind and generous woman and I liked her very much.

Now my husband, Brian was raised as an only child and had never had much to do with little children, so he wasn't bothered about having his own for a while; however, when Lindsay and Marjorie came for the wedding, she managed to change his mind. From clapping eyes on her for the first time, he fell in love with her, as she did with him. He was 'Unca Byron' to her the three weeks she was in England, and we took her everywhere we went. All of our friends thought she was adorable and Brian said if he could be guaranteed a child such as Lindsay, then he was all for starting a family. He and I were married 2½ years and still living in East Law when I became pregnant and we were both ecstatic. Our lives seemed to be going forward by some grand design; we were married, had our own home, were living in a beautiful area, Brian had great prospects, I was the little housewife, and now the promise of children. Perfect? That is, until I was 3½ months pregnant and miscarried.

It's hard to explain how much this affected me, and nobody who has never lost a baby can possibly understand the full gamut of emotions that a woman has. First of all, there is the promise of hope of your own child. This was my child, nobody else's, at least mine and Brian's! From the time I first knew I was pregnant, I already had the child's name picked out; if it was a boy then his name would be David; and if it was a girl then her name would be Allison Lindsay. In my mind's eye, I had already done the nursery, bought the baby clothes, had the child christened, and booked it into Infant's school. Then nothing! All hope gone, with only a visit to the hospital to have the remains of the child cleaned out of the womb. I didn't mention my miscarriage to many of my friends, because all it seemed to do was embarrass them. They didn't want to know about it because they had no answers. They had no inspirational words of wisdom or reassuring comfort to give me; no, miscarrying early was just an ordinary everyday event and something to be got through on your own. Miscarrying a baby in the north of England at that time was just like having a good sneeze, "go get yourself cleaned out, and try again!" Not much point on dwelling on something we couldn't do anything about, so Brian and I put it behind us, and got on with our lives. Every so often one relative or another would ask, "How long have you been married?" and when given the answer would say, "Well isn't it time you had children?"

Rather than go into detail about what had happened, I'd always agree with them, it was the line of least resistance.

Gran, Lorna and Ted emigrate to Canada

We were still living in East Law when Lorna finally made the decision to immigrate to Canada to be with Marjorie and Ken, and it took a while for the rest of us - Billy, Jimmy, Nora and I, to get used to the idea. It seemed so far away, but if Gran had the courage to go and live in Canada at the age of 78, then the rest of us could find the courage to get on a plane to go visit her.

L to R: Nanna Lowther, Lorna, Gran and Ted just before they left for Canada.

Lorna sold the house on behalf of Marjorie and Ken, cleared everything out, packed up their suitcases and they came to live with us until it was time to leave. As the day of departure drew near, Gran kept changing her mind about wanting to go and finally she asked if she could stay with me; of course she could, for as long as she wanted, forever if she wanted, she was my Gran. Once Lorna knew that Gran was having second thoughts about going, she said she could stay behind, but that her and Ted still had to go. She had given up the house, sold or given away all the furniture, and had resigned her job. She had to go. I had some heart-breaking conversations with Gran during the two months they stayed with us. Not wanting to persuade her to go, and not wanting to encourage her to stay because I knew she'd would be very unhappy without Lorna and Ted, I finally wised up and gave her a lifeline in England by telling her that if she didn't like Canada after she'd been there a while, then she could come home and live with Brian and I. I don't know if they were the magic words she needed to hear, but she cheered up, and said she was going to go with Lorna to Canada now. Maybe it just put her mind at ease knowing that she would always have a home in England, who knows?

We invited all the relatives to our house for a farewell party for them, and I remember I had made individual plates of cold cuts and salad when Billy's wife, June, came into the kitchen and asked where the children's plates were. "Pick any one of those on the table, they're all the same," I said. "But the children can't eat all that, they'll waste half of it!" she replied. "In my house, everyone is treated equally, and if they waste it, then they waste it, but children get the same as adults," I said. June just shook her head and said, "You'll learn Nan, when you have your own, that it's very wasteful to give children more than they can eat." I know what she said was right, and at that time I was perhaps a bit overboard in my belief that children should be dealt with courtesy, respect and

June & Billy Buckett, 1975

treated as junior adults. Maybe it had a lot to do with my childhood of being seen and not heard, but every child who came into contact with me was treated especially nice and if that meant a full plate of food, just the same as the adults, then so be it.

A couple of days after the farewell party Gran, Lorna and Ted left for Newcastle Train Station to catch the train to Liverpool where they would board the ship for Canada. How Lorna got herself, Gran and 12-year old Ted, plus all the suitcases and her dog Kim, from England to Canada without losing anything is a miracle. Even after arriving in Montreal in Canada, she had to get them all on a train to Toronto and as none of us had telephones at that time, we had to wait anxiously for a telegram to say they had finally arrived safe and sound at Marjorie and Ken's house. As I said, Lorna's been an organizer all of her life, and she excelled herself in this trip.

Life took on a new normal. I can't say it got back to normal, because three of the women who raised me, Gran, Lorna and Marjorie, were in Canada and not likely to come back. Grandad was dead; Nora and Stivvie and son Anthony, lived in Durham city; Billy and his wife June and children Billy, Keith and Susan still lived in Consett; but Jimmy and his wife Ruby and baby Fiona had moved way up country to Carlisle. We heard more news of Billy and Jimmy from Lorna in Canada, than we heard from them locally. Now that most of the women in my childhood were no longer in England, everyone gravitated to Aunt Mabel and Uncle Joe's house. They had just moved from Castleside to Shotley Bridge where Uncle Joe secured the job of part-time Gardener, and the bungalow that went with it, working for an important Surgeon in the local hospital, but he still kept his job driving shunt trains for the Company.

Aunt Mabel & Uncle Joe, 1976

With my house in East Law being slap bang in the middle of Aunt Mabel in Shotley Bridge, and my mother Beattie, in Ebchester, I now had a choice of whom to visit. It was brilliant! I'd always loved Aunt Mabel; she has been very special to me from being a very small child, so having her live so close was a dream. I would walk along to her house, have a good natter, then walk home again, or walk to Beattie's and do the same. I was spoiled for choice. I don't mention much of their third sister, Aunt Gladys, because after swiping me across the head at Grandads' funeral, I did my best to keep out of her way so didn't see much of her.

My mother, Beattie.

Life became a series of letters back and forth from Canada. Lorna took over the job as family correspondent from Marjorie, and remained the strongest letter writer over the years and if it weren't for periodic dispatches from her, then we'd all have lost communication with each other a long time ago.

Nora and I had a very good relationship, she was my sister, so it was a given. She was definitely somebody I took for granted in my life, and I never gave it a thought about how she'd feel when Brian came home from work one day to tell me we were going leaving England also.

PART 2 - AUSTRALIA

We're going where?

We'd been happily married for four years when, in February 1967, two Australians visited the Company and Brian was asked to show them around and explain all the processes that went into making steel, and he did it so well that the Australians offered him a job on the spot. He said he'd discuss it with his wife and get back to them, to which they responded, "Just tell her she's going mate." I was thrilled when Brian came home and told me that people from the Broken Hill Proprietary Company in Melbourne, Australia, wanted to hire him to work in Whyalla, South Australia, and that he wanted to go, but I was shocked at the same time, "Australia. Why Australia? I didn't want to go to Australia. If I had to leave my beautiful home to go anywhere it would be Canada. Canada, where the other half of my family live!" Brian thought for a moment, "How about if we go to Australia for a couple of years then go to Canada? I'd like to see something of the world before we settle down."

It seemed as though everybody was jumping this ship called England. Marjorie, Ken and children and Gran, Lorna and Ted had all gone to Canada and here I was about to jump in with both feet and agree to go to Australia. When I think about it now, most of the momentous decisions of my life have been made on the spur of the moment and this proved to be no exception. I never gave it another thought but said, "Okay then, but after two years we're going to Canada, right?" I suppose if I'd argued against going we wouldn't have gone, but when you've been born and raised in a small village, to have the opportunity of going to the other side of the world when somebody else is paying for the trip was exciting. It was like something you read in a novel. Of course I was going. Wherever Brian was, I'd be right behind. Both of us agreed that we would look upon our time in Australia as a two-year holiday, nothing more and nothing less; after all, we weren't like ordinary immigrants, we weren't really going to settle there, were we?

We broke the news to Nora and Stivvie first and even though I was a bit apprehensive about telling her because she was my nearest and dearest relative, she took it very well and said, "You only have one life to live Nan, go for it!" I should have known she'd be okay, because by now going abroad to live was nothing new. Marjorie, Gran and Lorna had moved to Canada. Cousins Robin, Peggy and Esther Barron had moved to South Africa as well as our best friends Anne and Alan, and cousin Sheila Maguire had moved to Queensland in Australia. So, Brian and I moving to South Australia surprised no-one in my family. Our leaving England was just going to be another letter with a foreign stamp on it and it wasn't a question of anyone being amazed anymore; it was more a question of, "Who's leaving next?"

Brian flew down to London to meet with the people from BHP to confirm his acceptance of a job, but we didn't tell anyone else until he received his Employment Contract sometime in March and only then did he give his mandatory three months' notice to the Company. Mr. Scott, his boss, was surprised to say the least and said, "I was grooming you for Head Office in London Brian, so if you ever come back, let me know." That was rather nice to hear, and it gave me a small measure of security that we weren't entirely burning all of our bridges behind us. So now it was done. We were both committed to leaving our homeland for another country, Australia.

Once Brian had put his notice in, we figured it was time to face the music and break the news to his folks, Tommy and Ella, something neither of us was looking forward to doing.

All my life I have been a very open and honest person, and to keep this particular secret until Brian decided when to tell his folks we were leaving the country made me really nervous. We'd gone to their house for the usual Sunday tea, and when Brian and I were clearing the tea things away in the kitchen I whispered to him, "Tell them Brian, or I'm going to have a heart attack because the suspense is killing me." "Okay, okay," he replied. "Just wait until we get the dishes out of the way. I need time to think of how to break it to them gently. He took no time at all because we'd only gotten through the door of the living room when he blurted out, "Mam, Dad, I've been offered a job in Australia and I'm taking it." He took me so much by surprise that I just sort of flopped down on the couch while exhaling a nervous laugh. Not a good thing to have happen. For a moment, there was a stunned silence and you could have heard the proverbial pin drop, then Ella pushed Brian to one side and ran into the kitchen and started to cry. Tommy sat motionless in his chair staring into the fire for a moment then slowly turned towards me and his whole body seemed to stiffen as he looked past Brian to me, and in a very rough and nasty voice said, "I'll never forgive you for taking Brian away, Nancy. This is going to break Ella's heart. I'm finished with you."

It was my turn to be stunned. He was my friend, or I thought he was. He was my antidote to Ella. I knew that from Ella's point of view I would inevitably be at fault, and I knew they'd both be upset at Brian leaving - he was their only child and they were going to be left on their own, and I'm pretty sure that, knowing most of my immediate family were now living abroad, it would have been natural for him to assume that it would be me taking Brian overseas – but only if it had been Canada we were going to! Yes, I had agreed to go to Australia with Brian so I was just as guilty of wanting to go there as he was, and if I could have gotten any words out what would they have been, "It's not my fault, I didn't offer him a job there." No, there were no words that I could say that would exonerate me, I was a willing partner, and if he chose to believe that it was me who was taking Brian away then nothing would change his thinking. There have been times in my life when I wished I were more articulate and this was one of them but before I could gather my wits to say anything, Tommy deliberately turned his back on me. I looked at Brian but he was as stunned as I was. I got up off the couch, collected my handbag, and in a quiet shaking voice said, "I'd better wait in the car for you Brian." Usually I could put other people's nastiness behind me until it wasn't awful anymore, but this time it was worse than awful, it was a terrible betrayal of my love and trust. As I waited in the car all I could see was the look on Tommy's face and hear his words, *"I'll never forgive you for taking Brian away, Nancy. This is going to break Ella's heart. I'm finished with you."*

For the past six years, I had looked upon him as a surrogate father and had loved him, but within the space of thirty seconds all that vanished. I'd meant nothing to him. It had all been a façade. All put on to please Brian. My stomach was bubbling and churning and my brain wanted to scream in protest to anybody who was listening, "WHAT DID I DO TO DESERVE THIS LIFE? Instead, I thought sadly, "Well, if he wants to blame me so be it. Both of them have let me know what they think about me now." Then the self-defense mental survival mode kicked in and I said to myself, "Well to hell with them. They don't have to have anything more to do with me. See if I care. I got along without them before I met them, I can get along without them now, and if they don't want me, then I don't want them." Oh, to be able to speak those words out loud, and not just in my head. To really not give a damn what other people thought. To be more like my sister, Nora, and show some defiance and guts. However, we're all shaped by events that happen in our lives and who knows, if I hadn't been shattered by Tommy's reaction I might have gone through the remainder of my life being a gutless wonder. To have someone I trusted implicitly turn on me, made me resolve to stop being a doormat for anybody who was in a bad mood to wipe their feet on – and Tommy now joined Ella in the detested hypocritical category.

Brian did his best to persuade me that it was unfortunate Tommy had reacted in the way he did, he understood more than I that Tommy still had to live with Ella and that visits from both of us were his only bit of relief. I know there is some sort of logic there, but he couldn't convince me. I wasn't as quick to forgive Tommy as he was, and even though Brian still visited his folks, my share of the 'Buckett' temper came to the fore and I stubbornly refused to go. Brian would tell them that I was too busy clearing out the house but I really didn't care what excuse he made regarding my absence, I only knew that I didn't want to have anything more to do with either of them. I'd had enough. I had visited them nearly every Sunday for six years and had held my tongue while I brushed off Ella's sly digs, just to keep the peace, but I was now past caring. I was right in thinking that they didn't believe any of Brian's excuses because about four weeks later I nearly fainted when I answered the door to find them standing outside unexpectedly. I say unexpected because it meant they had to catch two different buses to get to our house in East Law, something Tommy said he'd never do. He was very polite to me and whereas in the past I'd have given him a kiss on the cheek and a hug when I saw him, I didn't this time, I was still smarting from the nastiness and finality of his, *"I'm finished with you"* comment.

Over the four weeks that I hadn't seen them I regurgitated all the rotten remarks that Ella had ever made, along with Tommy's pretty nasty comment, so both of them were treated very coolly while we waited for Brian to come home from work. I remembered my manners and offered them refreshments that they gladly accepted but it was a very awkward and strained atmosphere until Brian walked in the door about an hour later. He came bustling through the door and stopped with a look of amazement on his face because he couldn't believe his eyes that his folks were sitting in our living room and the first words out of his mouth were, "Hello there, what's wrong?" The assumption he made was natural because they never visited us by bus and always made Brian go and pick them up when they wished to come to our house. It went very quiet for a moment, "Well, Mohammed won't go to the mountain, so the mountain has had to come to Mohammed. We've come to visit Nancy," Tommy replied.

I was absolutely flabbergasted and my mouth dropped open but I couldn't say anything. For the first time in my life, somebody other than my husband had to take into account my wishes and feelings. Finally, I was somebody to be reckoned with. It was like a light bulb lit up inside my head and row upon row of sizzling waves of electricity shot up from my toes to the end of the hairs on my head. Tommy Shaw, tough as nails, hardline union man, had to swallow his pride to meet a 24-year-old slip of a girl on her terms. What a bitter-sweet moment. It flashed across my mind that he had the ulterior motive of pegging me as the letter writer in the family but all I said was, "Thank you very much," and went into the kitchen to compose myself. If Tommy had apologized to me for being nasty to me in the first place I'd have forgiven him anything, but he didn't. He just assumed that everything would get back to normal now that he'd made the first move, but he let me down so badly that I never totally forgave him or trusted him again for the rest of his life.

From the moment Brian signed on the dotted line, BHP started pressuring him to fly to Australia as quickly as possible, to the point where I was starting to feel very uneasy about what he had committed us to and started to panic. After all, we were leaving the 'cradle to grave' security blanket of the Company for a 'quantity unknown' employer and they wanted Brian to leave immediately instead of honouring the three months' notice he'd had to give the Company. I couldn't sell the house without his signature plus I needed help getting rid of furniture and the car and help with filling tea chests full of stuff to send out by boat. Moving overseas was a brand-new experience, and I wasn't confident enough to manage things on my own, and I was feeling very apprehensive about going there at all. Brian may have been used to high-pressure tactics from senior executives, but I certainly wasn't. For one thing, I needed time to get used to the idea of even going to Australia because it was in the opposite direction to my preferred destination of Canada and I was very nervous about being on an airplane for three days. When Brian's new bosses heard that I was nervous of flying, they decided to let us come by ship instead. Just what I wanted – four weeks on a ship should let me get used to the idea of going to a country that was at the opposite end of the world and the people I wanted to be with.

Our home was sold within a very short time of it being put on the market and the first thing Brian did was to pay Bill back the deposit money we had borrowed from him. We now could concentrate on clearing the house and as weren't sure how much it would cost to transport our possessions, we decided to rid ourselves of everything but necessities. We had sold or given most of our things away before BHP told us they would transport our belongings for us, but the only things we were able to salvage and send was the washing machine, and about six tea chests of soft furnishings. We still had Brian's Steinway piano that we could have sent out, but Aunt Mabel suggested it might not make it in one piece so we donated it to Castleside Women's Institute along with all the paraphernalia such as the music stool and a 20-year collection of sheet music. One of our sentimental possessions that we just couldn't part with was Brian's writing bureau that his folks had bought him when he was five years old. It was a lovely piece of furniture so we asked Ella to look after it for us until such time as we could retrieve it from her.

The only other notable possessions we had were also Brian's. He had started collecting records when he was a teenager and had a huge collection of all the old opera singers including Caruso, Gigli and Tauber but, as they were very fragile '78s, he gave them to my sister Dorothy and her husband Barry. About a year later, we received two recorded tapes through the mail and couldn't believe our eyes - Barry had recorded eight hours of our records onto tape for us - what a lovely gesture. Every time I put the tapes on I thought about how he would have had to sit quietly watching the tape, get up, switch off both the record player and tape player, change the record, ensure the tape was in the right spot, then start recording again; what an extraordinary effort he had to have put in to make those tapes. We still appreciate the fact that he did this, and still have the tapes.

On the one hand, it upset both of us to get rid of our home and beautiful furniture but, on the other hand, it liberated us for life. No other house or piece of furniture that we have ever owned since East Law has owned us. We certainly admire and appreciate what other people have but since experiencing freedom from earthly possessions, we've not put much stock in keeping up with the Jones's.

Our most emotional possession to find a new home for was our dog, Chick. He was only about 6 months old at the time and if we'd taken him with us he'd have had to be in quarantine for 6 months which would make him a year old before we got him back, so we thought it better to find another home for him in England. After interviewing three families we finally chose a young couple with a large house and big yard, and two small children. When the mother came to get Chick, we parceled up his food and dishes into two bags, put his leash on him and petted him all the while taking him to the front door. He knew something was wrong because he kept looking back at us with big soulful eyes while walking down the path to the front gate. I have never felt so bad in all my life as the time we let Chick go to another owner; he'd been like a baby to us, and it was extremely emotional giving him away. It was so disturbing that after his new owner drove away both Brian and I sat before the fire and with tears in our eyes vowed we'd never have another pet.

While we were packing up and getting rid of stuff in the house, Beattie was an enormous help. With living a short distance away, it was easy for her to get to our house, and I don't know how I'd have done everything without her. She had jokingly said a couple of times that she'd better come with me to help unpack because I'd not find anything again, and I had lightheartedly agreed. But her tone became much more serious when she mentioned it for the third time, "Nan, I don't know how you are going to manage without me; I'd better come to Australia with you." I didn't know how to respond because I thought she was still joking so I pretended I hadn't heard. However, a couple of days later, Bill said nearly the same thing. He said, "How do you feel about Beattie and me coming to Australia with you? I've always wanted to go there." "How do I feel? Great! I'm having trouble believing what I'm hearing, but that would be great," I replied in astonishment. We had all gotten along like a house on fire since we moved to East Law and over the last three years all four of us had become firm friends. "Yes," I said, "That would be fantastic, and we'd love you to come with us."

Bill said that since the Roman Remains had been discovered on the property he'd had some interested buyers; one in particular being a garage franchise. The franchise was especially interested because their property was sort of triangle shaped on a corner lot on the low road to Newcastle and it would have been a perfect set up for them – they could catch the motor trade while people dropped in to see the Roman Remains. Bill said he was really interested in this particular sale because the amount of money they were offering would have let him retire at 55 instead of 65. Although I was not going to argue them out of going, I couldn't understand why they wanted to leave England at this time in their lives. Brian and Rose had new baby Gary, Nora and Stivvie had new baby Anthony, and our mother was a loving grandmother. I couldn't *really* believe that she'd *really* want to leave the grandchildren - not *really*. Nevertheless, they appeared to want to go to Australia with us and were making plans to do so, when they decided to wait until Brian and I settled out there first, then they would follow later. By now we'd gotten all of our belongings sorted out, the house was gone, as was the furniture, and all the stuff that was going to Australia was being transported to a cargo ship and would arrive about two weeks after we did. So, all that was left to do was to move into Beattie and Bill's house and stay there until it was time to catch the train for the first part of our journey to Australia.

We had just settled into their house for our last couple of weeks in England when we had a call from our local newspaper, The Consett Guardian, who had heard through the grapevine that we were going abroad and they wanted to interview us. Brian was 27 and I was 24 when the news that we were going to Australia made front-page news, and apart from a huge picture of us both, the headlines read "Local Couple Emigrate. Brain drain hits Consett," that made us feel as though we were going to drop off the face of the earth and, when we got to the Outback we were convinced we had.

Australia here we come

We held a bon-voyage party in the local pub and invited family and friends for final goodbyes and the next day we readied ourselves for our departure from England. We were up bright and early in order to get to Delves Lane to say our very last goodbye to his folks. I really didn't want to go, but Brian said he needed moral support so I felt obliged to go with him. Understandably, they were very upset; it's not every day that your only child takes off for the other side of the world with the intention of never coming back. So, with Ella hiding her tear stained face in her apron and sobbing that it was terrible, just terrible, Tommy wished us all the best and a safe journey and, as an afterthought turned to me and asked me to write to them and I said I would. Hardly an unexpected request.

Now it was time to go. Time to leave our homeland behind. Time to embark upon our great adventure. Paul and Allison drove us to Newcastle just in time to catch the train to London then we'd have to change trains to get to Southampton where we'd set sail. Here we were, a young married couple, lovely home, secure job, great future ahead of us, and we'd just thrown it all away for the mysteries of the wild blue yonder, and neither of us could have possibly guessed we were about to experience the adventure of a lifetime.

At Southampton, where the Titanic had sailed from, we boarded the Fairsea, an Italian ship that had been used to transport soldiers and equipment in World War II and it hadn't changed a bit – it was built to hold about 1,200 people but we totaled 1,200 passengers plus 600 crew. Nowadays the world is so small and foreign lands are just a few hours' flight away, but in the mid 60's the world was still a mighty big planet, and to sail on a ship for nearly four weeks to get from one country to another was a huge undertaking. We were experienced 'tourists' in Britain, but going up that gangplank knowing we were going to be on an ocean for so long and visiting foreign lands where they didn't speak English was a heart-stopping moment. The question arose in my mind, "Do I really want to do this?" We were leaving everything behind us, job, house, family, security, everything, and nothing would ever be the same again. With a jumble of thoughts running through my head with each step up the gangplank I finally said to myself, "What the heck, we're here now; we're going to see something of the world that we can't read about in books. We're young, we will survive!"

It seemed to be a huge ship when we looked at it from the quayside and it had three decks above the waterline. The very top deck housed the quarterdeck where the Captain steered the ship. The second deck was where the swimming pool, table tennis, shuffleboard and quoits were, and the third deck, which was mostly enclosed, had a 12' corridor running around the outside of it, and had two lounge areas, a children's play room, and the main eating area, and on the fourth deck which was below stairs there was a small movie theatre, a hairdresser's and barber shop, and laundry facilities.

Our quarters were another three flights of stairs down into what we felt were the bowels of the ship and to say they were cramped and noisy was a gross understatement. It was the smallest room I have ever seen and even though it was no bigger than a walk-in clothes closet it held two bunk beds, one wardrobe and a set of drawers. I gave Brian no choice but claimed the bottom bunk for me because there was no way I was going to sleep on the top bunk in case I'd fall off during the night, and given the rough seas that were to come, that was a good decision on my part. We could hear the loud pulsing rhythm of the engines quite clearly and both of us wondered if sailing to Australia instead of flying was a good thing because we thought we'd never get to sleep in that noisy sardine-can of a room. Its only saving grace was that there was a ceiling fan to keep the air circulating and when we switched it on it muffled the engine noise slightly. Brian looked at me and we both burst out laughing. "Well." he said, "it's only for sleeping – we'll be up on deck all day and you'll be so tired with all the activities on board it'll not bother you where you're sleeping after a couple of days." Laughingly I agreed, "Okay then, I suppose you're right. We really have no choice but to put up with it, so just let's enjoy ourselves with other things."

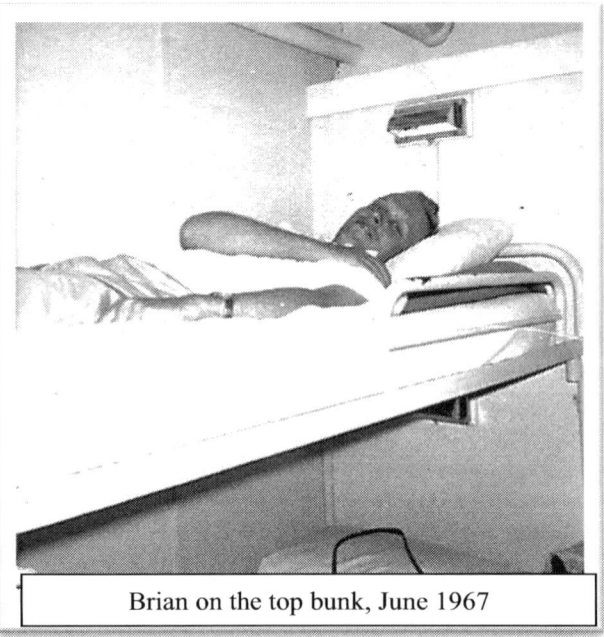
Brian on the top bunk, June 1967

All of this had taken place with one of us standing outside the door, as we'd had to take turns looking in. We could stand side by side in the room but if you wanted to move around then the other person had to get onto the bottom bunk and pull their legs up out of the way. Before we entered our room, we were introduced to a young man called Virgilio who would take care of us during the voyage. Fancy that. We had our own steward whose sole purpose for being on that ship was to look after us during our journey – what pure luxury. He was Italian who didn't speak much English and all through the journey he tried to teach me to speak his language but apart from being able to say good morning, good evening, and thank you, I never mastered it, although he appreciated my efforts. He was always smiling and was very helpful, and every time we left our room we'd come back to find it tidy and the beds made, even if we'd only just sat on the bottom bunk it was tidied up all the same. He certainly took his work seriously.

Brian left me to unpack and went to reconnoiter the ship and when he came back about an hour later it was to tell me he'd made his way around the ship twice so there was no fear of getting lost because the ship wasn't so big after all. He also told me that there were no baths on board only showers, and as I'd never seen a shower before I had to ask another woman how to use it and it was such a wonderful experience after all the years of freezing to death in an unheated English bathroom that I took two showers a day just for the fun of it. This journey was to be a lot of 'firsts' for me, but not all of them so enjoyable.

Never mind from day one, from minute one, I was seasick. The ship was doing a rock and roll and an up and down all at the same time - and that was in the harbour. I never even saw the ship leave Southampton because I was too busy lying on my bed feeling ill and by the time we had reached the coast of Spain I was so thoroughly seasick that just the thought of food was enough to make me throw up, and I wasn't the only one. Eleven hundred and eighty-seven other passengers were seasick. Twice, during that voyage, the seas were so rough that every passenger, except for thirteen, were seasick and, incredibly, Brian, who really disliked being on water, except for the rowing boats in the Lake District, was one of the thirteen passengers who never had any problems with seasickness, and it was the same thirteen people who showed up for supper both times. Unbelievable! I had been flat on my back in pure misery for two days before stalwart Brian manhandled me upstairs, sat me in a deckchair in the warm sunshine, and made me eat. "You've got to eat something Nan, or you'll get really sick!" he said. "I can't eat anything, Brian. Just the thought of food is making me gag." I replied. "Try this," he said. It was a bread roll. A freshly made bread roll with absolutely nothing on it, but after tasting a little bit, it slid down my throat like hot butter off a griddle. It was manna from heaven. After feeling really sick, that simple little bread roll got me back on my feet, and as we had put the coast of Spain well behind us, I found my sea legs and started to enjoy the journey.

The main dining room only held enough tables to seat 600 people and as there were 1,200 passengers it meant two sittings –5 pm or 7 pm. We were given the early sitting and the added challenge of trying to physically eat while the seas were still rolling fairly heavily. The very first night that I made it to the table, the ship rocked so unexpectedly that all the soup plates, some filled and some not, and the cutlery, slid off the tables onto the floor. Most of the younger crowd thought that it was hysterically funny but I was concerned because I could see water halfway up the dining room porthole and I really thought we were going to tip over. The waiters, who were all Italian, tried to steady themselves while holding a soup tureen and with one arm gesticulating wildly in the air screamed to everyone, "hold plate, hold plate in future!" We thought it was a bit futile trying to eat at this early hour, and Brian managed to switch our sitting to 7 pm when the night calmed the sea down a bit.

The cuisine was magnificent and I sampled foods that I'd never heard of before such as spaghetti and linguine, and that fantastic Italian bread. Brian didn't fare so well because of his allergy to onions, and I think he lived on bread, ham, cheese and apples for most of the trip. There were lots of really nice people in our cliché and two groups are worthy of mention because we kept our relationship going for quite a while after we landed: Joyce and Sheila, who were nurses from

Cumberland and were really gentle girls well suited to nursing, and George and Barbara, and their five children. George was a butcher from somewhere in the south of England and they had decided to move in order to give their children a better future. They were all going out to Australia on the Australian Plan, meaning you paid 10 English Pounds towards your fare and the Australian government paid the rest, but you had to stay in Australia for two years, and you had to surrender your passport to the authorities to make sure you did stay. Our fare had been fully paid for by BHP but the commitment to stay two years was the same.

We traveled through the Mediterranean, down the Suez Canal and into the Red Sea and over the Indian Ocean to Perth, in Australia. Stop! Hold on a moment! Lots of things happened after we left Southampton and before we reached Australia, lots of things, and not all of them nice. The first thing of any real significance was that we were all totally out of our depth with respect to the weather and had to adjust both mentally and physically to the considerable heat that most of us we were experiencing for the first time. The weather in England was notorious for being overcast and raining with only the promise of a warm sun at the best of times, and clothing was mostly heavy cardigans and jackets. However, you've never seen outerwear come off so quickly as when we rounded the coast of Spain and the sun started to get uncomfortably hot.

Brian changed into the white shorts and short-sleeved shirts that he wore to play Badminton, but I was not so lucky. I'd never owned a pair of shorts in my life, so had to be content with cotton dresses. Most men rolled up their shirtsleeves and trouser legs and plunked a white handkerchief tied with knots in the corners on their heads, and a lot of the younger women literally stripped down to bra and panties. Noel Coward when he wrote the song, "Mad Dogs and Englishmen go out in the mid-day sun" must have been sitting on a deck on our ship, because I've never seen so many near-naked bodies happily burning under a hot Mediterranean sky. Maybe being raised by grandparents had something to do with it. Being brought up in a village atmosphere instead of a big city must have clouded my outlook because I didn't understand the 'swinging sixties' at all and I found this near-nakedness to be very embarrassing, so I kept my eyes averted whenever I had to pass them. I'm sure Brian didn't.

Sometimes Ignorance really is Bliss

We'd been on the ship for about nine days and we were supposed to stop in Port Said, but the Captain announced over the loudspeaker that terrorists were shooting at English ships, therefore we weren't stopping but sailing for another week to Cairo to replenish supplies. The supplies had been getting low, not so much the food as the water and with temperatures in the 100's every day, I was drinking a lot of it and I didn't know you could get sick from drinking water. The water at home was safe to drink, but not on the ship. Unknown to me they were down to the bottom of the barrel so to speak and the more liquid I drank, the more I threw up and because they feared dehydration in all that heat, the more liquid Joyce and Sheila tried to get down me again. After seventy-two hours of violently and deliriously throwing up and down, Brian physically carried me to the Doctors who took one look at me and diagnosed a severe case of gastroenteritis and shot me with a double dose of something from a syringe. I was extremely dehydrated but was told not to drink the ship's water but to drink bottled soda water instead, and I believed Brian when he told me later I was close to death because I really felt like it. However, the injections the Doctor gave me over the next three days started to work and I was able to go up on deck and sit in the shade with George and Barbara.

I'd no sooner started to feel better than we reached the Suez Canal and lines were thrown down from our ship to tugboats fore and aft. The ship nearly filled the width of the Canal and if we'd been on a lower deck, I'm sure we could have reached out and touched land. The tugboats were small, relative to the ship, and it was a bit hard to believe they could possibly have enough power to take us where we needed to go, but they did. We sat idly on the deck and marveled at the way they maneuvered the now silent ship slowly through the Canal to the dock in Cairo. We moved to the bow and were instantly mesmerized by on-shore activities. Without the noise and pulsing rhythm of the ship's engines to cause distraction, the whole scene was like a moving painting on a sand canvas and so different from anything we'd ever encountered that everything was fascinating. In the distance, there were about six men in long flowing black robes leading well-burdened camels away from a small village into a wide expanse of desert. Nearer to hand young boys paused in their job of knocking dates out of palm trees with long wooden poles to wave to us, as another couple of young boys busied themselves herding goats towards a well off to our right.

George, with Barbara at his side, stood quietly to one side, with a puzzled look on his face. He gave a sigh and Barbara turned to him and asked him what was wrong. He replied, "If I didn't know better, I'd swear those bunkers lined up along the bank were ammunition and weapon dumps but they can't be, because if I remember right, they were all demolished at the end of WWII – but something's not right." George had done his National Service in the Middle East so we figured he knew what he was talking about, but it was hard for us to give much credence to his comments. I mean I didn't think it mattered to us that Egypt was stockpiling weapons and ammunition, it didn't affect us, we were just passing through. The world was at peace, or so we thought.

The tugboats took no time in maneuvering the ship into its position at the dock and, before we knew why, small baskets came flying over the side onto the deck. Dodging the incoming projectiles, we were surprised to see hordes of small boats filled with men and boys and later learned that the boats were called Felucca's and that people made a living this way. They'd throw baskets of trinkets onto the deck with the expertise of years behind them, shout to get attention, and barter and bargain with a relentlessness that had to be seen to be believed. Once the ship was secured and the gangplank lowered, younger boys scrambled onto the deck and began pestering everybody to buy something, so Brian and I figured it was best to get out of the way and disembark.

Most people got off the ship to do the tourist thing and to see the Pyramids and other Egyptian wonders but Brian and I just went into town to the nearest market place as I was still not feeling my best and wasn't up to being trashed around. The market place was only about a ten-minute walk from the ship and after weaving our way through a few side streets, we came out into the open area and it was just like something you'd see in the movies; there were lots of covered stalls with fruit and vegetables, different kinds of baked breads, woven baskets of every shape and size, tourist models of the Pyramids, the Sphinx and King Tuts' sarcophagus. Men and boys, in knee length robes over their trousers, shouted and waved their arms and tried to bring attention to their stall or sat about in doorways smoking long pipes attached to narrow necked vessels or drank tea out of glasses at the tables. All the women walked together in pairs and wore head to toe robes, and didn't speak to each other but walked quietly, with their heads down, or stood silently at a stall until the vendor chose to acknowledge their presence. It felt as though we'd stepped back into a land that time forgot.

There were so many people and the aisles were so narrow that it was hard not to be carried and jostled along and with the noise and heat it was all a bit confusing so we pulled ourselves to one side to get our bearings. As we did so the noise of the market stilled and it seemed as though everyone collectively held their breath. In what seemed like slow motion, stalls were silently closed and vendors either melted into shop doorways or disappeared into the nearest alley as hundreds of armed soldiers pushed and shoved their way into the market place from the dozen or so streets around. After a second or so of shock at the transition and not knowing quite what to do next, it seemed as though hundreds of eyes turned to stare in our direction. In reaction, I turned to see what they were looking at, and standing just behind were another four Englishwomen, all momentarily paralyzed like us. From out of the mist in my mind it dawned on me why we getting those really nasty looks – none of us were dressed in the all-encompassing robes of an Egyptian Lady. We were Infidels. "Brian, let's get back to the ship, something is not right." He agreed.

It didn't take a genius to realize that the street scene had changed far too quickly for it to be normal. The others obviously thought so too, and the six of us were among the first people to make it back on board. We found the Captain and crew scurrying around like mice, and we all thought they were going to cast off there and then but had to wait for the other passengers to return first. We had no sooner pulled up the gangplank and were being pushed out into the Canal and on our way when the 1967 Arab/Israeli war started over our heads and even though we were sailing away from the troubles everybody was on edge for the next few days. It was only after we reached Fremantle in Australia that we were told of the very dangerous situation we'd been in. All the while we had been docked; BHP had been in close contact with the British Consulate in Cairo. They wanted the British Consulate to put pressure on the Egyptians to make sure our ship was released before any fighting started, but neither the Egyptian government nor the British Consulate could guarantee that we'd be allowed to leave. We had been perilously close to being stuck in the Canal for the duration of the war. How much more excitement do you need in your life?

Our last stop before the long haul to Australia was Djibouti, just on the edge of Africa and it was with great trepidation that we left the ship to do the tourist thing but it was going to be a long time before we hit land again. It was nighttime and the docks were dark and eerie and there was an unpleasant damp sticky heat rising from the water, and all we could see were the silhouettes of a few street vendors lounging around waiting to take advantage of innocent tourists. We teamed up with another couple for safety and walked down the ship's gangplank into a long narrow street of dark doorways and out into an open market place where there were a lot of men in the same long flowing robes that we'd seen in Cairo. It was quite unnerving seeing so many people hanging around in the darkness of the night just doing nothing. Who knew what was being hidden under those robes, especially when we knew they were shooting English people in Port Said and that there was a war going on behind us in Egypt. Not a very brave soul at the best of times, I was quite relieved to get my souvenir carving of a native lady that we didn't even barter for, and to get back to the ship to the 'comfort' of our quarters.

No sooner had we left Djibouti and sailed into the Indian Ocean than I, and the other eleven hundred and eighty-seven passengers, became seasick again. For the next few days I did nothing but stay in my bunk praying that the ship would go in one direction only, because not only did it lurch from side to side but, without warning, it would drop like an elephant into a trough. I was spread-eagled in the bunk trying to stop myself from rolling onto the floor while making sure I didn't hit my head on the top bunk when Brian insisted I go up on deck with him. I was still muttering under my breath something about letting me die in peace when we came out into the sunshine and I found out why he was so persistent. I could feel my eyes opening wide and my mouth dropping open as I walked slowly to the handrail of the ship. I looked at Brian then down at the sea. It was the most beautiful shimmering, iridescent green and blue colour; the sun was really hot and it was bouncing off the waves, catching each wave and making it sparkle and shine. I was speechless, totally speechless, for when my eyes came into focus there must have been at least ten or twelve whales swimming really close to the ship, keeping us company. Their beautiful sleek and streamlined blue and black bodies dived in unison, came up for air, blew their spouts, came right up out of the water and splashed down again sending a spray of water up and over the handrail and wetting most of the spectators. What an awe-inspiring sight of these magnificent and totally fascinating creatures of the water world. Their spectacular show kept us all entranced for about four hours until they changed direction and kept everyone talking about them for days.

By now we had left the Northern Hemisphere of Europe far behind and were in the Southern Hemisphere so could see the Southern Cross, the one depicted on the Australian Flag, and once the sun had gone down and the sky was dark we would go up on deck each night. When you live in a civilized country the lights of the houses and street lights mask the stars so you don't ever see them clearly, but when you're out on the ocean and the ship dims its lights for bedtime, the stars come out in all their glory and they look like very expensive diamonds being moved tantalizingly right or left to catch the moon's rays to exquisitely sparkle for an appreciative audience. To see the vastness of the heavens for the first time was more than merely spectacular. The brilliance and clarity of the stars as they hung like dazzling orbs of light in the sky before dancing along the horizon and dipping into the ocean for a moonlight bathe was breathtaking, and just lying on a deck chair viewing the immenseness of the heavens confirmed God's presence and each evening it felt as though we had visited God in his house and saw all the lights shining from the windows of his many mansions.

While we were up on deck admiring the heavens, experiencing what we felt was an awesome experience, a lot of other young people were busy drinking themselves silly below deck. It wasn't that we minded having a drink but having come from a 'drinking man's town' we couldn't figure out what the attraction was in 'drinking to get drunk' and so for the most part kept away from these people, but it was interesting to see how civilized behaviour went out of the window along with the rules. When we entered the Indian Ocean, the clock had to be stopped at midnight each night so that we could catch up on Australian time, which was about a 14-hour time difference. This was great news for the people who enjoyed a drink because the bars were supposed to close at midnight but with the clock being stopped it remained midnight for one whole hour and all the 'boozers' were allowed to drink for an extra hour and most of them drank more in that one hour than in the preceding eight which didn't make a whole lot of sense to us, but each to his own entertainment. I thought star gazing was best because it didn't wake you up with a headache the next morning and there were certainly some grumpy young people at lunch over the next few days.

We had no sooner stopped talking about the whales than we had another glimpse of the wonders of the sea. Brian and I were up on deck when, to our initial consternation, scores of fish started leaping out of the water. My initial reaction was that something was very wrong with the ocean, but someone more knowledgeable laughed and said it was okay, they were flying fish. "Flying Fish!" "Fish that can fly?" I'd never heard of flying fish before and if I hadn't seen it with my own eyes I'm not sure if I'd have believed it, but there they were. Scores and scores of flying fish. As soon as I knew it was part of their nature to jump out of the water, they were fascinating to watch. As they left the water the sun's rays glistened on their scales and we were treated to a rainbow of colours. All you could hear from people around was, "Ooh, did you see that one?" or, "Ah, what beautiful colours," or, "Just look at how high that one flew." It was a delightful afternoon and we all wondered why they had picked our ship to entertain.

There were lots of organized activities on board the ship, and you could join up to play table tennis, shuffleboard, quoits, card games by the dozen, or volunteer to help with the nightly entertainment of musical numbers, dance competitions, or just plain disco dancing. There were swimming pool games, walk round the deck games, and any other kind of physical activity games you can think of. In fact, there were too many organized things and it was just nice to sit on a deck chair and relax for a while. The crew certainly tried to keep everybody occupied and one of their organized charades was that everybody who had never crossed the Equator before were invited to join in the 'Crossing the Equator Ceremony.' We had to line up before King Neptune, the ruler of the sea, and the equivalent to Mother Earth and in order to permit us lowly air-breathing humans to sail over his oceans, we had to appease him by having our faces and hair painted with a mixture of ketchup, brown sauce and salad cream, then we were 'dressed' in all the leftover salads from the galley and dunked into a bathtub of water and only when you completed this ceremony were you given a "Crossing the Equator Certificate." Not everybody did it because they didn't want to get dirty, but I remember we did it and it was great fun.

Just outside of Fremantle we had our last surprise from the ocean when a school of porpoise came to the ship and entertained us. As soon as we saw them we ran to the bow of the ship for an uninterrupted view and watched in awe as these marvelously entertaining creatures kept pace with the ship. It was amazing to see those mammals surfacing the water while crisscrossing in front of the ship's bow; and it was incredible to see how fast they swam while performing for our enjoyment. The Captain said he had never seen whales, flying fish and porpoise one after the other in all the times he'd sailed the Indian Ocean and could only congratulate us that we were very lucky to have been able to see so much of the ocean's wildlife on this trip.

Preferential Treatment

Within no time at all and yet it seemed as though we'd been on the ship forever, the shoreline of Australia got nearer and nearer, and as soon as we got within docking distance of Fremantle, it was announced over the loudspeaker that a representative from BHP had arrived by tugboat and was now on board to meet with Brian and Nancy Shaw, and would we go to the lifeboat station on Deck B to meet with Mr. So-and-so. He was a very nice man who explained the immigration process to us and gave us both a BHP pin to wear in our lapels, and special papers to present to Customs when we reached our final destination, Adelaide. This caused a bit of a stir among the people we had gotten to know on the ship that someone from BHP was there to meet with us. Most of them were surprised, and a little jealous, to hear that we had previous employment and a house waiting for us and were a little bit annoyed that we'd never mentioned it to them. All we knew from other people was that they had made the decision to emigrate to a new life in Australia and we didn't know if anybody else had employment or houses waiting for them, we'd never felt the need to ask, so were surprised when we realized that we were indeed privileged people and that nobody else had the comfort of knowing what was going to happen to them. Other people on the ship had just taken the chance and emigrated to Australia on a wing and a prayer but no job, and they would be disembarked at their previously specified destination and taken to an 'immigration area' with communal housing until they could find a job and a home on their own.

We had not realized that with Brian already being employed by an Australian company, we would have preferential treatment but both decided that we were not going to feel guilty about it, but would enjoy the experience. I would certainly not rub other people's noses in it, but neither was I going to let them tarnish our good fortune and the best bit of advice we ever received from anybody while going to Australia was from Mr. So-and-so when he said, "If you take my advice, keep away from other English people, they are a pain in the backside, always saying that they lived in palaces or some other such luxury before coming here and unless they fall on their feet straight away they do nothing but moan and groan about Australia." We certainly took advantage of his advice and kept away from 'moaners.'

After docking in Fremantle, Perth, we decided to take the opportunity to stretch our wobbly land legs for the first time in about two weeks and to have a look around once we'd gotten off the ship. To our surprise the town of Fremantle was only a short walk away and that is where we headed. It was a real pleasure walking in and around the docks because they were extremely clean and the streets leading to them were very wide and open, nothing at all like the shabby and dirty docks of Southampton, Cairo and Djibouti and we both decided that if these were just the docks, then the rest of Australia must be pretty fantastic. Even though we had been gradually getting used to hotter and hotter weather we'd had the breeze from the ocean to counteract it, but in Fremantle not only did the streets give off a heat haze that was new to us but the air was extremely hot, and after walking around in the heat for a while I became desperate for a drink so we went into the nearest pub. If I had had two heads, green hair and saucer shaped eyes I couldn't have caused more of a stir with the locals. Women didn't go into pubs in Australia, at least not through the front door, but I didn't know it at the time and ordered lemonade. Never before, and never since, have I tasted anything more refreshing and mouth-watering delicious than that glass of lemonade. I don't know what made it so special other than it was made from fresh lemons, served in ice-cold glasses straight from the refrigerator, and you could hear the tinkle of ice cubes against the cold glass, but it tasted like nectar from the God's to my overheated body. I wanted to take some back to the ship for Joyce and Sheila but it didn't come in bottles. What a pity. I think the landlady could have sold her recipe in the marketplace and made a fortune, it was that good.

All too soon we were back on the ship for the last couple of days of our journey to Adelaide and all we had time to do was to catch up on our laundry and pack our suitcases. Then suddenly we were there. We had made it. The vast majority of people were getting off in Adelaide so there was quite a crowd on deck when we made our way upstairs. The sun was shining and everybody who was disembarking was lined up against the handrail with suitcases ready to leave as soon as they could. After nearly four weeks at sea and all the trials and tribulations we'd gone through, we were about to be welcomed to our new homeland. Sure enough, there was another representative from BHP who made his way on board to meet us and he hurried us down the gangplank before anyone else, whisked us through customs and out onto the main street where there was a taxi cab waiting to take us to our hotel. One minute we were on the ship; the next minute we were on land – as quick as that.

It was early Friday evening when we were booked into a lovely hotel in the center of Adelaide and the hotel receptionist gave us the airplane tickets that she'd been holding for us for a flight to Whyalla on Monday morning. We left our suitcases in the room for the time being and set off to explore Adelaide. What a beautiful city, very clean, very open and enthusiastic. People actually spoke as you passed them by, "G'Day Mate" was the usual greeting and we'd answer, "Hello." What a friendly place. We took our time looking in shop windows and furnished our as yet unseen house with this, that, and the other, and had a great time and must have 'window shopped' for about two hours until we started to feel our sea legs going a bit wobbly and headed back for the hotel. After a lovely meal in the hotel restaurant we went straight to bed and hoped that during the night our sea legs would become land legs and that the bed would stop rocking long enough for us to get to sleep.

Whyalla, South Australia

All I really knew about Whyalla what that it was another Company steel town much like Consett, and that it was somewhere in South Australia at the top of a gulf stream near to the city of

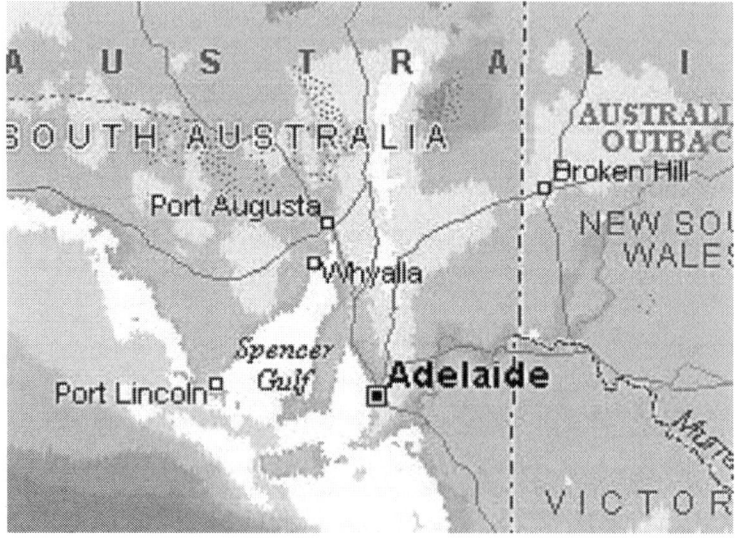

Adelaide, and I had gone on blind faith and Brian's word alone that we were heading for some sort of civilization. So, when the hotel receptionist told us that Whyalla was about 400 kms north of Adelaide and virtually an oasis in semi-desert country I was more than a little apprehensive. "Pardon me, it's what?" I looked at my husband, "Brian, where on earth are we going?" By now we'd spent Saturday and Sunday looking around Adelaide and liked the wide streets, modern stores, lovely bungalows, and the fantastic sea shore, and would have enjoyed living there, but we were only staying there temporarily until we caught the plane to Whyalla. After the response I got from the hotel receptionist, now I knew why we'd been given quizzical looks from some shop assistants when we asked if they had any information about Whyalla - they knew we were heading for the back of beyond but didn't like to tell us.

We were up early on Monday morning to make sure we got to Adelaide airport in plenty of time for our flight to Whyalla and while we were there, mounted on a stand, saw the very first plane to cross the Indian Ocean. I've forgotten who flew it but they must have been crazy because the balsa wood and paper plane looked as though it was held together by glue and bits of string and thin wire; it certainly didn't inspire any confidence in me for what was going to be my first flight ever and I said to Brian that if our plane was similar to that one I'd walk to Whyalla before I'd get on it. However, to my delight we were flying on a very modern 18-seater DC3 propeller plane, and when the pilot asked if this was anyone's first flight I stupidly raised my hand. Quite unexpectedly, he turned to me and said, "Just so that you know, please lift your feet up when we take off, it will help us get off the ground." And I did, and it was only when everyone around me started laughing that I realized how naïve I had been and it took about half an hour for my embarrassment to fade.

On the one hand, we were very lucky to be flying to Whyalla because it gave us a very comfortable bird's eye view of the South Australian landscape as opposed to all the other people who had made Whyalla their destination but had to travel by ordinary bus. But, on the other hand, having lived all my life surrounded by sumptuously green countryside, being able to look out the window and see a very forbidding and austere landscape made me very nervous; very nervous indeed. As far as the eye could see the earth was scorched red and barren and for mile after mile there was nothing but scrub brush and a few leafless trees that gave little or no shade, and no creatures moving around. I couldn't see any green anywhere, and I must admit my uneasiness was growing, and more so when we circled Whyalla Airport to land because all I could only see was row upon row of houses with corrugated iron roofs. Lordy! Lordy! I had come to live in a shanty town. Our village in England was an oasis of beauty and culture compared to my first impression of Whyalla.

There was another representative from BHP waiting to meet us on the tarmac right beside the plane and as I reached out my hand to shake his I missed the bottom step and fell flat on my face. I lay there for a second thinking that the people traveling with me must have thought I was the biggest twit they'd ever had the misfortune to come across, what with believing the pilot and lifting my feet up and now falling out of the plane. People behind me started to laugh when the BHP man, who was having an awful time trying to keep his face straight, said, "Welcome to Australia Mrs. Shaw. You know it's not everyone who has the good fortune to fall out of an airplane and live to tell the tale." Good point, although I didn't fully appreciate his humour at the time. I'd scraped both knees and laddered my nylon stockings – all the while hoping like mad that he wasn't Brian's new boss and that the people on the plane weren't going to be Brian's new workmates or he'd have never lived it down.

On our way out of the airport the BHP guy told us there was a change in plans and that we were not going to our new house but were going stay at the Whyalla Motel instead. We'd filled in the forms while still in England and applied for a rental house from the South Australian Housing Trust who built new houses as needed. They would clear an area of virgin brush and build a very simple timber frame house, on about ¼ acre of land, and had gotten behind in construction because the volume of families choosing to work and live in Whyalla were more than they could cope with. Brian read my mind and expressed his concern about the expense of staying in a motel for an unknown period of time and the BHP man said not to worry they would pay for our accommodation. Even though the news that our new house was not ready was a bit disappointing, it was beneficial to us. After all, we'd no furniture coming by boat, only soft furnishings and a washing machine. We had nothing to sit on or sleep on, so we thought spending time in the Motel would give us time to get ourselves sorted out, and after thanking the man for coming to pick us up at the airport, we settled into our temporary home.

Far too excited to just sit around, we unpacked and hung up our clothes, and took a taxi into town to find out what the stores had to offer. We desperately needed to buy cooler clothing, because even though we arrived in July, which was in the middle of Australia's winter, our English summer clothes were still too robust for the current climate. We also needed to find furniture shops so as to mentally, if not physically, furnish our new house. A new house! Our last house in East Law, had been built at the turn of the century and as we'd made the quantum leap in furniture, now we were on the point of making a quantum leap in houses. It felt great. There weren't many shops along the main street in the small town, and as it was early in the afternoon and a bit too hot to spend much time window shopping we ducked into a gift shop called 'Hooper's.' Our very first purchase in South Australia was a large stuffed Koala Bear toy that we parceled up there and then and took directly to the Post Office and posted to Marjorie's daughter, Lindsay, in Canada.

We had a great time during our first shopping expedition and I say expedition because it felt as though the Australian language didn't belong anywhere in an English-speaking world. Mind you, when I first opened my mouth to ask for something I was greeted with a reciprocal blank glazed look – I'd never given my north of England accent much thought before, but it dawned on me that they didn't understand me much the same way that I didn't understand them, and it took a while for me to slow my speech down and to correctly pronounce all my words so that I could make myself understood. Once in a while I'd forget myself and would drop words 'a mile a minute' but given no response would have to start from the beginning again.

The rest of the day flashed by, and in no time at all that same BHP man knocked on the door on Tuesday morning to pick up Brian to start his Australian working life. When he came home from his first day on the job it was to tell me that he'd met some great people and that his new boss was holding a 'Welcome' party for us on the Friday evening at his home. What a lovely gesture. I can't remember doing much for the rest of the week other than exploring about 100 yards either side of the motel; watching the television when it came on after lunchtime; and using the laundry facilities to catch up on our washing, and it passed by inauspiciously.

Friday evening we excitedly went over to Brian's new boss's house where we met some people who would become close friends all the time we lived in Australia. Our first impressions of the Australians, which never changed the whole time we lived there, was that the Australian culture was the most relaxed and informal way of life in the world and the Australian people were among the best in the world. We found them to be friendly and sociable, extremely generous and extraordinarily laid-back. They don't worry about a thing. If it doesn't get done today, then it will get done tomorrow. They work hard and play hard and we decided that if the people we had met so far were typical Australians, then this was indeed 'God's own Country' with sunshine and sea thrown in as a bonus and definitely a great place to live. The party was a 'theme song' party and as we'd never attended such a thing before, I hadn't a clue what to wear, so we gave it our own interpretation. I just attached a map of the world to a piece of string and went as, 'I've got the world on a string,' and Brian went as 'Greensleeves' by wearing a tube of green cloth on each arm.

They were a terrific group of people all about the same age as us, and once we tuned in to their Australian accent they were really fun to talk to and we found out a lot about Whyalla. I was really surprised to learn that we had houses in England that were older than the city of Whyalla as it was only settled in 1880, and I'm pretty sure my first home in Templetown was built around that time. Whyalla's first name was Hummock Hill after a small hill in the area, and they only had about 50 people living there who were known as Hummocky's. What with living in tents and having no natural running water – all of it had to be brought by ship across the bay in Port Pirie - it must have been pretty tough for the first pioneers. In 1914, its name was changed to Whyalla which is aborigine for 'place of deep water' and that's pretty accurate because they built and launched ships there. Until 1945 it was a Company town totally owned and operated by BHP until a local council was elected and again, it was similar to Consett, as it still relied upon BHP as the major employer. It won the right to become come a city in 1961 with only about 14,000 people, and even though it was growing by leaps and bounds, it still had only had about 25,000 inhabitants by the time Brian and I arrived in July, 1967.

Even though it was surrounded by desert on three sides, the fourth side of Whyalla was bounded by the upper Spencer Gulf and has the clearest water in the world with the most beautiful beach you'd ever find anywhere in the world. Geographically speaking, to the west of Whyalla were the Middleback Ranges, rich in iron ore, and across the water were the magnificent Flinders Ranges. The place was growing like crazy but it still had the lovely feeling of 'small-town' community. It was large enough to have most of the major conveniences such as a bus service, child-care crèches, a library, a big shopping center and a couple of parks and even though its backyard was outback with scrub brush and scorched earth, the older part of the City of Whyalla had plenty of trees, plants and grass.

After living in the Whyalla Motel for nearly two weeks, Brian came home to tell me that we were leaving the next morning and, as the new house was still under construction, we'd be moving to the Iron Knob Hotel on Eyre Highway, about 50 kms northwest of Whyalla, in the real outback. "Why do we have to move there Brian?" I asked. "Because Whyalla Races are on," he replied. I'd seen a poster in the reception area of the motel but was still puzzled as to why we had to move. "The Whyalla Horse Races are the biggest social event of the year and as the motel has been fully booked for over a year, we've got to move out of town because there is nowhere else to stay," he said. Then he continued, "My boss wants me to do a costing job at that site, so it will be handy if we stay in the local hotel, at least until the Races are over." By now I was starting to get pretty fed up with living out of suitcases but, undaunted as ever, I readied myself and started packing.

Iron Knob – the Real Outback

Somebody from BHP came to pick us up the next morning to drive us to our new destination and that particular drive was an experience never to be forgotten. It wasn't as though the vastness of the outback was totally unexpected, after all, we'd flown a couple of hundred miles above it to get to Whyalla but sitting in a car and driving through it was a different feeling altogether. It is impossible to describe how enormous it all was; or what it felt like to drive 50 kms on a fairly straight road through miles of open bush and not see another human being or another car.

My mind fluctuated between being excited at the openness and of being terrified at what would happen if the car broke down. It wasn't as though there were garages on the street corners – there weren't any streets to have corners on. I had come from a small village, where everybody knew everybody else, and if you sneezed the neighbours knew about it, and here we were being driven through miles and miles of Australian outback with not another soul in sight. I thought we'd landed on another planet and when we pulled up to the hotel, I was sure we had, because apart from the hotel and thousands of miles of open bush, there were only about thirty other houses scattered about. From recollection, the hotel was two stories high with a wide veranda running along the upstairs front. It was built of red brick with at least 30' square rooms, with two windows to each room, and every room was furnished in mahogany panels. While we waited for the receptionist, I looked out of the hotel window across miles and miles of scrub brush and thought, "This is an oasis in the desert," and wouldn't have been a bit surprised to see a couple of sheiks on stallions riding up to the front door. The hotel was furnished with highly polished leather couches and chairs, and it had the feeling of small-scale Cathedral to it, and another few people staying there must have thought the same, as they talked in whispers also.

Outside, even in the heat of the day, loud cackling and chattering noises came from some Kookaburras, Budgerigars and Cockatoos sitting in a few trees across the road and I quickly hid behind Brian as a beautiful male peacock strutted into the hotel lobby. "That's okay dear," said the receptionist. "That's just Charlie. He comes in here to cool off. Just give him some room to move and he'll not touch you." "What about those kangaroos and emus?" I asked her as I remembered seeing a couple of 'roos and emus either lying or strutting off to the side of the main front door. "Do they come inside?" I asked. "Oh no, they are not allowed in here, but don't worry, they'll not bother you," she replied. "They are as tame as house kittens," she laughed. "Just keep out of the way of the big red bugger, 'cos if you get too close he'll thump you. He has a bloody mean streak sometimes!" By now we were walking up the stairs being led to our bedroom and as the door opened, both of us gasped in surprise. The bed was so high off the floor there was a stepping stool to get into it. The receptionist, who was also the hotel owner, chuckled at our reaction. "Keeps any creepy crawlies from getting into the bed dears!" she said. "Do you get many nasty insects here?" I asked. "Well, you're in the bush now. You've got to be more careful because we can't keep the doors shut all the time, we're a hotel," she answered. "Just make sure you shake your shoes before you put them on, because scorpions love moist dark places!" she went on to say. I guess there was a lot to learn about the outback, much more than I realized.

The room was pretty dark not only because of the heavy paneling, but also because the owner hadn't fully opened the floor to ceiling curtains. We took her advice of leaving them closed so as to keep the heat of the blaring sun out, in an effort to keep the room cool and after unpacking once again, went downstairs just in time for lunch. The hospitality of the owners was unbelievable, as I have never seen so much food served to only two people. They must have thought we were ditch diggers with extra-large appetites because we were served steaks as large as dinner plates and shrimp as big as baby lobsters. There were so many desserts that they had to be wheeled around on a trolley and no sooner had they taken them away, but they came back to the table with a garden salad, cheese, crackers, and coffee to finish the meal. To say it was just 'sumptuous' is an understatement. Wives in Templetown could have fed a family of six on what we were given and, needless to say, it was impossible to finish a full meal. Everything was of the highest quality, from the lily-white table linen to the crystal glassware and silver cutlery. This was a hotel the rich and famous could easily have frequented and we were spoiled rotten.

Everything about the Australians was over-generous and over-simplified. We were greeted with, "G'day Mate," by all and sundry and thought them all very friendly. That is until we met with the man who was picking Brian up for work the next day. We were up early and were sitting in the main lounge when we saw a man stop at the reception desk and heard him say, "I'm here to pick up Brian Shaw. Call the Pommy Bastard down will you?" Upon hearing his name, Brian rose to his feet and walked over to him and he jumped slightly as Brian touched his shoulder. "Hello there, I'm Brian Shaw and this is my wife, Nancy," he said. Totally ignoring me, the man said, "Sorry mate. I didn't mean for you to hear that, but you might as well know that every Englishmen over here is referred to as a Pommy Bastard." "Why is that?" asked Brian. "When Australia was first discovered, England used it as a dumping ground for convicts and they were known as POMES which is an anagram of Prisoner of Mother England, and as some English who come over here are real bastards, the name stuck. Don't worry about it though, because we've also got chinks, wops and paki's," he laughed. All the time he'd been talking, he had totally ignored me and I stood quietly to one side not knowing how to respond to this man's ignorance. Apart from the time I'd gone through the front door of the pub in Fremantle and met some slightly hostile stares from the local men for invading their territory, I'd never met such a rude and chauvinistic male in all my life. Not only was he lacking in manners, but I didn't like the way he made reference to other people. What was a chink, wop or a paki? Brian saw the look of consternation on my face and said, "It's okay Nan, there are a lot of surprises yet to come I imagine." Later that night he told me that the man had referred to Chinese, Italian and Indian people. What an ignorant man! Thank goodness he was in the minority.

While Brian worked, I found it hard to occupy my time and one afternoon, while I was sitting in the lounge just staring out the window, the local policeman came and joined me for afternoon tea. "G'day Nancy, have you got your Australian driving license yet?" he asked. "No, I've done nothing about it because I thought we'd have to get back to Whyalla first," I replied. "I've brought you the booklet and if you study it, I'll test you," he said. After having a driving license for more than six years I wasn't too worried about a driving test, but his suggestion was brilliant. To be able to take a driving test where there were only a couple of streets, practically no stop signs, and definitely no traffic lights was just too good to miss, and both Brian and I got our Australian driving licenses within one week. Now we could buy a car instead of having to rely on other people to get around. Great!

Shunt trains had run along the bottom of my garden carrying coal to the Company, and iron-ore trains stopped traffic in town and it suddenly dawned on me that I'd seen neither sight nor sound of either type of train. Where were they? Supposedly, Iron Knob was named after a mountain in the area, and it was made of pure iron ore which belonged to BHP, so where were the trains that carried it to the steelworks in Whyalla? Here I was, living in the only hotel within a 50 kms radius, theoretically not far from a BHP-owned mountain of ore, but there was no sight of it, nor any sign of red menace dust anywhere. This is when the horizon shifted a bit more.

When Brian came home that night and I asked him about it, he said, "You'll not believe it Nan, but the trains are not like the one's we've seen at home, maybe twenty wagons or so at the most, these trains are at least a mile long." "A mile long. That's impossible!" I cried. "No, it's not. Remember the land is very flat and at each end they have two engines pulling, and two engines pushing, and once a day the wagons are driven down to Whyalla full, and using the same line, are brought back empty ready to be filled for the next day's run. The size of the operation is mind-boggling!" he said. "But where is it?" I asked. "Way back in the bush, way, way back. You'd have to be in a helicopter to actually see where the site is, because you'd never see it from the road," he replied. Well no wonder I'd never seen any red menace dust if it was that far back and it could stay that far back as far as I was concerned, because I loved the beautiful clean environment.

While we were staying in the Iron Knob Hotel we had the chance to meet with the boss of the Iron Baron site. Now this doesn't seem much of an announcement, until you learn that this man very rarely came into town, and when he did, he kept very much to himself. However, he'd heard of Brian from the boss of the Iron Knob site and made it his business to meet him. He invited us to join him for supper and was so impressed with Brian's knowledge of iron and steel, open cast and underground coal mining, that he drove both of us to see his incredible operation. If Brian was wowed by the Iron Knob site he, and I by osmosis, were overwhelmed by the size of the Iron Baron site. They had been working for more than ten years at that site, just removing surface ore to get it ready for open cast blasting, and you could hardly tell where they'd been. Each Mack truck was capable of holding 250 tons of iron ore, and the wheels were so large that Brian stood inside the rim of one wheel and could hardly touch the top. What an experience! When Brian told his boss at the Whyalla office that he'd been to Iron Baron, he made the comment, "Nobody is allowed to go there. That boss doesn't like anybody to visit, and he makes the excuse that it's because it's a 60 kms round trip into the outback on a dirt road. You must have impressed him, Brian."

Building a New Life

We lived in the Iron Knob Hotel for two gloriously pampered weeks and, finally, in late July 1967, and after living out of suitcases for seven weeks, we were given the keys to our brand-new semi-detached house in 7 Mepstead Street, Whyalla Stuart, Whyalla, South Australia. At that time, our house was located right at the edge of the city limits and from the bottom of the street you could see about 100 miles across the bush into the Nullabor Desert. The main door was on the side of the house and you walked directly into the living room complete with a small wood burning stove in the middle of the long wall. On the right side was a door into a huge eat-in kitchen and through the kitchen you turned left to go the bedrooms and bathroom, or right to the laundry and separate toilet. All the floors were wooden planks ready and willing to be sanded, stained and polished which is what we did, except for putting pale blue linoleum on the kitchen floor and there was untouched virgin soil that constituted a garden to the front and back of the house. We had made friends with a few couples at our 'Welcome' party, and through Betty and Steve Knight, we bought a fairly new, sandy coloured, leather couch and two chairs from friends of theirs who were returning to England. Although the rest of the house did feel a bit sparse, the living room, complete with my home made heavy gold brocade curtains, and highly polished floor, did give us some measure of comfort, not only to sit, but also to sleep. The couch turned into a double bed that we slept on each night, and our clothes were hung on hanging rods Brian had inserted into some of the empty tea chests. This was 'minimal living' thirty years ahead of its time.

Over the next few weeks the rest of the street filled up with some of the families we had traveled half way across the world with and it took a while for a few of them to be civil. Once they found out, not from me, that we'd been flown up to Whyalla and had waited for our house in a comfortable hotel, they weren't too happy. I commented at the time that we were in a bit of an awkward situation with our fellow Brits, but Brian reminded me of the good advice given to us in Fremantle so I steered clear of the 'moaners.' However, I felt sorry for a young woman with two small children when she told me they'd had to live for 4 weeks in an old army hut in Adelaide that was riddled with mice and insects, followed by a heat-exhausting six-hour road trip up country in a dilapidated bus. Some of my fellow countrymen that I did enjoy calling friend were Pat, my neighbor from three doors down, and Betty whom we'd met at the party, and through Betty, Iris and Marion. I also met a lovely Australian girl, Yvonne Ross, at that same party, and we became firm friends.

We learned very quickly that social life was just as important as working life and took our turn holding barbeque parties in the backyard. Because we were new arrivals and didn't have a nice back garden we held most of our parties indoors to start with and they were called 'pot luck suppers,' meaning you brought food and drink with you and shared it, and that was okay. It meant you could entertain a lot more without incurring a great deal of cost. Our particular group of Australian friends included us in everything they did, even if it was just shopping in Adelaide, and we'd either drive down on the Friday evening or fly down and stay in a hotel overnight. It just made a change from the local scenery. It didn't make a whole lot of sense when I think about it now because the shops closed at lunchtime on a Saturday and if we wanted anything in particular we'd have to dash around like crazy - but it was fun all the same. One of the crazier things we did was to drive about 100 kms just to get a drink of beer on a Sunday. The pubs were traditionally closed on Sundays but, trust them, our friends found out if you showed your driving license - proving you lived so far away - to the owner of the pub in that little bush town you could get a beer so, every once in a while, when we got bored of doing other things, we'd do that – drive a round trip of nearly 200 kms just to get a beer.

It didn't rain much in Whyalla so outdoor activities could be planned weeks in advance and we took to the Australian way of life immediately. Lots of times we'd be part of a convoy of about six cars and head off into the bush to various places of interest because you never went into the bush on your own, it was much too dangerous. The outback wasn't like a walk in the park, I mean if you broke down and hadn't taken plenty of provisions with you such as gas, food and water, you could die within three days, especially if you strayed off the beaten path because there were thousands of bush trails and a distinct possibility of never being found, so no-one was ever stupid enough to go into the bush on their own.

We were pleased to have made friends early because they re-educated us very quickly about how to live in South Australia, and I mean re-educate. Everything we'd learned from growing up in an over-civilized non-dangerous society was thrown out the window because we had to learn from scratch of the everyday dangers that were around us. We learned about deadly 'outdoor' snakes and spiders which lived in shady areas – and it scared me so much that I never planted any trees or flowers near to the house, and I always made sure that the grass was cut so short that no shelter could be offered to such species as the deadly Brown Snake, the Red Backed Spider, or to the most dangerous of them all, the Funnel Web Spider. This was a creature that looked something like a Tarantula and it would dig a hole just under the surface of any loose soil and then jump out at its prey's throat with its lethal bite. Needless to say, our garden was the only one in the street with solid grass – nothing but grass. My logic was that if there were no trees, flowers or loose soil then no snakes or spiders could live there.

Two 'indoor' insects to really watch out for were the mosquitoes and blowflies. I never ever got used to the mosquitoes, because there seemed to be zillions of them, and it didn't matter how much we secured the house they always got in and made directly for me. They drove me absolutely crazy as they left a red itching and burning lump on every part of exposed flesh and at times you would have thought I was covered in polka dots. Irony of ironies, they never affected Brian, just me. The last pests that I could have lived without were blowflies. They looked just like a bluebottle fly until you killed them, and in death they released the next generation of wriggly white maggots from their bodies and I was never happy until I found the fly that I'd swatted and gotten rid of it and it's offspring.

I remember my reaction the first time I saw a House Spider that I thought was my first sighting of a Funnel Web Spider. I was heading from the car toward the front door with my arms full of groceries and you couldn't miss the thing, it was big and black and about the size of my fist. It was huge. To me it looked similar to a Tarantula and I was so startled that I yelled and dropped the groceries and Brian came running to see what the matter was. He looked at me as though I'd gone deranged in the head but could see that I was greatly agitated, and while he was trying to calm my fears, the spider totally ignored us and continued spinning its web in the corner of the porch above the door. Brian tried to remind me that Funnel Web Spiders didn't spin webs but dug themselves into the ground but I was scared of the thing and was only too pleased when he made a swipe at it and it scurried off along the wall and around the corner, but when I was telling Betty what had happened I couldn't believe my ears when she scolded me and told me not to do that again as this spider spun its web in a shady corner and ate mosquitoes. I felt so stupid that I wanted Brian to find the damn thing and put it back.

We learned that when you live near the outback it is a matter of everyday survival to keep a spare can of gas and a can of fresh water in the car at all times since you never knew when a Kangaroo would jump across the road in front of you and unless you had a roll bar fitted to the front of the car you were no match for a Kangaroo, and could end up crashing into the bush somewhere, so everybody was prepared for an emergency at all times. No kidding.

I remember one time when a young couple newly arrived from England joined our group and were traveling with us through the bush to visit Point Lowly lighthouse, which was reminiscent of an English seaside, and they were in the car in front of us when they suddenly stopped and got out to look at something. Because of the dust that was kicked up on the bush trail, the car behind gave the car in front a fairly wide berth so as we were driving up to them we could see why they'd stopped. To our horror, they were watching a Brown Snake lying about 10 feet away from them - one of South Australia's most deadly snakes - so Brian started banging on the car horn to get their attention and when we were close enough for them to hear he leaned out of the window and shouted, "Get back in the car now. That's a killer snake you're looking at. One bite from that thing and you'll be dead in a few minutes and drive away as quickly as you can so that it doesn't get a chance to wrap itself underneath your car." They didn't need to be told twice but dashed back to their car and shot off in a cloud of dust. The snake barely moved from its position under the scrub brush at the side of the trail but both of us heaved a sigh of relief as we left it behind.

In addition to our social life in the backyard of other people's houses, we joined the 10-pin Bowling League as well as the Whyalla Badminton Club and before we knew it we were First Couple on the tournament team. The other local clubs were Port Augusta, about 60 kms away, and Port Pirie, about 120 kms away. About once a month we'd travel to one of these clubs for a tournament and we hadn't lived in Australia very long when the annual South Australian Badminton Championships were being held in Adelaide. The same couple had won the singles, doubles, and mixed every year for the past five years and were expected to win them again and probably would have done if not for Brian and I. We traveled with the rest of the team down to Adelaide and Brian won his singles match, while I lost mine by one point; then we each went on to play the ladies and men's doubles and won those; then Brian and I won the mixed doubles, in the year of 1967. Even now, all these years later, I still have my original badminton racket with catgut strings in my carryall, but I'm afraid the 24" waist badminton skirt hit the garbage bin quite a few years ago.

Boosting the Population

Four months after we arrived in Australia, in early November, nearly at the height of an Australian summer, I fell pregnant, but it wasn't until December, when my elderly doctor, Dr. Muir, originally from Scotland, thought I was, but told me to come back in a month's time. We kept the news to ourselves so as not to jinx anything, and after my pregnancy was confirmed Brian started fussing around me like a mother hen with a chick. "Brian, there are about six other women in this same street who are pregnant, are you going to fuss them too?" I laughingly asked. "How come there are so many pregnancies?" he queried. "The doctor said that it was normal for young women coming out from England, in particular, to fall pregnant once their blood started to thin in all this heat," I replied. Neither of us had heard of this before so had to take his word for it.

Thrilled to be pregnant, but anxious at the same time given my previous miscarriage, I was also a bit nervous since I'd only started work in the Invoice department at BHP two months earlier and I thought Joy, my boss, would be less than pleased to hear my news, and there were other things jumping around in my mind. The thought of bringing a baby into a house with very little comfort disturbed me and I cast my mind back to a period only six months earlier, to my lovely fully furnished home and couldn't help but wish I was still there with my sister Nora. How could I have gotten myself into such a position? We had a couch that turned into a bed; we were using the tea chests as wardrobes; and we ate off trays on our knees. Something had to change. This was our defining moment. Big decision time. We were going to make a go of it and settle in, or pack it all in and return to England. This was it. Time to put our money where your mouth was Brian! 100% commitment or, "Home James, and don't spare the horses."

We weighed the pros and cons. Brian was enjoying great success as Whyalla's first ever Cost Accountant. We lived about two miles from the ocean. The weather was brilliant – guaranteed blue skies and hot weather every day. We had a fantastic social life; and now there were other streets behind us so the place was growing very rapidly and it was a growth experience like no other. Nowhere else in the world could you feel the throbbing energy of a vibrant and visibly expanding city. We decided to stay, to give it our best shot - at least for the next two years. We were 20th Century pioneers. The cons – no family at hand if we needed help of any kind.

We made up our minds to stay and modestly furnished the rest of the house, and now we were proud owners of a bedroom with two single beds in it, and a wardrobe. We'd bought single beds because of the heat but ended up pushing them together to make a King-sized bed for snuggling. Lovely. Then we bought a six-seater table and chairs for the kitchen. Again, lovely. It meant we could actually sit at a table and eat for a change. We deliberately didn't furnish the baby's room because we didn't want to tempt fate. Coming from a small village, it was superstition not to have everything ready for a new baby just in case something nasty happens.

Our first Christmas in Australia was upon us, and even though it was as hot as Hades, we invited Yvonne and her husband Ian to our home to celebrate with us, and to enjoy a traditional English early afternoon meal of Turkey with all the trimmings, and Sherry trifle. I should have known better. The sun was high in the sky at 6 am, and the perspiration started rolling off me as I put the Turkey into the hot oven to roast. I spent most of the morning preparing salads, main course and dessert, and the whole table was laden with food, but by the time we took our places, the house was so hot it was impossible to eat anything other than the salads and dessert. Yvonne, who was Australian, had no idea what to expect and gasped at the sight of all the food, then laughingly said, "Nan, I bet this is the one and only time you ever make a big meal in the middle of the day. We'd better come back at midnight to enjoy all this." She was right; everything was topsy turvy when it came to entertaining, and nobody entertained in the middle of the day, only in the coolness of the evening.

I was enjoying a very healthy pregnancy when catastrophe struck. Joy, who had been off work sick for two weeks, came back and said to my friend, Yvonne, who was also pregnant, and myself, "Ladies, I'm very sorry to have to tell you this but I have had silent German measles – you'd better call your Doctor." Never mind call him! I dropped what I was doing and went quickly over to Brian's office. I told him about Joy, and during the drive to our Doctor's office he managed to calm me down a bit before entering. That was a waste of effort, because Dr. Muir, while injecting different medicines into my backside, started listing out about a half-dozen birth defects that could happen to my unborn baby and he had my emotions sky high again. Once he finished, he looked at my unshed tears and said, "Don't worry, they may never happen." I don't know whether it was the stuff he pumped into my system or not, but for the rest of my pregnancy I had morning sickness right through the afternoon and well into the evening, and after another month, I resigned from working fulltime in the workforce for the next twelve years.

We had lived in this house for seven months, and I was four months pregnant, with just enough furniture that would do us until the child was born, when the doorbell rang and I opened it to find Joyce and Sheila, the two nurses from Cumberland whom we'd met on the boat, standing on the porch. The girls had originally gone to Sydney but decided to explore the country before settling down and they stayed with us for about a month until they got their own apartment and jobs at Whyalla Hospital. Very politely we gave them the main bedroom and we, once again, slept on the couch. Within days of Joyce and Sheila moving out, George, the butcher from the south of England, knocked on the door. He and Barbara, and their five children, had also gone on to Sydney but hadn't liked the big city atmosphere, so the next thing I knew we had seven lodgers. But Brian and I decided to keep the main bedroom for ourselves this time and let the other seven take over the rest of the house and within a couple of days we felt like we were the lodgers.

Of all the people who have ever lived with us over the years, this family was perhaps the most trying. Maybe it was because they were from the south and we were from the north but communication was a real problem. Barbara had been a cook in a hotel so was used to giving orders left, right and centre, but in my own home, I felt she crossed the boundaries at times. She had had five pregnancies and never a day's sickness with any of them, so couldn't understand why I was ill so often and would make veiled remarks about people who just want to be waited on, meaning me. I'd had toxemia from being three months pregnant and that was practically unheard of, being more normal at the six-month mark, and it got to the point that I kept to my bedroom out of her way as I couldn't stand her pointed comments any longer. It wasn't the most pleasant time I can tell you. Luckily for me, by the time I was seven months pregnant, George finally found a job in a butcher's shop and they were able to rent their own home and move out. I thought they'd have been appreciative of the fact they'd had free lodgings for three months, but they never thanked us and we never saw them again. The good side to all of this was we'd gotten our lives back and I was hoping no more people would show up needing accommodations for a while.

Once we had the house to ourselves again Brian thought he'd make a start on the garden and if he'd known what he was letting himself in for it would have stayed as it was. The house was built on virgin soil and nothing had ever disturbed it in history so it was as hard as rocks. Brian did his best to loosen the soil in the front and back gardens to sow grass seed and after many trials and tribulations, and birds showing up to feed on the seed, we managed to get a decent showing, but it was the most backbreaking job he'd ever had to do. Even with all of his efforts it never came close to looking like a real garden, and they say if you can't grow a garden in South Australia you'll never grow a garden anywhere. But knowing that Whyalla didn't have its own source of water and that every little drop had to be piped in overland from the Murray River in Melbourne, a distance of about 800 kms, made it hard to justify 'wasting' it on a garden.

Although every house had running water piped in, all houses were equipped with a free-standing 500-gallon water storage tank standing in the back garden, attached to the roof of the house by a pipe and this is where we got our actual drinking water from. I'd boil the heck out of it, strain it a few times through clean cheesecloth and put a jug of it in the fridge so that we had clean pure water to drink. When the rains came, a couple of days a year, the tank would fill up again but to stop mosquitos from breeding, a small cup of kerosene had to be poured in and it floated on top of the standing water. Not wanting to ever taste kerosene I was very careful not to run the tank dry. It was cause for great celebration when the rains came, not only for the gardens and drinking water, but the children would be out in the street in their swimming costumes splashing and frolicking about and thoroughly enjoying the tremendous downpour of cold, cold rain. Coming from a climate of constant rain, and water that could be drunk straight from the tap, this was quite an eye-opener of what the priorities in life are.

After being in and out of the hospital for numerous health problems during my pregnancy, I was actually at home when I started having contractions. I had gone to bed early around 9 pm, but by midnight had to wake Brian to tell him I thought the child was on its way. "Oh no!" he said. "What's the matter," I asked him. "I forgot to fill the car up with gas and I don't know if I have enough to get you to the hospital," he replied. "Do you think we should call a taxi?" I asked. "Well by the time I drive to the Shopping Centre to call for a taxi I could have you to the Hospital. I'll get you there!" he said. If I had known just how little gas was in the tank I'd have never gotten into the car, because Brian's total focus was on the gas gauge whereas mine was on the contractions which were coming fast and furious. I thought we'd never make it to the hospital and had visions of giving birth in the car, where it had run out of gas on the side of the road.

Brian pulled up to the Emergency door of the Maternity Hospital and the nurses whisked me onto a Gurney and told him to go home. I wanted him to stay with me, at least in the waiting room, but the hospital staff wouldn't let prospective fathers anywhere near where they were working. I was admitted at 1 am, and by 2:07 am on 26 July, 1968, practically a year to the day when we arrived in Australia, I gave birth to a beautifully healthy baby boy, David Scott Shaw. Dr. Muir walked through the door of Delivery, and half-jokingly said, "Didn't I tell you to give birth before 2 am because I didn't want you to interrupt my sleep?" At 8 am, Brian came to visit and said, "Have you had the baby yet?" Well I guess he wasn't to know that it takes a while for a woman's body to go down again but still, I could have clobbered him for his question and for a split-second I was tempted to say, "No." But I couldn't do that to him and to see his face and watch him rise about 10' off the floor when I told him he was now a father with a son was incredible. He walked around with a dazed look on his face for the next couple of days and you'd think nobody in this world had ever had a child before. But it was amazing to think that after five years of marriage we'd had to come all the way to Australia to have a child but for some reason it felt right. Brian sent telegrams to Lorna and Marjorie in Canada and to Ella and Tommy and my sister Nora in England telling them that we had a brand-new son. In reply, Lorna sent a beautiful shawl that she'd made. Marjorie sent a big blue Panda Bear, and a box of Lindsay and Nancy's baby clothes, and because they were mostly girls things I passed them onto my friend, Yvonne, who had had a baby girl a month before me, but I kept the muslin diapers for my baby. To our great surprise, Ella and Tommy sent a handmade pram set of satin and lace that she'd had especially made, and lamb's wool blankets and some baby clothes. It was nice to know that my family had not forgotten me even though I was thousands of miles away from them.

Brian had grown up as an only child and had no experience with either babies or children, but he was soon to learn because David was only three weeks old when I was rushed back to the hospital on the brink of death. He had gone out to his regular weekly Bridge Club meeting and if he hadn't mentioned my discomfort and pain to his bridge partner, who happened to be Dr. Muir's wife, and had left me for another 24 hours they wouldn't have been able to save my life. Neither of us knew that it was not normal to have such pains after giving birth. I didn't, so how could I expect Brian to know any different. She insisted he leave the Bridge game immediately and take me to the hospital, which he did. When the Emergency Doctor examined me, he found that toxic afterbirth had been left inside me causing a deadly infection to rage throughout my body. In the process of admitting me, Dr. Muir came walking up the corridor to me, and wishing to possibly embarrass Brian he shouted, "Brian, I see more of your wife than you do." To which Brian replied, "That's fair enough because I see more of *your* wife than you." It lightened the mood somewhat and I couldn't help but think Dr. Muir would have to get up much earlier in the morning to get one over on Brian.

I was deathly ill but didn't know it, and neither did Brian until much later in the week. They wheeled me off to an isolation room where everybody had to be covered from head to toe in sterilized gowns just to come into my room, and everything I touched was sterilized within my room. I felt as though I had the plague or something but, in the beginning, I didn't care about anything. When I asked what was going to happen to the baby because I was breastfeeding him, the nurse said, "Oh you can't have the baby in here, you're highly contagious. We wouldn't dream of letting a baby come in here, and you can only see your husband once a day. Nobody else will be allowed in." My poor husband. A three-week old baby at home and his wife, once again, back in hospital for goodness knew how long. Talk about getting thrown in at the deep-end. This is when I really missed my family. If it hadn't had been for God and good neighbours, I don't know how we would have managed. Brian had to work and David had to be looked after. Thank God for my neighbor Pat, and friend Betty Knight. Betty came to the rescue in the daytime while Brian was at work and Pat came to the rescue at night while Brian made a flying visit to see me. How he coped is anybody's guess because I was out of it and too ill to care for the next few weeks. However, once on the mend and out of hospital again, we settled down and enjoyed being first-time parents.

Brian had taken advantage of one of my hospital visits, and had painted the third bedroom lemon and white, because we didn't know the gender of the baby at the time, and it was beautiful. He'd also gone shopping for a wardrobe for baby clothes, but decided it wasn't worth the money, so bought two 6' tall broom closets instead. When he told me what he done I was a bit hesitant, but he painted them lemon and white, put shelves inside, and put pictures of panda bears on the outside, and I absolutely loved them, and every other young mother who came to our home wanted some. The only time I have ever put my foot down about wanting a specific piece of furniture happened in this house. I wanted an Australian bassinet for my child. Nothing else would do. It had to be a bassinet. It was an item of pure luxury at a cost of $600, instead of a $300 crib, but I wanted one so badly because I had never in my life seen anything so beautiful as an Australian bassinet. It was a beautiful and intricately woven basket with each strand covered in white plastic. It sat inside a stainless-steel stand on wheels, with a stainless-steel rod rising about 3' up and over the back of the basket to hold mosquito netting which then draped over the whole thing. On the outside was a cover made of nylon and lace and a frill that went right around the edge of the basket and it was absolutely gorgeous. The basket could remain stationery or, with a flick of a switch it could rock back and forth, or it could be lifted out altogether and brought to wherever we were. It was the most perfect sleeping quarters for a baby, and for that climate, I could ever have wished for, and I really loved it, and David grew out of it when he was 3 months old.

Now even though I loved the Australian bassinet, I didn't care much for Australian prams and through Betty we purchased a second-hand English Silver Cross pram from a couple she knew whose child had outgrown it. Not to say that the Australian prams weren't functional, they were probably better for the climate, but since pushing Marjorie's Silver Cross pram when I was very young my wish was to have a pram like that of my very own one day. There's something so majestic in pushing a Silver Cross pram around, they are so high off the ground with four wheels as big as bicycle tires and it just felt more grand than pushing an Australian pram around which is nothing more than a clothes basket on wheels. David and I thoroughly enjoyed that pram and if he wasn't outside because it was too hot, then he was parked in his pram in the laundry because that was the coolest place in the house.

We learned that the most similar church to the Church of England was Anglican and we went to see the Vicar to ask him to perform the Christening Service for David. He was a most peculiar man and it sort of stopped us in our tracks to see his mode of dress. He had the recognizable long black robe and collar of a Vicar but had opened-toed thongs, or flip-flops they call them there, visible on his feet, and for some reason he didn't strike me as being very serious. However, he was, and he insisted that the godparents must to be confirmed in the Church of England and as two of our friends, Betty and Steve Knight, were we asked them to stand for David. David was christened at three months old and his party turned out to be much bigger than our wedding because we had more than 60 people show up. We had a 3-tier christening cake made and he wore his very own beautiful christening gown of lace and silk that I still have. It was a great party maybe because we were the first people in the street to buy an air-conditioner for the living-room window so we partied in air-conditioned comfort. Betty used her movie camera to record the christening and our home and Whyalla but, as she was in the process of moving back to England, asked to borrow the film to show her folks when she arrived. Then she was supposed to send the tape onto Beattie and Bill, who would then forward it to Canada, but she never did, and we never had any replies to our letters. I still feel bad that I don't have any record of my first child's christening other than his Baptism certificate.

You're moving – didn't you know?

All this time we'd been living in Mepstead Street and Brian had been working for BHP for nearly a year and a half when he got promoted to Manager, Costs, Prices and Special Expenditures. What a title eh? He was good at his work and his bosses knew it and only days after his promotion his boss called him into the office and asked when we were going to buy a house. Buy a house? We hadn't gotten this one broken in yet. Nevertheless, he was told in no uncertain terms that as he was now a Manager, and BHP Managers didn't live in rental houses alongside the employees, we must move. Silly us. We thought we'd left the social class system behind in England.

It was okay for them tell us to buy a house in the 'management' side of town; they were the ones with plenty of money. We had spent our savings on this house and in all the paraphernalia that was needed for a new baby, so how earth were we going to find a house that we could afford? BHP already had the answer. They owned a lot of houses that they used for temporary housing for other area managers who came to Whyalla for short periods of time; and they just happened to have one of these for sale. It was nearer the center of town, park, zoo, and shops. Lovely. It needed a lot work done to it because nobody had ever cultivated the half-acre garden and the grass and weeds were as tall as the 6-foot fence surrounding the property and the house wasn't in much better shape either. But, I have to hand it to them, BHP bent over backwards to make sure Brian and I liked that house and they paid for their staff to paint the inside and outside for us, and even though they had removed most of the furniture from the house, they left a bedroom suite which we refinished, a big kitchen cabinet and a washing machine. They arranged our mortgage with the bank and sold the house to us for $8,000 that was $2,000 less than the market value, so all we had to do was sign the papers and move into our beautiful freshly painted detached bungalow in 10 Neill Street, Whyalla Playford, Whyalla, South Australia.

And it really was detached. On the left-hand side, there was a 10' wide drive leading up to the house and on the right, there was another 10' between the house and the fence, and every other house in the street was the same so we actually had about 20' between houses. It was another well laid out and very functional house in the shape of an 'L.' On the short part of the L was the living room, with the kitchen, laundry and toilet behind it, and the three bedrooms and bathroom made up the long part of the L. The outside of the house was changed enormously from a very ugly dark green and mustard trim to a deep blue and white, and we asked the painters to paint the inside pale blue and white so as to cool the house down at least visibly. The only painting job that Brian had to do was to paint the roof with aluminum paint. When I asked the painters why most of the houses had aluminum roofs, they replied, "Because it reflects the hot sun away from the house, but you have to keep it in good condition and paint it every so often." And when I asked them why it wasn't on their list of things to paint, they replied, "It's too bloody hot to get up on the roof when we start work. Brian needs to get up there at about 4 am before the sun comes up!" Poor Brian!

We settled into our new home very quickly and the first thing we did was to hire a man with a mini bulldozer to come and bulldoze out the wild grass and weeds from the ½ acre back yard so that we could sow a lawn. Here I go again – just lawn, nothing but lawn. But it worked for me. I remember him knocking on the door and asking me if I knew any Aborigines because in digging up the land he'd found a whole load of Witchetty Grubs that were a real delicacy to them and basic Bush Tucker and he didn't want to waste them, but I couldn't help him, I didn't know any Aborigines personally.

We loved everything about Australia, except the insects mentioned previously. We loved the area where we now lived; it had been settled for years so there was lots of green grass and fruit trees in other people's gardens; beautiful sunshine, lots of fresh fruit and vegetables which they used to share with us; we had a lovely home and great neighbors. I was still good friends with Yvonne and her new daughter Leanne, and they would regularly visit me or we would visit them or meet somewhere for lunch. Getting tuned into the Australian accent was one thing but learning all the colloquialisms was another. I remember the first time Yvonne said she would,

"Shout me lunch" and I didn't know what she meant. Maybe the chef was deaf and she really had to shout - I didn't know, and it was only in response to the dumb look on my face that she repeated, "Buy you lunch, treat you to lunch." I learned a lot about living in Australia through Yvonne, she was a very good friend all the time we lived there but I was about to leave her behind in the baby producing department.

Congratulations, again!

I'd had so many health problems when pregnant with David that Doctor Muir insisted that I take the birth control pill straight away to ensure no more pregnancies for a while but I'd only been taking it for three months, less one day, when something dreadful happened. I'd been feeling very uncomfortable during the night but it was only when I awoke the next morning that I discovered why. I tried getting out of the bed but couldn't and anxiously said, "Brian, something is wrong with my left side, I can't move!" "What." He came running around to my side of the bed and sure enough, the left side of my face had collapsed and my left arm and leg were flopping around seemingly unattached to my body. He ran to the phone box and Dr. Muir advised him not to waste any time waiting for an ambulance and that he would meet us at the hospital. By now I had the good fortune to make friends with a lovely Australian lady, Kay Golding, further along Neill Street, and Brian bundled David up and took him along to her house. After putting me through a battery of tests at the hospital, neither Brian nor I could believe it when they told us I'd had a stroke caused by an allergic reaction to one of the basic ingredients in the birth control pill. I was only 26 years old! Luckily, I came through it okay without any complications that they told me about, but the Specialist said that given my recent medical history we should take other precautions to avoid another pregnancy. However, I think God had other plans in mind for us.

David was only four months old when I started feeling ill and throwing up again and Brian gave me no choice but to see Dr. Muir who, after examining me, totally embarrassed me when he said, "I envy the passion of you young folk because you're pregnant again." Good heavens! It had taken us five years to get David and now we were about to have two babies, in two years. When I went into the waiting room to Brian, Dr. Muir came with me and with a big silly grin on his face said, "Congratulations Dad, you're about to become a father again." Brian nearly dropped David and both of us looked a bit sheepish at the news. I had hoped for another child, to give David a brother or a sister, just not this quick.

We left the Doctor's office and once in the car Brian very quietly told me that he had something important to tell me when we got home. I asked him why he couldn't tell me on the way but he replied that he needed to look me in the face when he told me. Very worried as to what he had to say I couldn't wait to get home. No sooner had we gotten into the house when he drew a quick breath and said, "Nan, we've got a big decision to make. The Specialist who looked after you in Isolation said that given the severity of the infection throughout your body it was touch and go as to whether he could save your life, and he thought it would be impossible for you to conceive again, and even if it was possible, you should never carry another child." The words seemed to tumble out before he could stop them, "He also asked me for permission to conduct a hysterectomy on you but then changed his mind with you being so prone to infection and offered to give me a free vasectomy instead." He drew another quick breath before continuing, "And I didn't tell you before, but Doctor Muir asked me whom I wanted to save, you or David, if it came to that, because with all the toxicity in your body he wasn't sure if only one of you would make it, and that we should definitely wait a few years before even thinking of having another baby."

Boy, he'd kept an awful lot of secrets to himself. "Shouldn't you have told me all of this a while back?" I asked. "No," he answered. "What would have been the good in telling you how ill you were; you'd have just worried yourself to death if you thought there was a chance of not being around to raise David, and what would have been the point in telling you may or may not be able to have any more children once they put you on the birth control pill to make sure you didn't? If you hadn't had a reaction to the birth control pill with that stroke, and gotten pregnant so soon, you need never have known any of this," he said sadly.

I suppose that, at just 26 years old, nobody wants to hear they nearly died, so he was probably right in keeping that to himself, but I was more shocked to hear the reasons why I couldn't, or shouldn't, have any more children. The more I thought about it, the more I put it down to God's intervention. After all, the Specialist and our own Doctor had expressed concerns about me carrying another child, and whereas one had said it was impossible, the other had put me on the birth control pill to make sure that I couldn't, but I had still gotten pregnant. "Brian," I said, "I'm not surprised you protected me from all that, it was probably for the best, but if I've gotten pregnant against all odds, then I'm keeping it. It may be our last chance to have another baby," I said. He came and put his arms around me and hugged me so close I could hardly breathe. "If you are certain, really certain you want to go through all that again, we'll go through it together," he said.

From the very first day of being pregnant again I was as sick as a dog and was in and out of hospital with such regularity over the next few months that I knew the hospital staff better than I knew David. If I thought I'd had medical problems carrying David, I had only scratched the surface because with this second pregnancy I dug the quarry. I'm not going to give you a blow by blow account of all the medical problems, only this one, because it affected me in a really bad way and nearly caused me to lose my baby. It all started when we received a letter from Tommy and Ella. It was just as I'd previously thought, Brian was not a good letter writer and it was left to me to keep him in touch with his folks, so this was just another letter I thought. Only this was no ordinary letter. This was an abomination of a letter! Pure venom! We had waited until David was seven months old before writing to tell them I was pregnant with a second child and their reply sent me reeling and I couldn't believe that anyone could be so asinine and cruel.

They actually had the unmitigated gall to write that they were disgusted with us and were not going to congratulate us on having a second child, because only animals had young every year! What a rotten thing to think, and worse still to write down on paper and send 12,000 miles. I couldn't believe what I was reading. How anybody could even think such a horrible thing bore no resemblance to a human being. What a thing to write to someone who had a history of bad pregnancies, and who was struggling with this pregnancy. Those words had to come from Ella, they just had to be Ella's thoughts. Tommy couldn't think such a thing, could he? No, they had to come from Ella. But Tommy did all the writing! He had to write because Ella never learned to write, but how on earth could he have written those words if he didn't believe them also? I was absolutely stunned and sick to my stomach.

When Brian got home and read the letter he was also stunned. We'd been married five years and had been together ten and although a bit worried, we were both ecstatic that we were about to have another child. Yes, maybe it was too soon for my body to cope with another pregnancy, but that didn't diminish our happiness at being able to have another child. From the minute we received that letter I told Brian that I was not going to write to them anymore. If they wanted to hear from him, then he'd have to write because I certainly wasn't going to. They had just shot themselves in the mouth. I was not put on this earth to be Ella's punching bag. They could both really go to hell now.

We received this horrible letter on Tuesday afternoon and early on Wednesday morning I started hemorrhaging and had to be rushed to the hospital. As I was still losing substantial amounts of blood on the Thursday evening the powers that be thought it would be best to abort the baby the next day. Now then, what do you think brought all that on? Hmm. Let me guess – Ella Shaw's letter? I was still in a state of shock over that letter and my mind had switched off somehow and I was just doing as I was told. They told me I'd lost so much blood that the baby must have been affected and as there was very little sign of life, there was nothing I could do but to agree to an abortion. I'd had an awful restless night and was quite exhausted when the nurses came to prep me for the operation but as I was still in nowhere land, it didn't seem to matter, and as I lay there, the thought came to me that this baby had been so special, being conceived the way he was against all odds, and now they were planning to take him away before he could be born. No sooner had I got that thought out of my head when he started kicking. He kicked so hard I could see the bed sheets move and although it took a minute for it to get through to my brain, probably because of the pre-op drugs they'd given me, I started screaming that the baby was kicking. I screamed so loud that two nurses literally ran down the corridor to find out what was the matter with me. "He's kicking!" I yelled. "The baby's kicking! You can't have him; I'm not going to let you take him. It's okay, it's really okay, the baby is kicking!" I cried through my tears. I felt a surge of energy rush through my body and if the Devil himself had been standing there, I would have thwarted him. "I AM NOT HAVING AN ABORTION! YOU WILL NOT GET YOUR HANDS ON THIS BABY! YOU CAN ALL GO TO HELL!" I cried.

One of the nurses ran back to the nursing station and phoned for Dr. Muir and the Gynecologist to come and trotted back with Matron Woods in tow. "Now what is this all about Mrs. Shaw," she demanded. "My baby is kicking. He is trying to tell me he is okay. He wants to be born," I cried. "Now don't be silly," she said. "It's doing no such thing. It's probably just some wind you have in your stomach!" she answered sharply. I knew better and I thought I'd trust my instincts rather than her opinion. "I am not going to have an abortion Matron. I want to keep my baby!" I said. "Well, we'll see about that when Dr. Muir and the Gynecologist come in. Come along nurse and leave Mrs. Shaw until later," she said, and with that she turned on her heel and trotted back to her office. I hadn't much liked the attitude of this woman when I was pregnant with David, but she struck me as being relative to a witch with this second pregnancy. A while later all three of them, Dr. Muir, the Gynecologist, and Matron stood over my bed while both male figures examined me. The bleeding had now stopped and they were genuinely concerned over the state of the fetus, but by now I was firmly convinced that I was supposed to carry this baby and hell could have frozen over before they would have convinced me otherwise. But in their wisdom, they decided to wait until Monday morning before carrying out the operation, because I was just too distressed and they hoped for an improvement to my mind, if not my physical wellbeing. Monday morning came, and with Brian by my side, we told all of them that we were going to see this pregnancy through to the end, and live with the consequences, if any. This was our baby and they couldn't have it, and neither could Ella nor Tommy Shaw!

During this second pregnancy, Brian was the only constant figure in David's life because I wasn't around very much. It felt as though all I had to do was hiccup and I'd be rushed back to hospital. BHP were so understanding of our predicament that they let Brian work flexible hours in order to take care of our young baby, but there weren't enough hours in the day. It wasn't all doom and gloom though, and I remember Brian telling me that when our friend, Marion was looking after David for the day, she was working at the kitchen sink, and kept hearing a 'plop, plop' noise. She'd given David some toys and put him to play in the laundry area where it was coolest, and when she went to see what the noise was, found him taking potatoes out of a small sack and giggling as he threw them down the toilet. Ken, her husband, had had to take the toilet to pieces to clear out all of the potatoes.

However, there was no doubt about it; Brian was reaching a state of exhaustion. Not only did he have to work for the money they paid him, he had to find babysitters for David, keep the house clean, shop for food, do the laundry and lastly, try and visit me. It was all getting far too much to cope with. We needed to come up with an alternative plan. David was seven months old; he'd had seven different babysitters in seven days, and he'd lost seven pounds in weight. Enough was enough. We needed to stabilize his world, let him stay in one place, let him get used to having a home and a room of this own, and so we hired a housekeeper, Mrs. Paris. Ah. What can I say about Mrs. Paris? She was a lovely old lady in her 60's; she looked after David; she cleaned the house - at least brushed the dirt under the carpet; she did the child's laundry - even if she did put all his diapers in with a red chenille curtain and died them all pink and read her romance novels all day long. It was the best decision that we'd made in a long time. It cost us all our savings, and then some, but Mrs. Paris was worth every penny and David was now secure in his own home. Brian established the routine of feeding David his breakfast and visiting me at lunchtime so that he could be home all evening to feed, bathe and be with David. It worked for us.

I had been a permanent resident in the hospital for the last two months of my pregnancy and was so fed up at looking at the same four walls that I signed myself out on the Saturday morning against the wishes of the staff. My baby must have liked it there, because my contractions started that same evening and I went back to the hospital the same day I signed myself out. After a very short three-hour labour, our second child, John Charles Shaw, was born at 1 am on the morning of 10 August 1969. He was also healthy and beautiful, and the Doctor's found nothing medically wrong with him. Thank you Lord and thank you John for letting me know you were okay at that most critical time! It was a different story with me, however. As I was packing up to leave the hospital after ten days, I was suddenly hit by pains in my lower abdomen. Exactly the same pains that I'd had after David's birth. The nurse who was helping me get my stuff packed looked at me as I'd bent over sharply and said, "What's wrong Mrs. Shaw? You've gone as white as a sheet!" "I've got the same pains starting again," I replied. It was a small Maternity Hospital and as all the staff knew me so well with being a frequent occupant there, they all knew what had happened to me after my first child had been born. "Don't do anything until I get Matron," she said. A few minutes later Matron Wood came to my bed. "You can't possibly have those same pains again Mrs. Shaw. We measured the afterbirth and it was all there. You are just imagining things!" she said in a very loud voice. Everyone in my small ward of four beds stopped to listen, as did the nurses and people going up and down the corridor as my room was next to the front lobby. "I'm sorry, but I do have those same pains Matron," I replied. Apart from the time I had screamed they were not taking my baby away, I'd not raised my voice to anyone outside of my immediate family so I had spoken quite quietly. "Nonsense!" she replied. "It is medically impossible for you to contract that infection again, impossible!" she went on.

Just as she spoke those last words the resident Gynecologist came through the front door and stopped. "What's the problem Matron?" he asked. She whipped around and very sharply said, 'Mrs. Shaw's convinced herself that she has those afterbirth pains again and I've just told her it's impossible." He looked at me, then turned to her and said, "Well, there is a simple enough solution Matron. Take a swab and have it checked out before Mrs. Shaw leaves." Then he turned to me and said, "Is that okay Mrs. Shaw? Will you wait around until we get the results?" "Yes please," I replied, "I have a one-year-old baby at home and I can't afford to end up back in hospital and leave my husband with two babies, so yes please, I'll gladly wait around. Thank you. Two hours later Matron came down the corridor to stand in front of my bed. Very softly and quietly she said, "You were right Mrs. Shaw. You do have that infection again. We'll give you some of those same pills to go home with and it should clear up." Emboldened by the news that I was not going crazy, I said, "Would you repeat that please Matron? AS LOUDLY AS YOU SHOUTED WHEN YOU TOLD ME I WAS WRONG!" And in as loud a voice as she used when she told me I was imagining things, she let everyone know that I'd been right and it felt good. But even though it felt satisfying, I couldn't help thinking that if I were to have any more children, I'd better not have them in her hospital.

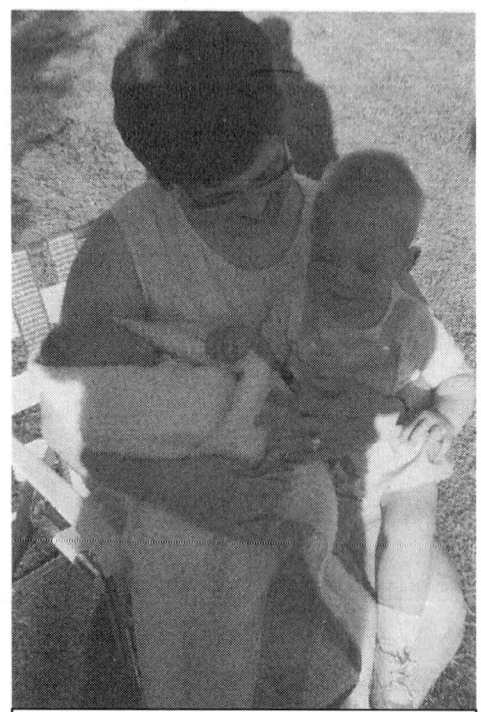

Nancy with newborn John and 1 year old David.

Our lives changed forever and I became a stay-at-home Mom while Brian could now concentrate on being the working Dad and although we loved each other very deeply, the children became our focal point because both of us absolutely loved them. They were ours. We weren't babysitting for somebody else. We were raising our own children and John was christened exactly one year and one day after David was christened. Well now, here I was, two years out from England, in a foreign country, new home, no other family members, health not very good, and a one-year old and a newborn. How's that for a challenging situation?

The road smooths out for a while

Because of our growing family, we bought a station wagon and quickly learned to put a mattress in the back for the children, and by the time we'd gotten to the outdoor party they would be fast asleep, but every few minutes we would check to see if they okay. It was a fantastic time to be young. I loved being a mother and being able to stay home with the children, and thoroughly enjoyed my life. Before the children awoke at around 6 am each morning, I'd have the house cleaned and breakfast ready for them. I never bought ready-made foods for them, as I much preferred to make my own, and whatever we ate, they ate. When David was just a newborn baby, Brian had bought me a 'Splurge' super mixer full of gadgets like a hand mixer, juice extractor, electric juicer, and a glass container for making milk shakes which was also fantastic for chopping up meat and vegetables meals to freeze for the children. We always had lots of visitors, and everyone was made welcome.

David was a beautiful child, full of chatter and curiosity, and I remember one time when I was in the living room feeding John, and because he was being too quiet, I went to look for him. I found him in the kitchen emptying the lower kitchen cabinet cupboard of all my Tupperware that contained rice, flour and cereals, into a pile on the kitchen floor. Not only had he not been content to do just that, but he'd gotten the tomato sauce bottle off the table, and when I asked him what he was doing, he replied, "I'm making cement Mommy, aren't I clever?" And at one-year old, he was, he was very clever. He could talk the hind leg off a donkey. He had started walking at seven months old, just holding onto the furniture with one hand, and the nurses in the hospital were astounded that the little boy who ran all the way down the corridor and climbed up onto my bed all on his own, was the same baby I'd given birth to a year before.

By now we had a lovely lawn back and front, nothing but lawn, and a great place for kids to play. We had an enormous umbrella with spokes that stood about 10-foot-tall in the back garden to hang washing on, and as Betty had returned to England and had no need for her heavy canvas cover any more, we bought it from her and it became our permanent fixture for shade. With John usually sitting on my knee, David and his little friends, played in the children's swimming pool under the shade of the canvas under my constant supervision. At that time, my friend and neighbour Kay had four children, Ian who was about 8, Louise about 6, and twins Andrew and Robert about 4, and whenever Kay needed to find a babysitter she knew she could bring them to me. Mostly I would just mind Andrew and Robert who were great playmates for David and John because Ian considered himself too old, and Louise would go with Kay.

My Australian friend, Kay Golding, 1968

Sitting under the shade with water being splashed on me periodically, I'd never notice the heat until Kay, when she came to pick her boys up, would invariably say, "Nancy, don't you realize it's 110 degrees out here. Aren't you hot?" I'd honestly not noticed the heat until Kay mentioned how hot it was then in no time I'd be sweating so we'd all head indoors to sit in the dark in front of the air conditioner. Normally people installed air conditioners in the window but I thought they were ugly and we had ours installed in the wall instead. The best way to keep the house cool in the first place was not to open the curtains and let the blazing sun in and that's what I learned to do very quickly. Doors were not left open either, not only to keep the heat out, but also the flying insects. Even with the curtains and doors closed the house got unbearable hot sometimes, and when I accidentally broke an egg in the stainless-steel sink I was amazed when it started to cook. Nonetheless, it was a great time and a great place to have children. Kay used to pop in now and again for a mid-morning coffee of beer and lemonade shandy because it was too hot to drink anything else, and for non-drinkers like us it was normal to have two dozen 3-Crown beers delivered every Saturday morning that was as casual as having milk delivered to the door in England.

We always had people popping in, and for the most part, I was pleased to see them. However, one person in particular is worth mentioning because I used to groan inwardly every time I saw him coming up the drive: Iris's husband, Frank, and it wasn't that I disliked him, he was just wearing out his welcome. He worked permanent nightshift and while Iris worked during the day time he looked after his three pre-school children. He got into the habit of bringing the children over to our house for me to feed, and then he'd sit half the day drinking cups of tea, before looking at the clock and saying, "Well, Iris should be home by now and have the supper ready so we're off." Honest. Some Geordie men. Of course, by now, my particular Geordie man was so well trained in making meals, looking after babies from morning till night, nursing a semi-invalid, going to work. He was Superman! Mostly to get out of the way of Frank, I'd get the baby ready and with David sitting in the front of the pram we'd go for long walks either to the shops or to a small park just along the road. I remember stopping at a shop one time to get David an iced lollypop when the shopkeeper yelled, "Your pram's fallen." I hadn't realized that without me being there to balance the pram, it became top heavy and 15-month-old David fell to the ground while 3-month old John slid right down to the bottom of the pram underneath the covers. I don't know who was more frightened, David or I, but John never made a sound.

The local park had a small zoo, and the three of us would spend a few hours and then walk home again just in time for Brian coming in from work. David was fascinated with the animals because most of them were so tame you could hand feed them and we'd take stale bread to feed the ducks in the pond then we'd go home, have supper, and most nights' head for the beach.

The beach at Whyalla is second to none and worthy of description and in all my travels worldwide, I have never come across anything more perfect. On one side of the jetty there was the harbour where BHP launched their ships, and on the other side was the public beach. The sand was a fine white powder and was extraordinarily clean; the sea was always a most glorious blue and you could walk out waist high for about ½ mile into the water. It is the most perfect beach in the world. Even Brian, who says he is allergic to water, used to love to swim there. We had a small lean-to type of tent that we used to put up to give us some shelter from the hot sun, and we would play on that beach and in that water until it was bedtime for the children. Having come from a land of spasmodic sunshine and lots of rain, this was a fantastic environment and we loved it.

When both children were out of infancy we used to pack picnic lunches and explore new places all the time. We even went as far as a couple of hundred miles away to the Barossa Valley vineyards and picked up boxes of wine at discount prices and we discovered a great love for the Kaiser Stuhl wines and sherries that Australia makes and to this day still think they make the best wines in the world. We had everything we wanted: a lovely home; great job; beautiful children;

terrific neighbors; fantastic environment; active social life. What more could I possibly want? Family!

Homesickness hits with a vengeance

My homesickness started with a telegram from Lorna in Canada telling me that Gran had died in her sleep the previous day. We still didn't have a telephone so the children and I walked to Barbara's house at the end of the street to use her phone to ask Brian to come home because I was so upset. She asked me what the matter was because I was still crying and I told her that my Gran had died. Then she asked how long it had been since I'd seen her and when I said it was nearly four years she replied, "Oh it's been so long since you saw her it won't hurt so much." How anyone could measure love by the distance of time is beyond me and as soon as I told Brian about Gran, we left quickly, never to speak to her again. I was heartbroken at the news of Gran's death. My anchor had gone. I had two beautiful children who would never know her as a grandmother. Who would never be able to sit beside her and cuddle her as I had done. Who would never know anything of her abundant love. My children would never have the opportunity of growing up in a family as I had done, whether real or pseudo. We were thousands of miles away from everybody who was important to me, and I suddenly felt very lonely.

Over the course of my two pregnancies, I had been so sick and BHP had been very understanding, but now they wanted their 'pound of flesh' so to speak. As soon as I was home after the birth of John they started to send Brian round all of their sites from Queensland to Perth to implement costing systems and profit reporting systems and he never knew how long he would be gone and as he never knew when he was going to be told to catch a plane that night, we had to keep a suitcase packed at all times. For the first year of John's life it was Brian's turn not to be around, and I found it very hard managing two babies all on my own and when Gran died, it triggered a tremendous feeling of isolation that even our fantastic life couldn't overcome.

I needed family. We had great friends and neighbors, but I needed family and I tried everything I could think of to persuade anyone to come and live in Australia. I pleaded and begged for nearly a year, offering to pay fares, housing and furniture, and to help them find jobs. I was willing to do anything short of selling my soul to have some family around. Beattie and Bill had changed their minds about coming as my brother Brian now had two children, Gary and Wendy, and my sister Nora had two, Anthony and Ian. Their final stake in the ground was that my sister Dorothy had just married Barry Kitchen and had bought a house not too far from them, so nobody from that side of the family planned on moving anywhere. Marjorie and Lorna had well and truly settled in Canada and didn't want to uproot the children again. Billy said if he was going anywhere it would be Canada, and Jimmy I lost touch with, and Brian didn't think any of his family would move to Australia.

Here I was in the land of milk and honey being torn in two. I really didn't want to leave, I loved it, but you know when you get a thought in your head and it just won't budge, it just keeps on nagging and nagging until you're driven mad by it? Well you'd have thought the record was stuck in a groove or something because I wouldn't let the 'family' subject die and I persuaded myself that I was all on my own in the far reaches of the earth with only two small children and an absentee husband. The other argument I used with Brian was that Australia was helping the

United States of America fight communists in Vietnam, and that my children were not going to grow up to fight in a war – even if they were only two and one-year-old at the time.

Brian thought moving from the isolation of Whyalla to the big city of Adelaide might give me a new lease on life, and help settle me down again, and he took some time off to find a new job and a new house. His boss at BHP did his best to dissuade Brian from leaving, and they offered to pay the airfare for me and the children to visit England for a while because, in his opinion, "When the homesickness hits, wives never settle until they've been home for a visit. She'll get over it Brian." And even though I greatly appreciated the offer there was no way I had the confidence to travel all that way to England on my own with two little children, so turned it down. We now had our own phone and within a few days Brian phoned from Adelaide to say he'd gotten a job and had rented a house, and he'd be home later than night, Friday, and that a moving van would be showing up at the door the next day. I had no idea everything would move so fast, so nothing was packed but once I'd told Kay what was happening she came along and helped me. Luckily Brian was not too late in coming back and had brought boxes with him, so between the three of us we managed to pack everything we owned that night, ready for the next day's move. We quickly made the rounds of our friend's houses the next morning and all of them, without a doubt, were shocked to hear we were moving and that it was all arranged.

We left the house in the hands of a real estate agent with an order to auction it to the highest bidder never thinking to put a reserve price on it, and who should buy it but our family doctor, Dr. Muir. He bought it for exactly one thousand dollars more than we had paid for it three years earlier. What a rotter! He lived not too far from us and when he asked me one time when I was in his office what we'd paid for the house I told him that we'd gotten it from BHP for two thousand dollars less than the market price. Stupid woman! I'll not do that again, no matter who is interested.

Brian rented a lovely three-bedroom bungalow which stood nearly opposite the historical cottage where Captain Cook, the famous explorer, lived, and for the first few weeks I enjoyed being there. It was fun having Brian to explore with and we both enjoyed shopping in the big department stores and having more than one department store to choose from. We lived not far from the beach – nobody did for that matter - and the sand was nearly as good as the talcum powder sand of Whyalla. There was a lot more choice in the stores and I remember going into a European Bakery for the first time in four years and ordering a dozen fresh cream cakes and nearly devouring the lot myself. Fresh cream cakes are practically unheard of in very hot climates, so coming across that little Bakery was a real treat and it tweaked memories of home.

Deep down, nothing helped to distill my feelings of loneliness for family. I really didn't want to leave Australia but after nearly five calendar years, homesickness was just building and building inside me. I had to be with family. I needed David and John to have Aunts, Uncles and cousins to grow up with – just as I did, and if family wouldn't come to me, then I would have to go to them. My mind was made up. Brian pleaded with me but I wouldn't listen. It was no use him talking any more, I was going home. Come hell or high water, I was going home. But where was home? My sister Nora, whom I loved dearly, still lived in England, but my other sisters, Lorna and Marjorie lived in Canada. Where was home now - England or Canada? We made the choice to go to England first because traveling 12,000 miles to England was cheaper than traveling 9,000 miles to Canada and by staying over the winter in England it would give the children a chance to acclimatize to cold weather then we could go on to Canada. We had arrived in Australia the first week of July 1967, and we left Australia in the last week of July 1971. David was 3 years old, and John was 2 years old and I was about to make one of the biggest mistakes in my life.

PART 3 - ENGLAND AGAIN

The Absolute Worst Journey anywhere, any time!

I had not written to Tommy and Ella since receiving their venomous letter and it was left to Brian to give them the news that we were coming home. He wrote and asked his folks to rent a house for us for the next six months, and both of us were bowled over at their response, "Well Brian, there's nowt to rent, so you can have your old bedroom back, but Nancy and the children will have to find somewhere else to live!" What on earth had I ever done to harm either of these people, apart from being born illegitimate, marrying Brian and having two babies in two years?

I knew I was over-sensitive. I'd had a lifetime of being over-sensitive. I was a product of my upbringing. I'd get all psyched up and feeling confident, then somebody would make some stupid remark that I'd take as a personal reference to me, and I'd stew over it for days. Except in this case there were no slyly dropped hints, there was no sophistication or subtlety whatsoever, it was out there, plain and simple in their letter, "Nancy, you'll never be good enough." And how did they expect Brian to respond to their moronic suggestion? Did they really think he would say, "Well goodbye Nancy, David and John, I'm off to stay with my folks? Sorry, but you have to fend for yourselves!" Did they really think he would do that? Neither of us could quite believe what they'd suggested, and even though it hurt me as I guess it was supposed to, Brian said he'd find another solution. One has to wonder what they really hoped to accomplish, but after writing to Beattie and telling her all about it, she wrote back and invited all of us to stay with her for however long we needed.

It had taken a few weeks to get letters back and forth so it was about six weeks before Brian once again wrote to his folks. He said, "Thank you for the offer of accommodation for myself, but I have a wife and two children, and where I go, they go. Nancy's mother has very kindly offered to accommodate all of us and we will be staying with her for the foreseeable future." I didn't want to come between Brian and his folks but I felt a lot better after he sent that letter. It was just as well they weren't the reason for my homesickness or I'd have stayed where I was. On reflection, it's a pity they weren't because it would have saved us a horrendous journey and a terrible homecoming. Still, at that time their letter hurt, but my attention soon shifted to Brian and the children. I think somewhere deep inside me came the first stirrings of real motherhood, like a mother bear awakening after a long winter of hibernation, only in my case it was a lifetime of hibernation. My husband and children were much more important than I ever was, and I determined that nobody on this earth would be allowed to upset them in any way, and nobody would be allowed to interfere in my little family circle, and at the top of the list were Ella and Tommy Shaw.

We gave ourselves four weeks to sell the car and furniture and, as usual, gave most of our stuff away to neighbors or to people who had come to buy one piece and got another piece free, and before long our rental house was empty and all we had left were soft furnishings that we packed into ten tea chests before arranging for them to be put on a cargo ship, then we moved into a motel for the last few days. We had arrived as a young couple but were leaving as a family of four. Thank you Australia!

It took a while to decide which way was the best way to travel home. The Suez Canal had been closed to all shipping traffic since the war in 1967, and ships had to travel to Europe via the Cape in South Africa. This made for a long six-week journey by sea, instead of our original four, and we thought that it would be too hard traveling with two small children, so we opted to split the journey into three parts, ship, land, and air. From Adelaide, we would sail to Singapore, travel by bus up the jungle of Malaya to Kuala Lumpur and catch a plane to England via Karachi in India. Simple but interesting we thought, and it would give us the opportunity to see something of the third world before getting back to 'civilization.' We paid for our travel in full and a few days later were advised by the travel agents that as we were traveling through 'disease infected areas' we needed to get a myriad of vaccinations including tetanus, yellow fever and tse fly in order to protect ourselves. Well, okay we thought, a needle is nothing much to worry about. The children were used to being vaccinated for one thing or another since being born, so we nonchalantly made the appointment to see the Doctor.

Within seconds of receiving the first set of injections our bodies started wailing in protest; and within minutes the slightest movement subjected us to ever increasing waves of undulating screaming tortuous red hot pain everywhere. It felt like hot lead was coursing through our veins. Even before we left the Doctor's office, Brian and I had tears running down our cheeks and the two boys' cries were earsplitting and I had no idea how we were going to be able to sit in the car and drive home, it was so painful to move. We felt every bump and crack in the road and even though the Doctor's office was only 15 minutes away, it took us nearly 30 minutes to get home. By now the two boys had literally exhausted themselves and cried themselves to sleep which we thought was the best thing for them, and after putting them to bed at 3 pm in the afternoon, both Brian and I inexorably slowly made it to the couch. We sat there in total silence for the next four hours making no movement that could possibly set off those unbearable excruciating pains again. Two weeks later we had to literally carry the children kicking and screaming into the Doctor's office for the follow up injection and, believe me, if we had had any inkling of the magnitude of that initial pain, we'd have opted for the six weeks on the ship – hands down!

Traveling anywhere in the world has been a mixture of pleasure and problem to me all my life. Anybody else can travel around the world with nary a hiccup. Not me! It should have been so simple; it was all pre-arranged and paid for. We were to catch the ship in Adelaide, pick up more people in Melbourne and Sidney, and come back around the coast for the last pick up in Perth, then sail the high seas for nearly two weeks and disembark at Singapore. Nothing is ever as simple as it sounds. The first strike against this journey was the vaccinations, and the second strike was that the ship was a day late in reaching Adelaide. Somebody on the outbound journey from England had fallen overboard just outside of Gibraltar and as they never found the body, the ship had to wait for the authorities to sort it out and to make up for the lost day, the ship was only stopping in Melbourne, and it was arranged that all the people waiting for the ship in Adelaide would now travel 12 hours by bus Melbourne.

David and John were brilliant and I have never been prouder of those two children than I was during that 12-hour journey because we kept to a grueling pace and I think we only made two or three stops during the whole trip. It was an awful experience having to drive like mad for hundreds of miles in order to catch the ship because they couldn't, or wouldn't, wait for us and I'm really pleased that both boys just snuggled into Brian and me and slept most of the way. Sitting right behind us were a lovely couple called Stan and Shirley who were also making their way back to England on the same itinerary as us, and they were so impressed with our boys they made friends with us. We were so glad they were very friendly because both were extremely helpful to us on board the ship. We made it to the quayside with about three hours to spare before the ship was due to sail and lined up before the Customs people and something that we didn't give much thought to at the time became very prophetic years later. Everyone had to fill in a Departure Form and Brian identified the children as being of British parentage but you should have seen the look on the Customs guy's face as he very definitely, and with great annoyance, crossed out 'British' and wrote 'Australian' against both boy's names. Eighteen years later with a choice of British, Canadian or Australian nationality, they chose to be Australian. Who knew? I guess that Customs guy did.

Nancy, John 2 yrs, Brian, David 3 yrs, and friend Shirley sailing under Sydney Harbour Bridge, heading for Singapore 1971

I think the ship we traveled on this time was a Greek ship but I'm not entirely sure, I only remember that it was a real passenger ship and much nicer than the one we'd traveled to Australia on. Our cabin, that had four bunk beds, was down a couple of flights of stairs which made it a bit awkward for carrying two small children, but they told us not to unpack anything because we'd be switching rooms in Sydney once some people disembarked. I couldn't wait until we reached Sydney! Only a few days then we'd have the luxury of having a room with porthole, and I had our suitcases ready to move the minute they said we could. What a difference a porthole made. As soon as I could see the sky and the sea I lost my claustrophobic and seasick feeling and had a really great time for the next two weeks, and the boys loved being on a ship and sleeping in the same room as us. Brian was once again on the top bunk and me on the bottom, and we 'topped and tailed' the boys on the other bottom bunk as I was nervous about David sleeping in an upper bunk after experiencing rough seas coming out. At the last minute, Brian had packed some of their toys in a suitcase and carried a briefcase full of their Dinkey Cars. These proved to be a great source of amusement as David lined about six of them up on the cabin floor and stamped his foot just as the ship rolled and the cars rolled from one side of the room to the other. "It's magik Daddy!" he'd exclaim, and John, who thought David was brilliant, kept clapping his hands in the air saying, "Do it agin Diadid! Do it agin!"

The third strike on this journey was that our designated meal time was at the same time as the children's so either the children could eat, or we could eat, and we couldn't change the schedule until most of the people got off in Sydney. What idiot made up this schedule? However, help was at hand and until we reached Sydney, Stan and Shirley who had a later sitting, took our boys for their meal while we ate ours. Mind you, I think with them not having any children, it made them feel good when they 'borrowed' our children for the pleasure they were. David had just celebrated his third birthday and John was just about to celebrate his second birthday on the ship. Both were able to eat with a knife and a fork, yes, a knife and a fork and were well mannered. They said 'please' and 'thank you,' without being reminded and if we had a dollar for every compliment we received when eating in restaurants with them, we'd have been very wealthy.

Everything was going along very smoothly. The July weather was good even though it was winter in Australia. It wasn't too cold or too hot and the breeze from the ocean was stimulating and refreshing. We spent most of our time up on deck playing with the children in the children's swimming pool or kicking a football around the deck. However, there is nothing so constant as change, and in any game of chance such as baseball, usually with three strikes, you're out! But with us, we didn't know we were playing a 'double header' and had another three strikes to come. We had been sailing into hot humid weather as we sailed nearer to Singapore and practically lived up on deck because there was no air-conditioning in the cabins below but, on the whole, we enjoyed the two-week voyage. Brian still didn't have much luck with the food and again, lived on ham and cheese sandwiches, and apples. But he especially enjoyed being able to spend so much time with the children after having to travel around Australia so much, that you'd have thought he was the only father in the world.

All through the journey the seas had remained fairly calm and as Singapore drew closer the ocean changed colour from a very deep black and blue to a translucent turquoise and green and it was so clear that we could see the ocean floor below. But disappointment set in as the tug boats pushed and pulled us to the dock and we saw that not only were the Singapore docks as dirty as the docks in Djibouti and Cairo but they had an added smell of festering rotten garbage. A foretaste of things to come! "All ashore who are going ashore!" was the cry and about six busloads traipsed down the gangplank and onto the nearest unoccupied bus. This was indeed a taste of the third world. The bus windows were all rolled down because that was the only air-conditioning available. It had cushioned seats but they were so old that they were compressed flat and we might as well have been sitting on bare boards for all the comfort they gave, and the bus, coupled with the permeating smell from the docks, told me that this was not going to be a very pleasant sightseeing journey, but rather a journey to be endured.

For a full hour, we traveled along roads with open running sewers dividing both lanes, before finally stopping at the Palace Hotel on 201 Jalan Munshi Abdulla, in Malacca, West Malaysia. The hotel was about 10 stories high and fully air-conditioned which was great after the hot and horrible smells outside and boasted an 'excellent cuisine for all.' But even after a bath and a change of clothes, none of us could eat much because we couldn't get past the virulent smells we'd had just driven through and I don't think any of us had more than a crust of bread which was all we could stomach. Brian bought a couple of bottles of Singapore's world-famous Tiger Beer because our friends in Australia said we should try it, and brought them to our room to enjoy, which we did.

Even though the air was atrocious we thought we'd better get used to it as we were scheduled to stay there for two days, and besides that, we'd probably never be this way again, and wanted to have a look around. A representative from the Australian travel agency was traveling with our group all the way to Kuala Lumpur and, along with a busload of fellow travelers, he arranged an outing. Apart from trying to con us into buying expensive jewelry at a pre-determined store, the sightseeing included a walk in Singapore's world-famous Hanging Gardens and they were indeed beautiful and magnificently laid out, and a visit to a tailor who could make and deliver suits the same day. Brian decided he'd like a made-to-measure suit and quickly paid his $100 Australian for a beautiful gray silk suit and it was duly delivered that evening. The material was so cool and crease resistance that, given the hot and sticky heat we were experiencing, Brian chose to wear it the next day for the next part of our journey – by bus through the Malayan jungle. We also bought the boys some silk pajamas and a pair of silk pants and a blouse for me and when we tried them on in the hotel room, we looked very Asian.

All the buses for the next stage of the journey were parked in front of the hotel and we sat in the first available seats and that was a pity because it meant we were on a different bus to Stan and Shirley. Nevertheless, we settled down and prepared to enjoy the journey. After all, it wasn't every day one traveled through the jungles of Malaya! Brian pointed out the British Barracks where my brother Billy served his National Service and it struck me that I was actually in the country near to where he must have bought my little monkey on a ladder when I was a small child. What an amazing coincidence. We started out traveling in convoy but once we traveled over the Straits of Singapore Bridge into Malaya, the bus driver put his foot down and took off hell for leather. Time after time other vehicles overtook us only to be overtaken again by our jealous bus driver. We were in a race to the finish, and it was the wildest, scariest ride you could ever imagine. What with having to steady ourselves and the children as he went around corners on two wheels and trying not to breathe in too sharply because of the sickening smell, it was the worst journey of our lives. Even though other people in the bus shouted for the driver to slow down, he took no notice and continued weaving in and out of traffic with no thought to anybody, either in the bus or on the road.

And the smell! Oh, my Lord, the smell! There has never been anything either written or said that could have possibly given us a hint or prepared us in any way for how physically gut-wrenchingly revolting the Malayan jungle smelled! We couldn't close the windows or we'd have stifled to death in the heat, and the stench of raw sewage as it mixed with the putrid smell of decomposing jungle vegetation made it all but impossible to breathe. There are not enough words in the dictionary to describe that ten-hour bus journey through Hell!

While Brian and I struggled to keep a handkerchief over our noses to filter the air, both children buried their faces into our chests for relief. Thank goodness they slept most of the way but I'm not sure whether they were asleep naturally or unconscious from the smell! After more than four hours of being bumped and bashed around on that roller coaster of a bus ride, the driver abruptly stopped just yards away from some roadside vendors and motioned for us to get out. Thank heaven the bus company had not prepared any pre-packaged food parcels because I couldn't have eaten anything from them after seeing the open sewers in Singapore and the run-down state of the bus. Brian managed to buy a couple of cans of warm Coca Cola, and some Lychee fruit which were remarkably refreshing. The only other food he bought was a big bunch of Bananas that he shared with everybody on our bus and, apart from a sip of warm Coca Cola, a Lychee fruit and a banana that was the only food we had during the whole road trip.

Finally, that horrendous journey came to an end and we gladly gave thanks and got off the bus and walked into air-conditioned 'clean air' comfort at Kuala Lumpur airport and had just got inside when John vomited all over Brian's new suit. Poor child, he felt so bad, but he couldn't help it. I thought he'd done well not to vomit on the bus because I'd been on the verge dozens of times. However, there was no way either Brian or John's clothes would clean up with just water; they had to have something different to wear. We had arrived there at 11 pm just in time to catch the plane at midnight for the last part of our journey home. By now both boys are crying and were very upset and when I asked David what was wrong he said, "John is crying so I'm helping him cry!" I was left with no choice but to open our suitcases in the middle of the airport to find clean clothes for both Brian and John and had no idea what to do with the dirty clothes other than throw them into the garbage bin. All the other clothes in our suitcases were clean and we couldn't put clothes with vomit on them in with them and we didn't want smelly clothes traveling with us on the plane, it would have been too embarrassing, so Brian's one-day old suit got thrown into the garbage along with John's clothes.

My lord! Could things get worse? Stupid me! I shouldn't have asked the question because they did! One by one the people who'd been traveling with us, all 6 buses, received their airplane tickets from the representative of the Australian travel agency and the Malaysian official. All except 13 of us! Where were our tickets? The Australian travel agency had told us when we booked and paid for the trip that we would receive our airplane tickets in Kuala Lumpur. Well, where were they! When asked, the two officials sheepishly replied, "Sorry folks! The airplane has been overbooked, there are no seats left. If you wish to travel to England, you will have to wait for the plane to make its way back here in three days' time and buy another ticket!" Pardon! What did I just hear! Excuse me? What did you just say? Stranded in Kuala Lumpur airport! All the money any of us had on us was traveling money, nothing extra. Including Brian and I and our two children, we totaled 13 people without a ticket to ride. There was Robbie and his wife and three children, a young couple with one child, and an old lady who had cancer who was going home to die. Robbie told us all to stay where we were and set off to find a telephone to phone the local British Consulate to see if they could exert any pressure on the travel agents. After an agonizing wait, he came back just over an hour later only to tell us that the British Consulate would lend us money to buy new tickets, but we would have to reimburse them upon reaching England.

Well, here I was, 28 years old, our plane had gone without us and I was left standing in a foreign airport trying to comfort two small crying children. I felt as though my country had deserted me. Apart from the time I threw the tantrum at Grandads' funeral, and the time I'd shouted at Marjorie, and the fight with Beattie over my wedding, and the one-sided fracas against aborting my baby in the hospital, I had never raised my voice to any other living person, ever. I had always been terribly shy. I was definitely not an assertive person and always preferred sitting in the background. I abhorred any kind of confrontation and would walk away rather than defend myself. However, that was all in the past and it was all about to change, big time! They were about to find out that Hell hath no fury like a full-blown 'Buckett' temper, and I was about to find out I had a fully paid up membership in the Mount Vesuvius club!

I slowly stood up and stretched myself, and in my best Australian upper-crust accent shouted as hard as I could across the concourse to where the travel agency guys were standing by a booth, "YOU BLOODY BASTARDS! YOU ROTTEN SWINE! COME BACK HERE! COME BACK, RIGHT NOW!" A stream of invectives including all the bad language I'd ever heard in my life, but never used, followed this and you could have heard a pin drop. I wouldn't have been surprised to see fire and brimstone coming out of my head. Brian's mouth dropped open; he just couldn't believe that all those terrible words echoing around the concourse were coming from me. Nobody was going to do this to us, to my children! We were not going to be stranded! We had paid our fare! I wanted our tickets! I'd had enough of this trip! More than enough! I wanted to go home!

The two travel agents tried to ignore me, but by now everyone in the line-up for the gates had fallen silent and turned to watch in stunned amazement. They had no choice but to come back, even if was just to try and shut me up. Good Luck with that! "Robbie! Go and get the British High Commissioner on the phone again, NOW!" He scurried off to do as he was told, while the sea of people parted to let the two agents through. Both of these agents were male, one from Australia and the other from Malaysia, and from the look on their faces I thought both of them had a patronizing attitude. I also think that if either of them had opened their mouths I would have gladly murdered one or both. My blood was up! "You owe us 13 tickets and we're not leaving this airport until we get them! Come with me while I talk to the British High Commissioner!" I brooked no argument. Myself, and the two travel agents, along with the other 12 people in our group tagging behind, made our way to the phone where the High Commissioner was on the phone - not an underling - *the* British High Commissioner himself! I was in full swing now. I've no idea where this iron will came from but we were all pleased it showed up. I introduced myself and explained the situation again, but he just repeated what had been said to Robbie that all they could do was advance our party the ticket money; however, the information I passed onto the travel agents and my fellow passengers was totally different.

"Okay, you agree then High Commissioner, that we do not leave this airport without tickets?" *"I've told you that all we can do is advance you the money for the tickets Mrs. Shaw!"* "Okay, and you agree that if we don't get the tickets, then we will inform Reuters, it can't be every day that decent British people get stranded in a foreign airport?" *"That's very drastic Mrs. Shaw and could possibly cause an international incident!"* "Well, drastic times call for drastic measures!" *"We can't make either the Malay's or the Australians do anything Mrs. Shaw, you're not the first people to be stranded here!"* "I think we can, seeing as how you're on our side!" *"Now, I didn't say that Mrs. Shaw!"* Well you get the picture, for nearly an hour we bantered back and forth over the phone but it wasn't until I said, "I don't think we're getting anywhere at all, it's time to bring in Reuter's!"

All the while I was on the phone with the High Commissioner Robbie was stationed at the next phone ready to call Reuter's worldwide news agency service and now I gave him the go ahead to ring them. He asked me what he had to say. I said, "Tell them that we are 13 British people including 6 children who have been stranded in Kuala Lumpur airport and neither the British

Government nor the Malaysian or Australian people will help us!" That did it! The High Commissioner started having convulsions on the other end of the phone and the Malay and Australian literally went white in the face. I'd hit the nail on the head! All three people, practically in unison said, "No, No, No, don't talk to Reuters!" Both agents scooted back to their booths to talk to their superiors. The first to come back was the Malay official who offered to pay all expenses and the hotel costs for the three days we were going to be stranded there. I told this to the High Commissioner and he chuckled. Then the Australian came back with an offer of airline seats for all of us, and when I told this to the High Commissioner he burst out laughing on the other end of the phone. At this point in the conversation I think I was practically walking on water because a mighty cheer went up from the crowd of people around us who had remained absorbed in the battle of words between one woman and three men. The High Commissioner's comment was, "Well, I would never have believed it had I not been a witness to it!" I thanked him most sincerely for staying on the phone with me, for understanding my double-talk conversation, and for not sending the police to pick up a mad woman at the airport.

Finally, at about one in the morning we had hotel rooms for the three days, and seats on a British Airways flight from Kuala Lumpur to Luton, England. Hip! Hip! Hoorah! Wait a minute! Hold on a moment! They said we had seats, but so had the Agency in Australia. It wasn't good enough just to be told anymore. I wanted a hard copy ticket and told them that none of us were moving away from the airport until we got them. They could make all the assurances they wanted, but I was not going to believe them until I had an airline ticket in my hand. When they said the ticket agents had gone home hours ago, I replied, "Well, hire a bloody taxi, wake them up, and bring them back!" And they did! They actually woke people up and made them come back to the airport to issue our tickets. It was nearly two am when we were issued our tickets and finally, after the longest day in my life, all thirteen of us struggled into the bus they provided and headed for the hotel. Brian and I had a double and two single beds in our room and the poor old lady in our stranded group was so frightened to sleep on her own that she begged to sleep with us, so we ended up giving her one of the single beds while David and John were topped and tailed in the other. For three days we were in limbo, unable to communicate with anyone at home, in the dirtiest, smelliest city in the world at that time.

I must mention that later that same day the Under-Secretary to the British High Commissioner actually came to see us in the hotel. He had been briefed on the details of what had taken place earlier that morning and seemed quite humoured by it. He said that lots of people had been stranded at that airport but never, in living memory, had anybody managed to get either new tickets or an all-expenses paid hotel. I asked him to once again thank the High Commissioner for playing his part and he said that his boss had thoroughly enjoyed the one-upmanship game and had passed the comment that maybe as a British Subject I should think about applying for a job in the Diplomatic Corp. We also had a visit from Reuter's. Word must have gotten to them somehow, because we never did phone them, just threatened to phone them. However, they came and interviewed me and apart from giving them the name of the travel agency that screwed us in Australia I thought I'd played the whole thing down.

For the whole time we spent in the hotel, neither Brian nor I could move either left or right without the rest of the gang being there because they clung to us like limpets. Where we went, they went. What we did, they did. I must have driven the hotel staff crazy as I was the orator for the group. "Your laundry's not ready – I'll see to it!" "What do you mean the sheets on your bed are not clean – I'll see to it!" "Your food is cold – I'll see to it!" I'm afraid anyone connected with this journey was treated with rudeness and disdain. They were all suspect and I trusted none of them, and I'm certain that once we boarded the bus to return to the airport days later all the people involved with me in particular must have heaved a huge sigh of relief. During that journey, Brian saw a part of my character that has never been repeated in its full force and we both agreed my share of the 'Buckett' temper was a dragon best left in its lair.

Bruised from the experience, and still very much on edge, we were the first people onto the plane, but sitting in our seats were people who had flown from England to Kuala Lumpur intending to get off at the next stop, Karachi. I stopped in the aisle. "There are people in our seats!" "Well, just sit anywhere for now," said the stewardess. "No, I've gotten these people this far, we're going to sit together for the last leg of our journey. They will have to move!" I admit now, that on looking back, I could not have been reasoned with. The poor stewardess didn't know what to do other than go for the pilot and he came storming down the aisle with a furious look on his face and asked what the problem was. When I told him what we had gone through for the past few days his look softened. "Oh! You're the people who got stranded in Kuala Lumpur! It's in all the English newspapers! I'm very sorry!" Then he turned to the people in our seats and asked them if they would please move to another seat for the rest of their journey. His manner and words were most comforting and he invited us to take our seats, relax and enjoy the flight. I could feel the tension and anxiety slipping away and started to unwind for the first time in days. Someone else was in charge now; we were on our way home and I could let go of the devil incarnate inside me. Well……...maybe not quite yet………we did have one more incident.

We'd been on the plane since 7 am that morning and it was now 12 noon but there was no sign of food. Our stranded group were the only ones on the plane with children and they were getting very hungry so I stopped one of the stewardess's and asked her when lunch would be served. "Oh, not for another couple of hours, we're on Karachi time now," she replied. "Well, may I have some biscuits and milk for the children to put them off until lunchtime then?" I asked. "No, sorry. They'll have to wait. Everything is rationed," she said. Talk about holding a red rag in front of a bull. Just tell me that my children and any other child traveling with me cannot have nourishment when they need it. I'm not sure if this was the same stewardess that I had a run in with, when we first entered the plane, and she was just being awkward, but I was not somebody willing to be pushed around anymore, and she was about to find that out. She was already halfway up the aisle when I shouted after her, "Just a moment please! "We've been up since 5 am this morning to be at the airport for 7 am to catch the plane. The kitchen at the hotel was not open so we've had nothing but a couple of crackers that we saved from our soup last night!" I drew breath, "I am sure I'm speaking for the rest of the adults in my group when I say we would very much appreciate it if you would find something for the children to eat. We will wait, but the children cannot!" Her face registered a mixture of shock and surprise and I'm sure she'd never had anybody speak so loudly to her before, but there is a first time for everything. Then I did shout, "AND, IF YOU CANNOT FIND ANY FOOD FOR THE CHILDREN, THEN I AND THE OTHER MOTHERS WOULD BE PLEASED TO HELP YOU LOOK!"

Eeh lad! Once again during this trip there was complete silence. Brian was no longer shocked at anything I said but was among the first to join the chorus of, "Here, Here! Feed the children!" And they did. They gave us just enough milk and biscuits to stave off the children's hunger pains until lunch. (Just as an addendum to all of this, I have never ever traveled anywhere without some sort of food in my possession since this time.)

After dropping people off in Karachi, we carried on to Luton in England and had been on the plane for 17 hours before we made our final touchdown. Even though the rain was coming down in torrents, I could have kissed the ground. I was home. Now all we had to do was to collect our suitcases, get through Customs, take the bus to King's Cross train station and catch the train to Newcastle. We had about 2 hours to catch the train, but as we were about 2½ hours' drive away I bribed the bus driver with 2 cartons of cigarettes to get us there in time and we made it with only seconds to spare. Brian had pre-booked second-class train tickets but as the stationmaster was in the process of sending the train out, he literally threw us into a first-class compartment and we gladly paid the difference to the ticket collector on board. It was the most perfect part of our journey, we were on the last leg home, and nothing could go wrong now. We had the compartment to ourselves, and all of us lay down to sleep on the bench-style upholstered seats; Brian and David on one side, and John and I on the other side and we slept the sleep of the dead for most of the 8-hour train journey.

What an Anti-Climax!

We had gotten along great with Beattie and Bill since we'd been married, and had corresponded with them on a regular basis all the while we were in Australia and as the taxi pulled into their driveway I could have wept with relief that our horrible journey was over. However, nothing in this world could have prepared me for the reception we received. Just as we were struggling to get the children and the suitcases out of the car, Beattie came storming down the path and with arms waiving madly in the air shouted, "Where have you been for the last three days! We expected you three days ago! It wasn't very nice of you not to let us know! Couldn't you have phoned to let us know where you were!" My heart fell to my stomach! No welcoming hug. No kiss on the cheek with words of, "I'm pleased to see that you made it safe and sound." Just arm waiving and harsh words. What a soul-destroying moment! They didn't know that for the past few months I had been driven in my desire to return home to family. They also didn't know that in the few seconds of her verbal attack, my vision of being welcomed home as the prodigal daughter evaporated swiftly into thin air. I could have turned around, got into the taxi, and headed back to Australia. In those few seconds, I knew I'd made the biggest mistake of my life. This wasn't home! This would never be home to me! I didn't want to be here! Oh, my God! What had I done?

It was all too much! I turned to Brian and broke down. I started blubbering, sobbing, and crying my heart out; the emotional dam of the past few months burst and water spurted out of my eyes, nose and mouth. Beattie and Bill looked on in amazement. They couldn't have possibly known what was going on in my head and my heart. They had no idea that Beattie's awful welcome was the last straw. They had no idea what we had gone through since I decided to uproot our family from Australia. No idea at all! By now David and John were clinging to me, crying loudly. Oh, my Lord! What a sorry sight we were. Brian hugged me close and replied, "Well, hello to you too. Sorry, but it was physically impossible to let you know that we were stranded in Kuala Lumpur and had to demand, threaten and blackmail British, Malaysian and Australian officials to get airline tickets out of there." This was, without a doubt, the worst period of my whole life. I had literally forced Brian to give up a brilliant career, a lovely home, and a beautiful environment, for what, a barren emotional wasteland? I have always said that regret is the cancer of life and, at that time, I had it in spades.

Beattie was shocked, "What! What on earth! Oh dear, I am sorry! I didn't know you'd had so much trouble getting here. We've been so worried about you. We didn't hear anything so we thought the worst! You could have been dead or something and we wouldn't have known!" She put her arm around me, "It's all right now though. Come on! Come on lass! Come on in and have a cup of tea!" A cup of tea! It is the Englishman's answer to everything. A cup of tea! All the problems of the world have been righted over a cup of tea and this was no exception. It is the panacea for anything that ails you. When you're stuck for what to do, or what say next, it gives a purpose -- put the kettle on to boil, warm the teapot, get the cups and saucers out, pour the milk and put in the sugar. It gives time to collect thoughts and to put a 'game face' on. After all, I had embarrassed everybody, including myself, when I burst into tears. Showing emotions is not very English you know. Stiff upper lip and all that in a crisis! Hence her enquiry, "How about a cup of tea?" I replied, between heart wrenching sobs, "Y..e..s.. please!"

Rebuilding our lives

We had caught the last train out of London for Newcastle, and it was around noon when we arrived at Ebchester and, less than two hours later, Beattie came to tell me that Ella Shaw was standing at the back door. How on earth she knew we were home I don't know, because we didn't know when we were going to get there, never mind anybody else. What should I do? Ignore her? Tell her to go to hell? Pretend she didn't exist? As much as I wished to confront her, I just couldn't. I was absolutely drained of emotion, and still hadn't gotten over Beattie's welcome. I thought about her only redeeming quality and that was in raising Brian. If Tommy and Ella hadn't raised him, I wouldn't have met him, courted him, married him, or had two beautiful children, and I was thankful for small mercies.

I really didn't want to have to deal with Ella Shaw just then, but I put a smile on my face as I walked to the door and lightly said, "Hello, how are you? Come on in and meet the children." She gave me a hug and a kiss as though we were the best of friends and I thought to myself, "Okay then, it's a new day, a new chapter." I wanted the children to have family and to all intent and purpose she was the only available grandmother on the Shaw side and, obviously, it would be better if we could all be friends; however, as I'm always learning, the road to hell is paved with good intentions. We walked along the hallway to where the boys were playing with their Dinkey cars on the kitchen floor, "David, John, come and meet your other grandmother." The words were still hanging in the air when she retorted, "Nanna, if you don't mind!" Oh man! Did she have to speak so sharply in front of the children! Why didn't she just say nothing and we'd have fixed it later?

The children turned and looked at her as if she were a fiery Dragon Monster and headed for my skirts. They were quick to recognize that the tone of her voice didn't fit the image of a perfect grandmother full of love and kindness, and once she realized she'd put her foot in it she totally ignored them and concentrated on making herself comfortable in an easy chair by the fire. The atmosphere was once again charged and Beattie asked the usual question, "Would you like a cup of tea, Ella?" "Yes please," she replied. I called to Brian who was watching television in the living room and he came through to greet his mother. "Nice to see you Mother! What do you think of the children?" "Well, I've only just met them; I don't think anything of them right now, except they don't look like you!" What a horrible woman! In two seconds flat, she inferred that Brian wasn't their father, and an icy band started to encircle my heart and I could feel myself going very cold as I turned from the sink where I'd been filling the kettle and retorted, "There is no doubt that he is their father! No doubt at all!" She looked at me as though I was somebody she'd never met before, and I guess she hadn't, as she snapped back, "I didn't mean that. I know he is their father; they just don't look like him!" Beattie quickly butted in, "Now, now, we'll have no arguing!" and looking directly at me said, "Now you just calm down, Ella didn't mean anything derogatory about the children, now did you Ella?" "No, not at all!" Ella replied sharply. I guess my nerves were just too much on edge but I knew Ella Shaw perhaps better than anybody when it came to making veiled remarks, and to my mind she was definitely casting doubts about the parentage of my children.

Ella got around David and John by digging into her humungous handbag and retrieving two large boxes of Smarties that she gave them. We'd never felt the need to buy sweets or candies before because they'd been encouraged to enjoy fresh fruit from our neighbours gardens so this was the first time in their lives that they tasted candy, and wouldn't you know it, they loved it and so she redeemed herself with them somewhat. However, after having a cup of tea and exacting a promise from us to bring the children to meet Tommy either the next day or the day after, she left to catch the bus home and the mood of the day lifted significantly. Nora and Stivvie and their children, Anthony and Ian, came in just as Ella was leaving, and before we knew it, we had a houseful of people when my brother Brian and Rose arrived with their two children, Gary and Wendy. I don't think we saw Dorothy and Barry until later in the week and they didn't have any children at the time. With six children ranging in ages from 5 to 2 running around, the house was pretty noisy; there was Gary and Anthony both 5, Ian 4, David and Wendy 3, and John 2, and everyone's attention was on the children which was a good thing because although I was happy to see everyone, my expectations had been so high that my homecoming was a colossal let down.

I was in big emotional trouble because I thought the families were far too casual at our arrival. I thought drums should have been banged, trumpets blown and balloons floated in the air. What a notion! All of them passed what I thought was the very offhand comment of, "Oh hello! You're back then!" and I felt as though I'd failed in some way and that I'd had to admit defeat by not staying in Australia but in having to come back to England. It seemed as though the unspoken word from them was, "Well, it's just as well we didn't sell up and go to Australia because you've had to come back!" If only I could open my eyes and wake up to find it was all a nasty dream and that we're all safe and sound in our home in Whyalla or, if I couldn't possibly survive without family, let me wake up and find myself in Canada! Why on earth hadn't I found the courage to just come home for a holiday!

It felt as though we had put everybody out and they wanted to get back to whatever it was that they were doing before we came. Somehow, and I couldn't say how, but they were different than I remembered. I can't say it was truly a case of, "I'm alright Jack," but that's the impression I got, and it was though we were now on the outside looking in. They had all gotten on with their lives and were quite settled, securely employed, and had nice houses. I felt as though the bottom had dropped out of my little world and I'd put my family in real jeopardy. We had no job, no house, no furniture, and from everybody's comments on the high unemployment in the area – very few prospects! Whether it was because my 'Dilly Dream' expectations of my children being immediately immersed into an openly affectionate and loving family were never realized, or whether it was because I couldn't let go of what we'd had, but I was grief-stricken. Even though we had written regularly over the four years I was away, I found it hard to verbally communicate or relate to either Nora or Beattie and it was just terrible. They were all strangers to me! And it was no better when we took the children to meet Tommy Shaw for the first time.

As we walked into the living room his very first words to the children were, "Well, hello there. Have you come for your pocket money then?" An innocent enough question, but to my 'highly tuned to the slightest insensitive remark mind,' his question seemed to emphasize our very vulnerable position of not having much of anything left, either home, furniture, or money, and I bristled. How dare he think that! We sold the house in Australia for much less than the market value. We gave away most of our furnishings. We'd spent thousands of dollars on the trip itself. Our money was running out at an alarming rate and he thought the only reason we had come back to England was so he could give our children POCKET MONEY! Talk about being over-sensitive. "No! They haven't come for your money; they've only come to meet you!" Tommy lifted his head toward me, "Well then, I won't give them any!" he replied.

I seemed destined to get off on the wrong foot with everybody and my dreams were being shattered left, right and centre. I had hoped that with not having any communication with him for two years that we could have left all the unpleasantness behind us and start anew but with his very first words I knew I had not forgiven him and it would be a long time before I did.

During the time we were away, Nora and Brian had built a family relationship between themselves and Beattie and Bill and both boys adopted them as Nanna and Grandad. I had enjoyed Beattie as an adult and I thought it was a shame that Nora couldn't feel Beattie's goodness as I had, so I was thrilled to learn through our letters that that she had been able to let go of the past and build a loving and sincere relationship with our biological mother, and I was really happy for her. But now that I had them both in front of me I discovered I was also jealous. I had been usurped and was no longer needed in either relationship, at least that's how I saw it, and for the next six weeks I convinced myself that I wasn't wanted by any of them, so I didn't want to be there!

I tried to keep myself occupied while Brian was doing the rounds of the employment agencies; I visited Ella and Tommy a couple of times a week but didn't get any support or sympathy from them. I took the children over to the playground and played hell with the local council to come and cut the tall grass so that the children could reach the swings. I played with them in the yard and didn't care if the ball went into the washing hanging on the line. I found myself making nasty remarks about the slightest little thing. I blamed everybody else for me being there, instead of me. However, I never expected both Nora and Beattie to team up against me when Beattie and I visited Nora in Durham and, while all four boys were out in the back yard playing, the two of them started. I must have been going through mental depression before it was medically identified as such because I could not get myself motivated about anything. I didn't want to be there; I hated being in England; I wanted to be back in Australia in my own house in Whyalla!

Lost in my own thoughts, I was sitting quietly on the couch when they started discussing me as though I wasn't there. Back and forth they went. "Why hadn't Nan stayed in Australia! Why doesn't she go back there! I don't understand her! She's making everybody miserable! It's time for Nan to get her act together! Start and take control of her life! Look after her boys!" On and on they went, repeating the same things over and over, and it was like everything about me shut down except my brain. Beattie started singing the song that contained the chorus, "I never promised you a rose garden!" which I've hated ever since, and Nora, who couldn't contain herself any longer, came over and slapped me hard across the face. "Sorry Nan, but I just had to do that! You're driving us all crazy!"

I was traumatized! I started talking incoherently and weeping which I seemed to do most easily these days, and my heart was breaking because I couldn't even explain properly to myself what the matter was, never mind explain it to anybody else, and it hurt like hell that my sister didn't even try to understand. Nora put her arms around me and said, "Somebody had to say something and we figured it was better we said it than Ella Shaw! You can't turn the clock back, you're here now and we're keeping you. Besides, nothing is ever the same when you go back!" She had never said a truer word! She was right, totally right! Nothing is the same when you go back! Although what she said and what registered with me were two different things. Nora meant that Australia would somehow be different even in this short time, but I registered the comment to mean that England was not the same, and it wasn't, not for me anyway!

They couldn't possibly understand the internal struggle that I'd gone through during the last few months of being mentally driven to return to family. They couldn't possibly understand how let down I felt by their offhand welcome. They couldn't possible understand the vast amount of emotions that threatened to engulf me every time I thought about Australia and how deeply I regretted leaving there, and then it hit me. No wonder I couldn't communicate with anybody! They still had the 'village' mentality. Nothing had changed at home. The places and people hadn't changed -- I had! I had left the 'village' behind. I had seen the world. I wasn't interested in talking about the price of cabbage any more. My vision was wider than that. I had been places, met people, done things I would never have done had I not left England. It was me that was different – not them. They hadn't changed – I had! Somehow, I was going to have to revert to the person I used to be if I had any hope at all of giving my children the family I'd hoped for. They were right! I couldn't go back to Australia, what was the point? I couldn't keep selling up and returning home every time I got homesick. My future was here, back in England, back where I started. Unknowingly, they chanced upon the only good reason to get me mentally back on my feet – my frozen attitude was hurting my children and for the first time since returning, I could feel the icy numbness around my heart starting to melt.

I had been mentally lost in a thick black fog for weeks and had been sinking deeper and deeper into depression but couldn't find the way out until now. With attacking me the way they did, they verbally smashed the 'displaced person' sign that I'd been carrying around in my head and I was so physically and mentally exhausted that I lay down on the couch and fell fast asleep. When I awoke a few hours later I stretched myself and started to giggle at the concerned expressions on their faces, and the oppressive black cloud that had hung over me for weeks dissipated into thin air. Nora turned to Beattie and said, "She's back. She's going to be okay.

We've got Nan back!" Now I knew I was home with family again and within a very short time, I started to feel like myself again. I wanted to be me again. I wanted to be the optimistic, full of cheer, happy go lucky, kind-hearted and good-natured person I'd always been, and as their warm and loving smiles warmed my heart, I could feel the last of the ice melt away. They loved me enough to be cruel, to be kind, and I let myself be accepted into the family fold again. That day turned out to be huge crossroad in our lives, not only for me personally, but also for my family because that was the day Brian got his old job back, with a substantial raise.

There was really high unemployment in the north east of England at the time, and it took a nerve-wracking six weeks before Brian got a job as Chief Accountant to a group of garages in Middlesbrough, about a 25-mile drive from Ebchester. He had been traveling back and forth for about a month and got the surprise of his life when he literally bumped into his old boss, Tom Scott, who was in the forecourt of the garage picking his car up after it had been serviced. Mr. Scott turned around to see who had bumped into him, "What the. . . . Brian! What are you doing here? I thought you were still in Australia!" Brian knew the Company had been nationalized into a division of British Steel and all the top executives had been moved to a new head office in Middlesbrough, and he wondered if he'd encounter any of his old colleagues but didn't expect one of them to be his old boss. He gave him a simplified version of our reason for returning home and when he asked how long we'd been back Brian replied, "About ten weeks now." Mr. Scott said, "You know where the new head office is? Well resign this job and let me know when you're starting work with me again but make it as soon as possible!"

All this time we hadn't known what to do for the best. We'd been back in England for 2½ months, still living with Beattie, and hadn't been able to save any money whatsoever. What money we had left over from Australia had gone, it had all been eaten up with living expenses and finding work so even if we wanted to, we couldn't afford to go overseas again, heck, we couldn't even afford to live where we were. We had no money left, only what Brian was earning each week, and the prospect of ever moving or owning our own home again looked decidedly grim, never mind furnishing it. What to do? However, when Brian bumped into Mr. Scott it seemed as though the decision of whether to stay or whether to go was made for us, and with him getting his old job back, we decided to stay, at least until we'd saved up enough money to go to Canada. Brian was quickly welcomed back into the fold and they certainly appreciated having him around. World markets were changing drastically and Brian was the only executive to have gained overseas manufacturing experience, not only in Australia but also in Japan. He'd been the project leader for a lot of Australian and Japanese business transactions and before very long he was 'fast tracked' up the executive ladder and invited to become a Board Member of the north-east Board of Directors. Definitely not shabby!

Settling Down

With the guarantee of a 100% mortgage from the bank now that Brian worked for the Company again, now known as British Steel, we searched around and bought a 1940's three-bedroom semi-detached brick house in the middle of a street of houses - 39 Rochester Road, Linthorpe, Middlesbrough. It was a big house with stairs at the front leading up to three bedrooms and a bathroom. There were two rooms leading off the downstairs hallway and to the left was the front parlour or living room, and the one at the bottom of the hallway was another living room and large dining room that took up the width of the house. Just about opposite the door into the dining room, on the far wall, was a door that opened into a small kitchen, built as an extension to the house. There was a small garden, and a garage that was accessed by using the narrow alleyway jointly owned with the house on our right. The inside of the house had seen better days, as had the carpets, but with a lick of paint and new carpeting throughout, it would do. It was in our price range and that's all that mattered, at least for now.

Six weeks later we moved our ten tea chests of soft furnishings into this empty house and staked our claim. Aunt Mabel gave us back a double bed we'd given her when we left the country, along with two newly upholstered easy chairs she and Uncle Joe had just finished, and Ella returned Brian's bureau, plus a hall table. We bought a second-hand dining room suite from my sister Dorothy's in-laws, two second-hand clothes drawers, and new single beds for the children. For the third time in my married life I proceeded to build a home from scratch. It was fairly meager, but so long as I had my own four walls and a roof over my head, comfort could wait except for my lovely gold brocade curtains hanging from the front room windows.

Our next-door neighbors, with whom we shared the driveway, were a young couple with two young children, just like us. Dora and Derek Aspry, daughter Janice who was about 8-years-old, and son Stephen a little bit older than David, at nearly 4-years-old. Dora was a stay-at-home mother just like me, while Derek was a blue-collar worker at the ICI, a few miles away, and whilst Derek had the most outgoing and fun personality you'd ever encounter, Dora was totally opposite with an extremely quiet and very shy nature. I'd thought I was terrible when meeting new people, but she was much more retiring than I was, by a country mile.

Now that I had put Australia physically, if not mentally behind me, I started to settle down and within a couple of days of moving into our home, made friends with Dora and Derek and their children. They didn't own a car, so with four adults and four children squashed into our little Mini car, we enjoyed our first autumn back in England exploring local beaches, and surrounding countryside. As we didn't have any furniture to furnish the front parlour we decided to turn it into a children's play room and bought a very old piano from an old man living across the road from us, just for the children to play with. I bought long handled artist's brushes, and some non-toxic paint, and David and John, and Stephen from next door, and another three regular kids from houses in our street, painted 'their' room to their hearts content. Whenever the weather was bad, which was often, our front parlour became a full-time babysitting service, but it meant that four other mothers always knew where to find their child.

All too soon the boy's first winter approached and I was concerned how they would manage the bone chilling winds and the waist high snow and had written of my concern to Lorna in Canada and to my great surprise, she sent me two Canadian snowsuits! Snowsuits were unheard of in England and I was constantly being stopped and asked where I'd bought them but they were only available in Canada at the time – pity! I shouldn't have worried about the weather, because the boys took to the icy cold English winter like ice skaters on a frozen pond simply because of those warm and cozy snowsuits. The minute they got into them all they wanted to do was hurry outside and play and I'll never forget David's words when he saw snow for the first time. It was while David, John and I were waiting at the bus stop to go into town to do some shopping and large fluffy snowflakes started to float casually down to earth. The three of us watched as the pavement became covered in snow and I was just about to tell David to put his glove back on because he'd taken it off to let the snow land and melt on his hand, when he turned to me and said, "Mommy, it's raining soap powder."

Our first year in Middlesborough passed very quickly not only with exploring and being the street's official child minder, but with painting and wallpapering and now the whole house, except for the front parlour, was lickedly split clean, although still practically empty. Summer rolled along, and we had our first visit from family in Canada when Ted, Lorna's son, came to stay which prompted us to buy bunk beds for the third bedroom which was very small, for the boys, so that we had a spare bed for him. Ted was 12 when he went to live in Canada and I hadn't seen him for six years, and he had just finished High School when he came home for a six-week holiday. What a handsome man he turned out to be and I really missed his growing years. He came to stay with us for a couple of weeks and we had a great time taking him around to all old and new places, and he enjoyed meeting David and John. All four sisters had kept in close touch over the years through letters, and when I passed the comment that I still really missed Lorna and Marjorie, Ted's appearance jogged Brian's memory of my original desire to move to Canada and seeds started germinating.

Ted, probably about 18 yrs old.

The children's early childhood was passing by very quickly and as the boys were conditioned to go to bed at 7 pm this meant they weren't seeing very much of their father. Brian was working longer and longer hours, and by the time he came home the children were already in bed and it felt as though he was just lodging with us, so we came to a compromise with his workload. He would come home around 5 pm each night so that we could all have dinner together, enjoy some quality play time, have fun with their bath time and when they'd gone to bed, he would go back to work for however long he wanted, usually until about 11 pm. It worked for us!

I'd reached an unspoken compromise with Ella and Tommy for the sake of Brian and the boys, and we had an 'arms-length' but comfortable relationship, made easier by her comment to Tommy that she now considered both David and John to be replicas of Brian as a young child. Even though Ella's dog came first, and she made that quite clear, she was kind to the children, whereas Tommy made no bones about it, he loved them. He was in his element when they were around, and teased them unmercifully, but so long as it was good-natured I didn't mind. We'd gotten into the routine of visiting Ella and Tommy every Sunday, and before long I was the designated cook of the Sunday dinner because Ella had lost her sense of smell years before and I think Tommy was fed up with burnt offerings. Ella was of the old school and not happy unless the vegetable pans were filled to the brim so that they'd be swimming in water, or she'd cook the vegetables in the pressure cooker and we'd end up with such unappetizing fare as brown cauliflower. I was not the world's best cook, but the vegetables did taste how they were supposed to and without fail Tommy would say, "My, I enjoyed that dinner!" Then we were expected to stay for Sunday tea and the whole day felt shot, because by the time we drove there, and drove back again, it was time for the children to go to bed.

This was our routine for the first year, before I said, "Brian, we need to make some changes to our weekend habits. We spend all day in the shops on a Saturday, and all day at your folk's house on a Sunday. When are we going to find time for the children?" So, even though his folks didn't like it, and the atmosphere chilled quite substantially, we restricted our shopping to a Saturday morning only, followed by a visit to his folks on a Saturday afternoon. This suited me fine because Ella usually shopped at Consett market on a Saturday afternoon and it meant Tommy could thoroughly enjoy the children without being told to, "Stop that carry on, you're messing up the seat covers." We also reduced our visit to three hours so that we could visit Aunt Mabel and Uncle Joe who were my touchstones, and after the chill in the air at Delves Lane, Aunt Mabel's consistent welcome warmed all of us. They were always happy to see us, and now that we had spare beds, we were delighted when they stayed with us a couple of times during the summer. The boys absolutely idolized them, as did I, and when they visited Uncle Joe was happy to stay with them while Aunt Mabel and I went shopping to either Stockton or Darlington markets. After leaving Aunt Mabel's house, we'd make a flying visit to Ebchester to see Beattie and Bill, and then drive over to Durham to visit with Nora and Stivvie.

Once Ella heard we had two spare beds, she decided to invite herself and Tommy for a holiday and enjoyed being waited on hand and foot so much, that every three months for the next three years, they came to stay for three weeks at a time. I don't think she really wanted to see either the children or myself, it was Brian, but to see him meant she had to 'put up' with the rest of us. It wasn't that she was impolite, although I must admit when I found her hand washing Brian's unmentionables in the kitchen sink I thought she had a nerve because she'd had to go through the laundry basket in our bedroom to find them, for one thing, and when I said, "Why are you washing Brian's socks and underwear in the sink?" she replied, "Oh I've always washed Brian's things by hand." Now if she'd started washing the children's things as well I might not have been so upset, but to pull Brian's things out of the laundry to wash individually irritated me. "Well please don't do that again, we have a washing machine, and his things get washed along with the children's," I said, and walked out of the kitchen without giving her the opportunity to respond. It was always one step forward and two back with her.

So long as she kept her snide comments to herself and showed me a modicum of respect I could put up with her but, more often than not, I struggled to keep my mouth shut because she was the most insensitive person I'd ever come across. We had not been back in the country for very long and were still trying to get back on our feet. The monthly house payment was huge, and the children kept growing out of their clothes and shoes. We also had a car payment to find, and we needed to put food on the table. We could have done without them mooching off us for three weeks at a time because not once did they ever offer to help with the expense of keeping them. Not once! I used to try and sneak out of the house to do the daily grocery shopping without Ella because if she saw me she'd say, "Just a minute till I get my coat on and I'll come with you." Knickers!

We didn't have a lot of money budgeted for food, and to have Ella put unnecessary luxury items into my basket, then scarper when the time came to pay for them, used to make me see red.

Believe me; we could have lived quite nicely without chocolate cakes, cream cakes and cream for her coffee. As soon as she was out of sight of the Cashier's desk, I'd put duplicates to one side, and she couldn't possibly have failed to notice missing items when we got home, but she never said anything. I think she got a kick out of putting me in the position of having to put things back on the shelves, because she did it to me every time I was unlucky enough to have to take her to the shops with me. I'd complain to Brian about her and ask him to tell her not to put extras in my basket, but he felt he couldn't upset her, so it was left to me to manage a tight budget. As soon as the three weeks were up the tension used to lift magically from my shoulders, until the next time.

Dora's child, Stephen, had been enrolled in a pre-school Kindergarten since the age of 4 and as David was nearing that age both Brian and I thought it was time to enroll David. I know as their mother I'm biased, but I thought my children were the greatest children ever born. From being small babies they had learned to share everything and didn't fight over things as other siblings did, and they were so close they even had their own language. David was so protective of his brother from the minute he was born that he had claimed him as his baby, and that we'd brought him from the hospital especially for him. He figured it was his job to bathe and feed the baby and as John was learning speech, David interpreted for him. There was nothing David wouldn't do for John and vice versa. Even when David went to pre-school Kindergarten for the first time he wanted John to stay with him and, "Help him play with the other children," but it was time for him to gain some independence, even it was only for a few hours each morning. John would watch the clock until it was time to go and get David, then practically dance along the street with excitement. You'd have thought they'd not seen each other for many years the way they'd greet and hug each other, and all the way home David would chatter away giving John a detailed account of everything he'd done that morning. They were growing up.

Before we realized it, two years had flown over. John was now attending pre-school Kindergarten, while David attended proper Kindergarten, and for the first time since they were born I had a couple of hours to myself in the mornings. Ah, the bliss of being able to sit and enjoy a mid-morning cup of coffee with no interruptions, except for Dora. Because it cost money for every second you used the phone in England, Dora and I had a secret signal that didn't cost us anything. Either I'd ring her three times and hang up in which case she knew to come to my house or she'd do the same and I'd go to her house. Coffee mornings! I loved them.

We had our first taste of the English National Healthcare System (NHS) in August of that year, when John's health took a turn for the worse. He'd been a bit of a sickly child when he was born and every two weeks the Doctor would stick a probe, covered with cotton wool, into his ear canal to remove whatever was in there. Seemingly the tubes in his ears hadn't grown properly and were very narrow which made him very susceptible to strep throat, ear aches and sinus problems. But it came as quite a shock when the Specialist said, "Well, Mr. & Mrs. Shaw, you have a choice. Your child must have his Tonsils and Adenoids removed as quickly as possible. However, it will be six months before I can schedule an operation under the National Health Services plan. But, if you like, I can do the operation this Friday if you pay privately." What choice was that? If we hadn't had the money, we would have begged, borrowed or stolen in order to pay privately.

Friday just happened to be John's fourth birthday and rather than let him suffer for another six months we chose to clean out our bank balance to relieve his suffering. As I was taking him down the corridor to the Nursing Station in Middlesbrough General Hospital on the Thursday evening prior to the operation, the Matron on the Surgical Ward came toward me and she must have been expecting us when she said, "Mrs. Shaw? Private patient, John Shaw?" "Yes," I replied. "I don't know what the world is coming to when nobody has the patience to wait any more, they all want to do it privately!" she said. "Pardon me? You've got the wrong end of the stick altogether! I don't think it's right to be blackmailed into paying $1000 to have our child's suffering relieved! The surgeon gave me a choice of waiting six months for the National Health Service to cover the costs, or he could do the surgery tomorrow if we paid him directly! Now if this were your child, what would you do? Wait six months or three days?" I asked. She totally ignored me as if I hadn't spoken but said, "Well come along with me then and we'll get him settled. You can stay until midnight but then you have to go. The operation will be at 7 am in the morning and you can come back around noon-time!"

I was back the next day at the allotted time and as I walked into his room I nearly fainted. Along one wall was a barrage of equipment, including what looked like a fish-tank with lots of tubes coming in and out and everything was covered with blood. John was lying in a pool of blood on his pillow rasping for breath and I stood there and screamed! Matron came running into the room and yelled, "Nurse! Nurse! This equipment should have been removed before Mrs. Shaw got here, and that child's pillowcase replaced!" She turned and caught me just as I was about to pass out. "Sorry Mrs. Shaw! We had a bit of a problem with John. He stopped breathing and we had to resuscitate him, but you wouldn't have known anything about it if we'd gotten the equipment out of here in time!" How unbelievably stupid and bureaucratic! They weren't going to tell me that my child had stopped breathing during the night and that they'd had to resuscitate him! I couldn't help but compare the English healthcare system with the Australian healthcare system, of which I was an expert, and decided the English system left an awful lot to be desired and I mentally resolved never to go to that particular hospital again.

As soon as they told me it was okay to take him home, I rushed him out of that dreadful hospital and with a lot of anxiety told Brian what had happened and both of us got really upset, and the next day David went very quiet and withdrawn and I wondered if he was sickening for something. It wasn't until I was getting him ready for bed that night when he anxiously asked me, "Mommy, is John going to die again?" that I realized he'd heard every word I'd said. Normally I was quite calm and quietly spoken around the children, and I hadn't realized that all the time I was ranting and raving David was standing to one side listening to me. Oh, the poor child! I took him in my arms and hugged him really tightly. "No," I said. "John is not going to die again. The nurse made a big mistake and didn't look after him properly, and that won't happen again, I promise you!" I didn't want him to be frightened either of nurses or doctors, and resolved to be much more careful in future, and not discuss anything really important in front of either of them. They deserved to be protected not terrified.

When lunchtime came around the next day, John decided he'd had enough of ice cream and wanted hot dog sausages instead. Music to my ears. After struggling to get any kind of food into him for nearly four years, he now had an appetite and after the sausages were hot enough David kept pushing them into John's mouth, one after the other, saying, "Eat another one John, eat another one." I think he must have thought that if John finished all 10 hot dogs, then nothing could possibly be wrong with him after that, and he was right. Neither John nor his appetite ever looked back, and it turned out to be money well spent, and I'd do it again in a heartbeat.

Not only were the children growing up, I was growing up too. I still wanted everybody to get along and be happy because that was my basic nature, but I'd never again be the semi-introvert who'd left England four years earlier. I was now very much aware that I had to mentally lie down to let people walk all over me and I wasn't about to do that anymore. This was 1973, still in the flower power era, with free speech and all that, and whereas I was still a pushover in a lot of ways, you could be guaranteed an argument or an unasked-for opinion where the welfare of children were concerned. I remember being on the bus one time with Dora and our three boys, and they were being a bit overly boisterous when a couple of old ladies who were sitting behind us said loudly, "They remind me of the noisy children that play in our street! They get on your nerves!" Well, should I ignore the comment or what? Not likely! Nobody gets away with anything when it comes to the welfare of children.

I slowly and deliberately turned toward them, looked both of them in the eye and said, "Thank you Ladies, I get the message. There is one thing you should keep in mind if you ever bump into boisterous children again. When you and I were young, we had green fields to play in and trees to climb on and lots of green grass everywhere. We had loads of outdoor activities that soaked up our energy. Farms to pick potatoes in. Gardens to play in. There was no traffic on the roads and very few streets. Think back. Think what it was like in your childhood. Nowadays, the children only have paved streets to play in and can't even relax doing that because they have to watch out for cars and trucks. Apart from an odd park here and there, there are very few 'green' activities to soak up any child's abundant energy. Think about it. Think about how you grew up and what the children of today are missing, especially living here in this steel town." I didn't say it nastily. I just gave them the facts of life that living in a town consisting of street upon street didn't make for a very pleasant childhood and that they should 'cut some slack' to all small children forced to grow up this way, and I must admit visions of our lovely big garden and radiant sunshine of Whyalla crossed my mind as I was giving them my lecture. They gave no acknowledgement of me having said anything to them until a couple of stops later when they got up to leave the bus and one of them just had to have the last word, "Well! Some people! It's as though I don't have any rights at all!" To which I quickly replied, "Yes you do! But so do children, and adults forget that!"

Our lives revolved around the boys. Those children were our pride and joy and we took them everywhere because I wouldn't trust anybody to babysit on an evening. If we got invited to some place that was going to be too late for their bedtime I turned it down. Sorry. No can do. Their wellbeing came first, and it wasn't until David was nearly 5-years-old that I was persuaded to let Dora's Aunt Alice, babysit for one Saturday night. Once I was able to trust her that she'd take care of our children we went dancing at Derek's place of work, in the canteen, of the Imperial Chemical Industry every Saturday night. It was great. There were door prizes, and without exception, either Dora or myself won one of the main prizes, mostly a roast of beef or pork, and whoever won it would cook it and all four of us would share it.

We had lived in Middlesbrough for maybe two years when our best friends, Anne and Alan and their two children, Leslie and Adrian, came home from South Africa, and stayed with us for about four months. Alan had been in charge of house and road building projects in South Africa for nearly six years, but now they were back and needed some place to stay until they got another house. I never fancied living in South Africa, and we did have the chance. When Brian told BHP that he was bringing me home to England they asked him to take a job with them in South Africa instead, but I wouldn't hear of it. I didn't like the way the coloured people were being treated and because I figured I couldn't do anything to help them then I was not going to take advantage of them either. Alan had some hair-raising tales to tell of their time in South Africa, none of them pleasant. I was particularly disturbed to hear that one of his neighbours in the distant township he was living in at the time had shot and killed a coloured man simply because he was too close to his house and at that time, in the early 70's, it was a natural thing to do. How awful, to treat some mother's son so cold-heartedly!

However, apart from hearing of all the horrible things that were going on in South Africa, we thoroughly enjoyed the time they spent with us, and it was great getting to know Leslie and Adrian and I consider them to be my nephews. Anne was absolutely fantastic to have around although she drove me crazy as she was a bundle of energy and it was hard to get her to stop and relax for a while. With living in a very hot climate the pace of my life had slowed down considerably and I liked it, but somehow hers had speeded up, and she was not at all happy until the house was cleaned from top to bottom, the beds made, and the supper prepared for the husbands. I used to say to her, "Good heavens Anne! Life is too short to worry whether the creases in the children's pajamas are perfect or not. Be thankful they have them! And no, I am not even ironing David and John's!" I am certain at that time I drove her crazier than she drove me, but she is my dearest friend in the entire world and I love her and there is nothing I wouldn't do for her. She has a personality, a presence and a purity of heart that everybody on this earth could learn something from.

Even though we used to visit Aunt Mabel and Uncle Joe quite regularly, both my sister, Nora, and I still got most of the news of Billy and Jimmy via Lorna in Canada and one of her letters caused us considerable concern. Jimmy was dying of cancer and had been hospitalized in Newcastle Infirmary but Ruby, his wife, had requested no visitors. Marjorie and Lorna ignored her request and came home from Canada as soon as they could to say their goodbyes to him, but neither Nora nor I were allowed to. Then they both came and stayed with me in Middlesbrough for a couple of days which was great, even though it was under heartbreaking circumstances, and they'd no sooner returned to Canada when Jimmy died, but Nora and I were not told. We only found out a couple of days after his funeral and were very upset when we were told that Ruby had requested that we not be told because, "they are not his sisters!"

He had been our brother all of our lives. As his sister, I had looked after his and Ruby's child for a year. He had given both Nora and I away at our weddings. How could we not be told? We were furious and hurt and couldn't believe that Ruby denied us the chance to pay our respects to our brother. It was okay when she was making use of me in looking after her baby, Fiona, but somehow, I wasn't good enough to be Jimmy's sister. Well, she was not going to get away with it. I told Aunt Mabel and Uncle Joe that I was going to write to her and let her know how angry we were. Aunt Mabel got herself all upset because she didn't think a letter to Ruby was appropriate so soon after Jimmy's death. Well, Ruby hadn't considered our feelings, so why should we consider hers? Uncle Joe asked to see the letter before I sent it and after he read it said it wasn't so bad, we had every right to be upset and what I had written just described how desolate both Nora and I were at Jimmy's death and that we were extremely upset that we had not been allowed to pay our respects, so he was okay with sending it. I never got a reply to my letter and until writing about it now, have never given her another thought, but for nearly ten years Nora never forgave Aunt Mabel or our brother Billy for not letting us know that Jimmy had died and I could never convince her that they had been put in a very awkward position and that it wasn't their fault, it was Ruby's.

Cousin Leslie, Uncle Joe, Aunt Mabel, and cousin Heather

Now and again, we had lightly touched upon the subject of moving to Canada but as we looked at the property market, not many houses were selling so we decided to bring our home kicking and screaming into the modern day 70's to better our options. I figured we had nothing to lose, either the renovations would help sell the house more quickly and for a better price or, if we really didn't go to Canada I would at least have a modern home, so we hired a building contractor to install central heating, new windows, new electric wiring, and new plumbing including a brand-new kitchen and a downstairs toilet. Because the garage was at the back of the house and we needed the driveway to store the demolished material for a while, Brian had to park the Mini on the front street beside our front door but when he went to get it the next morning he discovered it had been stolen. The police found it after about three days but it was so badly damaged that it was a write off and we had to buy another car so this time we bought a Maxi and I thought after the smallness of the mini that I was driving a luxury car until I went around a corner and the wheel dropped off. A bearing had collapsed and you've never seen anybody in more shock than I was. Thank goodness I was going slowly or we could have been really hurt and even now if there is a rattle or squeak I am not happy until the garage has looked it over.

David frightened both of us during this renovation because, unknown to him, the builders removed the old iron banister rail on the stairs after he'd gone to bed, ready to install a modern-day ranch style one the next day, and when he came out of his bedroom and went to jump over it, it wasn't there and he crashed about 10 feet to the floor and knocked himself unconscious. John yelled for me and I came running to see what had happened and my heart just about stopped because I thought he was dead. I phoned Brian who immediately came home from work and we rushed him to the nearest hospital, which unfortunately, was the same hospital that John had been in, The Middlesbrough General Hospital, and he lay on a stretcher in Emergency for nearly four hours before being seen to. After waiting such an agonizing length of time both of us were extremely agitated, and maybe Brian used too sharp a tone of voice when he asked a Nurse who was walking up the corridor when a Doctor was likely to come and see our unconscious five-year-old. She spitefully replied, "Who do you think you are then, bloody miners? You want preferential treatment?" The coal miners had been on strike all summer and as the reserves of coal dwindled so did household electricity, and it was being rationed to a few hours a day to each household, so everybody was really fed up. Nobody had much sympathy for the coal miners who kept on demanding more money and holding everybody hostage, so I understood her comment. But Brian, who was never at a loss for words, shouted back as she was walking away from us, "Aye, I'm a bloody coal miner and I've got a bloody pick axe in the car, do you want to try it for size?" Tempers were definitely flared and other people stopped to listen. But all that shouting brought the Doctor out into the corridor to see what the matter was and after being told by the Nurse that, "They've only been waiting four hours, I don't know what they are complaining about!" he came to examine our unconscious child. He immediately sent him for x-rays, and although they couldn't find anything wrong they admitted him for overnight observation, and both of us slept in the chairs beside David's bed while Dora looked after John. We fervently hoped that we'd never have to go to The Middlesbrough General Hospital for anything, ever again.

Not Again!

With both children in regular school now, I started working as a temporary secretary from 9 am until 2 pm, so that I could be home before them. I was finally getting out and about in society, upgrading my office skills, and contributing to our savings account. Lovely! We had been back in England and settled down now for about three years, and the boys were doing well in school and we thoroughly enjoyed visiting all our relatives, including Ella and Tommy.

I still wasn't too happy with the English weather after that fantastic weather we'd experienced in Australia, but as the boys couldn't remember anything different, it remained just wishful thinking that just for once I'd open the curtains and find brilliant blue skies and hot sunshine, instead of constant rain. Brian was doing well in his job, so well in fact that he had to go down to London every few weeks with Mr. Scott and have meetings with the big boss's in the Head Office. Some big shot down there had been told that he'd lived in Australia for a few years and on one of his trips asked him if he'd like to go and work in Saudi Arabia. "To do what?" asked Brian. "Well the Shah of Iran wants us to build him a Steelworks and we think you'd do a great job at managing the project. Why don't you talk to your wife about it?" I thought about it for a while and asked him if he seriously wanted to go. I didn't mind the hot weather, in fact I quite liked it, but I didn't fancy having to wear head-to-toe clothes and to raise the children in such a dictatorial and fanatically religious country, so I said no, it wasn't for me. If he wanted to go, then he could go, I would keep the house and our way of life, and he could come home on holiday every so often. Ha! Where was my brain when I said that? What on earth was I thinking? Now it was his turn to dig his heels in. "I'm not going without you. We're either all going or none of us is going!" he said. "Okay, okay. Just tell them thanks, but no thanks, because your wife won't leave England" I replied.

Brian turned down their request and our lives settled down into a comfortable routine again for another six months. David was just 6 years old and John 5 when Brian, whose 'itching to move' seeds had been germinating ever since Ted's visit, unexpectedly said, "You know Nan, this isn't where we wanted to be! This isn't where we wanted to settle!" I looked at him, very puzzled, "What on earth are you talking about?" I thought he was going to bring up Saudi Arabia again, but he continued, "We didn't intend to stay in England this long. We were only going to stay long enough for the children to adjust to cold weather!" Ah, now I've got it. Now I'm on the same page as him! I replied, "Yes! Yes, that's right! You're right! Yes! We had made that decision before we left Australia -- three years ago! Brian, how could you possibly want to move now?" It ran through my mind like a bush fire that we managed to buy a house with no money. We'd renovated it from top to bottom. We'd furnished and refurnished it. The children were doing great in school. Brian had an executive's job with a secure future. Canada! Why on earth would I possibly want to go to Canada? I still had half my family living in England, so why would I want to throw everything away again and move to another country? This is the third home I'd built from scratch. I was not moving anywhere! Ah! What a very persuasive husband I had. Here I go again! I hadn't given it much thought as to why we should even be thinking of moving countries again, but it was Brian who could see the writing on the wall; I was much too busy with everyday living.

England, in the 1970s was losing manufacturing jobs like water down the drain. Wages were climbing sky-high and investors wanted a good return on their money and were clamoring for lower costs and higher profits, so companies started offloading manufacturing jobs to the Far East where wages and overhead costs were very low. It didn't take long for people to realize that the demand for cheaper goods meant that their jobs were headed where the cheap goods were being made such as Hong Kong, Taiwan and India but it was too late, the cycle had started. You either paid the higher price for goods 'Made in England' which not many people wished to do, or you got the cheaper goods made in the Far East at the cost of your job. The repercussions of offloading manufacturing jobs overseas weren't going to be pretty for anybody, either in the steel industry or the mining industry. It was such a vicious cycle - there wasn't going to be the demand for coal to fire the furnaces to manufacture the steel to make the finished product anymore and lay-offs and redundancies were becoming daily occurrences in the north east of England. Brian, as a member of the Board of Directors, knew that British Steel had been over-producing steel for years and were going to close a lot of manufacturing sites to try and remain competitive in the world market. He would be okay; he'd have a job forever even if it meant moving to the few specialized steel sites remaining in the country, he would be employed. But what about our children? What would happen to them when they grew up? It was time to seriously think about where to give them the most secure future.

Not so fast though! I wasn't selling up and moving anywhere until I'd seen the environment first. I wanted my own firsthand experience of the next move, if there were to be any, and I persuaded my sister Nora to vacation with me in Canada. We would stay with Lorna and Ted and visit with Marjorie and Ken and family and 'case the joint!'

PART 4 - CANADA

'Casing the Joint'

When I was born, if I could have looked in the Book of Life against my name, what would have been written there? I think it would have been something like this, "You will be raised in the village of Templetown, marry a local boy from either the steel industry or the coal industry, and have 3 children. You will rent a house in a street, live a long industrious life making ends meet, and be buried in Blackhill cemetery." Period. End of story. Never in my wildest dreams could I have ever have imagined it would read, "You will marry a man with a sense of adventure and will live in different countries. You will have two living children and numerous homes and just when you get them reasonably furnished, you will move. You will be a modern-day explorer." If I'd known what sort of life I was to live, I don't think I'd have believed it. Ordinary people like me did not constantly move. The people I grew up with got married, furnished a home, and stayed there until death. Brian's folks lived in the same rented house for more than sixty years, whereas it was my destiny to be a Nomad and move every two.

Nancy & Nora, 1974

It was 1974 and I was 31-year-old and the mother of a six-year-old and a five-year-old, and it felt as though my life was going by at the speed of light, but it was an exciting time to be alive! Class barriers, both physical and mental, were being broken all over. People were enjoying a much higher standard of living and, where there was more money, there was more freedom. Countries were finally getting back on their feet after World War II; and traveling between them was now so simple that it was a normal every day event to just hop on a plane and go wherever you wanted. Once Brian gave me the facts of manufacturing life in England, and painted the picture that our boys, living in the north east of England, were not going to have a brilliant future, it motivated me into action, and six weeks later, my sister Nora and I sat on a plane on the tarmac at Middlesborough airport, waiting to fly to Toronto, Canada, where we'd spend three weeks visiting Lorna and Marjorie, so that I could check the place out.

Nora had never flown anywhere before and was pretty nervous about flying, but as I was now considered a seasoned traveler I assured her there was nothing to worry about and told her to settle down and enjoy the experience. Before we took off, the Air Hostess came around with boiled sweets to suck so that the cabin pressure didn't build up in our ears, and throughout the whole flight, walked up and down the aisle with a stream of cold drinks, hot drinks, food, and snacks. We were two mothers who had fetched and carried and had run after our families and now somebody was pampering us. It was great, and we both determined to enjoy everything they put in front of us. Now whether it was just her fear of flying, or whether it was because the cabin had gotten too hot and stuffy for her, but just as Nora turned to say something to me, she threw up all over me. I personally think it was the anchovies on a garden salad that did it. But now I felt how Brian must have felt when John threw up all over him in Kuala Lumpur airport, stunned and a bit embarrassed and I was not quite sure what to do because all of my clothes were in a suitcase in the hold of the plane. But I couldn't just sit there; I had to do something, so I went to the bathroom at the back of the plane, holding the contents of Nora's stomach between the folds of my polyester dress. Thank heavens somebody had invented drip-dry polyester because once the contents had been flushed down the toilet, the dress rinsed clean and the smell went, but it took quite a while to dry. I felt sorry for Nora because she was still feeling nauseous and suggested that she put her head on a pillow and try to sleep through it but, "Please face the cabin wall, just in case."

I thought back to my seasickness and gastroenteritis on the ship going out to Australia. I thought back to when I naively lifted my feet on the plane, then fell out of it at Whyalla. I thought back to the ship that now wasn't docking where we wanted it to dock and remembered the hectic overland bus drive to Melbourne. I thought back to the horrendous journey through the jungles of Malaya, and I thought back to the long, very long, plane trip to England. It was though my Book of Life page had an addendum that read, *"Oh, and by the way, traveling by land, sea or air will not be easy for you. You will have indescribable experiences that will be hard for even you to believe."* I must have traveled at least three times round this planet in my lifetime in airplane mileage and, without exception, I've had something unusual happen to me on every trip.

We finally taxied into Toronto airport and both of us could feel the excitement grabbing hold. We were in Canada. Canada, a place we'd only read about in school and Lorna and Marjorie's letters, and although both of us were happy to be there, my main purpose was to see if there was a future for my family there. Even though we'd kept in touch through letters and had seen Lorna and Marjorie when they'd visited England a couple of times, they had stayed primarily with other relatives, so neither of us had seen much of them, but now we had them all to ourselves. It crossed my mind that I had a lot to do within the next three weeks. I needed to find out if Canada was the place for us; that there was a future for my children, and that I'd get on okay with Marjorie, in particular. I gave myself three weeks to find out everything I needed to know in order to make an informed decision as to whether Brian and I ought to uproot our family once again. More like three minutes I'd say.

We got off the escalator after collecting our suitcases and were immediately surrounded in grins, arms, hugs and laughter from Lorna, Marjorie and Ted. What a fantastic feeling, and what a welcome. It was like coming home. Within seconds of seeing them, I remember thinking that I'd wish for nothing more in this life, if only the four of us could be together, forever. Within a few minutes, it seemed as though the invisible tear in the fabric of my life had been instantly mended as all four parts bonded. Everyone hugged each other as though it had been years since we'd last met, and when I walked outside and felt the hot July sun I just knew this country would be the best of all worlds. As I stood outside, I welcomed the clear blue skies and hot sun of 'my' Australia and threw away the heavily polluted and gray skies of Middlesborough. It was perfect, just perfect!

Marjorie and Lorna both lived and worked in the city of Toronto, the capital of the Province of Ontario. But it was to Lorna's home we were going, and my eyes were as big as saucers as the taxi drove us from the Airport through the city to her home in the suburbs that looked like a cross between a Swiss Chalet and a country cottage. Maybe it was because I was a driver that I noticed it, but I'd never seen so much traffic, with cars constantly overtaking from both the left and the right sides. Lorna assured me that once we got off the highway and onto side streets, the volume would fizzle out, but I couldn't help but compare the roads of the countries I'd lived in. England still had one-lane country roads that meandered all over the place; Australian roads were predominantly two-lane highways; but Canada beat them both with its six-lane highways and that's a lot of traffic!

Lorna and Ted's apartment was in the upper half of an ordinary house and you went up the stairs to their front door, as if you were going to bed. It had a living room that was quite large, a small bedroom, and a kitchen and bathroom. The owners of the house lived downstairs and had rented the upstairs so as to help with the mortgage, as houses were very expensive, especially in the city. Marjorie left to pick up 11-year-old Lindsay, and nine-year-old Nancy from her child minder, and when Ken came home from work, all four of them came back to Lorna's for supper. Both of Marjorie's boys, David and Ian, were now grown men and although both of them had called us 'Aunt' when they were small because of our age difference, this was a new era and we acknowledged each other as cousins, as did Ted. It was all a bit confusing for their sisters, Lindsay and Nancy, because they were introduced to both Nora and myself as, "This is your Aunt Nora and Aunt Nancy," whereas their brothers were our cousins. Talk about a brain scramble. It was marvelous reconnecting with our Canadian relatives, which was how we referred to them in England, and the next few hours passed in the blink of an eye, and both of us were sorry when Marjorie said it was time to go home but that she'd see us tomorrow.

Ted slept on a bed chesterfield in the living room, while Lorna, Nora and I all slept together in the bedroom, just like we did when we all lived in Templetown. Except instead of two old squeaky double beds, there was a single bed, plus bunk beds that Marjorie had passed on. I quickly grabbed the bottom bunk, just in case the seas were rough again, and before long with Nora above me, Lorna gently snoring on the bed opposite, drifted off to sleep. Both Nora and I awoke around 3 am, which to our bodies was 8 am, because of the five-hour time difference, and as neither of us could get back to sleep, we started talking in what we thought were

Marjorie & Lorna in 1974 at Centre Island,

whispers. After a few moments, Lorna, tiredly but good naturedly said, "Go back to sleep you two. It's not time to get up. We're going out in the morning." In an instant, she mentally transported us back to when we were small children who constantly talked in bed in Templetown and she would shout up the stairs, "Go to sleep you two. Don't make me come up there!" "Quick, blow the candle out before she comes up," Nora said, and we all chuckled at the memory.

We were up and about at daybreak too excited to try and sleep more, not wanting to miss a moment of time with Lorna and Marjorie and wanting to see everything we could possibly see while we were there. Lorna and Marjorie lived within walking distance of each other and as neither of them had a car, we examined each and every house as we walked over to Marjorie's home. The streetscape had nothing in common with either England or Australia as no two houses were the same. Detached houses were mixed in with semi-detached and small apartment blocks dotted most corners, and where there was a house on the corner the bottom floor had been turned into a convenience store, and everywhere we looked there were stores selling donuts and coffee, ice cream, Pizza, hamburgers, fried Chicken, or sandwiches. There were restaurants run by every nationality under the sun, such as Indian, Chinese, Greek and Japanese. I'd never seen so many places to buy ready-made food in my life, and most of them were open 24 hours a day. Both England and Australia were not as food friendly as Canada, as most of their stores closed promptly at 5 pm, so it was quite an eye-opener for 'the village kids' and both of us thought we'd ventured into an American movie set.

Marjorie and Ken had rented a whole house for their family of six, in the 'Beaches' area of Toronto and even though it was supposed to be a nice area, the house had a 'run-down' feel to it. They had done their best to spruce it up but as they didn't own it obviously didn't want to spend their hard-earned money on it, and the owners let the overall house run into disrepair. It was located in a street of houses that ran down the side of a long hill, and the bus ran along the bottom, which meant it was quite a hike from the bus stop to their bottom step. Just looking up from the street to their front door was enough to give anyone palpitations, because there were two sets of concrete steps running up the middle of the garden, each with its own landing and railings to hold onto, and both sets were extremely steep. I wondered how on earth Ken managed to cut the grass on either side, and figured he must have had a rope tied round his waist from the rail for safety, while he hung off it. We made it to the top of the steps and flopped down on a bench outside the front door. "You should have an escalator instead of steps Marjorie, that's a heck of a climb," Nora said.

Marjorie's daughters, Lindsay and Nancy, were beautiful girls. Both of them had long blonde hair in pony-tails, and Lindsay let me brush her hair and braid it around her head so that she looked like a Swiss milkmaid. They were easy girls to love and I wished I could have been around them in their infancy. I'd always wanted a daughter and if John had been a girl he would have also been named 'Allison Lindsay', but it wasn't to be, and it came as quite a surprise when Marjorie gave birth to her next daughter, and she asked Lindsay what she wanted to call the baby and Lindsay said, "Nancy" after Aunt Nancy. We would be forever known as 'big' Auntie Nancy, and 'little' Auntie Nancy. Sorry 'little' Nan.

Toronto had so much public transportation, that nobody really needed a car. Apart from the bus, there were streetcars that ran along tramlines hooked up to an overhead electric cable, plus subways and trains. The choice was amazing and, for the first week, we made great use of it.

Both Lorna and Marjorie had taken time off from work, so with Lindsay and Nancy not needing a child minder because both were on school holidays, we totaled seven people who constantly hopped on and off public transportation like pro's. There was Lorna and Ted, and Marjorie,

Lindsay and Nancy, and Nora and I, and there was so much to see and do that it was unbelievable and everything was practically geared for children.

During the first week, we visited Pioneer Village that I initially thought was a replica of some outlying areas of Templetown. However, it was actually a theme park that demonstrated how immigrants to Canada survived in the 19th century. There were over 20 buildings on the site that had been transported from all over Canada to be conserved, such as a Blacksmith's, a one-room schoolhouse, a Doctor's house and a hotel which had a restaurant in the basement that made meals out of the village's produce. People in period costume sheared sheep, milled flour for bread, grew vegetables and herbs, and took care of a multitude of animals such as horses, goats, sheep, hens and chickens. It was fascinating, once again, to watch women in long heavy dresses covered in pinafores, bake bread in front of an open fire with an oven to one side – shades of my youth.

Lorna and Marjorie crammed as much sightseeing as possible into the first week of our visit because the newspapers reported that Toronto's public transportation workers were threatening to go on strike which would have made it very awkward to get around. We went by bus to visit Casa Loma, a huge European-style castle built right in the middle of the city, and both of us wondered why this was on the list of things to see until it was explained that this was the only castle to ever be built in Canada. It had been built to the specifications of a very, very rich man who went bankrupt, and the place was abandoned and given over to neglect and decay. Years and years later, a group of civic-minded people, the Jaycee Lions, raised enough money to start restoring and furnishing the castle in the era it was built and they made history come alive. When enough people gathered in each room a voice, pretending to be the original owner came over a loud speaker and described the room in detail. The Jaycee Lions mentally transported us back to the turn of the century and to the castle's historic importance in the settling of Toronto. What realism! I couldn't help but wish England would do something similar to all the castles and cathedrals they had. It would have made them much more interesting.

We also visited Ontario Place, a government owned recreation area, mostly for children. It consisted of a large group of predominantly glass buildings, connected to each other by walkways with glass walls and each building, consisting of numerous rooms, stood on stilts in the waters of Lake Ontario. Each room had a different theme, and the children could find themselves playing with Lego blocks in one room, and racing cars in another. There was also a different kind of building, shaped like a 10-story high golf ball that held the biggest movie screen known to the world at the time. To one side of the buildings, pedal and rowing boats were contained, while on the other, sailing yachts lay moored for easy access to the lake. There were lots of things for children to do outside also: climb the rigging of a pretend ship; run through an open building while trying to miss huge punching bags; go down the big water slide; picnic with your own food or buy food from lots of vendors dotted around the big grassy areas. It was a fantasy play land and I loved it. Everywhere seemed to be directed at children, and Ontario Science Centre was no different. It meant a much longer bus ride along the top of the city, but it was absolutely worth it. It was another children's paradise. Different rooms had different activities and they reduced the mystery of science to actual 'hands on' play. It was a fascinating place and it would have taken two or three days to see all of it. In England, we were used to telling the children not to touch anything and to only look with their eyes just in case it broke and we'd have to pay for it, but that wasn't the case in Canada. They encouraged children to see, feel, touch, and smell, and built specific facilities to ensure they did.

There was so much to do and to see it was impossible to fit it all in, and we opted to visit the Toronto Islands which were not too far from Ontario Place. Lorna and Marjorie put a picnic together and we all caught the streetcar down through the middle of the city to the lakeshore where we caught a ferry across to the islands. What an amazing place Toronto turned out to be.

Everything just got better and better, and the next place to visit was more marvelous than the last. It was only a 10-minute boat ride from the mainland to the Islands but it gave us the opportunity to study Toronto's skyline of high rise buildings and apartments dotted along the lakeshore. The buildings were so clean they sparkled and various sizes of yachts bobbed up and down at moorings in front of them. Fancy that, you could be sitting at home one minute, and then jump into your boat the next! The Toronto Islands consisted of a small light-wing airport and a few cottages that had been settled years before which the owners wouldn't give up, so the city built the park of a few hundred acres of grass and trees around them. It was a great place to relax after the hectic pace of the city, or to picnic, or swim on the beaches at the far side. Except for Marjorie who stayed with the bags, the rest of us hired bicycles and rode around the bike paths, before having our picnic on the beautifully manicured lawns. We even saw signs that said, "Please walk on the grass." What with our senses being assaulted at every turn, it was an exhausting but exhilarating first week and I remember writing a tongue-in-cheek postcard to Brian which said, "Not coming back, send the children on!" I loved everything I saw, from the busy shops lining the streets to the huge department stores. We were spoiled for choice as to what to do, and I loved it.

Nora and I and 12 of my Canadian family travelled by car 1-1/2 hours from Toronto to see Niagara Falls in all its glory, and although I'd read about them as a small child, nothing could compare to the actual sight. The Niagara Parks Commission had cultivated the surrounding land with eye-pleasing lawns, trees and flower beds which created a perfect setting for a unique jewel. It was truly breathtaking. To be able to stand so close to the edge of the Fall's and watch the dizzying volume of water go thundering over the edge was hypnotic, and I could well imagine that if the half wall and strong steel railings weren't in place it would have been easy to fall in. Obviously, the main attraction in Niagara was the Fall's, but some very enterprising people had converted the rest of Niagara into a permanent recreation town, and the streets were filled with such attractions as The Haunted House, Madam Tussard's Wax Museum, and Ripley's Believe it or Not. There were tacky souvenir shops everywhere, along with fast food outlets, and the whole place somehow tarnished the image of the magnificent Fall's and I was a bit disappointed. I much preferred sitting on the cultivated grass lawns eating our picnic to scurrying in and out of the amusement arcades.

The next week of our holiday was taken up with traveling further afield, and the same family members piled into cars and headed off for Ottawa, the capital of Canada. Ottawa was another beautiful city, with architecture much older than Toronto's, and a huge tourist attraction, and both Nora and I must have forgotten our history lessons in school because both of us were surprised to learn that Canada was only 200 years old. The tour guide had only just gotten the words out of his mouth when Nora turned to me and whispered, "I have some antiques nearly that old." It certainly put into perspective how really young Canada was.

Our next stop was the very old city of Kingston. This was a border town between Canada and the United States and if I remember right, it was one of the first places to be settled in Ontario, and I think it was originally the capital. From there it was possible to take a boat tour all the way up the river, past thousands of islands, and into the States, but it wasn't allowed to stop as there was no definite border up river. It just did a three-hour round trip. The boat tour was known as 'The Thousand Island Tour' and these islands were so famous they even had a salad dressing named after them. One has to wonder why anyone would want to sit on a boat for three hours just sailing up, and back again, until you learn the secondary reason that all the islands were inhabited. Now, grant you, the whole area was beautiful with lots of islands in all shapes and sizes, but the definite attraction were the buildings on them. This was where the rich and famous built their holiday homes, ranging from cottages to mansions and it must have driven them crazy when boat tours gawked at them all day long. Nora and I thought it must be similar to bus tours in Hollywood, "And this is Marilyn Monroe's house and the next house is John Wayne's," and so on. It did feel a bit strange watching people go about their business on their own island, but it was fascinating all the same. Some of those houses were so huge we mused how it was possible to build such big places on such a small plot of land. I mean, it must have been quite an exercise in juggling building material, as most of the houses only left room for a path around the outside, before they'd drop into the water. Where the island was much larger, we'd see much bigger houses, harbours with much bigger boats, and tennis courts, and the outsides were so magnificent with ornamental balustrades we wondered what the inside must look like. On the other hand, there was one small island maybe only 12 feet square, with a house on it and we wondered how long it would be before a surging wave from one of the tour boats would swamp it into extinction. It was all so fascinating and everyone enjoyed it.

Exhausted from a long six-hour drive home, we thanked our drivers, and decided to take it easy for a couple of days. That is, until Lorna decided to take us shopping. Now if I have one hang-up in life it is shopping. Contrary to every other woman on this planet, I just hate having to elbow my way around stores trying to find the most perfect this, that or the other and get no pleasure out of it whatsoever. I tried to get out of it, but after much persuasion by the others, decided not to spoil their shopping trip so I acquiesced. Lorna had worked for the Canadian head office of Sears since she'd arrived in Canada and decided that we couldn't go home without shopping at her favorite Sear's outlet store. It was an American company, with a huge following in the States and in Canada, and they sold everything from household furniture and appliances to clothes, and from gardening equipment to hammers, all at reasonable prices, and if you couldn't find what you wanted in Sears, you weren't looking hard enough. Their outlet store was different to their main stores in that it was stocked with 'end of lines' and slightly damaged merchandise, all at rock bottom prices. That suited me just fine. With Lorna's help in browsing around, I bought the best of the best to take home for gifts, and it was such a great shopping experience, I went back two more times with them.

I liked everything I saw and experienced about Canada. I liked the fresh air, the sunshine, the friendliness of the people, the places I'd been, and the family I'd been with. I liked everything. When I asked Lorna if she thought moving to Canada would be right for us, she said, "You have to make your own mind up Nan. I cannot tell you one way or the other. If you want to come here, you have to make the decision." I was a bit taken aback by her response because I thought she'd say, "Yes, come. It will be great having you here. Come as soon as you like!" But when I thought about it later, it dawned on me that she was right. She couldn't make that kind of decision for me. What if it didn't work out? What if I had to admit defeat and go home again? She would feel awful if she'd encouraged me to come and after leaving everything behind again, ended up hating it. This was one decision I would have to make on my own. It was up to me to decide my family's future. All too soon it was time to pack our suitcases ready to leave the next day for Toronto airport to fly home to our families. It was a bit heart wrenching for both of us, saying goodbye to half of our family, not knowing when, or if, we'd see them again, and both of us were in tears as we made our way onto the plane.

We spent the first few hours sitting quietly in our seats discussing the merits of Canada when I noticed an unusual smell. I tracked it down to one of our flight bags that were tucked under the seat in front of us, and as I lifted the bag up, the smell took off and permeated all around us. "Oh, my Lord," I said. "It's the egg and onion sandwiches that Lorna made. The heat of the cabin must have warmed them up." By now, Nora was having a fit of the giggles. Both of us had hoped nobody would notice we'd brought our own food, just in case it wasn't allowed, but it was impossible to ignore the mouth-watering delicious smell. "We'd better eat them really quick," I said. "Before anybody asks where it's coming from." Well, I hadn't gotten them unwrapped before some people behind us stopped a Hostess and asked what they were cooking in the galley because something smelled wonderful, and with very guilty feelings, we stuffed those sandwiches down us and looked the picture of innocence when the Air Hostess asked, "Who's been frying onions then?"

Once back on English soil, my thoughts and feelings of Canada had to be put into words, and before we even got off the tarmac Brian wanted to know all about it. "I liked it Brian. It's a great place for children. It feels a lot like Australia with a bit of England thrown in. I really liked it," I said. Nora's husband, Stivvie, apart from giving us a hug and a kiss, was very quiet during the drive to our home in Middlesborough and I understood why. He really didn't want to hear that Canada was a great place and that we were thinking of moving away again. Nora had said on the plane that although she'd like to live in Canada, she couldn't. Stivvie had a very secure job working for Barclay's Bank, and as his mother was now a widow he would not leave her and, as she got on so well with our mother, Beattie, she could not bear the thought of leaving her either. So, both of them had looked on Canada as a vacation only, whereas I had gone to reconnoiter on behalf of my family. We had totally different viewpoints and there was a touch of sadness in the air as they left to drive home to Durham.

Now that the excitement of visiting Canada was over, there was a lot to think about, and the decision to sell everything and move once again was not going to be made lightly this time. For one thing, it was very expensive. The real estate market was still down and houses, even if they managed to sell with all the unemployment in the area, were not selling for anything like they were worth, and if we didn't get a decent price for the house we couldn't afford to ship many of our possessions, so my mental questions started, "Why am I even thinking about doing this? Do I really want to start again? Would we give the boys a better future? Would we have a better standard of living than what we had? Would Brian be able to get another job? Would we be able to buy another house? How long will it take me to furnish it again?" Like a mental broken record, they played over and over in my mind. I'd argue with myself, "Brian has a great job with a secure future. *Yes, but for how long really?* We have a nice house. *We can get another one.* The children are settled in school. *They're young, they'll soon settle in another one.* We don't need to go anywhere else. *There's more family in Canada.* We're all happy here. *We could be happy there."*

Over the next couple of weeks, Brian and I examined every question inside out and backside foremost, until we decided there wasn't much point in trying to guess what kind of life we could expect to live in Canada, if we weren't going to be allowed in. We needed to take it one step at a time and apply for Immigration before we drove ourselves crazy wondering if we were doing the right thing. This wasn't the same as moving to Australia when, as a young couple, we threw our destiny to the winds. Or even in making the decision to winter in England with our children because we knew we had family there. This was a really big decision because the children and I had settled and built a new life in England, in my homeland.

Oh Canada!

We both decided that as children in Canada were six years old before they attended regular school, we would put any thoughts of moving there to one side until John, at 5 years old and already attending school could slip into the Canadian education system, and practically six months to the day, Brian came home from work and said, "Nan, it's time to apply for Immigration to Canada." "What's happened?" I asked. "Nothing in particular, only we had planned on going to Canada after Australia, and I think it's time to go now," he replied. Then he paused before saying, "I don't want to be on my deathbed saying I wish we had......., I'd much rather say, pity we did......." Well there wasn't much I could say in response to that. After all, what were a house, job and country between friends? So, with my predestined fate of either moving houses every two years, and countries every four, we sent off our Immigration application.

Things took off at a gallop and after visiting Canada House in Manchester in January, being interviewed and completing our medical examinations, we were informed in March that we'd been accepted and were told to take up residency in Canada within twelve months. Twelve months, great! What a difference from the five months' notice I'd had to go to Australia. Twelve whole months in which to plan things! Twelve months in which to sell the house, get rid of furniture, pack up our belongings and book our travel. But only twelve inadequate months in which to find a way to tell Ella and Tommy we were leaving them again! Well, there was no time like the present, and the sooner we moved the less anxious I'd get, and we planned to move when the children's schooling finished for the summer, at the end of June or beginning of July. So instead of having a very long twelve months, we reduced it to four months and that made things very tight. Brian had just enough time to give three months' notice and he needed to do it practically straight away. But we agreed not to tell his folks until much nearer the time. Looking back, I think we should have removed July from my calendar and I'd never have moved anywhere at all.

The 'For Sale' sign was put up in the front window of the house, and numerous people came through, but no offers. This was quite upsetting because we'd spent a fortune renovating the place and I thought it would have been snapped up. After all, French doors and new wall-to-wall carpeting weren't exactly normal in the north east. The house had all new windows, plumbing and electric wiring, plus a brand-new kitchen and toilet. It was reasonably priced, and I thought people were getting a bargain. What more did they want? They wanted the lot! Two female schoolteachers bought our house and once they heard we were emigrating asked what furniture we were leaving behind. I said I'd leave absolutely everything if they allowed us to live in the house until the very last moment, and they agreed. We gave them a set of house keys and in return for buying our house, we left all the carpets and curtains, the bedroom, living room and dining room furniture, two television sets, refrigerator, stove, washing machine, toaster, and an iron. We left the whole house fully furnished except for the two beautifully upholstered chairs that Aunt Mabel and Uncle Joe had given us and, after Aunt Mabel said we could, we gave them to Dora's Aunt Alice who had regularly babysat for us, who loved them.

As soon as the house was sold, we wondered how to tell Ella and Tommy about our plans. We knew they weren't going to say, "Good for you, that's where you should have gone instead of coming back to England." No, they were bound to be upset and there was no easy way to tell them. They had gotten used to the idea of being grandparents, and Tommy really did love the children. We'd all gotten along fine since the first holiday they spent with us in our home and it was like lambs to the slaughter driving to Delves Lane to break the news. "Mam, Dad, I have something to tell you," said Brian. Both stopped what they were doing to look at him. "We've sold the house and we're moving to Canada," he continued. Ella took off to the kitchen as her usual exit, and Tommy exploded, "You're what! How can you do this to your Mother again!" And, turning to look at me he uttered, "I will never forgive you for as long as I live Nancy!"

Although upset at his outburst in front of the children, I wasn't totally surprised as I knew he'd blame me again, only this time he would be justified to some extent. There wasn't much point in hanging around, so I helped the children into their coats and we said goodbye. They would have to deal with the heartache of Brian and the children leaving, all on their own. Since their obnoxious letter to me in Australia I had pushed them to the periphery of my life, as I knew neither of them wanted me as a daughter-in-law, and although I did feel sorry for them, I wasn't going to let either of them brow-beat me anymore, and for the next three weeks I refused to visit them, until Brian practically got down on his hands and knees and begged me.

As our remaining time in England decreased, Ella's spiteful comments and crying increased, and after living through some very emotional visits, I just had to put my foot down. My family came first. Basically, I was still a quiet, non-confrontational person, but I'd grown a backbone in Kuala Lumpur and I realized I didn't owe them any consideration at all, not even a courtesy visit since they were being so horrible. The atmosphere was electric as I sharply told both Ella and Tommy that I was not going to let the boys visit any more if things didn't improve, and you'd have thought I'd just slithered out from primordial ooze from the look on Tommy's face. No words were spoken, but his look said it all, "Who the hell are you to tell us how to behave!"

I suppose my ultimatum must have been quite shocking to them. They weren't used to me venturing an opinion or stating the obvious. In all the years I'd known them, I'd never voiced my real thoughts, I'd laughed at Tommy's silly jokes, I'd listened to him ramble on about anything and everything and I'd put up with disrespect and innuendo's thrown at me by Ella. I didn't like being put in the position of having to tell my elders that their behaviour was unacceptable. Shouldn't they have known that themselves? Weren't they raised in the same way I was, to respect the rights of others? They were very surprised and it went silent for a moment. Then Tommy quietly said, "Well you've got to understand that Ella is really upset he's going away again. She's just got used to having Brian back, and now he's leaving again. I don't know what to do about it." Well, out of the mouths of babes and drunks comes the truth. They weren't bothered at all that I and the children were leaving the country, only Brian.

Hearing Tommy say those words out loud hurt me to the core, and I gathered the children's coats and started getting them dressed to go home. Nobody was going to make use of me, or my children, and if it was only Brian they wanted, it was only Brian they'd get in future. "Where are you going?" Tommy asked. "We're not wanted here, so we're going home," I replied. Tommy must have played his words over in his head because the next thing he said was, "Sit down lass. I didn't mean it like that. We love the bairns." Yea, right! I'd once accused Ella of loving her dog more than she loved the children and she replied, "Well I've known the dog longer!" It was on the tip of my tongue to lash out at him but I couldn't. I wasn't very good at the thrust and parry of verbal swordsmanship. I was more like a Lancaster Bomber who just dropped the bomb and flew away, then went back in a couple of weeks after things had settled down again, because absolutely nobody in the north east would be so dishonorable as to resurrect an argument.

It took me such a long time to get over confrontation. First, I'd get mad at myself that I'd even said anything. Then I'd get mad because I'd not said what I really wanted to say. Then I'd go over both sides of the argument in my head and find the most perfect words that I could have used, and just after I'd gotten the argument won, I'd see it from the other person's point of view, and within no time I'd convince myself that I was totally in the wrong and would apologize. It never failed, I always gave in first. True to the working man's code of ethics of arguing one day and of paying for a round of drinks the next, nothing was regurgitated on our next visit and they gradually accepted the fact that we were leaving the country once again. We arranged, and paid for, a telephone to be installed in their living room and promised to phone them at least once a month, and I know it was going to be hard on them not being able to see Brian, but at least they could still speak to him.

To our great surprise, Ella accepted the fact that we were moving away again much quicker than Tommy, and on one of our visits she went into her bedroom and came back with her Beaver Lamb full-length coat hanging over her arm. She loved that coat and had worn it to our wedding 12 years previous. "Here," she said, handing me the coat. "You're going to need this in Canada. I've heard that it is snow and ice for most of the year. You'll need it more than I will." I'd have never guessed in a million years that she would give me one of her treasured possessions, and all I could say was, "Thank you very much. That's very nice of you." And not having experienced a Canadian winter, her guess was as good as mine as to how cold the weather would be. Maybe she knew something I didn't! When we said our last goodbye, Tommy really surprised us by saying, "I've had time to think about you moving away again and I think you're doing the right thing. The way things are going here in the north east, there'll be nowt for anybody soon, much less the children when they grow up. Just keep in touch." Ella, although in tears, promised to come and visit us after we'd gotten settled, but Tommy said he'd wait until he got his own wings because he didn't trust any airline.

Because we were leaving the house totally furnished we didn't have the frustration of finding new homes for our big stuff and with mostly soft furnishings to pack, it didn't take long. I'd given most of my fine crystal to my friends and neighbors so that they would remember us, and we surprised Aunt Mabel by giving her our Australian 99-piece dinner, tea and coffee service that she'd always admired. Once again, Brian's bureau was given to Ella to look after until such time as we could retrieve it. Dora loaned me some sheets and blankets for our beds, and on our last morning in England I returned them to her, locked the door behind me and put the key back through the letterbox before getting into the taxi for the airport. It was the least aggravating time I'd ever had when moving countries.

We arrived at Middlesborough airport for the first leg of our journey to Canada only to find that the baggage handlers had gone on strike that morning, and if we wanted our luggage to travel with us we'd have to physically put it on the plane ourselves. So, with the children and me standing beside the carry-on bags, on the tarmac next to the plane, Brian had to struggle to get two steamer trunks and two large suitcases into the hold all on his own. "Thank goodness I won't have to do that in London," he said, as the luggage was booked directly through to Toronto, and I agreed. Then with our two boys, aged nearly 7 and 6, each carrying their own teddy bear, we helped them up the steps into the plane and sat down. It was only a one-hour flight to London and we'd no sooner got on the plane and settled down, when we had to get off, to catch an Air Canada, 747 Jumbo Jet, flight to Toronto, in Canada. Excitement was beginning to build in all of us, and the boys were wide-eyed at all the planes waiting at Heathrow Airport. We had time on our hands, and once we got our boarding passes, we relaxed by the big windows and watched the boys as they enjoyed the planes coming in to land, or taking off. We had two lovely children. They were well behaved, and well mannered, and a real pleasure to be around. Not only did Brian and I chuckle over some of their comments to each other about the different planes, other people did the same. They were our pride and joy.

New Beginnings

The Air Canada flight was nearly empty, and we had two rows of seats all to ourselves, and after a marvelously comfortable and relaxing flight, we arrived in Toronto, Canada, in July 1975. After collecting the luggage, we had to wait quite a while for Custom's clearance, but with both boys carrying their own teddy bear, and with David helping Brian to push the luggage cart while John held my hand, we all walked optimistically towards a bright new future. We went through the double doors into the terminal to find Lorna and Ted standing right in front of us wearing the biggest grins on their faces you're ever likely to see. "Welcome to Canada," Lorna said, as she thrust a bunch of red roses into my hands, all the while grabbing me and hugging me as though she'd never let go. Flowers, and love's red roses at that! What a lovely gesture! I just knew we were all going to be happy here. "We thought you must have changed your minds about coming," she said. "No, no," I laughed. "Sorry about the long wait, but the Customs people kept us for over an hour while they checked our papers," I said. "Well, you're here now, and we're keeping you, and to make sure you don't go anywhere else, we've got some bags of cement to put in your shoes Brian," she chuckled.

The boys were excited to meet up with 'Uncle' Ted and Aunt Lorna again, and they chattered away telling them all about the two planes we'd been on. Thank goodness Ted had a lot of patience with children, because he listened intently to all they had to say. For the time being, it was arranged that we'd stay with Lorna and Ted in their apartment, and I wondered where we'd all sleep, but Lorna had that covered. She had rented another room from the owners, in their part of the house, and Brian and I would sleep downstairs while the boys would sleep in the same bunk beds that Nora and I had slept in. Later that evening, Marjorie, Ken and the girls, Lindsay and Nancy, and their son David and his wife Donna, came over for supper, and we enjoyed a lovely family reunion. After they'd gone home and it was time for sleep, I remember standing at the bottom of the house owner's bed and saying to Brian, "Well husband. It's not every wife who, at 32 years old, can say that after 12 years of marriage she has no house or furniture and a husband with no job, and two children, and that all her worldly goods are stashed into 10 tea chests sailing the high seas, and there is only $800.00 in the bank, and that she is starting from scratch for the fourth time." He laughingly joked in response, "Well you must be getting used to it by now."

It took the children and me a few days to recover from the time lag but not Brian. He was dressed and out of the door the very next morning before we were even out of bed and within the first week he and Lorna found a whole house to rent between us, and we moved. I think, at that time, if Lorna had known how her and Ted's lives were to change because of our arrival, she might have been slightly more hesitant in her welcome. Brian set about finding work. He explored Toronto all on his own and walked up and down Bloor Street where the employment agencies were and got the same response from practically every person he met, "No Canadian experience, no job!" That was a bit discouraging to me and I did start to worry about it, but not Brian. He knew that if he pounded the pavement and knocked on enough doors, he'd find work of some kind, and in repeating a visit to one employment agency, he chanced upon an American company wanting to hire a Controller. They wanted somebody with international finance and manufacturing experience and Brian fit the bill, and within two weeks of us arriving in Canada, he started working for a company manufacturing cosmetics, just a bus ride away. I had faith in my husband's qualifications and abilities, but it was a bit nerve-wracking until he found work and was able to take the pressure off.

I spent the first three weeks in Canada frantically scrubbing and cleaning the rental house from top to bottom, and painting and wall papering because Billy, June and their children, young Billy, Keith and Susan were due to arrive on holiday at any moment. Now, having another five family members come to stay at the same time as my four had just arrived would have been enough to panic any normal woman, but not Lorna. Not only had she found permanent shelter for my family, but she had everything planned so that we'd all be comfortable. She had been collecting and storing furniture for more than six months and from her tiny little single bedroom apartment, she furnished a three-bedroom house. Every time a friend of hers got a new piece of furniture, Lorna would either buy their redundant piece, or they would donate it to her for us. What lovely friends she had, and the nicest piece of furniture we were given was a settee and chair from my Anteloper, Isabella Crowther.

Lorna and Isabella had been best friends since they were teenagers and had met up again years later in Canada and Isabella and her husband, Ron, were naturally adopted into our family. Isabella always referred to herself during family gatherings as an interloper until one day she was referred to as 'Anteloper Isabella' and the name stuck.

Lorna, 90 yrs old, 2020

Anteloper Isabella Crowther, 88 years old, 2020

It was a bit of a puzzle how we'd manage to find places for 11 people to sleep in only three bedrooms, but Lorna had a plan. Our two boys slept in our bedroom in the back of the house, on the mattress off our bed, and even though the base was a bit uncomfortable, we managed just fine. Billy, Ted, young Billy and Keith slept in the large front bedroom; either on shaky-downs which were a few blankets heaped one on top of the other and was quite comfortable, unless you happened to roll around the bed, or in sleeping bags, and Lorna, June and Susan slept in the third bedroom next to the bathroom, on the single bed and bunk-beds. There now, everybody had a bed, and with so many people and children in the house, it was full of fun and laughter.

As I had discovered on my vacation to Toronto, there was so much for everybody to see and do, and even though Brian was at work, the rest of us hopped on and off streetcars, buses and subways and had a fantastic time. David and John thoroughly enjoyed all the places we went to and whereas the others had a limited time to see and do everything, my two boys rejoiced that they'd be able to go back, time after time. All too soon it was time for my English relatives to return home, and although I was sad to see them go, I was happy to remain with Lorna and Marjorie as I had now joined the ranks of the Canadian relatives, and for the rest of the summer Lindsay and Nancy walked over to our house to be with us, instead of their normal child minder.

Brian was itching to get his own transportation after 'window shopping' at various garages with new and used cars for sale, but since neither of us had a Canadian driving license, it seemed a bit pointless to have a vehicle sitting in the driveway that nobody could drive. We had no idea at the time that our British driving licenses would let us drive in Canada for our first three months. But even if I'd known that, I wouldn't have been very happy getting into a car with someone who'd had no experience of driving in Canada. English and Australians drove on the left-hand side of the road, which was normal to us, whereas everyone in Canada drove on the right-hand side and it was just too disorientating, so I insisted we each take six driving lessons from a driving school, just for safety's sake, and within another three weeks both of us passed our driving tests with flying colours, and headed out to buy our first Canadian car. We could have bought a small car for just my family, but as neither Lorna nor Marjorie had cars, we ended up buying a second-hand 10-seater station wagon that would enable all of us to go out together. What a huge car, and although it was a gas guzzler it was the most perfect vehicle to transport all 10 of us wherever we wanted to go and now that we had the freedom of the roads, we went everywhere. Lorna and Marjorie and families saw more of Canada driving around with us during those first few weeks of our arrival than they'd seen in all the years they'd lived there without us. Ah, the luxury of four wheels and a driving license!

September came and it was time for the children to attend school, and the house we rented was just walking distance away. I remember dressing them in their English school uniform of short pants, shirt and tie, knee socks and polished leather sandals the first morning, and when they came home at lunchtime David insisted on changing into the same kind of jeans, t-shirt and sneakers that the other children wore. He didn't want to be different, he wanted to fit in and not stand out as a newcomer, and he was right. It was a different country with different ideas, it was more cosmopolitan and relaxed, and I agreed never to dress him in a school uniform again.

Once the children went back to school I had time on my hands and apart from cleaning and cooking I wondered what to do with myself. Yes, having 60 channels on the television to choose from instead of the three I'd had in England was great, but it was hardly productive. It wasn't adding anything to our savings, which were just limping along. We needed to give our bank balance a shot in the arm, so I decided to find a part-time job that would allow me to make some money but would allow me to be home with the children also. Apart from a few weeks here and there, doing temporary secretarial work after both children had started regular school in England, I hadn't really worked since my first pregnancy, so I wasn't overly confident about finding something suitable. But Marjorie came to the rescue this time. She worked for a temp agency called Office Overload and persuaded me to take their typing test just in case something came up. Typing was something I loved to do, and I remembered when I'd just started work at the Company and was volunteered to help in the secretarial pool. I stood beside the Company Director's secretary waiting for her to finish a document and was just awestruck watching her hands fly over the keys on the manual typewriter. Just as she finished, I mentioned that I'd never be able to type that fast and she said, "It's all in how you hold your hands over the keyboard, and years and years of practice, practice, practice." Even though my typing skills might have gotten a bit rusty since the last time I worked, I thought with all the practice I'd had over the years, it would just be like riding a bike, you never forget, so I took the test.

They gave me a manual typewriter and I achieved 102 words per minute, which I thought was pretty decent, seeing as how I'd not used a manual machine in more than 10 years, and when I mentioned it to the supervisor she said, "Why didn't you say you could use an electric typewriter? Please do the test again." And this time I achieved 120 words per minute, and from the comments I heard, that score was practically unheard of. They gave me a one-week assignment within the Marketing Department of Canada Post Office down by the lakeshore, and I think the boss's name was Paul Martin and as I shook his hand I said, "Mr. Martin. Did Office Overload tell you that I can only work until 2 pm each day because I must be home for my children when they come from school?" His face sort of scowled as he replied, "No they didn't and that's going to be a problem because I need somebody here until 5 pm each day." "I'm terribly sorry," I said, "They were supposed to have told you, but if you phone them they will replace me, but it will probably be tomorrow before they can do that." He looked at me with some annoyance, "Well, if you can stay for today I'll ask them to send somebody else for the rest of the assignment!" he replied. He took me over to a desk with a huge pile of correspondence on it, and I must have been getting through it much quicker than he expected, because before lunch he came back and said, "Nancy, I've never seen anybody type so fast or so accurately before. If it's okay with you, I'm happy to have you work just five hours a day for as long as you want." Except for school holidays when they temporarily replaced me, my one-week assignment lasted ten months until we moved to the suburbs.

I also made a good impression on Office Overload because they persuaded me to work from 5 pm until 10 pm every night in their head office. I'd arrive home from Canada Post around about 2:30 pm in the afternoon just before the children came home at 3 pm. Then I'd make supper and we'd eat ours just as Lorna came in the door at 4:30 pm, then head off to start work again at 5 pm in the big city of Toronto, and Brian would come and pick me up at 10 pm. It was very hard work, but both of us knew we'd never be able to afford to buy another home on just Brian's savings. We had taken to heart Bill Dodd's advice of years before, when he said we'd be better off buying our own home, rather than paying the mortgage for someone else, and with the intention of doing just that, we scoured the housing market for something we could afford. Even though I liked the amenities Toronto had to offer, I really didn't want to raise the boys in another 'street' environment after having that experience in England. I was rather hoping we could find an environment similar to what we'd experienced in Australia. Yes, the house was in a street of maybe 16 houses, but it did have 20 feet of land on either side and sat on ½ acre that gave lots of space for young boisterous children to play.

Given our budget, our search took us further and further away from the city, to the outlying suburbs of Mississauga and, in particular, to the small town of Meadowvale that was still in the early stages of being planned and built. We stopped at an information centre and were delighted to see the whole area at a glance, complete with models of houses, schools, churches, and even a man-made lake in the centre of town. Each area had distinct housing of no more than 100 dwellings of either detached or semi-detached houses, bungalows, townhouses or small apartment blocks, and were connected to each other by parkland and bike paths, or little overhead bridges where the road encroached. It promised to be a safe and secure environment for young children to play and to attend school and we all thought it was perfect.

We went through pamphlets regarding house details on upcoming housing projects, and over the next few weekends did some serious research into the quality of their homes. We visited model houses completed in other areas and really put them to the test, and the people in charge of these homes must have thought we were mad. Whereas other people would look at the overall size of the house, and check out the lovely model furnishings, we checked the basics, "These floorboards squeak. Those stair hand railings are loose. There's not much water pressure coming out of those taps. They didn't do a very good job installing those light fixtures." We picked at the bones of each house, and the finishing work they did, before settling on a builder called 'Philmore.'

Practically every house in Canada has a basement that is basically another room the length and width of the house, rising from the foundations of the house. They need a basement so as to house the huge central heating furnace and the foot-square ductwork that runs like spaghetti underneath the ground floor, before running up inside the walls to the living quarters. Most builders ensure this room is raised sufficiently above ground so that windows can be installed and instead of having a dark deep dungeon, people 'finish' their basement so as to add extra living space to their homes. Our original intention was to find a home with an upstairs large enough for my family, and a huge basement that we could have 'finished' for Lorna and Ted, plus their two small dogs. Coming across this new town was the best thing that could have happened to us at the time, because with a bit of juggling in the finance area, both Lorna and I were able to buy a home of our own. We each bought a brand new three-bedroom Executive Townhouse – sounds grand, doesn't it? And it was. Even though we owned the house and could do whatever we wanted to the inside, the residents collectively owned all the land with strict rules as to its upkeep, and each homeowner paid a monthly fee to cover the cost of maintaining the exterior of the house, plus snowplowing, and landscaping. Lorna and Ted bought #33, we bought #34, and my cousin David and his wife Donna bought #36, and we all traveled the 30 miles or so from Toronto to Meadowvale over the winter to watch 'our' houses being built. It was very exciting.

Our first winter in Canada was an experience none of us will ever forget and thank goodness, if not mentally then at least physically, we were prepared. Luckily for us, Lorna and Ted had taken us shopping for suitable winter clothes, such as hats, scarves and gloves for all of us, knee-length boots and a fur-lined knee-length jacket with a drawstring hood for Brian, boots for me, and snow suits and boots for the children. We passed the comment that they'd be much too hot to wear, but they knew better and we needed everything we bought plus much more. Canada had the worst winter in over 50 years with record snowfalls and daily temperatures of minus 40, and I thought hell had frozen over at last. It took everybody by surprise and I began to think Ella had had prior warning when she gave me her fur coat. Nothing moved on the roads, no bus or tram was running, and no car was able to get out of a driveway, all of which contributed to an eerily quiet winter scene. The trees were laden with snow, and everywhere looked like a winter wonderland picture postcard. The sun, even though it had no warmth in it, was shining brightly and making everyone's eyes squint against the dazzling white of the snow. It was beautiful to look at, and I'd have been happy to stay in the warm indoors doing just that, until the children asked if they could go out and play in it.

Once warmly dressed in heavily padded snow suits, which was just as well, because the snow came up and over their shoulders Ted and Brian decided that as they couldn't possibly get to work, they'd go out and play also and persuaded me to come. Trussed up with no part of my body exposed to the cold, except for my nose, I wore knee-length lamb's wool lined leather boots, and Ella's fur coat over the top of my winter jacket held together with a belt around my middle, and I must have looked like the original Abominable Snowman. I'd just gotten outside when it started snowing again, and in no time at all I was completely covered in snow and the hairs in my nose froze, so I hastily beat a path back indoors. If this was a normal Canadian winter, then give me back my Australian winter of plus 60 degrees, or even my English winter of two inches of snow. The boys, on the other hand, all four of them, absolutely loved it. Ted and

Brian even built an ice rink in the back yard so that they could all play hockey outdoors and I thought they were all quite mad.

The extreme weather slowed down the completion date on our house by three months to July, but we'd rather they built it correctly than rush to complete it, so patiently watched for the weather conditions to improve and, when possible, drove up to Meadowvale to see what progress they'd made. Home-ownership wasn't new to us anymore, but buying a townhouse was, and especially one built inside a park system. A series of steps and landings led to the front door and, once inside, four steps led down to the above-ground basement, while four steps led upstairs to the open plan living room, dining room, and kitchen with large patio door, and small bathroom with just a toilet and washbasin. In one long continuous movement, the stairs continued on upstairs, in another series of steps and landings to three bedrooms and full bathroom. Our basement had a large window in the front underneath the living room window and a small window in the rear underneath the dining room window, and it was totally empty except for the central heating furnace and hot water tank. It was a very large house, much larger than any other townhouse in the area and being located where it was, it fit our young family requirements perfectly. In between my house and my cousins David house at #36 were three single garages and house #35 sat on top of my garage, their garage, and David's garage. It was a novel set up, and the only way they could get to their front door was to walk up a flight of stairs that ran beneath David's living room window, to the patio on top of the garages and in front of their door. Lorna had the same set up to her right, with the house to her right being accessed in the same way. All three family gardens backed onto the park walkway and bike path system and about four hundred yards away were three public tennis courts and a large open grass area.

Buying a new house in Canada is a fantastic experience, one like no other I've ever had. A certain percentage of the overall house money paid to the builder, allows new home-owners to choose from a range of fixtures and fittings that go into the home to a basic standard, and if you want more expensive fittings, you can pay the difference. We chose the basics because we couldn't afford to upgrade anything at the time. The year was 1976, and we chose to have a bathroom suite, consisting of bath, toilet and sink in the height of fashion, gold. We chose wooden doors for the kitchen cabinets, in a light brown colour and again, in the height of fashion, an Avocado Green refrigerator and stove. In the hallway outside the living room and dining room was another bathroom, containing a toilet and sink, again in our lovely gold colour. The 'stick-on' tiles for the bathroom, toilet room, kitchen, and behind the front door were all in the same off-white colour. The three bedrooms' upstairs were fitted with white shag carpet, and the main floor plus all the stairs were supposed to be fitted with shag carpet called Burnt Sienna. It was supposed to be a brown colour, with a slightly orange tinge, but it wasn't like that at all. When we opened the door to our new home, both of us were dazzled at the sight. It was bright orange. Absolutely bright vivid orange! They must have put the wrong carpet down, and I headed off toward the Site Office at the end of the street to ask them to change it. He arranged for us to go back to the Samples building, and the guy brought forward the Burnt Sienna carpet sample to show me once again. "Yes, that's the one I chose – various shades of brown with a faint tinge of orange, that's it!" I said excitedly. "Just a minute," said the salesman. "That's not the real colour you know!" "Pardon?" I said. "Well, that sample has been around for years and it has gotten dirty, it should be bright orange!" Oh no! They were technically correct, I had chosen that carpet, and because we couldn't afford to replace a brand-new carpet, I had to live with that damned orange carpet for the next ten years, before we replaced it – a month before we sold the house.

Two weeks after our final inspection of the house, in late June, and just before the children finished school for the summer, I packed in my temporary job in Toronto. Mr. Martin didn't want to see me go, and persuaded me to continue working for Canada Post by arranging a job with the same hours, in a subdivision on Finch Avenue, about a ½ hour drive away from my new home, after the children went back to school in September. I said I would try it, but wouldn't make a long-term commitment to him before I'd experienced driving back and forth in heavy traffic on those busy highways. Part-time work had not been on our agenda as we wanted to raise our children ourselves, but needs must when the Devil drives, and had I not found some work it would have been years before we could have become homeowners again, and the end result was worth the sacrifice.

We arranged to move into our brand-new house on July 1st a three-day weekend national holiday, and with lots of family to help, we filled the moving van to its brim. It was déjà vu with respect to our second move within Canada. Lorna had amazed us by furnishing the three-bedroom rental house from top to bottom from her small single apartment, but that was nothing compared to the amount of stuff we'd collected since then. I swore somebody must have been bringing stuff in the back door as we were taking it out the front because it seemed never ending, and both Brian and Ted had to drive all the way back to Toronto for a second full load.

We were only the third set of families to move into the estate, and because the majority of the other houses were still being built, obviously no landscaping had been done, and everywhere around the house was still loose damp dirt. It had been a very long and busy day, and the boys were just getting in the way so I sent them both outside to play, and to watch for Brian and Ted to come back. I didn't have as many boxes or as much furniture as Lorna had so it wasn't long before my furniture was in place, and most everything was unpacked and put away. Then I concentrated on making a play area in the basement for the children. We had brought a shag area carpet, designed in multi coloured squares, from England, and as the rest of the house had wall-to-wall carpets, the only place it could go was in the basement. Lorna had saved two old customer counters from being thrown away by Sears, and as each counter had four compartments, it made them ideal for toy storage. So, within a very short time I had the rug rolled out, the counters in place, and all the toys unpacked and stored in each compartment. It looked like we'd been there for months. Then the children came in.

If I hadn't known they were of the Caucasian persuasion, I'd never have been able to tell as they had so much muck and dirt all over them. "Stay right where you are until I run a bath for you, you scruffy pair," I said, thinking of our brand-new carpets. I ran up the stairs to the bathroom and turned the tap on but there was no water. What! This is a brand-new house, where is the water? Here we were, on a Saturday afternoon, on a long weekend, and no water. Lorna didn't have any water either, so I ran down to the Site Office and told them, and the response I got was, "Oh, you'll have to wait until Monday, until the Consumers Gas Board officially cuts the seal on the water heater." Man alive. Don't tell me that the welfare of my children has to wait for anybody. "Excuse me!" I said abruptly. "You're telling me that we will have no water until Monday. What are we supposed to do before then, for drinking, bathing, and flushing toilets?" I asked. "I don't know," he said offhandedly. "Well, I'll tell you what I know. This Site Office has a bathroom because it is also going to be a Model house when you've finished some more houses," I said. "And as it has a bathroom, and obviously running water because you're using the toilet, I will bring the children here to bathe," I continued. "You can't do that," he exclaimed. "Can't I? Just you watch me!" I said angrily, and with that I turned on my heel and trotted back to my house to get the children.

I was just checking the last of the unopened boxes for some bath towels when a knock came on the partly opened front door. "Hi there! Anybody home?" shouted a male voice. "I'm down in the basement," I responded. "Stay where you are and I'll come down," the voice continued. Once in front of me, he introduced himself, "I'm Philip Morris, the owner of Philmore. I understand you have no water and want to use the Site Office facilities," he said. "That's correct Mr. Morris. I have two really dirty children thanks to no landscaping, and they need a bath, and your guy was no help at all. He told me I'd have to wait until Monday to get water, and that's unacceptable," I said. "Well, I'm not supposed to know how to do this, but I've brought some tools and I'll turn the water heater on for you, just don't tell the Gas Board that I've done it, will you?" he said. "Well, let me put it to you this way, Mr. Morris, either somebody fixes the water heater, or I'm bringing the boys to the Site Office, or to your house now that I know your name," I grinned, and that was many a true word spoken in jest.

What a lovely man, and so different from his agent in the Site Office. He found the valve for the water main, and turned it on, and grunted as he got down on his stomach to cut the official seal of the Gas Board, before lighting the water heater from the whoosh of gas. What a lovely sound! "Give the heater at least an hour to let the whole tank get hot, then your boys should be able to soak some of that dirt off them," he said. Then as he looked around the open basement, he commented, "It hasn't taken you long to settle in, has it? That's a nice play area for the children." Then he checked for running water in the kitchen, and in the upstairs bathroom and seeing that the beds were already up and made and the living room furniture was in place he made another comment, "Most people don't get unpacked for weeks. It's nice to see someone so organized." To which I responded, "We've only been in Canada for a year, and we've been living out of boxes and suitcases for most of that time, so I want the children to settle into their own home as soon as possible." I didn't tell him that I hadn't had very many boxes to unpack. I escorted him to the front door, and his last comment was, "That's a nice orange carpet you've chosen, very cheerful, I like it." I didn't know him well enough to gauge whether he was pulling my leg or not, so bit my tongue and politely said, "Thank you very much." Then I remembered that Lorna didn't have any water either and asked him to turn her water on also, which he did.

The town of Meadowvale was nearly the size of the city of Whyalla in Australia, and it gave off the same air of vibrancy as building sites popped up all over the place, and it grew in leaps and bounds. It was the best of all worlds for young children such as ours and as more young families moved into the area the boys made life-long friends.

Once we'd paid the deposit on the house and the lawyer's bill, we didn't have any money left over and, on one wage, we were just managing to pay the mortgage and put food on the table, when the boys asked us to buy them a bike each. It was the most awful feeling I'd had in a long time, but I had to tell them we just couldn't afford it at this time. They would have to wait.

However, they had another solution. They would buy their own bikes, if we would let them. All the time they had been attending school in England we had given them money each week to put into their school savings account, which was transferred into their own bank account in Canada and this is what they'd use. Well, it might as well serve some purpose, and they'd only be this age once, so both children bought their own bike, and had a lovely summer exploring the bike paths and parks of Meadowvale.

Marjorie and Ken preferred living in Toronto near their work, and as neither of them drove, they liked the convenience of city life with its streetcars and subways. So, with Brian driving, Lorna and Ted went back and forth to Toronto each day to work, while I minded 8-year-old David and 7-year-old John, along with my school holiday visitors, 13-year-old Lindsay and 10-year-old Nancy. We all loved Meadowvale. It was the safest place you could think of for children to live and play and both Brian and I resolved not to move from that house while the children were growing up. I could safely let the four children explore the area without any fear of anything nasty happening to them.

Very soon, Lindsay and Nancy went home, and with David and John settled into their new school, I went back to work for Canada Post. It was only for five hours a day but driving back and forth during horrible rush hour traffic got the better of my nerves and I left after six weeks and became a full-time mother again. Two weeks later, after settling down into my homely routine, I answered the door to find Mr. Morris once again standing on my doorstep. Puzzled, I invited him inside, and he took me totally by surprise when he offered me a job working in his new Site Office, at the other end of Meadowvale. I was more than dumbfounded. He'd only met me that one time, when he'd personally turned on the water and lit the water heater for me, when I jokingly, but fairly seriously, suggested I'd bring my boys to his home for a bath. "Thank you very much, Mr. Morris, but I have no experience with trades people," I said. "Oh, I think you'll do just fine. I've seen you in action," he said, "I need someone who is organized, someone who is not frightened to talk back to people, no matter who they are. It's not hard work; you'll just be checking deliveries of building material to the site. It will only be for a few months, probably only until Easter, and we close down over Christmas so you'll be home for your children," he continued.

It all sounded very good, and when he told me he'd have someone pick me up so that I didn't have to drive my little car over rough dirt roads, and that same someone would drop me home at 4 pm each day, I agreed. All I needed to do was to arrange for the children to stay at school for lunch instead of coming home and they didn't mind at all. It was a unique experience working on a building site, especially in the winter. The roads in and around the site were not maintained and were banked on either side with snow and ice. This had the effect of making the road feel and look more like a bobsled run. My initial driver spoke very little English and he had appalling driving habits. Whenever he was faced with an incline, he'd take the pick-up truck out of gear and let it freewheel down before slamming it into gear to take the corner. I had visions of always missing the corner and of either being killed, or ending upside down in a ditch, and my knuckles were constantly white from hanging onto the dashboard, much to the amusement of this particular driver. After a few days of hair-raising rides, I mentioned it to Richard who was my supervisor, and he changed the driver, thank heavens.

Easter came and, as promised, my services were no longer required, and I have to say that, apart from the first few rides with that crackpot driver, I thoroughly enjoyed the experience. I met truck drivers, designers, salt of the earth trades people, owners checking out their homes - just like I did. I checked and added up roofing trusses, windows, piping, and wood by the truckload. I told drivers that they couldn't take anything onto the site before I'd checked it over, and they were very nice about it. They showed me much simpler ways to check the quantities, such as count one row down and ten rows across to get the number. I checked everything for quality and accuracy and, without a doubt, that job was great.

However, that was all finished now, and for the next four years, I enjoyed being a homemaker for my husband and two boys, and Marjorie's two girls whenever they weren't at school. I had had to get a car in order to go back to work at Canada Post, and if nothing else, it was worth working for that reason alone. It was a third or fourth hand, very small, red Toyota, which Lindsay nicknamed 'Oyota' because it was missing the letter 'T' and all four children and I would squash into it and take off for the day. Depending upon how much gas was in the tank determined how far we could go, and if there was sufficient, after rush hour was over, we'd drive across the top of the city to Ontario Science Centre as it was everybody's absolute favourite 'hands-on' activity. Then, after paying for admittance, I'd check to see how much money I had left which was never very much, and tell each child, "You can have a hamburger and fries, or hotdog and fries, plus a drink, but don't ask for souvenirs please." I never felt very good about having to restrict them, as I personally would have given them everything they asked for, however, with four children to feed during ten weeks of summer holidays each year, it was financially impossible to give them everything they would have liked.

Our family motto was that we were a 'share' family, and we shared what little we had, and didn't feed meat to one child and fowl to another. Everybody was treated exactly the same. All the children who stayed with us came under the rules of the house, and if David and John couldn't have something extra, then neither could anybody else. All four children understood the 'share' concept and not one of them ever put me in the embarrassing position of having to refuse to buy something I couldn't afford. Every other week I'd try and afford to visit Pioneer Village, Casa Loma, Ontario Place, Toronto Zoo, or some such place they hadn't been in a while but on hot summer days they much preferred to go swimming. Since Kenneth's death from drowning, Marjorie had made sure that Lindsay and Nancy were taught to swim, and they swam like fish. We had also made sure David and John learned to swim at the indoor pool in Middlesborough during our last year there, so all four of them were in their element in water, they just loved it. We spent a lot of days either at the outdoor swimming pool at our local conservation area, Eldorado Park, or at the swimming pool in Streetsville, a small old-fashioned village that bordered the town of Meadowvale. I'd nearly always make a picnic to take with us, and with blankets and towels to the ready, they had their choice of which swimming hole to use. Both places had rivers running through the parkland, and if they weren't in the water, they'd find some other way to amuse themselves. It was the best of weather and the best of days.

One of my pet peeves was that I absolutely hated having to come back to a messy house and kitchen and have to clear everything up before I could start supper. It just took the joy of the day away from me, and even though there was a little grumbling, the children made their own beds and cleared away toys or games lying around, while I washed the dishes and generally tidied up before leaving. As we shared everything else, we shared housework, and I'm sure none of them liked it. To sweeten the job slightly I drew up a chart of chores, each with its own monetary value, and each child put a checkmark beside the chore they did and it gave them the incentive of making more than just pocket money. Invariably, Lindsay and David turned out to be the workers, and whether it was because they were a little bit older than their sibling and much faster at the job, but they earned much more money than either of the other two. I felt sorry for the two youngest siblings because they'd stand in front of me and say, "Well so-and-so did the job before I could do it," and both Lindsay and David would share some of their money with the others. Not quite the 'learn the value of a dollar' that I'd been trying to teach, but they certainly lived up to the 'share' motto.

They had rules to live by, and they knew just how far to push me without getting into any trouble. There were certain standards of behaviour that were acceptable and those that weren't, and if it reached the point of unacceptability, then they got a smack on the back of the legs with a wooden spoon. They knew that 'No' meant 'No' unlike other children who would whine on and on until they got what they wanted. Invariably with two girls and two boys there would be disagreements, and I always figured there were three ways to look at things, first there was her point of view, then his point of view, and somewhere in the middle was the truth. If one child came in crying that the other one had hit him, I'd get them both together and say, "Now what did you do to him that got him so angry that he hit you?" Once given an explanation, I'd make them both shake hands and hug each other, then they'd start to laugh at the silliness of making them do that, and they'd be friends again in no time.

The other motto that we adopted was, "We don't need anything that badly that we'd steal to get it!" And with six of us living on one income, there wasn't much left over for treats, but I knew without a doubt that they were all honest and trustworthy. When the boys were little they were encouraged to always tell the truth even if it meant not punishing them for what they'd done. I'd say, "Tell the truth, you won't get wrong, just tell the truth!" I thought it was far more important that they tell the truth without fear of punishment because having to own up to doing something wrong was, in itself, a form of punishment. But as they grew older it changed to, "Tell the truth, and you'll get a punishment that fits the crime." Mind you, if they hesitated, I'd remind them that if I had to find out on my own what they'd done, they'd be in real trouble then.

I figured to be the best parent in the world you needed to be born with the Wisdom of Solomon and the Patience of Job, and as I had neither, I did the best I could. I wasn't their best friend. I was the parent and it was my job to see they were raised with love, kindness and consideration, and they were. My children were taught everything that it was possible to teach them, either by word or by deed, with a measure of discipline thrown in. There were a number of rules that Brian and I had agreed upon when they were very small children such as, "Never argue in front of the child. Never threaten the child with the other parent, a policeman, or a bogeyman. Only one parent at a time can be angry. Never hold discipline until the other parent comes home. If you make a threat, carry it out. If you've made a mistake, then apologize. Don't let a child play one parent against the other. One parent cannot contradict the other, and never ever talk down to a child, they are people too." I'm not saying I had all the answers because I didn't. I hoped they would learn more by example than lecture, although I was prone to the odd one. I encouraged them to speak up, but to be respectful while doing so, and not be frightened by anything, or anyone, including me.

Since I'd found my temper in Kuala Lumpur, it spurted now and again, and I never knew why I got irritated or angry because that was out of character for me. It wasn't until a few years later that I found out I had been suffering from pre-menstrual syndrome each month. But well before then, both Brian and everyone else knew to keep out of my way for a few days, since they never knew when the volcano would erupt. I remember one time David was sitting on the couch watching television when the door opened, and as Brian walked in, the first words out of his mouth was, "Dad, you'd better run for the hills, the Indians are on the warpath!" I never stayed angry, it was more like, "I'm okay now kids, the top has blown, things will settle back to normal." Every day was a new learning experience and for the most part I thoroughly enjoyed it, but sometimes I wish they'd have been born with a blueprint that would have made my judgment calls much easier. I found it tough to keep them close for safety's sake, but to let them go so that they could stand on their own two feet, and if I'd had my way, they would have remained at the permanent age of 8 and 7.

With three families all living in close proximity; we had the most marvelous times together. My cousin David was an excellent cook and he'd invite us to his house to enjoy a barbeque on the back patio overlooking the parkland, or they would come along to our house for a meal. His wife, Donna, and new baby Letisha, and I used to get together most days, to enjoy coffee mornings that would last all day. I really loved Donna. She was the most generous person you'd ever wish to meet and would literally give you the shirt off her back. She had a tough outer skin, but a really soft centre, and some people found her hard to get along with because she could be quick to take offence, and it would take her a long time to forgive what she perceived as slights to her. That was unfortunate, because as Marjorie, Lorna and myself were raised in the north east of England where a spade was a spade and not a bloody shovel, plain blunt speech was the norm. We said what we meant, and we meant what we said, with not a lot of room for misinterpretation, but Donna would often read alternative meanings into what was said. I had no idea that I'd said something to upset Donna until she'd gone very quiet, and once I got to know her better, I chose my words more carefully, and she became less sensitive. Sadly, she died of a heart attack in her early 40's, but she is someone I will never forget.

Letisha, or Tisha as she is known, was a lovely child. She was the newest member of the family for me to babysit and, as all the other children were much older, John was seven at the time I think, she was spoiled rotten, but in a nice way. It had been a struggle for Donna, who was a brittle diabetic, to get her strength back after the birth of Tisha, so I'd bring the baby along to my home and Donna would join us later. Tisha was a gorgeous, placid child, who reminded me so much of her father when he was a baby, and I loved her like crazy from day one, and still do. She would lie on the rug and gurgle away quite contentedly as my boys kept her amused and she loved them both. When she got older and could walk she used to follow them around and pester them all the time and I think that it's quite apropos for children to be tagging along behind children, there's something quite down to earth about the next generation following the last – keeps everybody grounded. Those days were the best of the best of my life.

Brian often brought Marjorie and Ken up for the weekend, and they'd sleep over at Lorna's house, while I had the girls staying with me, we have numerous family outings together, still in our big 10-seater station wagon. Somebody only had to say, "Oh, I've always wanted to go to such and such a place," and we'd go. No sooner said than done. I remember the first time we went to visit Marjorie & Ken's friend, Brian Foster, and his new wife Jane, in the country town of Stayner. They had met Brian while traveling on the same boat to Canada, and when it came time to disembark, the purser said, "Families first please, families first," and Brian sidled up to Marjorie saying, "Hi there, I'm your new son." And with those few words, he attached himself to her family and they became lifelong friends. Brian had done well for himself in Canada, as he'd progressively bought and sold shops and stores, until finally settling down to owning a very large nursing home. We had a lovely visit, and night had descended when it was time to leave, and Lindsay started to cry. When I asked her why she said, "I'm frightened because there are no lights and Uncle Brian won't be able to see the road to drive home." The girls had lived within the city limits all of their young lives and had never experienced the total blackness of night without streetlights. I assured her that Uncle Brian's headlamps would be sufficient and that we were used to driving on roads without lights, and that she shouldn't worry and cuddled her into my side, but it was ages before she stopped shaking.

Out of all my cousins Ted has been the most consistent presence in my life. He and I get along like a house on fire, and there is nothing I wouldn't do for him, and vice versa. At 22 years old he was still a big kid at heart with a love of nature and was in his element in the summer if he could borrow the boys to go swimming, fishing, hiking, or camping. Or on some winter nights, a knock would come on the door and Ted would be standing outside all geared up to play road hockey in the main street, "Are you coming out to play?" he'd ask the boys and Brian, and within seconds, they'd all be playing outside. He was a fantastic 'Uncle,' to my boys, and they loved him, as did I.

It's strange how some events remain so vivid in memory, while others fade and have to be prodded and poked to come to the surface, but I remember the day my mother died in 1976 as though it were yesterday. It was about 7 pm when I got the call from England, and when Nora came on the phone I knew something had to be drastically wrong, because with the time difference it was 12 pm her time. She was sobbing and found it difficult to get those awful words out, "Nan, Beattie's dead. She died this afternoon. There was nothing anybody could do about it!" What a scream I let out. Brian came running into the kitchen where I'd slumped to the floor, "Beattie's dead! I can't believe it! Beattie's dead!" I yelled. Beattie had promised me that as soon as we were settled both her and Bill would come and visit for a few weeks, so how could she die? She was in her early 60's. How could she die so young, so unexpectedly? How can you be fit and healthy one minute, and dead the next? Brian took the phone off me to ask Nora what had happened. "Beattie was having lunch at home with the village doctor and she just keeled over. There was nothing the doctor could do as he thought she'd had a brain aneurysm. We'll have to wait to find out for certain," she cried. We found out later that she had died of a blood clot to the brain and the doctor had been right, there was nothing he could have done to help her. Our patio door was open, and when Lorna heard the commotion in our kitchen she came to see what the matter was and learned that her sister, my mother, had died that day. She put her arms around me and asked me if I was going to be okay and I remember howling through my tears, "How can she be gone? I'll never get to know her as a mother now! I'll never get any answers now! How could she have left us without telling us what happened!"

Somewhere in the back of my mind I had hoped there would come a day when all three of us, Nora, Beattie and myself, would be able to sit down and discuss the events of our birth's. It wouldn't be an easy discussion, but nothing less than the truth would suffice. Nora and I would demand to hear the unmitigated truth about our fathers. We'd want to know everything, good or bad! Unfortunately, our mother died before we could reach that plateau, and as she left no letter explaining the facts, we were destined to never find out. Both Nora and I had a million unasked questions that we'd had dragged as a heavy chain from childhood to womanhood, questions that would forever remain unanswered, and I resolved to never hold anything back from my children.

I don't know whether I was sorrier that my mother had died, or sorrier that I wouldn't have a chance to know the truth. I really couldn't say. Brian tried to comfort me, "Do you want to go to home for the funeral?" he asked. "Yes, but we don't have any money for the airfare!" I wailed. "We'll find it somehow!" he replied. Air travel was still expensive, with the return flight being the equivalent of two months' mortgage, and we just couldn't afford it, and even though Brian suggested we borrow the money from the bank I wouldn't let him. Beattie, and the rest of them, would just have to know that I wanted to be there, but I couldn't put my family into debt. Nora was surprised that I wasn't flying home for our mother's funeral, but as it turned out it was a good thing I wasn't there because I was able to keep out of the fracas that followed.

What a long time ago it is now but some events just stay with you. Nora phoned a few days later to say that our mother's funeral had been well attended and that services had been held in Ebchester Church just across the road from her home, Mains Farm. Then the family had gone back to Mains Farm to celebrate Beattie's life. Celebrating a person's life is something I truly believe in. I believe the body is just a vehicle for the Soul, and once the body dies the Soul returns to our heavenly father and after being released from earthly cares, it is cause for celebration. In other words, went you've done your time on earth, your reward awaits you in heaven, and everybody should be happy for you. However, the celebration did not go as smoothly as planned and Nora and my brother Brian got into a terrible argument about the estate. I don't know exactly what was said; only that Nora was intensely upset when she phoned me days later. She said that our brother Brian had taken his father and our mother's husband, Bill, to see a lawyer to ensure that she and I did not inherit anything from the estate, and what did I think about it? I'm afraid I replied, "Well, you know what Gran would have said, "If nobody gives you anything then you have nobody to thank." That wasn't what she wanted to hear and I totally misunderstood how deeply she felt about it. Since my leaving England the first time, she had forged a very strong relationship with our mother and felt as though she had finally been acknowledged as their eldest child. But with Bill stipulating that we were to be excluded from his will, she lost her place in the hierarchy, and was rejected all over again, and it haunted her until her dying day. The law had changed in England to include any illegitimate children as stepchildren into the marriage and all she wanted was to be acknowledged. She didn't care about the size of the estate or the money; and if Bill had arranged to leave her just pennies from our mother's portion, she would have been okay.

I wasn't upset for me, although I was upset for her. Nora accused me of not understanding what she was going through and she was right, I didn't understand, because at that time I would have considered any inheritance to have been charity and I was still nobody's charity case. I'd had no expectations so I could hardly say I was disappointed. It had never dawned on me that I should have expected something from all the hard work my mother had put into that estate, in order to make up for all the wrongs that were done to us. It seemed natural to me not to expect anything because Bill wasn't my father. If he had died first and left everything to our mother, then I would have expected to be recognized as one of her four children. There was nothing we could do other than pay expensive lawyers to fight it through the courts for the next few years, and I don't think either of us were in a position to do that, so what was the point of letting it sour the rest of our lives. None at all. I was really sorry that she took it so hard, but as I hadn't much communication with my other siblings, Brian or Dorothy, since we'd become adults, I couldn't guess what they were going through, so it all went on the back burner. Nora, Stivvie and Anthony and Ian still visited Bill, as he was considered their grandfather, and things must have settled down with Brian and Dorothy because they went quite often.

My life went back to looking after the welfare of my children, and with them in mind, looked around for activities to help them settle. Meadowvale was such a new town, and not many sports activities were set up so Brian and I, and five other parents got busy. We were a bit late getting all of our children into organized activities the first summer and decided to go full steam ahead and get them pre-booked into sports activities for the next year. We arranged for Streetsville, the town bordering Meadowvale, to incorporate us into their soccer schedule as we had a couple of soccer pitches, and we managed to find soccer coaches.

We were early enough to enroll the children in winter sports though. The City of Mississauga, which was where Meadowvale resided, bought the Meadowvale Four Rinks after its builder went bankrupt and seven parents set about organizing a hockey club. Brian was the Treasurer and I became a fundraiser, while my cousin Ted signed up to coach a team and designed the club's logo that is still in use today. We expected about 50 children to show up and were absolutely astounded when over 300 enrolled. Talk about instant hockey club! And because most of the children couldn't skate at all, I arranged for a professional figure skater to teach them the basics. Next came the boy scouts only there weren't any openings available. There were plenty of parents wanting their children to join the boy scouts but nobody was prepared to start another group in Streetsville. I went home a bit discouraged until I talked to my cousin David and he volunteered to organize a brand new 1st Meadowvale Boy Scouts group, with me as the second-in-command, and my cousin Ted as an occasional helper. After that came school activities. It was a brand-new school, and this time there were lots of volunteers for every position, be it school trustee, lunch room organizer, or play time supervisor and Brian was chosen as the Treasurer of the school lunch program. With our little group of seven people, we helped set up the Homeowners Organization; canvassed people for support of a high school even though our children were still very young; and I reported on the whole sports scene for the Meadowvale World newspaper. We were very busy parents. We encouraged our boys to try every possible sport available so as to ensure strong healthy bodies and a life-long love of sports, and within the space of two years, we had two sets of equipment for tennis, badminton, soccer, hockey, baseball, basketball, fishing, and skiing. All of which was scattered around the basement and if you can name it they tried it on for size, before finally settling on soccer, hockey and the boy scouts.

My second summer in Canada was taken up with child minding all four children, soccer practices and games and enjoying our overseas visitors. Aunt Mabel and Uncle Joe flew over for a three-week visit and stayed with Lorna and Ted for the first time. She had gotten into the habit of paying Marjorie & Ken a yearly visit, but now that Lorna had a larger home with room to spare, and Ted could drive and had a vehicle, it made more sense for them to stay next door to us. Besides which, there are only so many times one can visit Casa Loma. I don't think Marjorie was very happy about it, but we did try and include her in the visit on a weekend. On Friday evenings, after work, Brian would bring Marjorie to our house, and as her son David and first grandchild lived only two doors away, she had a choice of whom to visit. Brian had built bunk beds in the play area of the basement, and that's where our two boys slept, while the two girls slept upstairs in the boy's bedrooms, in single beds, and if Marjorie came on her own, she slept on the couch in our living room. By far the most consistent overseas visitors were Aunt Mabel and Uncle Joe, and their visits got progressively longer each time, with four months being the longest. They were absolutely fantastic with all the children, and everyone loved them very much. If Uncle Joe was up before the boys he used to quietly come into our house and sneak over to the bed and scare them half to death by shouting, "Are you lot not up yet? The day's half over! Come on you lazy buggers, get out of those beds!"

Both of them loved visiting Canada, and as cousin David had been one of her favorite nephews, she, like Marjorie, reveled in the fact that all she had to do was pop along the street to see him. Aunt Mabel got along great with Donna, who also loved her very much, and thought the world of new baby, Tisha. She just loved the fact that there was family next door and up the road, and everyone's doors were open to her and Uncle Joe. That summer, the residents' association gave permission to build a fence around our back garden, and that's what we did, except Uncle Joe and Ted took part of the fence down between our two houses and made a gate making it easier to get into each other's kitchens. Now we could pop in and out of each other's houses without the long walk to the front door of each house and back.

Our second winter in Canada was nothing compared to the first, with snowfalls and temperatures nearly back to normal. It was still cold, with lots of snow, but most people cheered the onset of winter because there were as many sports activities taking place during the winter as in the summer, with the most popular sport being downhill or cross-country skiing. In the city, most boys belonged to a hockey, figure skating, or skiing club, and if not interested in ice, there was indoor volley ball, basketball, badminton, or soccer. In the country, boys were also interested in ice hockey, hunting of any kind, ice fishing, and snowmobiling. A snowmobile was like an old-fashioned dodgems car on skis, and there were hundreds of miles of properly made trails set up on country properties.

Two nights a week, and twice on a weekend, all four of us would head for the Four Rinks for either a hockey practice or game, and I'd sit in the stands quietly freezing to death. I always enjoyed watching the boys play ice hockey, either defending the goal, or trying to score and, contrary to other parents, would clap my hands for whatever team scored. Those were great days when both boys played in the same hockey arena, because it meant that if I didn't feel like

Ella Shaw at Niagara Falls, 1976

getting my bones frozen, Brian would take the children on his own, to practice. I always went to see them play in an official hockey game against other teams in the area, but as they got older and the play got tougher, it wouldn't have been my first choice of sport. However, the boys loved it. Both played 'Defense,' and even though they were still very young, both of them were tall and well-built and I used to cringe when they body-checked other kids against the boards. If they were the ones to be body-checked I had to hold tight to my seat so as not to jump over the glass partition between the stands and the ice, to see if they were okay. I once told a coach that he shouldn't encourage the children to be so violent on the ice, but he said it was a Rite of Passage for Canadian children, and that my boys were the worst offenders. What a cheek! My boys weren't rough; they were being raised in a secure, loving environment, with the emphasis on kindness and consideration for others. What did I know? When I told Brian what the coach had said, he laughed, "He's right, haven't you seen how those two nail other kids against the boards? They've got half the kids in the league scared to death of them. Would you prefer them to get smashed against the boards?" "No," I replied, "I wished they'd joined a Figure Skating Club instead."

Our third summer came very quickly, and we had a visit from Ella that we paid for, and because she'd never been overseas before, she traveled with Aunt Mabel and Uncle Joe on one of their annual visits, and we all had a terrific time. I didn't know what to expect, but during our monthly phone calls to them, we'd had some very nice conversations and the old saying of absence makes the heart grow fonder must have been true, because we all looked forward to her visit. She was the nicest person I'd *never* met, and helpful beyond words. She absolutely loved the sun, and for someone so straight-laced and uppity I couldn't believe my ears when she asked to borrow a pair of shorts and a t-shirt. Who would have believed it? Not I! It was as though the sun melted the ice in her veins, and she relaxed, played with the children, helped with the chores, and was a joy to be around. Her and Donna became firm friends, and she was ultra-pleasant to everyone. If only she'd been like that for the first 15 years of my marriage we'd have had a lovely relationship, and I was really sorry to see her leave, but she promised to return.

For our third winter in Canada we gave the boys, as a Christmas present, the choice of either returning to England for a vacation with the grandparents, or go to Disneyland in Orlando, Florida. It was no contest, Disneyland won hands down. It was only a four-hour flight away from Toronto and the winter snow, and we landed in a gloriously sunny and very hot Orlando, rented a car, and stayed in a hotel about an hour away from the amusements. The next morning, we were up bright and early, to get into Disneyland as soon as the doors opened, and were just amazed at how organized everything was. The car park was so huge that Disney provided open-sided trains to transport everyone to the park entrance, and after paying for three days' worth of fun, we caught the ferry from the mainland over to Disneyland's Island. What a phenomenal experience for both children and adults! Apart from the weather being absolutely terrific in the middle of winter, the boys were absolutely thrilled with the individual rides, and cartoon characters roaming the streets.

It was marvelous seeing all those Disney characters come to life. Someone had to be the best organizer in the world, because even though there were lots of people lining up to get into some of the buildings, the lines ducked in and out of areas set up to amuse people while waiting.

One of the more memorable rides was Space Mountain. It was a roller coaster built on the inside of an alpine mountain and we were seated in two separate cars, each like a small canoe without seats and with rounded ends, metal wheels gripping iron rails. In pitch darkness, the cars rocketed away, screaming and whining as metal touched metal. We couldn't see a hand in front of us and everything was experienced through the pit of our stomachs. We were pitched left or right as the car screeched around corners or flung either forward or back as it either dropped like a stone or accelerated up a hill. It was a ride filled with terror. The boys were strapped in between our legs, and Brian had wrapped his arms around David because we were going so fast that the speed had whipped his sunglasses and cigarette lighter from his top pocket. He yelled for me to hang onto John and when I put my arms around him I found his straps had started to loosen and had I not held him so tightly, he'd also have been forced out. Finally, after what seemed like hours, that nightmare ride came to an end and we were flung forward as the car screeched to a grinding halt at the bottom. I had to be helped out of the car because my legs and arms were positively shaking and, Brian, who had spent a month climbing death defying mountains in the Lake District with the Outward-Bound Mountain School in England, agreed with me that, in this instance, once was definitely enough.

Thankfully, none of the other rides posed such a threat to life and limb. Our last day at Disneyland was Christmas Day, and we were all thrilled to watch an enormous parade down Main Street in Never-Never-Land. We took the last ferry back to the mainland, to where the car was parked, and from the stern of the boat, watched as Disneyland disappeared into the distance. We were just about to turn away from the rear to start walking to the front, when the sky lit up with a huge assortment of fireworks. For nearly 15 minutes they burst up and over the Castle similar to the fireworks shown on the Disney show on television and the children never shut up about it for weeks.

Unfortunately, our trip was marred slightly because our return travel arrangements were changed while we were on the plane. It was announced that Toronto was socked in with snow and no plane could land, so our plane was now going to land in Montreal to wait for a break in the weather. The airline arranged for hotel rooms for the night, and early next morning we were back at the airport waiting for the runways to clear in Toronto, and we sat in the waiting room for nearly six hours before the airline decided to transport us by road. and after nine hours of traveling on a bus in horrendous road conditions, we finally made it back to Toronto airport and I swore that I'd never ever travel anywhere during winter again. Poor Lorna and Ted had fought their way to Toronto airport the night before in a full-blown blizzard to pick us up before finding out we weren't going to be there, and they'd had to make the same trip again the next day in the same awful weather. Altogether, it was a Christmas to remember.

Toronto and suburbs are nestled around Lake Ontario, and the heavy winter snowfalls usually come up and over the lake to fall in what is known as the 'snow belt' about an hour north of Toronto, where people would go to ski. Apart from private resorts, the government let people use conservation areas for picnics, swimming and boating in the summer, and for skiing and ice-fishing in the winter, and with so many people traveling on the roads, snowplows keep the roads clear, most of the time. February came and, along with my cousin David, and four other parents, we took our scout troop to experience a weekend of outdoor activities, lodging in a Scout Hut, in the Snow Belt area of Collingwood, about a two-hour drive north of Meadowvale. That turned out to be another experience never to be repeated. Along with my cousin Davids' car, which had a trailer towing a snowmobile, four other cars loaded with children and stuffed to the gills with basic necessities, we tortuously drove through 15-foot high snow banks on either side of country roads, to the scout hut. We could see it in the distance, but as no road had been plowed out, we were suddenly faced with trekking ½ mile through five feet of pure untouched snow, with 14 children tagging behind, carrying sleeping bags and all the food we'd need for the weekend. David told us to stay where we were, and he unhooked the snowmobile and went to reconnoiter, to see how deep the snow actually was, and if the last person had left the key to the hut. Then he came back and organized the children into groups, made them carry their own things, sent them toward the hut, and started loading the snowmobile with stuff from the cars. I stayed behind until the last of the cars were emptied then, dressed in my big boots and fur coat tied in the middle with a bit of string, headed out on my own.

I wish video cameras had been readily available in those days, because for sure someone would have won a Favorite Video's top prize if they'd shot me trying to make my way through all that snow. David hadn't made much of a pathway with the snowmobile, and as soon as I stepped through the front gate, I sunk up to my waist in snow. I didn't know whether to laugh or cry at the thought of having to struggle all that way to the hut and for a moment decided to stay with the car. "Oh, come on, you can do it!" I said to myself. "Everybody has made it, including most of the children." Trying to balance myself, I yanked one foot out of the slushy underlying snow, and when I broke the suction, the momentum threw me backwards into a spread-eagled position. Now I was soaked from top to bottom. After much struggling to get up, I rearranged my clothes and, after lifting and thrusting one foot forward like a Ballet Dancer, I ended up doing the 'splits' and couldn't move either forward or backward. Comic relief at its finest. I decided to give up and shout for help, and soon three or four boy scouts came back to look for me. To add insult to injury all of them danced around on the top of the snow as though it was made of brick, and it was only me who was buried in it.

David had also wondered where I'd gotten to and he arrived just after the boys. "You lot get back to the hut and I'll bring Ballou," he said, and I really did feel like Ballou the bear, which is what my second-in-command title was. "Hop on the back of the snowmobile and I'll take you in," he said. I gingerly lifted one foot over and while still not quite seated because I was adjusting my clothes for comfort, he decided to show off his prowess by gunning the machine and taking off. As soon as the damn thing leapt away I did a complete backward somersault and my coat got caught somewhere and I was dragged through the snow for about five feet before it released. David came running back, "Oh my God, I've killed you!" he exclaimed. As I lay there, with snow jammed inside my coat, sweater, trousers, and in every open orifice in my body, I thought, "Why, oh why didn't I just shut up when David was looking for volunteers?" I thought I'd better put him out of his misery and made a move to get up. He grabbed me by the arm and pulled me to my feet, but I couldn't see his face because snow was jammed between my eyelids and my glasses. "Are you okay?" he asked nervously. I could have played it up, given that he was just showing off, but I just laughed, "You don't expect me to get back on that thing again, do you?" I asked. "I promise to go slow this time, promise," he said, and just about at walking pace, he drove me to the hut. I was the only mother there, and I got the job of trying to keep the children dry and fed. For two days, I wrung out wet clothes and tried to dry them in front of electric heaters or slaved away in the kitchen trying to make enough food to feed 20 people. On the return trip home, which took four hours to drive through a horrendous snowstorm, I vowed to my cousin David that I'd never volunteer for another weekend excursion. Summer, maybe. Winter, definitely not!

Ted had bought himself a small fold-down trailer/caravan that he was able to tow behind his car, and most weekends he and Lorna went camping. They would venture further and further afield, until they chanced upon Manitoulin Island, about a 9-hour drive away, and it was the biggest island in the world to be surrounded by fresh water. They spent their two-week vacation camping on that Island for the next few years, and I must admit it was gorgeous. It was a beautiful scenic drive up through northern Ontario, but wanting to get there as quick as possible, they would drive to Tobermory, the nearest mainland to the Island, and only about 5 hours' way, where they'd catch the Chichiman ferry for the 1½ hour lake crossing. If Brian could wangle the time off we would join them on their camping vacation otherwise, for two weeks every summer, they'd just borrow our boys.

We had arrived in Canada when our boys were nearly 7 and 6 years old, and we had enjoyed everything we had experienced since getting off the plane. All of us, including the boys, now 11 and 10, were well and truly settled, we loved our home, the environment, and all the activities we were involved in. We loved the yearly visits from Aunt Mabel and Uncle Joe, and nobody had any thoughts of moving anywhere ever again. So why did Brian's American boss ask him to move to the United States of America? Why did he have to upset the apple cart!

Brian came home one day to tell me that his company had asked him to move to the United States of America, and they had put it in such a way that if he refused to go, he was also refusing to work for the company. "I'm not moving anywhere else! We both agreed that the boys should stay in one place and make life-long friends, just like we did growing up, so you'd best start looking for another job because I'm not leaving Canada, and that's all I have to say about that," I cried. What an awkward position to be put in. "You either work for us in the States, or you don't work for us in Canada!" I went and told Lorna what had happened, and she was most concerned, "Brian, do I have to get the wet cement for your shoes?" she asked. He laughed and replied, "No, I don't really want to go there either, but I had to ask." And with that decided, he looked for another job within Canada. After 16 years of marriage, the four-year cycle of moving countries was finally broken.

Returning to the workforce fulltime

Brian took a phone call from our best friend, Anne, in England, and after only talking with her for a few moments, he had tears in his eyes as he came into the living room and said, "That was Anne on the phone with some devastating news, Alan's had a heart attack and he's dead." Alan and Brian had been best friends since they'd been old enough to go to school together, and it hit him really hard. How could anyone die of a heart attack at just 37 years old? "Anne is frantic, she hasn't worked full time since her boys were born, and she doesn't know how she's going to manage," he continued. Anne had two boys, Leslie 13, and Adrian 9. Apart from the terrible news that he'd just lost his best friend, all Brian could think about was I'd be in the same boat as Anne, if he died suddenly. I had also been out of the workforce for over 12 years, except for the few and far between part-time jobs I'd had. What would happen if Brian just keeled over? Up until Alan died, we'd always thought it was more important that I stay home and raise our children, instead of paying somebody else to raise them with different values to ours, and we referred to these as, "we deliberately choose to be poor" years. Brian's earnings were always considered to be 'the bread on the table,' whilst any I'd earned were 'jam on the bread,' and as we'd lived without jam all the years our children were growing up, maybe it was time to get back into the workforce. Maybe it was time to ease the financial burden at home and set something up to secure a future for me. We both discussed it over the next few weeks and even though he increased his life insurance coverage substantially, we decided it was time for me to look around for a job while he was still around, and before I really needed one. We talked it over with the children, who were now 11½ years old and 10½ years old, and as they had no objections, the only drawback I could see was that, at 36 years old, I was a bit long in the tooth to start and build a career.

It was my last full-time summer at home with the boys, and they had just returned to school in September when, with half a heart, I applied for a secretarial job at AES Data. They were a modern company, located not more than ½ mile from my home, in the business area of Meadowvale, and they were just setting up a company to manufacture state-of-the-art word processing machines intended to replace electric typewriters in the office. Not quite sure that this is what I wanted to do as it meant learning new skills, they offered to hire me as secretary to the software engineers in the Research & Development department. I thought it would have taken me much longer to find work, and my mindset was still at home with the children, but with the company being so close, Brian persuaded me to 'give it a go.' I was able to drop the boys at school in the morning, pick them up for lunch at home and drop them back again, all within my lunch hour. They got out of school at 3:30 pm but by the time they walked home it was nearly 4 pm, and as I got in just minutes after 5 pm, they were only on their own for an hour, and for the next eighteen months until my boss, Peter, got fired, it worked like a charm.

In my lifetime, I had gone from using a manual typewriter to an electric typewriter to a computer and I loved it. We hired only the very best and brightest graduates from Universities all over Canada to create new software and because the technology was so new, they used me a guinea pig. They needed an ordinary secretary, just like me, to test all the software used to create a document. Programs came on individual diskette, and if you wanted to create a spreadsheet, for example, then the machine had to be rebooted with the Finance diskette. Or if you wanted to print a document in its finished form, as opposed to one long ribbon of pages, then you had to reboot with the Repagination diskette in order to split the document into individual pages. Given the functions of personal computers today, those word processing machines were certainly clumsy, but it was fantastic being able to store the document on diskettes for re-use, and not have to retype them word for word as I'd had done when in the Invoice department of the Company. What a fantastic time to re-enter the workforce. I was in the forefront of computer technology, receiving on-the-job training, which meant I was light years ahead of anybody else in the secretarial field, light years!

I took to everything like a duck to water and within six months of precision typing reams and reams of one-line data entries, such as "if this is so-and-so, go to such-and-such, or if it is this, go to that," they promoted me. The day of the dedicated secretary was coming to an end, and multi-tasking was taking over. AES Data sold thousands of those new machines with the promise that the typing workload would be cut in half allowing secretaries to become administrators which would reduce the workload of the boss. At least that's what they promised, and in order to test their theory, they promoted me to Software Supervisor which meant a lot more administration work than usual. That was a heck of a quantum leap from secretary, I can tell you. As well as scheduling nearly 30 programmer's time on just a few research machines, they persuaded me to take over the time-consuming task of configuring hexadecimal language into binary computer language. Then I'd put the finished program onto a Master diskette, and after creating a number of individual program diskettes, I was in charge of point-of-sale and troubleshooting programs to the public. I really enjoyed the job, the people, and the close location to my home and everything was working out really well. The boys were still well cared for, and the next summer holiday was no problem. Lorna and Ted took them two weeks camping on Manitoulin Island, then Brian took his vacation, and I took mine, and we filled in another two weeks for them at hockey camp. That meant only two weeks out of the ten-week summer holiday to fill in, and I still came home for lunch, even though the boys could have managed quite nicely.

In addition to holding down a full-time job, I was Chairman of the local boy scouts chapter, as well as Ballou for our scout troop. I was still a fundraiser for the hockey association, and driver for my children's practices and games, and still reported on the sports scene for our local newspaper, but everything else fell by the wayside, and after being involved with the boy scouts for more than three years, I figured it was somebody else's turn to run the thing. I appealed to the City of Mississauga residents through the auspices of the local television station, and received so many responses from qualified people, that I was able to replace more than 30 people who wanted to move on to other things, and I was one of them.

I've no idea why Peter got fired, except that in North America, you're only as good as the last project you complete and that he had been having trouble creating 'bubble' memory for the computers, whatever that was. He was an excellent boss with a brilliant mind, and well-liked by all his staff of more than 30 people, and it came as a shock when he left. I know I could have stayed with AES but, within a couple of weeks, Peter phoned me at home and offered me the job of Office Manager, working with him in downtown Toronto. I told him I'd think about it for a couple of days and get back to him. My concern was for the boys who, at 13 and 12, hadn't been on their own very much and, as I'd be leaving before they went to school and wouldn't get back until much later in the evening, I felt as though I was abandoning them. Brian interjected into my thoughts, "It's time to start cutting the apron strings. The boys need some independence, to find out what they are made of. You've trained them well, they'll survive," he said. So, it was decided that I'd try it out and if it worked for everyone then good - if it didn't, I'd either look for other work, or stay home again.

I loved working with Peter again, he was so supportive and appreciative of my skills, and he encouraged me to get involved in all aspects of running the company, except the Finance department. I can't say the same about the owner, and I didn't like him very much at our first meeting. He was a loud-mouthed know-it-all and very pompous. He went on and on about how rich he was or was going to be at the expense of the taxpayer. It was a software engineering company with about 20 employees, who created computer signs for public places such as highways and train stations. Office personnel could change the signs over the telephone lines instead of manually having to change them, and as the government owned most of them, the majority of the workload was contracted to the government.

Two months into the job, Peter asked me to produce a document within three days that would have taken three weeks, and I just couldn't do it. There was no way one person could have typed it in time, so he suggested that I take it to a local typing service, to a lady called Maggie. I drove over to her office, about ten minutes away, and was awe-struck at the set up. She had maybe six AES word processing systems, two in each room, and had built a lucrative business doing overload typing for numerous companies who, instead of hiring another full-time person, periodically sent large documents to a typing service. I had never heard of such a thing, as I'd always done my own typing, even working overtime to complete it. But what a brilliant idea! I got along great with her, and she explained the set-up. She'd get the work, hire a temp to do it on her machines, charge the company, pay the temp, and keep the difference. Money for old rope I thought, and I wondered if I could do something similar. I resigned from my permanent job, as I just hadn't felt good about working there since first meeting the owner. He just struck me as a dishonest person, someone who would have been at home with the criminal element in the back streets of Toronto, and about two years later I was proved right. Because software programs took so long to write, and before they received the final program, the government allowed companies to invoice them periodically by building up Science Credits, and the owner had been inflating the amount of credits owed to him and got caught. I watched the television news as he was sentenced to eight years in prison and was really happy that I'd only spent three months working with him.

Buying a machine of my own was hard to justify when just starting out, and after Maggie agreed to me finding my own work she'd rent me one of her machines in her office, at her normal hourly rate, and within the next few weeks I became a freelance operator. Maggie also taught me how to charge for my services. She said that it was acknowledged in the industry that an average typist could only type four pages in an hour, and that was what she based her charges on, and as I was a much faster typist, and could type six or even seven pages an hour, I had a lot of leeway when it came to charging for my skills. I got the work, rented one of Maggie's machines, did the work, charged the company, paid for the machine rental, and kept the difference. An entrepreneur was born! For the next few months, I had great fun being a freelance operator. If needed at home, I'd refuse the work, or if I couldn't get out of it, Brian picked up the slack. I either worked in a temporary capacity at other companies on behalf of Maggie, or I rented one of her machines and did the work that came my way through advertisements. It was a marvelous way to make money. It meant I could contribute to the family's finances, but could choose when, where, what, and how I did it.

It was around this time that my sister Nora and Stivvie made the decision to come and live in Canada. They had all visited as a family, nearly four years earlier, just a year after our mother had died, and as Stivvie had lost his mother, Ivy Stephenson, just weeks after our mother, Nora had wanted to pick up sticks and move to Canada as soon as she could. However, as children, Anthony 10 and Ian 9, were well and truly settled in school, and after losing both grandmothers, it would have been too much of an upheaval, so they waited until Anthony was just about to leave school at 15 before applying for immigration. They had done some preliminary investigation and found that although working experience counted for you in the points system, if you weren't far enough up the corporate ladder and didn't have enough points, you were automatically disqualified, and although Stivvie had worked in the Bank since he'd left school, he was quite content to be an Assistant to the Manager, and not a Manager in his own right even though he could have done the job. We had talked to each other on the phone lots of times in the past few months and I had described Maggie's word processing service bureau, and the fact that I'd made more money working as a freelancer than in a permanent job, and it was not long after that conversation, Stivvie wrote to say that the only way they would be accepted for immigration was if he started his own business and employed Canadians, and was I interested? Of course I was. I'd do anything to help them. I would help him set up and run a word processing service bureau to employ Canadians, and a few weeks later he called us to say that he had been given an appointment with Canada House in Edinburgh, Scotland, and was it possible for us to fly over and sign an Affidavit confirming our intentions. No problem. Brian took unpaid time off work, and we splurged on a four-week vacation to England, arriving the first week of December, and flying back to Canada on New Year's Day.

For the first and only time, both boys played on the same 'rep' team together, as John was considered good enough to play with older boys, and the coach was most upset at losing both great defense players during league play. He pleaded with Brian to leave the boys behind and even offered to have them stay with him, at his house, but there was no way I would consider going anywhere without them. Our suitcases were packed, including the boy's hockey skates, and we promised to take the boys to Durham Ice Rink three times a week so that they could practice. Three days before we were to catch the plane, David came down with Chicken Pox, and my first thought was that the coach had wished this upon us, and then I thought, "Well, I'm traveling by plane again, I shouldn't be surprised at strange things happening, and they always do."

Brian decided that as it would be me starting a business with Stivvie, I'd be the one to sign the Affidavit, so he'd stay home with David, and so as not to spoil everyone's holiday, I should take John with me. "Well, let's see what the Doctor has to say about David first. You never know, John may be coming down with it also," I said. The Doctor said, "You know the foundation cream that woman put on their faces? Well plaster his face with that and nobody will know, and put a baseball cap on his head." I wasn't quite sure I heard correctly and repeated what he'd said, "Cover his spots?" "Yes, that's right!" he replied. "But what about other people on the plane catching Chicken Pox? What if there is a pregnant woman sitting next to us?" I said anxiously. Obviously, my mind was remembering the time Joy told me she'd had silent German measles for two weeks when I was first pregnant with David. "Oh, Chicken Pox is nothing to worry about, and the chances of a pregnant woman sitting next to you are zero and even if there was one, it wouldn't do any harm to a fetus!" he said. Okay then, if he's not worried then why should we be, and that's what we did. Poor David. Apart from feeling really rotten and ill, he sat all during the seven-hour flight with his face plastered in foundation cream, his jacket collar pulled tight around his neck, and his baseball hat jammed onto his head. I felt as miserable as he looked. He really wasn't very well during the first week back in England, and Tommy was frustrated that all David seemed to do was lie down on the couch. I finally had to tell them that our boy was just getting over Chicken Pox and it would take another couple of weeks before he felt like himself again, and Tommy stopped chivvying him into doing something he didn't feel like doing. He had an awful time getting through the Chicken Pox but cheered up about it when he found out after returning to Canada that he'd passed it onto his cousin, Ian.

Ella and Tommy insisted we stay with them, which was a real surprise, and while Brian and I slept together for the first time in his old home, both boys slept in sleeping bags on the bedroom floor. Even though the house had been renovated and modernized, all the floors were still concrete, hidden underneath about six thin carpets, and I was quite horrified the next morning to find both sleeping bags damp on the outside. The Council had installed central heating radiators in all the rooms but Tommy thought them unnecessary and wouldn't turn them on, so I had no choice but to ask Aunt Mabel if the boys could sleep in her house each night, in Consett. Stivvie had arranged to have a rental car waiting for us at Durham train station, and each night Brian bundled both boys into it and drove them up the hill to Consett to stay with Aunt Mabel and Uncle Joe, and each night Aunt Mabel asked the boys if they'd had anything to eat, and of course they hadn't, so she cooked hamburgers each and every night they stayed there.

We attended the Immigration interview with Nora and Brian, and duly signed our Affidavits, confirming our intention of starting a business with them in Canada, and then settled back to enjoy the rest of our holiday. There wasn't much to do in England in December, just visiting other family members, hanging around Ella and Tommy, or taking the boys to the ice rink three times a week. Word had gotten around to the younger members of the Durham Wasp's Hockey team that two 'Canadian' boys were practicing, and after a couple of sessions, about six of them asked Brian if they could join them. Our boys lived and breathed hockey and were years ahead of the much older English youths in hockey and skating skills, and I think both of them were surprised to find out how really good they actually were. Except for Brian and Stivvie chasing around the countryside on Christmas Eve to find a village butcher selling fresh, not frozen, turkeys for Christmas dinner, nothing much exciting happened. The only other thing worthy of note, was that while sitting on the bus on our way back to Heathrow airport, I asked the boys if they had enjoyed anything about their vacation and John stood up in the aisle and yelled, "Yes, this bit. We're on our way home to Canada!"

After working freelance for about four months, two ex-colleagues from AES Data, Neil and Doug, gave me the job of typing up a Business Plan for a joint venture company being created by two of the biggest companies in Canada, and after spending the next three months glued to a machine in Maggie's office, they offered me the position of Branch Administrator with an annual salary impossible to turn down. Neil and Doug had already found a location specifically to house all the computers and software engineers, and it would be run with me in charge of all administration. The timing was perfect, and it was a great opportunity to gain experience in setting up a company practically from scratch. Just what I needed to learn before Nora and Brian came to Canada, and the only other thought I gave to them was that for the next year I'd also be earning a great salary while waiting for them to arrive. I told my new boss, Fritz, who was the General Manager, or Managing Director, that I could only commit to working for him for a year because of my prior commitment to Stivvie and he agreed that once I had gotten things up and running, it would be okay. Ah, the best laid plans of mice and men etc., etc., everything was constantly multiplying, the premises, the computer mainframes, the workforce - it was a groundswell of forever expanding technology.

Fourteen months after I started working for Neil and the rest of the gang, Nora and Stivvie, with Anthony and Ian in tow, arrived in Canada, and after a few weeks of everyone living with Lorna and Ted, Anthony and Ian moved next door to live with me, and that was the situation for the next six months. I knew I had made a commitment to Stivvie, and when I reminded my boss he said, "Oh, that was just a ruse to get them here, they'll manage fine without you," and I let myself believe him, for the most part. However, working away from home where they were not in sight, and then being in close proximity with them after work, caused a great deal of conflict.

I kept looking for legitimate reasons to leave my job and let myself believe there were none; I loved the job and was earning great money for a woman; but things came to a head when Fritz told me he'd asked for a really huge increase in salary for me but had only been given a fraction of it, that I now had an excuse to leave. I had put my heart and soul into that job and had worked all the hours that God sent to the detriment of my family, and I felt as though they slapped me right across the face with that insulting amount, which I hadn't even asked for. It was time to leave.

The Word Wizards

But, because of my hurt feelings over that piddling amount, I was free. Free to do whatever I wanted. No more driving downtown, no more late nights or weekends, and no more bosses to please. It also meant no steady income. Still in heartfelt terms, it meant I could look Stivvie in the eye once more, so in March, 1982, we proceeded to incorporate a word processing service bureau known by the name my nephew Ian gave it, 'The Word Wizards.' For cheapness, we could have found a room in the back of a building as was usual, but I wanted to be different. I wanted the business to be visible to the public, to reduce the cost of advertising, and we rented a small store along the main street of Streetsville, next to a three-way set of traffic lights. There was a lot to do in setting up a business; we needed machines and furniture, as well as telephones, wandered around an empty room, but with the help from contacts I'd made in my last job, we commissioned an office supplies salesman to find us reasonably priced desks and chairs. We also needed a word processing system, and we purchased a second-hand machine from a company where I'd previously done some temporary work. An old clunker, a prototype we thought, but it worked and served us well for the first few weeks. We even got overload work from the company as they knew we had the machine, and within three weeks we were up and running.

It was through Maggie that we got our first major client, Atomic Energy of Canada (AECL). She phoned me and asked if I could spare some time to help them with a huge document they were putting together, and for the next couple of weeks I worked in the AECL offices on her behalf, and it was only when I told them that I had my own business to look after and that I couldn't come back after my commitment to her was over, that they asked me to take over the whole assignment with my own people. I told them I'd speak with Maggie about it, and as AECL was located more than 50 miles away from her and she was having trouble getting girls to go there, she gave me her blessing to take it over. They were putting together a proposal to sell a Candu Nuclear Reactor to Mexico when they asked me to supply temporary word processing operators for both day and night shifts. We managed to supply them with the couple of girls they needed for the day shift, but the night shift looked to be impossible until I phoned some of my ex-colleague girlfriends from AES Data. Within a few phone calls I convinced six of them to work from 6 pm until midnight, five nights a week and all weekend and for giving up their time, we gave them the full hourly fee except for two dollars an hour. This covered our costs of paying them up front before being repaid by AECL. After two weeks, AECL decided to increase the workload and we were asked for one more day time operator, and with nobody available, I volunteered myself.

I got on so well with the head guys, who were English/Canadian, and against the wishes of the Supervisor who worked there; they put me in charge of organizing the enormous quantity and quality of documents that came from all over Canada. I certainly earned the money they paid me. No two documents were the same, they had different line spacing, different margins, different indents, different character fonts, different font sizes, and with so many variables it was very time-consuming trying to make one cohesive document out of thousands of previously submitted pages. But as soon as they put me in charge, the first thing I did was to give all the operators, in all the sites, including the head office where I worked, a sample document detailing the standards which they were to follow and that simplified things enormously.

There were perks to this tremendous task, because when it was finished, they asked me to accompany the document to Mexico just in case there were any last-minute changes. AECL had already decided that I was going, and had an American and Mexican Visa all prepared, but didn't tell me until two days beforehand. My response was, "Gentlemen, I can't go because my British passport has expired, and it will take at least six weeks to get a new one." Panic stations!
They'd not thought about sending anyone else, and Mexican Visa's took nearly a week to get. They phoned the British Consulate in Ottawa, and as I was still working hard putting the document together, they were assured that if Brian and Stivvie took the overnight train, with all the forms and pictures they needed, then they would renew my passport while they waited. It was a rush to get everything done, and Brian phoned me the next afternoon to say he'd got it, and

that he and Stivvie were on their way home. I was due to fly from Toronto to Houston, then on to Mexico City, less than four hours after they arrived back with the means to do so.

It was the first time I'd ever traveled anywhere on my own, and I wasn't very happy about going, but I'd been put in a position where they needed my services and were willing to pay handsomely for them. In any case, I was only going one way on my own, because after the document arrived in Diplomat Pouches and was housed in the Canadian Embassy, the Lear Jet would have room for me on the way home, so I thought I'd look upon it as a personal adventure. The flight from Toronto to Houston, Texas, on the Air Canada flight was pretty uneventful, and I looked forward to changing planes to an American plane to fly into Mexico. I was not impressed. Not at all. It wasn't a very large plane and, as I sat just behind the propeller, the noise was absolutely deafening. Before very long my head was pounding, and a Stewardess with a trolley stopped to offer me a cup of coffee. I thought it was just what I needed but couldn't believe my eyes when she handed me a thin plastic cup. This plane belonged to an American airline who constantly bragged that everything was bigger and better in America so why didn't they have proper cups to drink from, instead of disposable plastic? The lukewarm coffee was drunk quickly, and as I turned to give the cup back, she motioned for me to put it into the green garbage bag she was holding, and to completely shatter any illusion that everything was bigger and better in America, that same Stewardess sprayed the whole plane with a thick disinfectant spray as we taxied into Mexico City airport, and I ended up smelling like a hospital orderly.

One of the last people off the plane, I followed behind the stragglers into what looked like an airplane hangar, and no sooner had I struggled to get my case off the roundabout than a Customs Officer stopped me and motioned for me to open my case. I had been busy looking toward the exit where somebody from AECL was supposed to meet me, and I wasn't expecting to be stopped, and he flustered me so much that I couldn't immediately find my suitcase key, and as I searched in my bag, not understanding one word of Spanish, but thoroughly understanding the arm waiving, he lost patience and pulled out a huge bunch of keys from his pocket and opened the case himself. He rifled through my things as though he were looking for either drugs or gold, while dropping everything onto a dirty conveyor belt next to him, and I started to get worried. Had somebody put something in my case that I knew nothing about? He made me stand there for what seemed like an eternity. My suitcase was now totally unpacked with clothes strewn about, and he very slowly looked me up and down as he examined my British Passport, American Visa and Mexican Visa over and over again. I was the only remaining passenger, and whilst other officials stood around talking to each other and looking in my direction, one came over and snatched my documents from my official, looked at them in a very haughty way and practically threw them at me, before waiving me away. Then, gauging by the angry tone in his voice, and the look on his face, he proceeded to chastise my official, all the while gesticulating for me to leave. I couldn't leave quick enough.

I managed to push all my stuff back into the case and drew a short lived sigh of relief as I went out of the terminal, where a second later a few taxi drivers surged toward me and jostled each other to get to my suitcase. I was very frightened, as I could only shake my head in response to their foreign questions, while hanging tightly onto my case. It hadn't occurred to me that it might be a Mexican meeting me because I was expecting an English-speaking AECL employee from their local office, and when one seedy looking character pushed his way through the crowd of drivers and grabbed my suitcase out of my hands, before taking off at a fast pace, I had no idea what to do about it. For a moment I was shocked, but I ran after him through the parking lot, and managed to grab his arm and stop him. "Where are you taking me," I asked. To my surprise, he spoke some English and as he pulled a piece of paper with my name on it from his trouser pocket, he replied, "Atomic. Atomic. You come! You come!" Oh, thank goodness, he'd said a word I could recognize - Atomic. He didn't slow his pace much, and with me jogging along behind him, he led me into a side street where he'd parked his car, and after literally throwing my case into the trunk he gestured for me to get inside. It was a very old car, with a huge amount of large dents and scrapes and I could understand how he got them, when he put his foot to the accelerator and went from zero to Mach 5 within minutes. It was a hair-raising ride, without seatbelts, and as we passed other cars in the same physical condition, I understood that the law of the jungle prevailed, and whatever car was left standing at the end of the day became the Lord and Master. With no thought to signaling his intentions, he swung in and out of traffic like he owned the road and after half an hour of hanging onto whatever was available, he pulled up to my hotel. Then he had the nerve to hold his hand out for a tip after shaking my insides to pieces. I didn't have any Pesetas so gave him an American $5-dollar bill, and with a big smile he said, "I drive you tomorrow." If I'd had any choice I would have turned him down, but he was an employee of AECL so had to use him. In 1982, there were about 80 Pesetas to the American dollar, and it turned out I'd given him nearly half a week's wages. No wonder he wanted to continue driving me.

The actual Candu proposal was not due to arrive in Mexico for another three days, and the reason they sent me down so soon was to let me get the brand-new word processing system up and running, in case of any last-minute changes. They had arranged for AES Data to install the system in the secure part of the newly opened Canadian Embassy and when I told them that I was not a Canadian Citizen and was not allowed in there they said, "Oh, you're British, that's good enough!" To actually test the system, it was necessary to do some work on it, and I volunteered to help the outgoing Canadian Ambassador send hundreds of 'thank-you' letters to all and sundry in Mexico. His assistant, who was to remain working with the new Ambassador, was so thankful that I'd saved her from an enormous amount of repetitive typing, showed her appreciation by taking me on a personal tour of Mexico City. One of the places she took me to was a huge indoor market near my hotel, and with her help, I bought four real Mexican sombreros, a Mexican blanket, and a few pieces of Mexican silver jewelry. After the rest of the AECL people arrived they asked me how I'd kept myself busy, and I told them that I'd worked for the Canadian Ambassador, and that I had gone shopping with his assistant's help, and they were curious to know how I was going to get it all home. In particular, they wanted to know how I was going to get four sombreros past Canadian Customs, and I jokingly replied, "Well, we're all going home on the same Lear jet, so I thought each of you could wear one!" They all had a good laugh at the idea of them wearing a sombrero, but little did they realize I was being serious.

We all had supper together that night, and I'd no sooner said goodnight to them and headed for my room, when a man followed me into the elevator. He'd been sitting at a table, just staring off to one side all evening, and I felt it was too coincidental that he should leave the same time as I did. Even though he made it to the elevator before I did, he waited until I'd pressed the button for my floor before he pressed his, and the hairs on my neck started to rise and I instinctively knew something was wrong. When I got out on my floor I stopped just beside the elevator to get the key out of my bag and he sort of hung behind me, and as I walked to my room he followed behind. Somehow, I had the sense to knock violently on my door and shout, "Brian, Brian it's me, open up will you, I can't find my key!" As I said that, the man turned and walked back to the elevator. I knocked on the door again and listened for the elevator doors to close before I opened the door with my key, and slammed it shut and locked it behind me. Shaking like a leaf, and even though I didn't drink, I poured myself a brandy from the miniature bottles in the small refrigerator in the room and the next day when I told the executives what had happened they made sure one of them walked me to the door of my hotel room each night after that.

I had been warned by AECL not to drink the water, as Mexico was notoriously known for giving people Montezuma's Revenge or, in plain English, gastroenteritis of the deadly black diarrhea variety, and had done very well for the week I was there. I'd used Coca Cola to brush my teeth morning and night and had been very careful not to eat salads or drink cold drinks with ice in them, and I thought I'd gotten off lightly. I never gave it a second thought but enjoyed some of the fresh fruit that was sitting on ice in the private Lear jet on the way home. Within a day of returning, I became violently ill with a severe case of gastroenteritis, which I thought was worse than I'd had on board the ship going to Australia. Once again, I was deathly ill, and into the second week I was so delirious that my sister Nora sat by my bedside and waited for me to die. I'd fought against going to the Hospital because I was too scared to travel away from the toilet and, as no Doctor would come to my home, I had to rely on homemade cures, and the only thing that got me through that horrible time was Lorna's Chicken soup. I kid you not. Even though I was throwing up and down violently, some small measure must have stayed in my system because that was the only food that would stay down. Once I was lucid again, and on the mend, Nora told me that I'd unexpectedly sit up in bed and hold conversations with an invisible Aztec Indian. I'd tell him I wouldn't be long in coming, and I remember laughing with her about it afterwards, but it must have been very frightening for her at the time. The only thing I can really remember saying was, "Hey look Nora, I've finally got skinny feet," because I was totally dehydrated and could see every vein.

A few weeks later AECL asked me to go down to Mexico again, this time to their office where they had arranged for two word processors to be installed and they needed somebody to train their Mexican office staff, Carmen and Josephina, and I agreed. It was only supposed to be for a week but the two girls asked me to stay for a second week to make sure they knew everything about the system so I said okay, no problem. I still had time on my Mexican Visa and never thought to check my American Visa because I thought with them being issued at the same time, they'd expire at the same time. Carmen and Josephine were really nice young girls, maybe about 15 years younger than me, and they must have thought they were entertaining royalty, instead of an ordinary person just like themselves. For the first three days, we ate lunch at a very posh hotel, and even though it was lovely, I said, "Ladies, I'm just an ordinary working girl just like you, is this where you eat normally?" When they answered, "No," we threw away the façade and for the rest of my two-week visit, we ate lunch at a little corner café with its chipped dishes on the tables, and I sampled the simple fare of the ordinary Mexican people. Evenings were different, and because they gave up their time to show me around, I sampled high-class Mexican fare in fairly expensive hotels. I insisted on paying for each outing, as their salaries were very low, and we all agreed that none of us had ever eaten such marvelous food in all our lives. I had a great time with those two girls and saw the real Mexico, not the tourist kind of Mexico, and fell in love with the place, and would have had no problem staying longer, but it was time to return to Canada.

At the airport, I received my boarding pass, and as I was waiting in line to pay my departure tax at a kiosk, in a different line, a wail of protest broke out from the young woman in front of me. She was an American, returning home from her first trip to Mexico, and hadn't known that she had to pay an $US 8.00 departure tax. She offered to pay it in Pesetas, or write them a cheque, but they demanded actual American dollars. As soon as I realized her dilemma, I gently nudged her arm and gave her the money, and she immediately burst into tears. She clung to my arm all the while I paid my tax and insisted that I give her my name and address so that she could return the money once she was home. I would probably have insisted on repayment as she did, but it was such a small amount that her behaviour was embarrassing, and after refusing to give her any personal details, I extricated myself from her embrace, and wished her a good journey home, to a destination different than mine.

My flight to Houston was called and I made my way to a seat about six rows from the back, just behind the propellers again, where else? All the seats except the two next to me were filled and the plane shuddered as it was pushed backwards in order to join the rest of the planes on the runway. Movement caught my eye, and I saw a young mother, with a young child in her arms, running down the aisle toward me, and I gathered she was heading for my row. Just as she slowed down and turned toward the seat, the plane lurched, and her grip on the child loosened and I caught him just before his head hit the headrest in front of me. He screamed not only because he'd fallen out of his mother's arms, but at the sight of a stranger catching him, and lost control of his bowels all over my skirt. He had Montezuma's Revenge and he started yelling and howling as though I were murdering him. His mother started crying hysterically and I honestly didn't know what to do. I was strapped into my seat, holding a strangers' two-year old child at arm's length, while he oozed black diarrhea all down his legs and all over me, and the mother didn't want to take him from me. Meanwhile, the plane was taxiing for take-off, and the Stewardess strapped herself into her seat and totally ignored what was going on. I had no choice but to ask the mother to fold my pleated skirt in on itself while I held onto a kicking, screaming child until the wheels left the ground and the plane leveled out in the air. The Stewardess brought a mountain of paper towels and, after the young mother put a wad of them on her lap so that she could finally take hold of her child, I gathered my polyester pleated skirt in one hand, and made my way tenuously to the bathroom.

For the second time on a plane, I stood in my underwear in an airline bathroom, flushing what I could down the toilet and washing my skirt in a tiny little sink. I laughed to myself, "This is becoming a habit, and maybe I should carry a spare set of clothes in my flight bag from now on." It took me quite a while to get my clothes clean, and as it was impossible to get all the water out, I made my way back to my seat with water dripping from the bottom of my skirt. The child was down to a dull sobbing, and the mother had cleaned him up, but he was still very distressed, and I felt sorry for him because I'd gone through the same thing weeks before. This time I had come prepared for my trip to Mexico, and on my Pharmacists advice had bought a bottle of Kaopectate as an antidote to the dreaded bacteria and, after retrieving it from my flight bag, I offered it to the young mother. She was naturally hesitant to give her child medicine she'd never heard of, but once I assured her that according to the label, it was safe for a young child, she gave him the prescribed dose and within minutes he fell asleep in her arms.

I'd just gotten wads of paper towel stuffed underneath my skirt to help dry it when the Stewardess asked me to move to another seat, to let the child stretch out and sleep comfortably. I didn't mind moving because it not only meant getting away from the noise of the propellers, but also the unavoidable lingering smell of the child's diarrhea. So, with my flight bag and handbag in one hand, and holding my skirt bunched up in the other, I bumped and bounced my way to the front of the plane. There was one seat left in the whole plane, right in between an American soldier and an obvious sailor, and when they both turned in my direction, they must have wondered what on earth was going on. I looked like a pregnant hippopotamus. It wasn't until I explained what had happened, that both men looked relieved, and with the ice well and truly broken, I settled down and enjoyed conversation with both men for the rest of the trip. Well, I thought, this has been a pretty eventful trip. First the young woman in distress in Mexico and now a young woman on the plane. But, as I was about to find out, distressful things always come in a set of three, and in my case I had another two to contend with.

Before we got off the plane in Houston, we were all sprayed with the same strong disinfectant that we'd been sprayed with on arriving in Mexico City and I was pleased to substitute that aroma for the lingering odor of diarrhea. My skirt was practically dry, and I looked forward to the last part of my trip home, from Houston to Toronto. Because I had flown back the last time in the Lear jet I didn't know Houston had no way of transferring my luggage directly onto the plane for Toronto. I'd have to collect my suitcase from the roundabout at Arrivals and find my way back through the terminal to Departures, all because they didn't have an area to hold people with connecting flights. Everything was open to the public, and it would have been very easy to get off a plane and vanish through an exit door, and I could see the logic of what was about to happen to me, but not until many days later.

I had just picked up my luggage in the Arrivals area when the biggest American Customs man you've ever seen, or ever will see, stepped in front of me. "Ma'am, follow me, you're under arrest!" Stunned, I just stood there until my wits came back, "Pardon me? Why on earth are you arresting me? I'm on my way home to Canada!" "You have no visa to allow you to enter *these* United States!" he barked. "You are an illegal alien! I cannot allow you to leave my sight because if you get outside we'll never find you again!" he sneered. "Excuse me! I do have an American visa, and a British passport, and I have no wish to remain in *these* United States at all. I have a return ticket to show that I am on my way home to Canada!" I said sharply. "Your visa has expired, and we don't want you here!" he replied offensively.

Oh, my Lord, how on earth had that happened? At that time, every country in the world except Canada had to apply for a Visa to enter the United States and unknown to me, with staying the extra week down in Mexico, the time on my American visa had run out. "Follow me!" he snapped, and that horrible man marched me over to the other side of the building. There was no way I could keep up with his long legs as I was also carrying my suitcase, and I kept lagging behind. "Put a move on Ma'am! I don't have all day!" he shouted rudely, as people cleared the way for him to stride through.

He got to the Departures desk well before me, and I could see him talking to his colleagues while pointing his finger toward me, and as soon as I got there they told me to open my case so that they could search it. This was in front of all the people waiting for their boarding passes, and I have never been so embarrassed in all my life. Once satisfied that there was nothing untoward in my suitcase, he hustled me through the building to where some office people were working and told me to sit on a bench while he phoned for an armed guard to come and watch over me. He gave the guard strict instructions not to let me out of his sight, and he even had to stand directly in front of the toilet door as I tried to relieve myself. I was absolutely mortified!

I had helped two American women in distress within the last few hours, and here I was, in their country, being treated like a scab infested low life. I didn't want to be here. I was on my way home to Canada, and I swore that I'd never get on another plane in my life. I had to sit on a bench, in front of an armed guard for four hours before my plane was due to board, and I could feel the steam coming out of my ears. I branded all Americans with the same brush I tarred that awful customs man with, and determined to see them all as the enemy, and when another armed guard, who just happened to be a Canadian working for the US customs people, came over and apologized for all the stress I was under, I told him in a loud voice, "It's too late for apologies. This is a lousy country and lousy people, and I can't wait to get out of it!" He accompanied me to my plane and with instructions to the Stewardess not to give me my passport back until we were over Canadian soil, he again apologized for the treatment, and wished me a safe trip home. That was, without a doubt, one of the worst travel experiences of my life.

Brian was waiting for me in the Toronto airport, and I could have wept with relief at the sight of him. Everything that had happened that day came bubbling out in a mixture of anger, embarrassment, principle and hurt, and only after I'd exhausted myself telling him what had transpired, he said, "Brace yourself, your horrible day is not over yet." With a dreadful sinking feeling in my stomach, I asked him what was wrong. David hadn't been very well for over a month, he was tired all the time and didn't have any energy so Brian took him to see the Doctor during the first week I was away in Mexico. The Doctor examined him and escorted him outside, and as he went back to his desk, he told Brian that he thought David had leukemia. My heart nearly stopped, *"David has leukemia!"* I screamed. "We don't know for certain until the results of the blood tests come back, but that is what the Doctor thinks. I didn't know whether to call you in Mexico or not, because there's really nothing we can do until we find out," he said.

"You should have called me the minute you thought something was wrong and I'd have dropped everything and come home on the next plane!" I gulped. My heart was racing a mile a minute, but Brian was right, the only thing we could do was to wait for the interminably slow test results to come back. "How is David feeling now? He doesn't know, does he?" I asked. "He's doing okay, but very anxious. I wasn't going to say anything to him, but he heard what the Doctor said," Brian replied. "What crass stupidity! What on earth was the Doctor thinking? Where were his brains telling a 14-year old that he thinks he has Leukemia?" I exploded. "Well the Doctor didn't actually say it to his face," Brian said, and went on to explain that David had heard what was said through the partially closed office door. "Even so, why did that stupid Doctor have to say anything about Leukemia until the blood test results come back?" I demanded to know. "Well to prepare us for the worst I guess," said Brian. "He should have made damned sure that the door was closed, because with only a superficial examination, that was a dreadful diagnosis for David to hear. He'll have himself convinced he's got it and is going to die at the ripe old age of 14," I cried. I raced through the door as soon as we got home, looking for David, and there he was, as usual, lying on the couch watching television. "Hi Mom, did you have a good trip?" he asked. Choking up, I couldn't answer for a minute, and as I put my arms around him and hugged him close, I responded, "It's okay son. You'll be okay. That man got his medical license from a cereal box. He doesn't know what the hell he's talking about!"

Our family Doctor had originated from Brazil, and with English being his second language, I was apprehensive about signing on with him in the first place. His office walls were covered in carved wooden ornaments, native curios, and blankets and he had a huge parrot in a cage just outside his door and every time I went there I half expected him to get his juju beads out and start dancing. But it was with more than normal apprehension that all three of us attended an appointment a week later to hear David's blood test results. Always a man of few words, the Doctor said, "Well everything is okay, David just has Sleeping Sickness, or Mononucleosis, so there is nothing to worry about. It will have to clear up on its own because there is no medicine I can give him, and he could be sick for up to a year."

Relieved that the diagnosis wasn't deadly after all, Brian and David left the room but I stayed behind. "Dr. V., have you any idea how much anguish you've caused my family? For the past three weeks you've had my son worried to death because he overheard what you had to say about him. Perhaps you should have waited until you'd gotten his blood tests back before putting a name to what was wrong with him," I politely, but very pointedly, said. The fact that he had caused so much suffering didn't faze him at all as he replied, "Well I can't help it if David overheard, he shouldn't have been listening." "You should have made quite sure that the door was shut behind you so that he couldn't hear," I quickly responded. He looked at me with a stony expression on his face, "If you've finished criticizing me, then perhaps you'll leave," he said.

No further response was required, only action, and I bounced out of his office, banging the door behind me, and one of his wooden pictures fell off the wall. But in the car with Brian and David, I really lost it. "He's nothing but a Witch Doctor! We're not having him for a family Doctor any more, him and his juju beads. It doesn't bother him one bit that he misdiagnosed David, not one bit! He told me to get out of his office, and I banged the door and one of his pictures fell off the wall," I laughed. "Are you okay David," I asked. "Fine, now that I know I'm not going to die," he replied. But he wasn't really. For the next four years, David had a regimen of physical fitness beyond belief. During the day, he'd spend hours either bike riding, skateboarding, or playing tennis, and during the evening, he'd be on roller skates at the local rink along with his friends. Every hour that God sent, David was on the go, and it was only when he was 18 and old enough to join the Red Cross Society to become a blood donor, in order to quietly get his blood checked every few months, that the strict physical and mental regimen loosened up, that David relaxed. Even though it was against my nature to hold a grudge, I was upset with that Doctor for a long time, and although I never wished him any permanent harm, somebody did. A couple of years later an article in the newspaper announced that his office had blown up, with him in it. Officials put it down to a gas leak, but we figured he'd done one witch doctor dance too many, and probably misdiagnosed a member of a local Mafia clan and they'd taken revenge.

Now that the huge assignment at AECL was over and done with, Stivvie and I concentrated on building our three-month old word processing service bureau. We mailed hundreds of letters to companies within a 40-mile radius and started getting positive responses, and within a few weeks we hired our first full time Canadian operator, which meant we had to buy another machine. Both of us found it very hard work. The very nature of the business was 'overload' so I found myself working longer and longer hours each evening and weekend, until all I seemed to do was go home to sleep and go back to work. Stivvie couldn't proofread the work until it was typed, so everything was a rush, and I didn't enjoy it very much. It was always a chicken and egg scenario. We had more than enough work for one person, but not quite enough for two, and then we'd have more than enough for two people, but not quite three, and so on, and so on. We never seemed to get ahead and neither Stivvie nor I took a salary as all the money that came in was plowed back into the business. By the time Stivvie and I had been in business together for three years, we had moved to larger premises in Streetsville, with store frontage, a downstairs training room set up, and a huge parking lot outside. We had over $100,000 dollars tied up in machinery and office furniture, a permanent staff of five people, including Stivvie and I, and a roster of 12 part-timers for our office, not counting the temporary operators we sent to other businesses, and I was exhausted. Mentally and physically, I needed a break. I couldn't continue working 7 days a week and all the hours that God sent just to cover the overhead. I just couldn't. I needed a break.

My husband, Brian, arranged for me to stay at a health farm for a few weeks. It was in Stouffville, about ¾ hour away from us, in the country. It was called Stouffville Health Farm, and little did I know that 'fasting' was a pre-requisite. I expected to be pampered and fussed over and was a bit shocked to find that no food was served, and there was only distilled water to drink and I thought Brian was trying to finish me off. But it's strange what happens when you stop eating food. Apart from being light-headed for a couple of days and spending most of the day lying down, it actually felt very good. It cleared my mind and body, and I'd have stayed there longer than the three weeks I did, but I started to experience pain all over. The Doctor told me I had fasted to such a state that residual pain left over from years previous was coming out of my tissues. I could feel the pain in my feet where my ingrown toenails had been removed two years previous and my teeth started to hurt where they'd been filled. I phoned Brian to come and get me. Enough was enough. I needed to get back to work.

The next year I worked myself to a standstill again, and when I got home late one Friday evening, Brian told me that he'd booked me to fly out on Sunday to Cuba for a one-week holiday. "Cuba? Did you say Cuba?" I asked. "Yes," he replied. "I asked the travel agent, where a middle-aged woman, traveling on her own, could have a week of peace and quiet without being bothered by other people, and they said Cuba, so that's where you're going," he said. "I can't go to Cuba. It's a Communist country. I don't want to go there," I wailed. "It's only for one week. You'll be okay, stop worrying!" he said. I don't know how I got to the gate for the flight to Cuba because my mind was not focused at all and it was a relief to sit down and just do nothing. It was only a four-hour flight and nothing unusual happened until we landed, and once everyone got their suitcase, the man in front of me got arrested because he had brought two suitcases of second-hand clothing for the women in Cuba, and that was not allowed.

I stayed in the Veradera Hotel, Cuba, west of the North Atlantic Ocean, east of the Gulf of Mexico, and south of the Straits of Florida, and the first night my room was next to the outdoor dance floor and bar, and the noise was so loud and unpleasant that I asked to have a change of room the next morning. They moved me to the very edge of the hotel, and for the rest of the week, it was fantastic. My breakfast and supper were included in the price, so I just had to buy my own lunch. I'd dress in shorts and t-shirt, take my book, and with a tall glass of Rum and Coke, make my way along the beach to a shady palm umbrella, and relax until it was time for either lunch or supper. The people were marvelous, very friendly, and nothing was too much trouble for them. After three days of peace and quiet, I decided to see something of the island and hired a taxi with a driver who could speak no English, and as I could speak no Spanish, we communicated in sign language. He took me for a two-hour ride, and apart from the beautiful scenery, he treated me to a drink of Sugar Cane from a street vendor. It was as though I'd stepped back into the much softer time of my childhood, when the skies were always blue, and soft dainty clouds drifted overhead. I loved it and promised myself I'd return with Brian and the boys.

In the middle of building a business and working myself silly, Brian picked up the slack at home. He made sure groceries were bought, the house was cleaned, and the boys looked after. At 17 and 16 years old, they were well able to manage on their own, as Brian had said when they reached their teenage years, "Sorry Nan, but you need to let go now, and let me take over." Fair enough. They still had rules to live by and a curfew to follow. Both had to be home before 11 pm and if they were going to be late, then they had to phone. Looking back at the big picture, I'm proud of the way my boys turned out. Both boys lived with principles and, in particular, the 'share' principle, which was "whatever we have, we can share," and both proved it at one time or another, beyond a measure of doubt. We were sitting quietly watching a show on the television, when a knock came to the garage door. We had previously commissioned a builder to 'finish' the basement for us in our Townhouse, and had built an extra bathroom, bedroom, and living room, which had access to the garage. Once fitted with a lovely carpet of mixed gold and brown colours, plus fully furnished, it was a more comfortable sensory environment than the living room upstairs, which still had the vivid orange carpet in it.

I opened the garage door to find a young girl of 15, called Stacey, and her 16-year-old boyfriend, Shawn, standing there. "Hi Mrs. Shaw. We've left home!" he said, "Our mothers have kicked us out and David says we can stay here." I'd known Shawn as one of David's closest friends, but didn't know his girlfriend, Stacey. "Well you'd better come in and we'll see what we can do about it," I replied, making for the couch. "Do you need anything to eat or drink," I asked. "No thank you. We've eaten at the Roller Skating Rink," Shawn replied. "Well make yourselves comfortable until we try and get to the bottom of this. But first things first, you must let your mothers know you are here," I said. "My mother won't want to know," said Stacey. "Well I'm afraid I can't let you stay here without your mother knowing, so it's up to you," I replied. I don't think I must have sat on the couch for more than five minutes before another knock came on the door, and when I opened it this time, there were two young girls that I didn't know standing there. "My name is Stacie, and I'm 16 years old, and this is Amanda, also 16," she said. "We have nowhere to live, and David said we could stay here," she continued. "Come in then," I said, more than a little bewildered. "Brian, do we have a 'Vacancy' sign hanging outside the door?" I asked. "Well if we have, you'd better take it down, we're full," he replied laughingly.

David came in a short while later, looking decidedly nervous. "Don't worry son, if they need a place to stay then they've come to the right house," I said. With that, he relaxed and said, "Mom, I didn't know what to do, I felt so bad for them and I thought you'd always find room for one more!" I turned to the four extra young people in our home and said, "Well, you're all very welcome to stay here, but on one condition. Even though you've fallen out with your parents, you must either phone them or let me phone them so that they know where you are. You can stay here until you get yourselves sorted out, but you must let your parents know where you can be reached. Okay?"

One by one they phoned home and after they had spoken to their mothers' I spoke to each mother and asked if I could do anything to help reconcile them with their children. Without exception, I was told they didn't want their child back. They were just too much trouble, and not worth the effort. How could you not want your own child? I didn't know any of the parents and didn't know what they had gone through, so couldn't venture an opinion. I only knew in my heart that the world would have to end before I'd give up on either of my children. I had a faint inkling of where the mothers were coming from, because having employed working mothers, I found most of them lived with different set of values than I did. Had Alan not died, I'd have probably still been at home, and never entertained the thought of going back to work, as I would have still preferred being a full-time mother, and to be fair most of the mothers' I employed had to work to make ends meet, but some of them just liked the extra money. Modern day families think they are giving their children the best of everything in life when they both work but what they don't realize is that by giving their children to babysitters to raise, it's the babysitter's values they are being raised with, and not their own. Suddenly the child reaches the age of 16 and doesn't know his/her parents because they have nothing in common, and the parent thinks, "I've given you the best of everything since you were born, and you treat me like dirt! Get out and look after yourself!" Stacey and Shawn stayed with us for nearly six months before vanishing to British Columbia, while the other Stacie took off for the streets of Toronto after only a few weeks, and the only one I managed to get reconciled with her folks was Amanda. Sad, isn't it?

The House that Jack built, or HMS Shaw

Four years into the business in 1986, when David was 18 and John 17, and after 10 years of living in the longest home we'd lived in throughout our marriage, we sold it the same day we put it on the market – one month after replacing all the upstairs carpets to a more neutral colour. We had paid for both boys to be professionally taught to drive at Young Drivers of Canada, and now that they had driving licenses they wanted their own wheels but there was no room to park any cars because we only had a single-car driveway, and the other reason I was persuaded to sell my lovely home was that my friend, Leanne, had just gotten her real estate license, and needed someone to practice on and it wasn't just that, of course, but peaceful little Meadowvale had been invaded by drug dealers, and I wanted to put some distance between them and my boys - it never crossed my mind that they'd also be able to drive - and for the next few years we did a 'nose sniffing' exercise every time we came home.

It was a lovely three-bedroom detached bungalow on about an acre of land, with a swimming pool, and, as the crow flies just about six minutes away from Meadowvale, but in the country, and although lovely to look at, none of us could have guessed that that house would become a nightmare. One week after we moved in, Ontario had a record rainfall that ended up in our basement among all the unopened boxes and furniture being temporarily stored, and we awoke to find boxes floating in about two feet of water. After a Building Inspector made an emergency visit, he discovered that the 'sump pump' was missing from the collection pit in the basement. We'd never heard of such a thing, and he went on to explain that as country houses are not attached to city drains, then the water that collects around the house has to go somewhere, and usually seeps into basements. Therefore, it was normal to create a weak point in the basement, such as a pit, then all the water can be pumped out again to where it would cause no damage. "Well, what happened to the sump pump if one is supposed to be there?" I asked. "I guess the previous owner took it with him, but as they are considered fixtures and fittings he shouldn't have removed it," replied the Inspector. Tom Hanks had just released a comedy called 'The Money Pit' and we swore it was based on our house because nobody laughed when we watched the movie. We became experts on swimming pools, septic beds, drainage of any kind, and leaky roofs because everything that could go wrong went wrong.

On our 23rd wedding anniversary, on December 21st, just before we were due to have 24 family members over for Christmas dinner, we discovered effluent coming up through the Laundry room toilet. Again, another visit from a Building Inspector. He told us that half of the original septic bed had been removed to put the swimming pool in and what bed was left couldn't cope with a family of four. His only suggestion was to find the cover of the septic tank and arrange to have the tank constantly pumped out until we could come up with another solution. Poor David. Apart from me, he was the only one at home at the time, and he got the job of removing about 40 patio stones in order to locate the tank lid. Once he figured out a rough location, he set about digging tons of wet, smelly sand off the top, and it was not a very pleasant task, but he accomplished it, without any grumbling. What a great guy! For the next two years, we had to have the tank pumped out once a month and apart from the inconvenience, it was very expensive. The Ministry of the Environment got involved and insisted we remove the swimming pool, but I refused. That had been one of the main attractions of the house, that, and the huge driveway. All my family enjoyed the swimming pool, so there just had to be another solution. After constantly battling with the MOE they finally conceded that it was possible to put an industrial septic bed into the land we had left, concentrated rather than spread out.

We also had water gushing from the road above us into the house and we had to dig a 30' long by 3' deep trench angled towards the forest and away from us. We had the master bedroom ceiling collapse after one of my relatives stood on the roof to clear out the leaves from the gutters and unwittingly pushed all the nails through the roof shingles and let the rain soak in. The swimming pool started losing water like crazy until John dug through to the pipes and discovered that 'Jack' had used ordinary screws instead of stainless steel screws to keep the pipes together and they had rusted away. Mind you, it did have its good points. It was a great house for large social gatherings and all our friends and relatives loved to visit. In fact, it wasn't unusual to have 10 or more extra people around the pool most weekends, for a swim and a barbeque, once I had a normal life again. That's not counting the hordes of young teenagers who adopted our house as their own. What an education and a huge expense that house was. I couldn't wait to sell it, but I couldn't in all conscience put it back on the market the way it was and it cost over $60,000 in repairs before I could look people in the face when we finally sold it four years later.

All the while I was trying to run the business, and trying to fix the house, I did my best to keep John in school. He just didn't like school. He had been totally misunderstood from the minute he joined school in Canada, and as each of his school reports marked him with a passing grade, I didn't know any different. I thought that both of my children were brilliant, and with John being able to read and write well before the age of 5, I thought he'd fitted into the school system brilliantly. Where was my head? It must have been buried in the sand. We only found out about John's lack of interest in school when his academic skills were tested before going into High School, where they were found to be deficient. I can roll with the punches on most things and turn the other cheek, but not where the welfare of my children is concerned. To be told by the Principal that he did not have the necessary education to attend an academic High School and would have to attend a blue-collar Trade School was absolutely unacceptable. I wanted him to make the choice as to what he wanted to do in life, not somebody else. If it was his choice to work with his hands, so be it, but he deserved nothing less than a Grade A education in order to make that choice.

I demanded a meeting with the Superintendent of the Peel Region of Schools, which is where his Grade schools were, and with every teacher and Principal, who had ever taught my son upon arriving in Canada. I wanted to know why they had consistently given him passing grades with no thought as to his actual skill level. With fire in my blood, Brian and I attended a meeting that included the majority of his teachers, three of his last Principals, a child psychologist, and the Superintendent of Schools. Each of his 'hands on' teachers agreed that he was a bright boy, well-mannered and well behaved while in their care and with more challenging work, which they thought he'd get in the next class, he should do well, and that had been the pattern, "Pass him onto the next teacher and see if they can trigger an interest in school." In other words, pass the buck! I was raised to respect other people, especially those with power such as Doctor's, Teacher's, Lawyer's and Policemen, and I would never ever question their abilities but for my back being against the wall. That meeting was different to any Parent/ Teacher meeting. Those ignorant people were about to pass judgment on my son's skills and toss him onto the scrap heap, and once I started questioning their basic ability to teach, the room came alive.

Again and again, different teachers made the same excuse, "Well if he doesn't want to learn, nobody can teach him," they said. "You could have called me if you were having problems teaching him. Each one of you has passed him through to the next class with no consideration for him at all and unless I know there is a problem, how can I solve it!" I said angrily. "Mrs. Shaw, we have large classrooms of children to teach, we can't spend time with one boy," the Superintendent haughtily replied. It was no use trying to talk to them. They just saw me as an ignorant mother shouting her mouth off. None of them would take ownership for their lack of teaching skills, and nobody came up with an academic solution other than to tell me to have his skills tested at a private school in order to reexamine his case. I'm afraid I was very rude and as I stood up to leave I said, "The problem with you lot is that teaching is just a job; it is just a way for you to collect a salary. In my day, teaching was a vocation, and it reflected badly on the teacher if the child wasn't taught, and those teachers didn't last long. You lot didn't give a damn that my child was not taught any academic survival skills other than what we, his parents, have taught him. Parents teach life skills, morals, values! You lot were supposed to teach his mind!" I said angrily. Nobody looked at me while I spoke, they all sat with their heads bent looking at paperwork in front of them and, as nobody responded, we left.

It cost nearly two months mortgage to have our son's academic skills tested, and we were given written confirmation that he had an extremely high IQ in the majority of the tests, and that the school system had completely failed him. It was the only time I ever regretted moving to Canada. For the next six months, privately paid for tutors brought John's grade levels up to scratch, but he was only given the option of attending Trade School. Well, he really didn't want to be a Chief Executive Officer of a multi-billion-dollar company anyway, that was just me wanting it for him. However, he attended Trade School off and on for the next four years and I'd constantly get phone calls from the Principal, to be told that he'd either not shown up, or that he'd had vanished after roll call. It was a good job I was in my own business, because I'd down tools, find him walking on the road home, and return him to school and threaten him what I'd do to him if he did it again. We played this game between us, with me pleading to the Principal at times not to expel him permanently, until he finally graduated. What with one thing or another, it was an exhausting time. A few years later, John actually thanked me for keeping him in school because he'd not have been able to realize his ambition of becoming an AZ truck driver without his Grade 12 Certificate, and when both Brian and I thought back on it, yes, from being a very small child all he wanted to do was to drive a big rig, and, given that the difference between the men and the boys is the price of their toys, he's very happy driving huge transport trucks for a living, and not many people can say that.

David, on the other hand, loved school. He graduated from High School with honours, and was accepted into the University of Waterloo, mathematical honours program. Children in Canada start school at the age of 6, and don't finish High School until the age of 18 then, if they have the qualifications, they go onto University and don't finish their education until the age of 24.

John was never interested in going to University other than when we all went with David to his campus, and all the young folk thought it was outgoing exuberant John that was staying, instead of the fairly quiet and reserved David, then he wished he'd achieved higher marks in his academic studies.

Life was never dull. It didn't mean because the boys were nearly grown that life was now quiet. No, it was exactly the opposite in fact. Both boys were very friendly, sociable, people and it wasn't at all unusual for me to take a break from work in order to get home and make supper that I'd find three or four extra people to feed. I had made the rule of, "If you bring people home around supper time, be prepared to feed them. Don't just feed yourself, that's very rude." Apart from my family unit, none of the other young people who made my home a second home for themselves had two parents, and I felt they had more stability in my home than in their own. They certainly had respect and were very polite in our presence. I know that for most of my boy's teenage years I wasn't around to do the 'motherly' things anymore, but neither of them suffered. I was only a ten-minute car ride away and able to drop whatever I was doing if they needed help, so it wasn't a case of putting them to the back of my life. They were my life.

I was still working hard in the business, and it came to the point when we realized that the business, functioning as a glorified typing service, was never going to be able to support two full-time owners. Stivvie had been taking home a small salary as everything was still being plowed back into the business, but I hadn't, so it was time to do something different, and he took a job working for a security company in Meadowvale, while I stayed on the premises. For the next year, Stivvie would come in after working a full day for somebody else to proofread for us, but it was physically just too much and after being 'on call' for emergencies for six months, he asked me to buy him out. To buy Stivvie out would be the easy route to take, but I didn't want all of the business. I wanted someone to share the responsibility with so that I could start and have a life. I offered a 50% share of the business to our first employee, for no money down, but it was refused. "All I want to do is to earn a weekly salary, and go home at the end of the day," she said. That just devastated me and I think that was the real beginning of the end of the business. A few weeks later they rushed me into hospital for an emergency hysterectomy and although I was supposed to be off my feet for three months, within three weeks I had no choice but to go back to work. It was a long holiday weekend and one of the big banks needed us to create thousands of individually addressed letters to their customers, and nobody wanted to work, so I had to do it. Whether it was because I was not in good health, or what, but suddenly I was fed up with the whole idea of being in business. I had given up a terrific salary five years before to work my guts out keeping other people employed and happy, whilst I earned very little for my efforts, and all the aggravation just didn't seem worthwhile any more. Unless I could expand the business into other areas then I didn't want to be there either.

One of the people whom we did regular work for owned a number of small businesses, and once John L., heard that Stivvie wanted out, he wanted in. He agreed to pay Stivvie a decent amount for his share of the business and, I figured that as he'd drawn a salary for a few years, I'd done right by him, and, in the back of my mind, if the business went in the direction I wanted it to then I would have personally made sure that he and my sister benefitted from it. John L., and I shook hands only, as he said if my handshake wasn't good enough, then no lawyer's paper would make us good business partners, and with that Stivvie and Nora, and Brian and I stupidly handed over our Share Certificates to the worst business partner in the world. He wanted to own 51% of the business to my 49% and convinced me that 49% was better than the 25% I owned right now. I said that I was only interested in him as a partner, if he would agree to expand the business, The Word Wizards, into other service bureaus as I needed to do something other than type for 18 hours a day. I wanted to create other service bureaus such as, 'Accounting Wizards,' 'Real Estate Wizards,' 'Legal Wizards,' and so on, and he agreed.

The first thing he did was to remove Stivvie's name from our Line of Credit at the bank and put his on, and at the time he 'bought' in, we had a fairly substantial amount of dollars in accounts receivable. He took over all the administration work, including payroll and office supplies, and told me that as he wasn't getting a salary, I wasn't getting one either. He also told me that he intended to reduce staff salaries and would save costs by buying a poorer quality of paper, and that he was going to substantially increase charges to our customers and refused to believe there was an industry limit as to what could be charged. I went along with the 'no salary' edict for the first three months, but would not agree to him reducing staff salaries, or his other changes. I had built the business on sound business practices, with honesty and ethics, and as every invoice that went out of the door had my name on it, I was not about to cheat my customers, nor was I about to use flimsy poor quality paper. My partner denied wanting to expand the business into other areas and admitted that he only wanted the business as a 'cash cow' in order to write off some business losses from his other companies. Once his true colours showed, I absolutely detested him. He had lied to me, and I was absolutely furious. I had been suckered into giving this man the business under false pretences and when I found out what he was really like there was no way I could work with him. He saw honesty in various shades of gray whereas I saw honesty as either black or white. You were either honest or you were not, and he was definitely not. I offered to buy him out three times, with interest, before finally losing my temper with him after three months. I put my coat on and walked out of the door while telling him he could have the lot. After I'd sold my home and gave away most of my furnishings when living in East Law to go to Australia, nobody and nothing would ever own me. I'd not gone more than a dozen paces when he came to the door and shouted, "You old cow, you'll be back! You can't walk away from all of this! Come back, you old cow!" Hardly words of endearment.

He kept phoning me at home, at first demanding and threatening, then begging and pleading but unless he was willing to let me buy him out, I just couldn't go back, and I really didn't want to buy him out if the truth be known. I had worked nearly seven days a week for 4 of its 5½ year history while the business multiplied each year, and I was on the point of collapse again, and after three weeks, I went to see my lawyer because I decided that he really could have it all. To my way of thinking, if he wasn't willing to expand into other areas, then the business had served its intended purpose of allowing my sister and her family to settle in Canada by employing Canadians for five years, and I was finished with it. My partner couldn't believe that I'd walk away from such a reputable business, and after trying to run it without me for a few weeks, with little success, rather than admit personal defeat and sell it back to me, he folded it, and that was fine by me. Unfortunately, while I was not in attendance, he ran our Line of Credit up to its maximum and refused to pay it from the receivables, and when I was talking to the Word Wizard's bank manager, he wanted to sue him, but I'd had enough and wanted out quietly.

I secretly sought offers for the equipment but could only raise a small amount so we redid our house mortgage to pay the remainder of the Line of Credit back to the bank. Even though he still wanted to sue my partner, I told our bank manager, it was through my name and home-ownership that we got the Line of Credit in the first place, and that my name was not for sale and I did not want it dirtied through the courts. Brian and I, and our two very tall and well-built boys, 19 and 18, showed up at my partner's home with a moving van, and demanded that he either release the equipment and furniture from his basement, or give me a cheque for its sale price. His face ran the full gamut of emotions as he looked into the aggressive faces of my family. He was a bully at heart, and he did what most bullies do when confronted, he backed down. "Now there was no need for this, Nancy. We could have worked it out." What on earth was to work out? He wouldn't give me back my business. He chose to fold it. He chose to put everything belonging to the business in his basement so that I couldn't get at it. He'd taken off with the accounts receivable invoices. He'd run up the Line of Credit and refused to pay it. What was to work out? I wanted nothing more to do with him, ever again. We parted on negligible speaking terms after he made the comment that I was the only person who'd refused to work with him in one of his companies. I told him he was the only person that I'd met in my whole life that I'd not found some redeeming quality in. He was such a despicable person who put no value on anybody other than himself. He'd had a robbery at one of his public houses the week before Christmas, and although very little was stolen, he gleefully told his staff there'd be no Christmas bonus, and admitted to me that he'd just saved himself a bundle. What a sorry excuse for a human being! It was worth giving up the business so as not to have any further association with him.

Still, there was a certain amount of sadness that it was gone, but as I've always said, "Regret is the cancer of life," and I resolved to only remember the good times I'd had. Different family members had helped during the previous five and a half years, and my son David, was predominant. He'd come in after school and on weekends and either help with the typing, or because he was training to be an accountant, he'd help with the books. He was always willing to learn and he learned practical business instead of just theory. Marjorie also worked with us a few times. She had been made redundant by Office Overload, and while staying with me on a weekend, would earn a few dollars proofreading. Even Aunt Mabel was roped in when she was over for a visit. One time she said she was getting worried that her money would run out before her holiday, so we kept her busy answering the phones for us for a couple of weeks, and she loved it. Needless to say, apart from Stivvie drawing a small salary, neither Nora nor Brian, who were sleeping partners, got paid when they helped out. Marjorie's daughter, Lindsay, came up and worked for us for a few weeks as a junior typist but, unfortunately, typing was not her forte and it didn't work out. However, she did live with us for nearly a year in order to attend Streetsville High School. That was because she wasn't doing well at home and we all thought a change of scenery might help her, and it did to some extent.

Starting again

Within one week of walking away from The Word Wizards, Neil my ex-colleague from AES Data, and the joint venture company, called me. He had wanted some typing done and once he heard I wasn't there, called me at home. He offered me the job of Office Manager to his new 'greeenfield' company, a communications software engineering company, newly started by a group of 10 ex-colleagues from the joint venture company, all of whom were known to me. As well as the role of Office Manager, I would also be the joint owners, Neil, Doug and Fritz's, personal assistant and as all three of us had remained firm friends throughout my business years, they welcomed me with open arms. I should have given myself time to grieve over the loss of my business, but I didn't. I jumped in with both feet and for the next two years traveled 1½ hours each way across the top of Toronto to work. I loved working there and for well over a year, until they hired a woman accountant, I was the only woman for nearly 30 men, and was spoiled rotten. It was thought consuming work, but just what I needed and, finally, I was putting jam back on the bread. The company was more a meeting of minds than a normal workplace, with so many highly intelligent people breaking new ground in the area of computer communications, everything was exciting. There was no such thing as normal business hours, because once they got into the middle of creating something, into the rhythm, I'd find them still at their desks the next morning when I came back to work and they took some persuading to have a break. There were a lot of bachelors, simply because they'd spent so much time in University, and building a career, that they didn't have time to find females, and some of the younger ones were lacking in social skills which I did my best to rectify. I was adopted as the mother hen by them and listened to their woes about the lack of females in their lives, but unfortunately couldn't help them in that area.

Other ex-colleagues from AES Data, such as Bijoy, were employed by Neil, and he and I would go out to lunch every day and became very good friends. Bijoy was originally from India and he had married Betty, an Englishwoman from London, England, and invited Brian and I quite often to his home for a meal, and whereas I loved the hot, spicy Indian food, Bijoy would make ordinary food for Brian and Betty. They were lovely people. The annual summer picnic was held at my home and all the families enjoyed our swimming pool. Bijoy cooked Samosa's, while others cooked hamburgers and hotdogs on our barbeque, and it was a great success. I would probably have been content to continue working there, had Ella not phoned to ask if she could come and live in Canada, and once she arrived I realized I couldn't continue to work and look after her at the same time. My colleagues and friends were very upset that I had to leave, and tried hard to persuade me otherwise, but I had no choice in it, Ella couldn't manage on her own. They gave me a fantastic 'going away' party which included all of their family members, and an 'all expenses paid' vacation to the Dominican Republic, at a time of my choosing. What great guys!

The road to hell really was paved with good intentions

The year was 1988, and Tommy Shaw had died two years previous. He'd gone to get coal out of the coal shed built into the side of the house and had slipped on the icy ground and lay there until Ella had gone to see where he'd gone. By now she was in her early 80's and very frail, and it was a struggle to get Tommy into the house. She should have called for an ambulance because once she got him on the couch he refused to move because of the pain as he'd broken his hip, although neither of them knew that at the time. It was only after he'd lain on the couch for three days that she decided to call for an ambulance but, sadly, it was too late, the damage was done, and within a week of being hospitalized he died. Brian made an emergency trip over to England, but Tommy died before he could get there, and no amount of pleading, persuading, or cajoling would convince Ella to come and live with us in Canada at that time.

My home had an open door to friends and family alike. Anyone who needed help was given it, with no regard to the cost. I even invited an employee to stay for as long as she wanted as her husband had battered her and, because she had no other family, she lived with us for nearly six months. So, when Ella asked to come and live with us there was no hesitation. All of our married life Brian had gone out of his way for my family, so the least I could do was to embrace his. If I'd known what was to come, hopefully I would have put my stupidly sentimental heart to one side, and really found out where she wanted to live, which wasn't with me, or Canada. After struggling on her own since Tommy died, Ella's health had really deteriorated and she was not able to feed herself very well, and when she said, "Nancy, can I come and live with you?" I immediately replied, "Of course you can!" And when Brian came home from work I told him about the phone call, and that we'd better start the paperwork to bring her to Canada. Because of her age, it only took about three months for official sanction and Brian brought 82-year-old Ella Shaw home to me in Canada on the eve of our 25th wedding anniversary.

When I went to the airport to pick up Brian and Ella I couldn't believe my eyes. If Brian hadn't been standing behind her, I'd have never recognized her and, while he struggled with the suitcases, Ella sat in a wheelchair that a Stewardess pushed toward me. The last time I saw Ella was about five years prior and she was still a tall strong woman, and to see this very frail and transparent, almost senile looking person, shaking uncontrollably, was very upsetting. I gave her a hug and a kiss, and almost immediately burst into tears. I didn't know her health was so bad, and I felt as though I'd neglected her because even though I phoned religiously every month she never once told me the state she was in, but I guess that, given her opinion of me that was to be understood. She would die before she would admit to needing my particular help, and she almost did. When Lorna and Nora joined me for a Chinese buffet at home the next day to welcome her to Canada, Nora asked me what Brian had bought me for my anniversary and I dryly replied, "My mother-in-law."

The first three months were hell on earth, because if I thought Ella Shaw was something of a trial at long distance, then up close and personal she was a living nightmare, and as much as I tried to make her feel welcome, she let me know that she didn't want to live in my house with me, only Brian, with the boys a distant second. I resolved to put the bit between my teeth and compromise, compromise, compromise. I coaxed her into eating invalid foods just to get some sustenance back into her body and, within a month, she responded so well that she was able to walk again with just the aid of a cane. I realized it must have been awful for her to leave her home of more than 60 years, as well as her homeland and friends, and I constantly reminded myself of what she must have gone through to make the decision to leave everything behind. It couldn't have been easy for her, and I really tried to help her fit in. Brian had arranged to bring some of her furniture, specifically her bedroom suite, and she thought I was stupid wasting money bringing 'old' stuff across the sea, until I said, "Whose furniture would you rather see when you open your eyes in a morning, yours or mine?" It didn't matter how much I did for her, she never liked me and never would. She wasn't a happy person and I am still sorry that she and I could not have had a better relationship because I think she missed out on the best daughter-in-law the world.

Ella Shaw – 82 yrs old, 1988

For the past two years, Nora and I had managed to get some sisterly time together, and if Marjorie wasn't visiting, we would go out on a Saturday to garage sales, auctions, or just have lunch someplace, but all that totally changed when Ella came. Brian had bought a wheelchair for Ella and as I didn't like leaving her on her own, I started bringing her with us and, on reflection, I don't think I should have done that. Nora didn't like Ella, but neither did anybody else for that matter, except my cousin David's wife, Donna, and I should have realized that whereas I had to put up with her, Nora didn't and she started to shy away. The other reason I think Nora faded into the background for a while was that I had wanted to leave Ella with some dignity and felt somebody other than me should help her bathe, and asked Nora to help. Once we had known Ella was coming, Marjorie's husband, Ken, renovated one of our bathrooms, replacing a bath with a walk-in shower so that it would be easier for her to bathe, but she wouldn't use it. She was only used to baths so I asked Nora to help her get in and out of the bathtub. Nora could see the predicament that I was in, being the hated daughter-in-law, and agreed to help. But when the time came, it was not an easy thing to accomplish. She got Ella into the bath but because she was so slippery, she couldn't get her out again, and had to shout for my help. I think Nora was so upset at not being able to manage Ella on her own, she never offered to help again and that's when I noticed her starting to make excuses not to come over any more. I couldn't get her out of the bath on my own either, and unless she agreed to Brian helping me, then she had no choice in the matter, she had to take a shower instead of a bath.

I asked her what was wrong with the shower and she said she didn't like the idea of water spurting onto the top of her head, so we replaced the fixed shower head with a flexible shower head that she could hold in her hands, and the problem was solved. We had previously made sure the shower was big enough to put a proper bath chair in, and after helping her to get in, she'd wash herself, except for her hair. Now and again, after she'd shout for me to come and help her get out, she'd turn towards me, and 'accidentally on purpose' soak me with the flexible showerhead. After she did that a few times, I cottoned on to her game and asked her to turn the water off before I entered the room. Mind you, to give her credit, she was a very clean lady, even though I had trouble persuading her to shower more than once a week because, as she very pointedly said, "I never go anywhere to get dirty." Ella was only with us for about six weeks when Nora faded out of the picture altogether. It just seemed to me that if I needed to include Ella in any of the family gatherings, Nora made an excuse not to come and because I was still trying to get Ella hale and hearty again, she took up most of my time, and although I missed my sister very much in the beginning, she wouldn't give me a straight answer as to why she wouldn't come any more, and after a few more weeks, stopped speaking to me altogether. I couldn't understand why, and I was extremely hurt about it. But, I must admit, I had so much on my plate that, finding out the real problem with Nora got to be a low priority and we actually went for the next five years without speaking. Unbelievable!

I didn't see much of Lorna during weekends simply because her time was taken up with Ted, and after they had bought the trailer/caravan, and had found a permanent spot for it in the lovely Scottish ancestry town of Kincardine, on the shores of Lake Huron, they'd travel the 2 ½ hours each way, every weekend to it, and who could blame them? It beat the heck out of the scorching hot pavements of the city. Winters were different, and once the trailer/caravan was closed for the season, Lorna and Ted would invite us for supper usually once a month, and on an opposite night to Nora and Stivvie. Nobody, other than Stivvie, knew why Nora wouldn't speak to me. She wouldn't even tell Lorna why she wasn't speaking to me, and I don't really think she knew herself. I think she'd just gotten herself into a bad mood because Ella was taking up too much of my time and she got her nose out of joint and was going to make me pay or something like that. But as Gran used to say, "She got herself into the stew, she'll have to get herself out of it again!"

Now that Nora wasn't around at all, Marjorie filled the gap. Nora had also fallen out with Marjorie a couple of years back after Marjorie had introduced her to some people as, "This is Nora, my sister/niece thingy," which did not go down too well, and forever afterwards, whenever Nora spoke of Marjorie she said, "My aunt/sister thingy, you know!" It wasn't that they weren't speaking, just that Nora preferred not to be in Marjorie's company. Mind you, we weren't the only two who had fallen out. Lorna and Marjorie had fallen out a couple of years prior. Honest. I don't know what it is about the 'Buckett' temper but those of us who belonged to the Mount Vesuvius club certainly had thin skins, and couldn't let an argument go without having the last word, and the two elders of the family were no different; however, Lorna and I hadn't fallen out so I used to tell her how Marjorie was doing, and she used to tell me how Nora was doing and the stubborn streak that we all had kept us apart for the next few years.

Marjorie and Ken had bought their own little house in the city a few years before, and while we were having major problems with our house, Ken helped us to fix them. Brian, who was now working as Corporate Controller to an international company not more than 30 minutes away from home, would drive down to Toronto on a Friday evening and pick them up, and then drive them home again on a Sunday evening. During the day, with help from the boys, mostly David and Brian, Ken would fix whatever it was needed fixing. Then the routine was for Brian to take Marjorie to the Bingo on the Saturday evening, while Ken and David and John built a bonfire in the back garden and with lots of their friends around, sit and enjoy the conversation and the beer. After he'd had put up with the young crowd for as long as he could, Ken would join me in watching a movie in front of the log fire in the basement living room. After a few months of these spasmodic visits, Marjorie, who no longer worked for Office Overload and Ken, recently made redundant by General Electric decided they needed to find an alternative way to live. All of their children, David, Ian, Lindsay and Nancy were married, and Nancy came up with the solution that if Marjorie and Ken would 'finish' the basement in their 'yet to be bought' house, they could live with her, so Marjorie and Ken sold up, stored their furniture in our double garage, and lived with us for six months until they found a house they all liked. They had only moved into their new home a few months before Ella came to stay, and even though Marjorie now lived only 30 minutes away from us, she stayed at my home every weekend for the next few years, rain, hail or shine, summer and winter.

Ella had been with us for three months now and, while I was sitting on the floor cutting wallpaper before hanging it on the wall, she fell over my leg and broke her hip. Oh man! Two steps forward and one back! An ambulance came and took her to hospital where they fixed her hip and for the next month I made two trips a day with home cooked food because she didn't like Canadian food, only English food and, once back on her feet and home again, she let everybody know that she hated Canada, but what she really meant was that she hated being around me. Marjorie was a great help while Ella was in the hospital. She would visit with me during the week, as well as the weekends, and both of us would go to the hospital together. On more than one occasion, she heard Ella tell me off because of the food I'd brought her. She didn't like it. She thought I'd put no effort into making it. "It's rubbish. I'm not eating that!" she'd say.

She didn't like the fact that I didn't spend hours with her, or that I left her in the power of horrible hospital staff who made her walk when she didn't want to. She was obnoxious and unfriendly with everyone in the post-surgical ward, and everyone felt the sharpness of Ella. The body might have gotten old, but the mind and tongue were as young and razor sharp as ever. One time when Marjorie was with me, Ella forgot she was there as she was sitting behind her, and as she started berating me for something or other, both of us were shocked to hear Marjorie burst out, "You should be bloody glad you've got our Nan, Ella! Nobody else would put up with you. I know I wouldn't!" And as she got to her feet she said, "Nan, give me the keys to the car,

I can't stand being around her any longer. I don't know how you put up with her, she's never changed. She's just a nasty *old* lady, instead of a nasty *young* one!" I know it was hard for Marjorie to be around Ella, because she knew Ella from when she was a very young child. She told me the story of having to pass by Ella's doorstep in Templetown on her way to school and of Ella viciously hitting her ankles with her broom for having the nerve to walk over her freshly swept path, and that Ella would hide in her doorway to catch any unsuspecting child that passed by but very quickly the children learned to cross the road rather than walk in front of her doorway.

After six months, Ella was back on her feet and fighting fit and Marjorie decided it was time for me to take my all-expenses paid vacation so we fixed a date and she came with me to the Dominican Republic. I must have infected her with my travel ailments because her suitcase went missing at the other end and we had to wait for hours before the airline found it. Then the Bronchitis I had before we left got worse, and I ended up in bed for two days while Marjorie amused herself, and finally, before we could fly back to Canada, we sat in the plane on the tarmac, for four hours in 100-degree heat, waiting for wing replacement nuts to be flown down from Canada. Not the best vacation in the world, but at least it gave me a break from Ella. I decided I had to get another job, as I couldn't continue being at Ella's beck and call all day long, she was driving me crazy. It wasn't as though I could get a break from her on a weekend, because if I arranged to go out with Marjorie I felt as guilty as hell leaving her behind, and if I did leave her behind for whatever reason, I'd spend the next three days being given the cold shoulder. I needed to find a job close to home in order to make her lunch, because she had to be coaxed into eating anything, and I didn't want her starving herself to death, and if anything went wrong I'd be there for her.

The best job yet

In 1989, when I was 46 years old, I applied for a job as Executive Assistant to Roger and John in the corporate head office of a packaging company about ten minutes away from my home, and I got it. Roger was on a temporary assignment from the corporate office in England to help in the finance department, whereas John was in charge of management development across the globe and was a permanent fixture. I wasn't at all sure that I wanted to work for this company long-term, as I thought they were a strange bunch of people, or paranoid might be a better word. The President thought industrial spies were stealing company secrets and gave the edict that everyone had to 'clear' their desks before leaving work, and early into the job I forgot, and left a binder on my desk with financial operating statistics in it and got hauled over the coals because of it, much to my chagrin. I'd never ever been told off in many years, and it rankled and I really debated whether this was the place for me, and there were other things going on also. My workstation was right outside the office of Mr. P., the Vice President of Human Resources, and after working there for nearly a month I was asked by another senior official if I was going to stay, and I bluntly replied, "I don't know. People don't seem very friendly. I've sat at this desk for nearly a month and Mr. P., hasn't even acknowledged my presence." And the very next morning, Mr. P., stopped in front of me and said, "Good Morning, Nancy. How are things going?" Some might say that was just a coincidence, but I think not, but I decided to stay until my three months' probationary period was up, and if they gave me a raise, I'd stay, and they did, and that was the best decision I'd made in a long time.

Personal computers had overtaken word processing systems a long time ago and because I was the only one in the office trained on an Apple Macintosh computer, courtesy of Neil et al, I was given the very first one. But once everyone could see the benefits, Apple Macintosh computers raced through the office like wild fire. My work was diversified. I worked for Roger on the finance side, pulling together monthly financial statements for more than 96 branches worldwide which got a bit boring, whereas working for John on the management development side totally stimulated my imagination. Within a year of working for both men, Roger was recalled to England, and I became John's full-time assistant.

Since rejoining the workforce fulltime, I must have typed thousands and thousands of pages from formulae for atomic reactors to legal aid documents, and from computer data entries to gold mine statistics. I must have typed every kind of written word, either through full-time employment, or through self-employment in business and I thought there was nothing else to do with a keyboard, but I was wrong. John stretched my mind and my abilities by taking me to the next step, that of desktop publishing. He had the most brilliant academic and conceptual mind of any person I had ever known in the human resources area, and it was his job to train every executive worldwide. As well as being a great author in this area, he raised the bar of excellence for me. Not totally content with the written word, John asked for, and got, charts and graphs of every possible size and shape. He was able to translate the written word into a meaningful piece of artwork that, although visually complex, was simple in its meaning. I loved working with him. Each day was a challenge because he wasn't content until the finished article was absolutely perfect from about a dozen different angles. I learned more about human nature working with him over the next few years, than I'd learned in the previous 46.

I'd been working for this company for just two years when Brian came home to tell me he'd accepted a redundancy package from his company and my first instinct was to panic. He had been the breadwinner for all of our married life and had worked as Corporate Controller for 12 years in this job. I couldn't understand why he'd accept redundancy until he said that if he hadn't accepted the package now, there wouldn't be one in a year's time. His company was owned by Americans, and the products that were being produced in Canada were going to be taken back across the border to keep their plants going, and the plan was to downsize the Canadian operations out of existence. What is it they say about work? "If your neighbor is out of work it's a recession, but if you are out of work it's a depression?" And in the early 1990's little did we know we had ten years of turmoil ahead. In the beginning, it wasn't as bad as I thought. Brian would continue to get his full-time salary for the next year, and on the promise of some consulting work for the American side of the business, we were optimistic for the most part. I was in a steady job, with no thoughts as to being laid off, so as long as I worked, we could manage.

Brian's other family

Brian's American boss asked him to take a six-month contract to turn around a failing company they owned in Cambridge, England and he decided that once there, he'd try and find his sister, Doreen. Ella wasn't too keen on him doing that, because she had harboured ill feelings towards Lewis for years, but Brian was determined. He found Lewis' phone number in Tommy's old phone book and from the hotel in Cambridge he phoned Lewis and asked for Doreen's phone number and address and that same weekend showed up on her doorstep and, from what he told me, Doreen was absolutely flabbergasted but highly delighted.

Doreen & Peter Robinson, 1990

With Marjorie taking care of Ella, I flew over to join Brian and to meet Doreen and her husband Peter and two of their three adult children, Martin and Keith, and Keith's partner Sally. We didn't meet Ian at the time because he was teaching English in Greece. We had been married for 27 years when Brian found his own family. You could tell Brian and Doreen were brother and sister, as they looked like two peas from the same pod, and it was quite a revelation seeing brother and sister together. You'd have thought they'd never been apart. For someone who was known in my family to be quiet and reserved, Brian was jubilant and it was Doreen who was quiet and reserved.

Brian & Doreen, 1990

My new brother-in-law, Peter, was quick witted, smart and very good-looking, and we all got on like a house on fire. We discovered a lot of similarities between us in raising our children, and our finances seemed to have run parallel. What a wonderful week we spent together. We didn't meet Ian until we went over to England for Keith and Sally's wedding and Ian, who was now living in Italy, was there with his new wife, Manuela. What a lovely family and I wished we'd known their children when they were small.

I had been invited to meet Lewis and his second wife Ellen at their home in Seaforth, near Eastbourne, in the south of England, which was a 4-hour drive away, and it was with some apprehension that the four of us, Doreen and Peter and Brian and I set off to visit them. Doreen was nervous because the three of them had already visited Lewis, and I gather the first visit between father and son was more like a boxing ring match. However, we received the nicest welcome. After all the horrible things I'd heard about Lewis from Ella, I found him to be the opposite. He had the same excruciatingly blunt approach to life that the majority of north of England people had, and I thought he was no different than the people I'd grown up with. I could tell immediately that he and Tommy were brothers because he had the same way of putting me on the spot with some of his questions, and if the answers weren't to his liking, he'd twist the meaning. I treated him just like I treated Brian at times; I let the whole thing go right over my head. If he wanted to spar with someone, then let it be with Brian who could think on his feet much faster than I could. Once he realized that he wasn't going to be able to get a 'rise' out of me, he settled down and we enjoyed lunch and, on the whole, I liked him and wasn't put off by his blunt manner. I'm sure that the people in the south of England come from another period in time. They haven't experienced the same raw hardships and rough life that northerners had, so most of them have a fairly calm manner, and how they put up with Lewis, I don't know. To have such a strong blunt northern character living among sweet natured southerners must have been akin to experiencing a daily tornado in the village pond. Lewis' sense of humour and sarcastic wit matched Brian's perfectly and to hear them together was brilliant! Tit for tat! Your point! Good rally! Game, set and match! Next! An outsider listening to father and son verbally duel would have thought 'pistols at dawn' was next on the agenda. We invited them all to visit us in Canada, and Lewis and Ellen said they'd love to.

Ella makes her final statement!

On the home front, the pattern was set. I'd put the food ready for Ella's breakfast, then hightail it to work, come home and make lunch for both of us, then rush back. Supper would be started by whoever was home first, whether it was Brian, David, John or I. David had done two years of study at the University of Waterloo, and to support himself during the second year had taken a part-time job in a video store and liked it so much that he decided to give himself a Sabbatical from studies and find a full-time job. His argument, which we argued against, was that he'd attended pre-school from the age of 3, then regular school from the age of 5, and he needed a break and, at the age of 21, we couldn't convince him otherwise. John had sailed through his AZ HGV truck driving license with flying colours, but as he was only 20, no company would hire him fulltime because the insurance for an under 25-year-old was horrendous, so he had to content himself with periodic work. But with both of them working at present, and at 23 and 22 years old, they decided it was time to leave home and set up a 'bachelor pad' and we agreed to help them.

We talked it over with Ella as to what to do with the house because it was far too big for just three of us and once the boys were gone, we didn't need a swimming pool anymore, so in our thinking, the obvious solution was to sell it, bank the money for emergencies, and move to somewhere smaller, but not if it was going to upset her. Ella said she didn't mind moving, as she'd like to be around other senior citizens and asked if it was possible to find an apartment for her in a 'seniors only' building. Since I'd gotten her back on her feet, I had arranged for a membership in an 'over 60's' club contrary to her violent objections and had driven her there every Tuesday morning and picked her up after work, and once settled in, she really liked it and as Meadowvale was predominantly British, it stood to reason that the local seniors building would house ex-patriots, so we started searching. We put the house on the market, and after a few months, it sold, and Brian started searching for new accommodations. At Ella's request, he found one double bedroom apartment for us on the end of the building, and a single bedroom apartment for Ella, two doors down. That was as near as he could get them, and as we were able to get Ella's apartment practically immediately, we set about furnishing it before she moved in. We asked her what she wanted for living room furniture and she replied that she wanted the same kind of dusty pink wing chair that she had at her senior's club. We furnished her place just how she wanted it with two lovely dusty pink velvet wing chairs and a dusty pink rug. Then we bought her a television and a small dining room table and chairs, and she used her own small china cabinet and bedroom suite. You'd have thought she was back in her little home in Delves

Lane, instead of an 8th floor apartment in a 10-story block, and she'd have moved into it right away, but we asked her to wait until we all moved.

The boys found a house to rent in Meadowvale, and we helped them as much as we could. We gave them practically every stick of furniture, except for our solid oak bedroom suite, and nearly every household appliance that we had, and for the first time in years, we bought everything new for ourselves and had it delivered to the new apartment. Before the boys even had time to settle into their new place, it felt like everybody they ever knew moved in with them, and before long they had a university 'Frat' house of young people who didn't contribute either to the rent or to the food. Our home felt like a supermarket because one or other of them would raid our fridge for something to eat or take a few bags of groceries with them so that everybody could eat. We thought our grocery bill would decrease once they'd left home, but in fact it increased exponentially because we were feeding all the 'freeloaders' living with our two sons.

It was just as well that the boys took most of the household stuff, because my gall bladder, which had started giving me pain a couple of weeks previous, decided that it needed to be removed, and I was scheduled for an emergency operation on the Thursday before we moved. Poor Brian was left to finish packing the rest of our stuff, including all of our crystal from our big china cabinet, our good chinaware, and lovely velvet curtains from the windows which unfortunately got stuffed into garbage bags and mistakenly got thrown out with the garbage. I was still in hospital when he and Ella moved into the apartments and I couldn't help feeling some relief that we'd set her place up previously.

I came out of the hospital after a week in post-surgery, and during a visit from Lorna and Ted, I sneezed and some of the staples came out of my incision. Brian took me back to the hospital as I was bleeding profusely, and after lying on a bed in Emergency until the following lunchtime, they admitted me for another week. I have never been as disgusted with the medical profession as I was at that time. It was as though I was blight on their surgical reputation. The surgeon who performed my operation never came to see me, even though my family doctor told him I was there, and after suffering a week of apathy, I couldn't wait to get home again. Home being the apartment with our stuff still in boxes lying around. The Victorian Order of Nurses came each day and put a fresh wick in my wound to drain it because they couldn't close it again with staples for some reason and for the next two months I was in a lot of pain and felt really miserable. Nora, who still wasn't speaking to me, sent a plant in a bowl, with a note attached saying, "Sorry, couldn't find any dead ones," and I asked Brian to drive over to her house and leave them on her doorstep because I didn't want them. Lorna said that Nora was just joking, but I thought it was in very poor taste, given what I'd gone through.

Ella, for the first time since she'd come to Canada, felt useful, and would slowly make her way along the corridor to see if I was okay. I didn't want to move an inch off the bed because of my open wound but had to, to open the door to her, and probably for the first time in our lives, both of us appreciated the other. Maybe she wasn't so bad after all, now that there was some distance between us again. Having two apartments gave us both a break. Ella liked being on her own, and I'd still cook, clean and take her out every weekend and as she was able to go upstairs to the social gatherings each day by elevator, I thought she really liked living there. It wasn't until we'd been there for six months that she told me she absolutely hated the place. I didn't like living in an apartment myself, especially a senior's apartment. Just walking from the elevator to our door was a trial, with all the coughing and gagging, and strong food smells in the corridor but there was nothing I could do about it at the time. Once back at work, life settled into the routine where I'd go home to make Ella's lunch, and sit with her until she'd eaten it because she'd gotten into the habit of putting most of it down the toilet. Then either Brian or I would take her evening meal along to her home and sit and chat for a while.

Both boys, but David in particular, was finding it very hard keeping things going at their rented house, with nobody contributing to the costs so David took it upon himself to pay for everything and with Ella stating that she hated the apartment, and as I didn't like living their either, we resolved to find another house that would accommodate all three generations. After keeping everything afloat for the next few months, we finally found a five-level house already split into two apartments, in Atherly Crescent in Meadowvale where we first started out. The idea was to remove the wall between the apartments and make it into one house again, but as the top half of the house was currently rented the boys would move into the bottom half before us, with Brian and Ella and I moving in two weeks later.

Ella's lease on her apartment ran out a month before ours, and as it would have meant renewing it for a full year, we moved her into our apartment with us until we all moved. She wasn't very happy about that and I was sorry we were going to have to move her twice. We could have moved her straight into the new house, into the bottom apartment, with the boys the next day, but I don't think that would have worked either. My cousin David and his wife Donna, came to visit us the night before the boys moved, and Ella complained that I was making her move against her wishes. She told Donna that she didn't want to move from the apartment, and that she really liked it there and Donna agreed that she should stay in the apartment if she wanted to. This was totally contrary to what she had been telling me for the past few months. She had made my life miserable by telling me constantly that she hated it there, that there was nothing to do, and no nice people to talk to. I could have torn my hair out in frustration. "Well it's too late to turn back now," I told her after Donna had left. "We bought a much larger house than we needed to have done with you specifically in mind. The boys will have the bottom two floors, and you will have the ground floor with the garden at the back, and Brian and I will have the top two floors. You'll be in the middle of the family. I thought that was what you wanted," I cried. "I want to stay here," she retorted. "Well I'm sorry but you can't. You shouldn't have made such a fuss about hating it here, and then I wouldn't have got another house," I replied. I thought Ella had no choice but to move with us, but she had other plans.

The next morning, I made sandwiches for Ella's lunch and reminded her she was going to be on her own until 6 pm that night because we were helping the boys move. I watched the clock all afternoon and made sure that we opened the apartment door punctually at 6 pm because I didn't want her to get worried if we were any later and found her semi-conscious on the floor by the bathroom. "Oh, my God! What's happened?" I cried. Ella turned her head toward me, her eyes full of pain, "I took all my pills!" she said. Turning to Brian I said, "You'd better call 911!" I felt absolutely dreadful. She'd rather kill herself than move into a home with me again. "Why did you do it?" I cried in anguish. "You don't want me around," she answered. "Ella Shaw, I've been married to Brian for 29 years and I can count on one hand the number of arguments I've had with you. I've loved you in spite of yourself. We only bought the house because you hated this place," I said. "No, you didn't. You bought it because of the boys," she responded. "The boys are big enough to look after themselves if needs be, it just seemed like a good solution. The family would be together, but separate," I said. She thought for a moment before continuing in another vein altogether, "Will you make sure David gets his birthday money tomorrow? It's in the back of my purse, and John's birthday money is there also." "Oh, you'll be giving it to them yourself, don't worry about that right now," I responded. All the time we'd been talking, I had been removing her pajamas because unfortunately she'd had an accident and very carefully I cleaned her where she lay, because I didn't want to move her just in case she'd broken something. I put a pillow under her head and wrapped a blanket around her, and although she flinched she didn't say anything. Because it was a 911 emergency call, the Ambulance, Fire Department and the Police came because they didn't know what kind of emergency it was and with a roomful of people standing around, the Paramedics got her onto a gurney and took her off to hospital.

Once I told the police that she had tried to commit suicide, they wouldn't let me go with her, only Brian, and he phoned from the hospital to find out which pills she had taken. She had been taking pills for numerous ailments, and the one's I can remember most were her heart pills and water pills. The other pills were more like placebos rather than heavy medication. I searched through the four bottles of medication, but her heart pills weren't on her bedside tray and I found them in the second drawer down in her dressing table, and as Brian always filled her prescriptions with the Pharmacy, he knew exactly how many pills were left in each bottle and was able to tell them. Within 1½ hours they had stabilized her, and the Doctors reckoned that she had only taken enough pills to make her sick, to make a statement. If she had really wanted to kill herself she would have taken some, or all, of her heart pills and would have been dead within minutes. So, when Brian phoned me at 7:30 pm to tell me she was okay, but that they were going to keep her in the hospital because when she'd fallen she'd broken her hip again, I felt a great relief. He stayed to keep her company, and when he phoned me at 11:30 pm to tell me she had died, I was devastated, and couldn't believe it. What happened? Nobody could tell us anything until an Autopsy had been performed. Ella Shaw had been a monkey on my back from the age of 15 until 49 and, by her own hand, she was dead! What a dreadful memory to leave anyone!

Because she had died under suspicious circumstances there was a Coroner's Inquest and a Police Investigation, both of which were totally foreign to Brian and me. Early the next morning two very young Policemen came to the apartment and started asking very pertinent questions to both Brian and I, but separately, and it came as a huge shock to realize they were trying to find out whether I'd murdered my mother-in-law or had contributed to her death in some way. I told them the whole story of what had happened since she came to Canada. I left nothing out. I even told them that they could check with our family doctor as she had threatened suicide before, by not taking her pills, and the last thing I told them was about Brian being adopted by her, and that his biological father, Lewis, her brother-in-law, was coming to Canada for a visit in two weeks' time, and that she hated the thought of being in the same room as him. The Coroner reported that she had taken just enough extra pills to make her sick, but with falling over and breaking her hip, some fatty tissue had worked its way up through her system and stopped her heart. She shouldn't have died but I think Tommy Shaw had something to do with it and from his place in heaven I think he came and said, "That's enough Ella. They've had enough. It's time to go."

Just before she died, she reminded Brian again about the boys' birthday money and for the second time in her life she thought of somebody other than herself – the first being the time she gave me her fur coat - and I hope both acts of kindness got her into heaven. The same two policemen came back just before her funeral and said, "From the Coroner's report we're happy to tell you that she died as the result of a self-inflicted accident, and that you had nothing to do with it. We're very sorry that you had to be interrogated but there are some nasty people out there who deliberately hurt old folk. But we're pleased to report that from our inquiries you did indeed look after the old lady very well. You're moving into a new home, so put the past behind you and get on with your life." That was much easier agreed to, than done.

John said he was just too upset to attend her funeral, the way things had happened, and I tried to understand. So, that meant only Brian, David and I would send her on her way. I asked Marjorie, Lorna and Nora not to come because I didn't want them to be hypocrites, because I didn't think it was right seeing somebody off when you didn't like them, and to our surprise my cousin David, Donna, Letisha and their second daughter, Krista, who was born when Tisha was 7, attended along with my friends Bijoy and Betty. Not a big send off, but at least a genuine one. It was a simple service, with cremation to follow, and all through it I was calm, until the time came when I put my hand on her closed casket and burst into tears. I did love Ella Shaw; I just found it difficult to like her at times.

Brian's biological father and his wife visit

Four years after Ella moved to Canada, and one week after her funeral, and just days after moving into our new house, Lewis and his second wife of 25 years, Ellen, arrived for a vacation. We sat at the kitchen table and discussed what had happened to Ella, and before I knew it, I was in tears telling them that all I had ever wanted to do was to help her in any way I could, but that she didn't want my help. She'd hated me all of her life and now she had left me with horrible memories. Ellen, who was extremely religious said, "Well now, God is always watching and he knows all that has gone on. We know Ella Shaw and how she was with everybody. Put the past behind you because you did your best and nobody would have been right for Brian, nobody!"

Brian & Nancy, Lewis & Ellen, 1990

Of all the people in the world I could have broken down with, these two people knew Ella Shaw the most. I mean really knew Ella and what she was like, and totally understood where I was coming from. Oh, what a relief to get everything off my chest to people who understood. It was like emerging from a four-year old hibernation and I could just feel my soul getting lighter. Thank you very much Lewis and Ellen. If I thought 34 years of association with Ella was torment, then Lewis, as her brother-in-law of more than 60 years certainly served his time with her and according to him he had nothing to thank her for because she stole his son. According to Lewis, he and his wife had moved from the north of England to Maldon, in Essex, where Doreen was born in 1939 and Brian in 1940. But with the war going on, the south of England was being bombarded by bombs and as Lewis was in the Army, the mother decided to bring both children back to the north east to stay with the grandparents where it was much safer. He said that as a 1-year-old and a newborn were too much for the grandparents, Ella and Tommy took newborn Brian but sent Doreen back to her mother. Then, when Brian was 3-years-old, and with the permission of Lewis's mother, Tommy and Ella adopted him. Lewis went on to say that as soon as he was discharged from the army, he immediately drove the length of the country to get Brian back, but it was too late. Brian was now five years old, and the grandparents insisted that he stay with Tommy and Ella, who were never able to have children. As Lewis said, he had no choice but to leave things as they were unless he dragged his family through the courts, and that's how Brian was raised in the North, and Doreen in the South. Now, having Ella Shaw as my mother-in-law, and knowing how she loved to be in the center of intrigue, hearing her version of what happened was totally different to the above. All of Brian's life it had been drilled into him that Lewis and his wife dumped the children with her and Tommy and never came back for them and, to quote her, "I never liked girls so I sent the girl back to her mother!"

Lewis's first wife was killed in a road accident and Lewis raised Doreen on his own but he used to bring her up north to visit both Brian and the grandparents, so they knew they were brother and sister from a very young age. However, the relationship between biological father and son was very strained due to the fact that Ella denigrated Lewis every chance she got and so Brian was raised to thoroughly dislike his 'father.' That was all about to change now that both Tommy and Ella were dead. Brian finally had the opportunity to start a relationship with his father, and with a much lighter atmosphere, we thoroughly enjoyed their company. We showed them all the usual tourist spots and traveled all over Ontario and one particular place that we visited still stands out. We took them to Pioneer Village to the country restaurant for a real homemade meal and my choice was beef stew but it had so much meat in it that I couldn't eat it all and asked for a doggy bag. "Are you going to get one then?" asked Lewis. I looked at him with a dumb expression on my face. "Are you going to get a dog then?" he repeated. We all burst out laughing and over the following years I came to expect the unexpected from Lewis all the time.

Our last family home

I couldn't help but think Ella would have loved the new house because she would have been the center of attention. The boys never had any food in their fridge and used to come and raid ours all the time so they would have had to speak to her any time they were in our kitchen. They used to get along with her and would fetch her drinks, cushions for her feet, change the channel on the television for her and, in her way, she loved them when we'd all lived together the last time. She had loads more patience with the boys than she ever had with me, and maybe Tommy was probably right when, years ago, he said that two women would never get along in one house and maybe that was the basic problem between us, especially in Canada, as we were two women used to running our own households. For the first two years, the boys had the bottom two floors, plus the middle floor that should have been Ella's, and more often than not we had a houseful of young people staying on a semi-permanent basis and I remember their friends Mark and Don as being two permanent guests. We also had a swimming pool with this house, an open-door policy, and a flood of young people every weekend.

By 1994 I had worked for the packaging company for five years, in one capacity or another, and had gone through two ownership changes. The first time, one of the original owners wanted out, so half the company was sold to an Italian company, resulting in staff layoffs. I was lucky to be kept on and moved into the Human Resources department, with a new executive, Pierre. I say lucky because Brian and both boys had been totally out of work for over a year and I was the only one keeping the home fires burning. Unfortunately for me, Pierre didn't like me and gave me the option of moving into one of the manufacturing plants, or of finding another job. So, I found another job and gave him one week's notice. I figured that's all I owed him, but didn't figure on causing such a rumpus with the rest of the executives who didn't want me to leave so I moved back under John's authority, and while working for him, also worked for the President & CEO, Sergio. Working for two of the most brilliant minds in business, was perhaps the most exhilarating and challenging job I had ever had. By now I had an IBM personal computer as it was thought, rightly, that they would take over the office business, and I was in my element creating one-of-a-kind graphic work for John, while typing top level secret documents for Sergio. Unfortunately, when the next takeover came, by a Swiss company, everybody in the corporate office was laid off, except for Sergio, who went to work for them in Switzerland.

I was now 51 years old, and really surprised to beat out much younger people, when I got a job as Executive Marketing Assistant to a global computer company, and I worked there for nearly two years. I liked my boss, Debra, but didn't like the cut throat atmosphere, and when she left to go to another company they laid me off. Actually, they didn't lay me off, they fired me. I remember sitting in front of Paul, her second in command, and of him saying, "We're going to let you go Nancy." And when I asked him the reason because I thought they would just replace Debra, he replied, "Well the quality of your work is not up to standard." Well, now, you can tell me my personality is not to your liking; you can tell me you think I'm too old; you can tell me that the department is downsizing; but you cannot tell me that my work is not up to snuff. "That's not a good enough reason Paul. I'll fight you in court if you make that the reason you're firing me," I said. While I talked very softly, his assistant, Barbara, was having apoplexy. "No, no, that's not the reason at all,"

Marjorie, about 75 yrs old, just before she died, 1996.

she said anxiously. "We're moving the marketing department to the United States, and we have no need of your services." "That, I can accept Barbara," I said, and collected my things and went home. I know Grandad said never to get fired, but there wasn't much I could do about it, so I put it down to a new experience, and learned a little bit more about human nature.

Life is strange with its twists and turns

1996 was both a good year, and a very bad year. A few months before I was let go from this last company I had taken three weeks' vacation but was spending it at home as I was redecorating and Marjorie spent the second week with me. It was a Thursday afternoon and I put the groceries away as she sat on the couch absentmindedly staring out of the living room window. There was no prelude to the conversation, no hint of what was to come, and as I sat down on the chair opposite her, she turned toward me. "Nan, I want you to do something for me," she said. "When I'm gone, I want my granddaughters to have these," pointing to her rings she'd just taken out of her purse. "What are you telling me for? Why don't you tell them yourself?" I asked. "I've just got a feeling," she said. "Marjorie, you're starting to frighten me. What on earth are you talking about?" I asked. "I just have a feeling that I need to tell you what I need done when I die!" Where on earth had all this come from? Did she know something that the rest of us didn't? "Marjorie, you're not going to die. I won't let you!" I cried. "Just listen to me please," she said. I couldn't have spoken now even if I wanted to; it was all a bit too incredulous and unbelievable. Still with a faraway look in her eyes, she continued, "I want a very simple funeral, the cheapest casket you can find. I don't want Ken to throw money away on an expensive one because I want to be cremated. I don't want to be embalmed, I don't like it, and I only want one red rose on my casket from Ken." Then she proceeded to tell me who owed her money and in what amount, and that I was to collect it, see that Ken had sufficient money in the bank, then disburse the rest between the grandchildren. "What brought all this on," I questioned. "I don't know, I just have the feeling that I need to tell somebody other than Ken what I want after I'm gone," she answered.

For a moment or two I couldn't have said anything or even moved. I truly believed in an afterlife, and had proof of it, so I couldn't have fluffed her strong feelings away. Nora and myself, along with Anteloper Isabella had, years before, gone to a meeting held by a famous English Medium, Doris Stokes, who was visiting Canada, and when she came over to us with a message, it would have been very hard not to believe. As the lady came towards us, Nora started shaking like a leaf. She hadn't been in Canada very long and was still not speaking to our brother Billy from the time Jimmy had died, and as he was due to come for another holiday, it was making things very awkward for any family get-togethers. The Medium, now standing directly in front of Nora and myself said, "I have a very old lady here saying she never made fish of one or fowl of the other. Is that you two?" All we could do was nod our heads in agreement, as she went on, "She has an uncle/brother, or brother/uncle with her but I don't understand the relationship." I said we'd grown up to call our uncle our brother, and she continued, "There's also a small child with them, maybe about 9-years-old, do you know him?" "Yes, you're looking at our grandmother, our uncle Jimmy, and our aunt Marjorie's son, Kenneth," I replied. Then, turning directly toward Nora she said, "I have a message for you from your 'brother' Jimmy. He says you need to 'let it go, let it go.' Do you understand?" Nora, who had turned into jelly, shakily replied, "Yes, I know exactly what he's talking about."

When Marjorie voiced her strong feelings, I hoped it was the distant future she saw, and not the present. "Now that that's out of the way, put the kettle on, will you?" she asked, back to normal. Marjorie was famous in our family for the amount of tea she drunk, and always, absolutely always, the first words out of her mouth when she got home were, "Ken, put the kettle on will you?" We had a cup of tea, the usual antidote for stress, and I never thought any more about the strange conversation other than to repeat it to Brian in bed that night.

Less than a week later, the very next Tuesday, I received a phone call from my cousin Ian telling me that Marjorie had been rushed into hospital that morning with what seemed to be a bad case of indigestion but was in fact a heart attack. As I drove into the hospital grounds that particular conversation pounded over and over in my head, and it was with some hesitation, I walked nervously into the Intensive Care Unit to visit her. Ken was already standing by her bed and he looked relieved to see me. Marjorie was conscious but didn't look very good and the only time we moved out of her sight was to let her family come in for a visit. She slept most of Tuesday and Wednesday but stayed awake long enough to tell Ken that she'd told me what she wanted done for her funeral and what was to happen to her things. Ken shook his head in disbelief, and I don't think either of us thought she was really going to die. Late Wednesday evening, after everyone had gone home, the hospital called Ken to say that she'd had a massive heart attack during the night and that she was now paralyzed down the right side of her body, and she was not going to recover. Everyone kept vigil all day Thursday and, during the afternoon, when Ken was standing to one side of her bed and I at the other side, she opened her eyes and said very clearly, "Nan, let me go. Let me go." I caught my breath as it bubbled up and promised to gush out in tears and I looked at Ken for direction, and he nodded his head. I turned back at Marjorie and when I found my breath said very quietly, "Marjorie, you can go whenever you're ready, just you go whenever you're ready." She left us early on the Saturday morning, exactly one week and two days after declaring to me what she wanted done when she died. Unbelievably heartbreaking!

Ken confirmed to David, Ian, Lindsay and Nancy that their mother, Marjorie, had instructed me what to do upon her death so Ken, David, Ian and I went to make the arrangements. I managed to comply with three of her instructions and that was the cheaper casket, the red rose from Ken on the lid and the cremation. Ian requested that his mother be embalmed because he didn't want a closed casket. He felt a closed casket was too final, and I told him what she'd told me only one week earlier but he insisted, so I mentally apologized to her and said three out of four wasn't bad. After her funeral, we went back to my cousin Ian's house, where Marjorie and Ken had been living in their 'finished' basement, for her farewell meal and we were all talking about Marjorie's good points which is our cultural custom at a funeral, and everything was fine until Ian's new partner, Debbie, looked across the table to me and said angrily, "Well I didn't like her! She could be really nasty! Even if she was dying she would still crawl up those stairs on her hands and knees just to show me she had done more crochet work than I'd done!" For a minute, I was stunned. I looked at Ian who was sitting next to her but his attention was elsewhere and I'm not even sure he heard her comments because there was no reaction on his face. But if looks could kill, she would have been dead in one second from the look on my face because I was absolutely horrified that she could be so terribly insensitive especially on the day of my sister's funeral, so Brian and I left. I was really surprised that Brian didn't say anything in retaliation, but maybe the dig in his ribs from my elbow stopped him.

I know Marjorie wasn't the easiest person to get along with; she had predetermined ideas about everything; she was opinionated and wouldn't ever back down from an argument but, as the elder of our family in Canada, and irrespective of what upset she caused, she expected to be treated with respect and common courtesy and was most upset when she didn't get it. On the other hand, she was the softest touch with her children and all their lives she never refused them anything. She would be the first one to put her hand in her purse to help them all out and yes, she'd expect to be paid back, but she wouldn't hesitate to help again. Even though there were lots of times that she and I argued and fell out, we never failed to fall in again and, as an adult, I loved her with all my heart and I think I was perhaps the only person who understood her deep down. We went shopping together, lunched together with me paying one week and her the next; went on vacation together and knew absolutely everything there was to know about each other's lives; we talked on the phone most days, or at least she'd phone me and say, "Hi, it's me," and I'd pick up from there and we'd talk about everything and nothing for ages and never ever finished a conversation without telling each other, "I Love you!" She was my best friend and confidant for a good portion of my adult life and I still miss her. All the time we were close as sisters I never once refused to do anything for her, but I really didn't want to comply with her last request of getting the loans back from her children and into the bank, and I couldn't help wishing that she'd asked anybody but me to approach them. I had loved her children as though they were my own and to have to ask them to repay their loans in front of their father, who knew nothing at all about them, was terrible. To their surprise, I told them about their mother's wish, and actually named the amount to repay to their father and I was very happy to hear that they all did!

It was only weeks after Marjorie died that I was let go from my current job which was supposedly being moved to the United States, and because Brian did not have a permanent job, only consulting work, I needed to find another job as quickly as possible, so I took temporary assignments. I had kept in touch with my ex-boss John ever since we parted ways, and through John, I was offered a full-time job with Jim in a division of the packaging company and, because Jim had known me while I worked at the corporate office, I was thrilled to accept his offer of Executive Assistant and Office Manager. He was the most marvelously kind man you'd ever wish to meet. He was very intelligent, and very much a 'people person' and we got on famously. I liked the way he dealt with people, fairly and consistently. Unfortunately, Sergio, who was now head of the Swiss operation, decided within the first two years that this division didn't fit in with his overall scheme and he sold it to an American company. Our three manufacturing sites were renamed, and our little division stood alone, with our office turning into the head office for the Canadian businesses. There were only five of us working there, Jim was the Vice President and General Manager, Duncan was the Vice President of Finance, Bob was the Vice President of Marketing, myself, and Brenda, assistant to Duncan and Bob. Brenda was a girl I'd gotten to know at my previous company and couldn't wait to hire. Between the five of us, we looked after everybody, and because we'd lost our Human Resources Manager who had been transferred to another division before we'd been sold, I took on that role as well. I had an extremely busy job, but I loved it.

Marjorie died in 1996. I started my last permanent job in 1996 and my son, John, got married in October, 1996 and, since John was no longer living at home his two friends who had been living with my boys, moved out of our basement apartment so we decided to demolish the wall between the downstairs and upstairs and make it into one house again. As with every other house we've ever owned, one little request led to major renovation. We had five bedrooms, three living rooms, three bathrooms, and two kitchens, and every room was pulled to pieces and rebuilt, even replacing all the windows and doors with new, modern ones. We had talked about selling it now that we were down to three people, but decided that while David still needed a home, we'd keep it. We'd only just got the place refurbished and new carpets installed, when he formally introduced us to Teresa, who turned out to be the love of his life, and they told us they planned to marry within a couple of years, and we were happy for them.

Early in 1997 Lorna phoned me to tell me that Nora had been diagnosed with ovarian cancer, and I didn't believe her. Our Nora with cancer, never! She'd absolutely refuse to have it. Not her! She was indestructible! She'd been a fighter all her life, she'd not put up with cancer! But sadly, it was true. I tried to be a good sister but whatever it was that I did to her years previous came to the front again and I had to be content hearing about her from Lorna. I did see her one night when Lorna and Ted asked Ken, Nora and Stivvie, and Brian and I to join them for a Fish and Chips supper at a local restaurant and as I sat down next to her I asked how she was doing, was stunned when she replied, "How do you think I'm doing. I'm dying of cancer!" I didn't know how to respond, so I turned toward Brian sitting across the table from me, but his attention was elsewhere. Ted had heard Nora's response to me, and I could see sympathy in his eyes but, he too, didn't want to acknowledge what she'd said, so neither of us said anything. I asked Stivvie later if there was anything I could do but he said no, for some unfathomable reason Nora wanted nothing to do with me, or anybody else for that matter, and that it was better if I stayed out of the way. Okay then, if that's what she wants, so be it. She had her mind up that nothing was going to save her, and she just got on with the business of dying.

David and Teresa were married in November, 1998, but Nora was just too ill to attend which was totally understandable. What was hard to understand however, was the fact that our brother, Brian and his family were flying over for the wedding, and she wanted nothing to do with him. He was staying with me and asked for Nora's address so that he might visit her. I tactfully tried to tell him that he wouldn't be welcome but he wouldn't believe it. She had not forgiven him since our mother, Beattie, had died and he walked all the way up to her house, knocked on the door and said, "Hello, I'm here to see you," but she slammed the door in his face saying, "Well I don't want to see you." He was trying to make amends, but she wouldn't let him. She knew she was dying, and it would have a great time to forgive him. I was sad for him, but as this was supposed to be a joyous occasion, that of my son David's marriage, I resolved to put it on the back burner, and enjoy the wedding, and all the family who were staying with me. Apart from Brian and his wife, Rose, and their daughter, Wendy and husband Derek, and grandchildren Ashleigh and Craig, my best friend in the whole world, Anne and husband Jimmy came.

Christmas of 1998 we had a big family get-together at my home for Christmas dinner, and it was only when Nora arrived that I could see how really ill she was. I had been too busy at work, renovating the home, and getting it ready for David's wedding, and while I got regular updates from Lorna, I hadn't seen much of Nora. She lay on the couch, as pale as a ghost, too weak to join in anything, and when I asked her why she had put herself to so much effort to come, she replied, "This is my last Christmas with all of you, and I didn't want to miss it." Her response just gutted me. Somehow, I'd been hoping for a miracle. I never really believed she was going to die. I didn't. I think the Dilly Dream part of my character just refused to accept the fact that my sister, who had been a second mother to me for most of her life, was dying a long drawn out death. It was not until the last month of her life that I was allowed to do anything for her.

Nora had been admitted to hospital because her body was breaking down and there was nothing anybody could do now; it was only a matter of time, and when she went into hospital for the last time, I asked Stivvie if it was okay to go and he said yes, I could. I walked into her hospital room and said, "Hi, how are you?" and her response was, "It's about time you came!" Straight to the point. "I'd have been here earlier if you'd have let me," I said. Ignoring that, she continued, "Nan, will you do something for me?" "Whatever you want," I replied. "I could do with a wash down, the nurses didn't have time today," she said. Stivvie left the room and suddenly there was just the two of us, two sisters who hadn't spoken much over the last five years but who had never stopped loving one another. I got the dish with the soap, water and washcloth and after gently washing her all over, talking quietly all the time, a serene silence drifted over us. Whatever it was that had caused the rift in our relationship was totally forgotten, and true to family principles of, 'Least said, soonest mended' nothing was ever mentioned, and to this day, I don't know for sure why she fell out with me for all those years.

Lorna and Stivvie went to see Nora at lunchtime, and Stivvie and I went every evening. He'd pick me up at home at 5:30 pm on the dot, and we'd stay until the nurses chucked us out at 10 pm. I got into the habit of bathing her, of making her as comfortable as I could, then of settling down in the bedside chair where Stivvie and I would carry on a conversation with her listening in. She found it difficult to talk so I brought books from home. I'd read a few chapters each night, and after a couple of nights, noticed some of the nurses coming into the room more often than previous. and when I asked them if I was disturbing them they said no, they were enjoying the stories. If I thought Nora was sleeping I would stop reading but she would either raise her hand or move her foot, to motion me to continue. I had chosen Lillian Beckwith's Hebridean trilogy to read because they were written near enough to our neck of the woods in England. We could all identify with a modern-day Englishwomen living amongst the Scottish highlanders whose way of life and outlook was stuck in the 19th century, and the short stories

My unforgettable sister, Nora. She died February, 1999.

offered a few chuckles rather than unremitting sadness. Because she was now in hospital her family doctor took a lesser role in her illness but she came in to see Nora one night because they needed to know the answer to one very important question, "Nora, do you wish to be resuscitated after you die?" It caught me so much by surprise that I'm afraid the tears came and even though I tried as hard as I could to stop them because I didn't want any attention on me, it hit me with the force of a sledgehammer that my sister was really going to die. The next question the Doctor posed was to Stivvie and me, "Have you given her permission to go?" Permission to go! No! I didn't want her to go! No, I haven't given her permission to go. I don't want her to go!

It suddenly struck me that the beliefs that I had spouted over the years were now on the line. In my heart of hearts what did I truly believe? When you're about to take that last breath, what happens next? Can I honestly say that I know? Well, I believe that the body is only a vehicle to carry the soul and when the body dies the soul goes back to our heavenly father. Simple as that! I believe that life on this earth is a test for the soul. I believe that we're put on this earth to learn lessons and when it's your turn to stand in front of God and he asks you, "Did you learn humility, did you learn kindness, did you learn generosity, did you learn, did you learn, did you learn…....?" and if you can't answer yes to all of his questions then you have to come back for more lessons. So even though I did not want my sister to leave, I had to let her go. It was her turn to go. It was obvious that her body was rapidly shutting down, and I couldn't ask God to keep her here and let her suffer. So, with a deep heartbreaking breath I replied, "Yes, she can go whenever she's ready!" Now where have I heard those words before? "Have her boys been to see her and given her permission?" the Doctor asked. "No, they haven't been yet," replied Stivvie. "Well, she won't go until her children tell her she can go. Be sure to tell them that they have to specifically tell her she can go," the Doctor said as she was leaving the room. Both of Nora's sons, Anthony and Ian, came the following night and Stivvie and I left early so that they could have a long visit with their mother and as they had both been drilled as to what to say, we hoped they'd not forget.

I had a very busy life outside of visiting Nora. The head office in the United States had been very busy buying up other similar businesses to ours and putting them under our control, and with me being the Human Resources manager, I was promoted onto the head office overall Human Resources management team. The team consisted of about 8 people, who set the standards for over 15,000 people across North America, and Nora had been in hospital for nearly a month when the head office decided that as I was the one representing our division, I had no choice but to go to a very important meeting down in Denver. I hadn't wanted to fly to Denver that night. It was early in the New Year, and the weather was atrocious and nearly every other flight than mine was cancelled. I couldn't believe that my plane was the only one flying south and I asked a passing Pilot why mine was flying while no other was. He replied, "Well we don't have that many planes flying north American routes that come equipped with 'some sort of' special equipment, it just happens that your plane has it, and can fly."

Lorna filled in for me at the hospital with Stivvie, and I phoned just before I boarded the plane to see how Nora was, and it was with a heavy heart that I left Canada behind. Nora's body was rapidly deteriorating to the point where her time was measured not in weeks, but in days and hours. Unknown to me, it was her last night on earth and when Brian phoned me the next day in Denver, to tell me she had died early that morning, the world stood still. Even though her death was now expected, it still caught me by surprise, and amidst a roomful of strangers, I burst into tears. It seemed as though everyone had conspired against me, the company, the job, and the airline. Everyone had made sure I couldn't be there when she died. She was my sister and I wasn't there. Memories of how things used to be between us, all the laughter we had, the daft things we did, how I trailed after her as a young child, how I relied upon her as a young adult, all of it came flooding back. It was as though I saw fifty-six years of my life with Nora played back to me in one second. I loved her, and I think she waited until I was out of the country to die, to spare me the picture of those last moments of her life that would have haunted me forever. Once her funeral was over, I threw myself into my job, in order to ease the pain.

Apart from the time I was a 'jack of all trades' when I owned the Word Wizards, I found myself wearing four hats in this job: I was Executive Assistant to the President & CEO, Office Manager, Desktop Publisher and Human Resources Manager and I reveled in it -- and as all these skills were learned 'on-the-job' without the benefit of formal education, I was pleased with my accomplishments. But about two months after Nora died, head office in Denver decided to relocate our head office near to them, and as Jim didn't want to move there, they let him go and, in 1999, at the age of 56, I was made redundant again. I remember speaking to an ex-colleague from the packaging company and when he asked me how I was doing I replied, "I'm making a living out of collecting severance packages."

Retiring from the workforce

Brian and I decided that it was time for me to retire. Both boys were married, and with only the two of us left, I had no need to work. We'd had some rough financial patches over the past few years, but no more than most people, and with him totally supporting us again I could put my feet up and that's what I did. It's been a long bumpy road full of adventure, excitement, uncertainty, happiness and tears, and if I could alter some things, I would. If I could live my life again, I would ask God to give me less of the 'Dilly Dream' character as I feel I've never stopped seeing life through her rose coloured glasses. I will never understand why people argue and fall out with each and never speak again, because life is just too short to hold grudges. I'll never understand some of the people who came into my life, and I can only guess they were part of God's tests. I tried to model my character after the goodness and graciousness of Gran as she was the greatest influence in my life showing love and kindness toward people. I also tried to be a good wife and mother, and as my boys were honest, loving, caring and decent men when they married, I think I did okay. After a lifetime of searching the world for roots, I woke up to find them inside of me all the time. My love for all my family whether there are actual blood lines or not is very strong, and wherever they are, those roots go deep.

EPILOGUE

I wasn't intending to add to my life story, I was just going to finish it at the age of 56 years old when I retired from the workforce, and I was only writing it to keep myself busy and to make a record of my history for my children, but as I am now 77 years old, many people have wondered what I have been doing with myself the last few years.

Update: When my son, David, married Teresa in 1998 they moved into our 2-level basement apartment but before long the Multiple Sclerosis that Teresa had been diagnosed with as a young girl really started to trouble her and she found it difficult to maneuver up and down between the two floors. So, as they were only intending to live with us temporarily, 6 months or so, and we would be left with a huge house of 5 bedrooms, 3 living rooms, 2 kitchens, 3 bathrooms and 2 laundries, they made a suggestion that we downsize and buy a more suitable brand new house between us, which we did; and because it was easier for Teresa to get around, now that she had a cane or a walker for support, they needed to be on the ground floor which had an extra living room that could be turned into a bedroom if needed, while Brian and I commissioned a builder to finish the basement into a self-contained 2-bedroom apartment for ourselves.

That worked out just fine for the first two years because when Teresa got pregnant I was there to keep an eye on her, and when she gave birth to my first grandchild, Breanna, everyone was so happy for them. Unfortunately, Teresa's health deteriorated, and when she fell pregnant again she wanted to move nearer her parents who lived about 40 kms away, which meant we would have to sell the house and find somewhere else to live. I voiced no objections, after all, I knew first-hand what hormones can do to you as I had experienced them in wanting to move back to family in England from Australia, so I was the last person to object to her wanting to be closer to her family, so I set about finding another home for us, a real retirement home this time.

I was now 59 years old, and my husband, Brian, who was 62 years old, was still working as a Controller for a transportation company but because he could do his accounting work from home, on the computer and over the telephone lines, I set about looking for a home somewhere out of the city; somewhere in the country, somewhere reminiscent of our 'village' roots of Templetown and Delves Lane. Our son, John, expressed an interest in us moving north, somewhere near him because he said, "Mom & Dad, you've lived with David and Teresa for two years, when is it my turn?"

Brian gave me three criteria for moving away from the city: the town had to have a golf course and a bowling alley, and a Doctor's office – not easy to find all three in the vastness of a Canadian countryside. Because Brian was working, my late sister Nora's husband, Stivvie, who was also retired, and I scoured the countryside in ever increasing circles from where my son John lived because as much as I love him, I didn't want to live in his back pocket, and decided on this 4.82-acre property, a 30 minutes' highway drive away from him in a 'village' of 1,000 people in the snow belt of northern Ontario. It's called the snow belt for a very good reason – it gets lots of snow. We have known snow to fall in October and last until June, and it is not unusual to have 2 feet of snow fall overnight so the skiers, snowmobilers, hockey players and, when the lakes freeze over, the ice fishermen absolutely love it – what summer is to us, winter is to the Canadians. The first snowfall we experienced here we immediately hired a man with a huge snow blower to clear our 100-foot drive or we would not have gotten out for a week.

I have no idea what I was thinking when I bought this house, sight unseen by Brian. Coming from a postage-sized garden I had no idea just how long it would take to mow 2 acres of grass around the house on a sit-on lawn mower but I found out really quick; keeping a steady pace it takes 2-1/2 hours, and a sore bottom. Why on earth did I think this was going to be a great retirement home? However, when Brian drove the 3 hours up the highway from the city to see the place one week later he absolutely loved it. He loved the little house with its two bedrooms, one living room/dining room combination, a kitchen and a bathroom, and he loved that it was surrounded by 2 acres of grass and 2.82 acres of trees. He thought it was perfect; yes, perfect to start off with, but not perfect to finish with, not while there are renovations to be done; the least of which was a new kitchen and a new bathroom. But, as usual, one thing led to another and before we knew it, the whole house was torn to pieces. I guess finding about 5 pounds of mouse-muck when the ceiling tiles in the living room were going to be replaced had something to do with the decision to renew everything.

I moved up here in February, 2002 and the builder who had been recommended to us by our son, John, started in June but he was so slow that he took 3 months just to strip this little five room house back to its wooden studs and when Brian drove up in August he fired him on the spot. We were nervous about accepting further recommendations from John about another set of builders that he was friends with, two brothers and a helper, but we hit lucky. They were the most professional men you could ever wish to meet and they were used to building and fixing homes for the millionaires who had cottages in the world-famous Muskoka resort region of Ontario, just a few miles away from us, and they agreed to rebuild our house from the basement up, putting in new plumbing and new electrical wiring. They also took some space from the two bedrooms upstairs and built a bathroom up there – very necessary when you get older. They also 'age-proofed' upstairs by putting very good quality pine wainscoting around the walls so that we wouldn't have to bend down to paint to the bottom of the walls in our old age; they finished half of the upstairs bathroom in cedar wainscoting so that we wouldn't get any insects making a home with us (we lived in the country after all) and the kitchen was rebuilt with light oak cupboards and the same good quality pine for walls. The ground floor bathroom was totally rebuilt in cedar, and they managed to find room to put a laundry in there also. Then, they turned an old barn that housed tractors etc., attached to the back of the house into a downstairs third bedroom, plus an office for Brian. We got the benefit of millionaire experience for pauper prices, and we referred to our home as 'elegant country.'

Thanks to Brian's sister, Doreen, who insisted the parents' estate be split between them, Brian got an inheritance from his biological father, Lewis, when he died (his second wife Ellen had died a few years before so he'd been on his own for a while). It was sad that he died when he did because Brian had arranged his flight home to England to see his father on his birthday in January and when I was talking to Lewis at Christmas I asked him what was wrong because he was talking a little strange; for someone so opinionated he just answered my questions in words of one syllable – "How are you?" *"Fine."* "Have you had Christmas dinner yet?" *"No."* "Brian will be there on your birthday." *"Fine."* "Is everything alright, just say the word and we will come and get you." *"The word."* "Can you wait until Brian gets there for your birthday?" *"I won't be here then."* Lewis had been diagnosed with Dementia and unfortunately Doreen had no choice but to put him in a nursing home, and that's where he died between Christmas day and his birthday, January 13. One often hears horror stories about old people being abused in nursing homes and I pray to God that nothing untoward happened to hasten the death of my favourite, highly opinionated, very vocal, pseudo father-in-law. However, with this unexpected inheritance Brian was able to commission some 'extras' for the house such as a huge double detached garage with a heated hobby workshop attached and a carport between the garage and the house. Well, it started out as a carport but a black bear decided to wander through from the forest and we got the builders to build it into something resembling a conservatory.

When we moved into this home Brian and I did something of a personality exchange. For 39-years' out of our 48-year marriage he was cheerful with family, but fairly guarded with strangers, and he described himself on numerous occasions as, "An optimistic pessimist," whereas I had been the eternal optimist since the age of 15, but very soon after we finished rebuilding the house and settling down I found myself with nothing to do, other than trying to do some gardening and writing my life story, whereas Brian thrived; apart from doing his job that he was getting paid for, he was either on the golf course with friends he'd made; bowling in three different bowling leagues in the local bowling alley, or having coffee with one or another he met in town. He'd go to the supermarket, a 10-minute drive away, to pick up bread and be away for 2 hours having gotten waylaid by somebody or other to stand and chat. I hardly recognized the change in him; he'd stop and talk to anybody who would listen and, after all the years of both of us being preoccupied with other things, to have the time to sit and talk in our screened-in porch was an unadulterated pleasure for the next nine years. We were always close and had great communication all our married life, but somehow living here we connected on a much deeper level. He was absolutely in his element in this country setting; it was as though his wheel had turned full circle. He loved the place and the people and swore he'd never move again; that he would never agree to sell the place, and that I'd have to take him out feet first.

We've seen some partner changes within the Canadian family over the last few years and it has been hard getting to know all the new partners, especially now that we are 300 kms away from my cousins. All four of Marjorie's children changed partners. However, after having been a confirmed bachelor all his life, at 50 years old, my cousin Ted married Beth, a lovely woman!

My son John's marriage failed and he has a new partner and my son, David's wife, Teresa, died after living here for four years. I'll tell you how they came to be living with us. David was having trouble taking care of Teresa who was bedridden with Multiple Sclerosis, their two small children, and working all at the same time, so we made them the offer of building a bungalow onto the back of our house and bringing them all up here out of the city so that David could look after Teresa 24/7 and that's what we did. We have the original two-storey country house at the front and a very modern open plan bungalow behind, but I lost the ground floor bedroom which was converted into a dining room for them. Both homes are totally self-contained but accessible through a door in my hallway; that way we could help look after the children while David looked after Teresa. I was 63 years old when they came to live here; Breanna was 5 years old, and Joshua was 3-1/2 years old, and they are now very mature teenagers and ready to leave home.

Sadly, Teresa died two days before her son Joshua's 7th birthday in October, 2009. Heartbreaking because her death came out of nowhere due to the sudden onset of pneumonia, and David was devastated and heartbroken. He had lost the love of his life. The children were

Teresa Flagello Shaw, 1968 – 2009

stunned and didn't know what to make of it, they were just too young to understand such a big loss and it took a while for it to sink in. Joshua maybe handled it the best of all of us because after Teresa's funeral, at the tea at her parents' home which is where most of her Italian relatives lived, Joshua said something, and I asked people to be quiet to let 7-year-old Joshua speak, so he repeated it in a very loud voice, "Why is everyone crying? If my Mommy is in heaven and out of pain, why aren't you happy for her?" What a touching question from a small boy, but he was right, if we believed that Teresa was in heaven and free from her horrible pain, then we should be happy for her.

Two years after Teresa died, and two weeks before his 71st birthday, my husband Brian died in May, 2011. We had been together for 53 years. He'd done his work for the day; gone out for lunch; voted as a Canadian Citizen for the first time; came home for a nap; got up and crashed to the ground like an old English oak tree. He was dead before he hit the floor and I can just imagine him standing outside his body saying, "What the heck! I told Nancy I wasn't leaving here other than feet first." He got his wish! But because of my firm belief in a life after this one, I couldn't begrudge him going; he'd been a loving caring husband, a fantastic father, and an adoring grandfather to Breanna, Joshua and Travis, and a very good friend to all he cared for. Three months later my brother Brian died of cancer; then a couple of years later my sister, Dorothy, died of cancer; my sister Nora having died of cancer 12 years earlier. Gosh, out of the four children my mother Beattie

My husband and partner of 53 years - Brian Shaw, 1940 – 2011.

had, three have died from various kinds of cancer and I am the last one living. I won't be placing any bets on the cause of my demise!

My grandchildren are all teenagers now and maybe because of the trauma they experienced when they were little, they seem to be more mature than their schoolmates. They certainly help around the house, and that was the deal when, after much begging from them, I bought them two puppies, Golden Retriever/ Labrador mix brothers, and they are big dogs now. I guess it helped fill a need for them. I also insisted in teaching all three grandchildren how to cook and bake from a very early age, that way they would always be able to feed themselves decent meals and not give in to junk food much. Brian had other ideas, he told them, "Don't worry about learning how to cook, so long as you know how to use a can opener you'll not starve." They didn't take him too seriously.

The first couple of years of my retirement were spent in the luxury of reading books, then the next couple of years were spent renovating my retirement home; then two years writing my life story, and another year overseeing the building of David's home and, finally, helping my son David raise my beautiful grandchildren – forever the old 'Nanny by name and Nanny by nature'. So once again, and I think I can confidently say this time is the last time, we have a big house of 5 bedrooms, 3 living rooms, 2 kitchens, 2 laundry's, and 3 bathrooms to house my son David and myself, and the two grandchildren, Breanna and Joshua; and the third grandchild, Travis, who visits as often as he can and we love him dearly. It's hard to believe where the time has gone, but in this year of 2020, granddaughter Breanna is 19 yrs old, and grandsons Joshua and Travis are 17-1/2 yrs old, and all of them are going to University, and for the second time in my life I will be an empty nester at 77 yrs old. As Brian would say if he was here, "You should be getting used to it by now."

It's funny the way my life has worked out because these 'golden years' are nothing like they were supposed to be, because as much as I love Canada, my sister Nora and I always fancifully intended to go home to England and retire to a cottage on Stanhope moors in the north-west corner of County Durham, just 'up the road' from where we started; unfortunately, she died too soon, so I'll stay where I am in my own little home in northern Ontario, because my son David and my grandchildren, Breanna and Joshua, still live in their home attached to mine. My guardian angel must have had something to do with this arrangement because it gives me the security of family in my old age; but I have told David that once I get too much to handle he can put me out on an ice flow for the bears, just like the Eskimo's used to do with their elders – in other words he has my permission to put me in a nursing home if I live that long.

Finally, to quote the famous American narrator, the late Paul Harvey, "and now you know the rest of the story."

Nancy Shaw, 77 years old, March, 2020

oooOOOooo

Nora Buckett Stephenson, 1941 - 1999

Nancy Buckett Shaw, 1943 -

Beatrice Maud Buckett Dodds' children

Brian Dodds, 1945 - 2011

Dorothy Dodds Kitchen, 1946 - 2013

"In with both Feet"

ISBN: 9781520258218

Printed in Great Britain
by Amazon